The Art of the American Musical

The
Art of the
American
Musical

Conversations with
the Creators

**Edited by Jackson R. Bryer
and Richard A. Davison**

RUTGERS UNIVERSITY PRESS
New Brunswick, New Jersey, and London

Library of Congress Cataloging-in-Publication Data

The art of the American musical : conversations with the creators / edited by Jackson R.
Bryer and Richard A. Davison.
p. cm.
ISBN 0-8135-3612-X (hardcover : alk. paper) — ISBN 0-8135-3613-8 (pbk. : alk. paper)
1. Musicals—United States—History and criticism.   2. Composers—United States—Interviews.   3. Lyricists—United States—Interviews.   4. Producers and directors—United
States—Interviews.   I. Bryer, Jackson R.   II. Davison, Richard Allan.
ML1711.A77   2005
782.1′4′092273—dc22
2004025319

A British Cataloging-in-Publication record for this book is available
from the British Library.

Manufactured in the United States of America

Contents

Introduction

In many respects, the impetus for this book was Oscar Hammerstein II's description of theater as "a nightly miracle." While Hammerstein undoubtedly was referring to any stage production, there is no disputing the fact that the most miraculous and mysterious theatrical form is the one in which he himself achieved renown—the musical. This is so because one assumes that in calling theater a "miracle," Hammerstein was more specifically highlighting its basis in collaboration; and in no theatrical enterprise is collaboration more essential and more complex than in a musical. With a play, the playwright, the director, the actors, the producers, and the designers somehow must work together to achieve a satisfactory production, but the Dramatists Guild contract explicitly gives the playwright the final word on what is said onstage. With a musical, those involved in its creation include a composer, a lyricist, a librettist, a director, a choreographer, an orchestrator, a musical director, a dance arranger, designers, producers, and performers; and while one person may, on occasion, fill more than one of those roles on a particular show, there is nonetheless no contractually defined indication as to whose word is final. To the outside observer, with so many opinions and talents clamoring for recognition, the key questions are how and why a musical ever gets produced and what aspects of the collaboration determine whether or not it will be successful.

In the search for answers to these fundamental questions, as well as others about the musical, we have interviewed for this book a group of individuals who are not only responsible for creating many of the great American musicals of the last sixty years but are also representative of the various talents involved in creating a musical. They include composers (Flaherty, Brown, Kander, Lane, Sondheim, and Strouse), lyricists (Ahrens, Brown, Comden and Green, Harnick, Ebb, Sondheim, and Wolfe), librettists (Ahrens, Comden and Green, Ebb, Laurents, Weidman, and Wolfe), directors (Laurents, Marshall, Prince, Stroman, Tune, and Wolfe), choreographers (Marshall, Stroman, and Tune), and a producer (Prince). In addition, Jason Robert Brown, John Kander, and Charles Strouse have worked as orchestrators, musical directors, and dance arrangers; and Brown, especially, speaks knowledgeably about how those less publicized artists function within the musical theater team. We are planning a second book of interviews about the art of the American musical that will focus exclusively on performers; but it is notable that, among those in this collection, Comden, Green, Marshall, Stroman, and Tune all have extensive experience as performers; Tune, in fact, won the first of his nine Tony Awards for Best Featured Actor in the 1973 musical *Seesaw* and won another one in 1983 as Best Actor in *My One and Only.*

We have focused on the American musical because, while it can trace its origins to European opera and operetta, as it developed during the twentieth century, the musical has rightly been designated as the only indigenously American theatrical form. While theater comedy can be traced back to Aristophanes, Menander, Plautus, and the commedia dell'arte, and tragedy has its roots in Aeschylus, Sophocles, and Euripides, all musicals, no matter their country of origin, owe a debt to the American version of the form, and any history of that form inevitably becomes a history of the American musical.

The great names in the early history of the American musical are composers Jerome Kern and George Gershwin, both of whom began their careers writing shows with memorable songs and forgettable books and both of whom contributed in the middle of their careers to works that changed the face of the musical. In Kern's case, the show was *Show Boat* (1927), which combined a great musical score with a story that confronted the serious and complex issue of racism in America and stands as the first great American musical. Gershwin contributed importantly to two landmark musicals—*Of Thee I Sing* (1931), the first musical to win the Pulitzer Prize for drama and a caustic, albeit satiric, look at American politics, and *Porgy and Bess* (1935), considered the greatest American opera but also a classic of the American musical theater.

Contemporaneous with Kern and Gershwin were such other major talents of the early American musical as Irving Berlin, Richard Rodgers and Lorenz Hart, and Cole Porter; significantly, like Kern and Gershwin, they were all composers or lyricists, because the score was, for many years, the only aspect that was important in musicals. This began to change with such shows as Rodgers and Hart's *On Your Toes* (1936), the first musical to incorporate dance as an integral component; it paved the way for later musicals in which dance played a major role, among them *West Side Story* (1957), *A Chorus Line* (1975), and *Contact* (2000). Three of the creators of *West Side Story*—producer Harold Prince, lyricist Stephen Sondheim, and librettist Arthur Laurents—speak about that show in this book, as do others interviewed. Susan Stroman, who conceived, directed, and choreographed *Contact,* and John Weidman, the show's librettist, talk at length about it here; and *A Chorus Line* is discussed by several interviewees, principally Tommy Tune. Rodgers and Hart's last show, *Pal Joey* (1940), was another advance for the form in its portrayal of a sexist, amoral antihero as its protagonist.

Richard Rodgers, however, achieved his greatest stature in the history of the American musical when, after Hart's untimely death, he teamed up with lyricist and librettist Oscar Hammerstein II, who had written the lyrics and book for *Show Boat,* to write a series of shows that transformed the American musical from a form that, with the exceptions noted above, had featured wonderful scores interrupted occasionally by frivolous and often preposterous dialogue into a serious art form. Starting with *Oklahoma!* (1943) and continuing with, among others, *Carousel* (1945), *Allegro* (1947), *South Pacific* (1949), *The King and I* (1951), *Flower Drum Song* (1958), and *The Sound of Music* (1959), Rodgers and Hammerstein dealt with such subjects as racism, spousal abuse, war, and conflicts between cultures and did so in shows that integrated story, music, and often dance in a fashion that foreshadowed and, in many ways, led to the "concept musicals" of Stephen Sondheim and Harold Prince. Sondheim speaks in this book of how much he learned from Oscar Hammerstein, and he also notes that *South Pacific* is the show "that changed Hal Prince's perception of theater."

Integration and interrelationship of the various elements of the musical have, since Rodgers and Hammerstein, become virtually a necessity for success; and, again, that is why the roles played by creators other than the composer and lyricist, who dominated most musicals before *Oklahoma!,* have become so important and are among the major concerns of this book. Before Agnes de Mille's dances became instrumental in the success of *Oklahoma!* and *Carousel,* who even knew the name of a choreographer for a Broadway musical? Since *Oklahoma!,* names like Jerome Robbins, Michael Bennett, Bob Fosse, Gower Champion, and, among our interviewees, Tommy Tune and Susan Stroman are familiar to all, and their contributions are indispensable to the success of the musicals they choreographed and, in many cases, also directed. In fact, the advent of the director/choreographer, which started with Robbins, is among the most significant developments in the American musical of the last half century. It is a testimony to the often acknowledged necessity of making the contemporary musical "seamless." Stroman, Tune, and the youngest director/choreographer we interviewed, Kathleen Marshall, all speak at length about their dual role. Another way of acknowledging the interdependency of the various elements of the contemporary musical is to note how many of our interviewees have filled multiple roles, often on the same production. Besides the director/choreographers mentioned above, Brown and Sondheim have done both music and lyrics; Ahrens, Comden and Green, Ebb, and Wolfe have been lyricists and librettists; Laurents and Wolfe have been librettists and directors; and Harold Prince has been a producer and a director.

Rodgers and Hammerstein's musicals also placed an important new emphasis on the book of a musical. No longer could it be foolish and unimportant to the success of a show—and unrelated to the musical numbers. In a Rodgers and Hammerstein musical, music and dialogue functioned side by side and, in some cases, indistinguishably. Musical theater book-writing became an art and a skill, and we interviewed several of its most accomplished practitioners. Arthur Laurents is responsible for what are generally considered two of the classic musical theater books, *West Side Story* and *Gypsy* (1959). John Weidman, working primarily with Stephen Sondheim but also with others, has written the books for *Pacific Overtures* (1976), *Assassins* (1991), and *Contact.* Lynn Ahrens has written the books for *Once on This Island* (1990), *My Favorite Year* (1992), and *Seussical* (2000); George C. Wolfe, who began his career as a playwright, has done the books for *Jelly's Last Jam* (1991), *Bring in 'da Noise, Bring in 'da Funk* [*Noise/Funk*] (1996), *The Wild Party* (2000), and *Harlem Song* (2002). All speak here about how they worked with the other creators on these shows. Because the contemporary musical resists easy rules of composition (this is another departure from the early musicals, most of which included such prescribed elements as an opening chorus number and two romantic couples, one of which was often comic), the experiences and work methods of these librettists of necessity have varied from show to show. Of particular interest is John Weidman's description of how he collaborated with composer/lyricist Sondheim on *Pacific Overtures, Assassins,* and *Bounce* (2003) and with director/choreographer Stroman on *Contact.*

There are certainly major figures in the history of the American musical since *Oklahoma!* whom we could not interview, usually because they died before this book was conceived or before we could talk with them; but many of them are mentioned, often by more than one interviewee, in this book. There is a great deal here about Rodgers and Hammerstein, Leonard Bernstein, Alan Jay Lerner, George Abbott, Frank Loesser, Jule Styne, Jerome Robbins, Michael Bennett, Bob Fosse, Zero Mostel, Ethel Merman, Peter Stone, Yip Harburg, and Gower Champion. As Kathleen Marshall reminded us, the history of the American musical as we know it is a relatively brief one. If we date the form's beginnings as early as Jerome Kern's first successes, *Very Good Eddie* (1915) and *Leave It to Jane* (1917), it is less than a hundred years old, and it has been a little over sixty years since *Oklahoma!* But, looking at it in another way, musicals like Kander, Ebb, and Prince's *Chicago* (1975), Sondheim and Prince's *Sweeney Todd* (1979), Sondheim and Weidman's *Assassins,* Kander, Ebb, and Prince's *Kiss of the Spider Woman* (1993), Brown and Prince's *Parade* (1999), Wolfe's *The Wild Party,* Stroman and Weidman's *Contact,* and Brown's *The Last Five Years* (2002) are far more distant in conception and final product than they are chronologically from the equally important musicals of the 1940s, 1950s, and 1960s. Because so many of our interviewees have been responsible for the rapid changes in the musical theater form, they are well qualified to define and explain those changes.

They are also able to take this sort of long view because their careers cover such a range of the history of the musical. Burton Lane began by writing songs for *Three's Company* in 1930; he knew George and Ira Gershwin well, discovered Judy Garland, and wrote scores for shows that featured performers like Al Jolson and comedians Olsen and Johnson in which, as he admits, "the songs wouldn't mean anything" and the book was "an excuse to do numbers." But he also wrote the score for one of the great musicals of the 1940s, and arguably of all time, *Finian's Rainbow* (1947), and he describes how different that experience was from his earlier work. Betty Comden and Adolph Green collaborated with Leonard Bernstein on *On the Town* (1944) and *Wonderful Town* (1953) and with Jule Styne on *Bells Are Ringing* (1956), but their careers also extended to *On the Twentieth Century* (1978) and *The Will Rogers Follies* (1991). Harold Prince produced four classics of the golden age of the American musical—*The Pajama Game* (1954), *Damn Yankees* (1955), *West Side Story,* and *Fiorello!* (1959)—but his work in the last decade includes directing a 1994 revival and reconception of *Show Boat* as well as *Parade* and *Bounce.* Arthur Laurents wrote the books for *West Side Story* and *Gypsy* in the 1950s; but he also directed *La Cage aux Folles* (1983), directed and wrote *Nick and Nora* (1991), and reworked his book for *Hallelujah, Baby!* (1967) for a December 2004 production at Arena Stage in Washington, D.C.

The work of John Kander and Fred Ebb, Sheldon Harnick, and Charles Strouse first attracted attention in the 1960s. Kander and Ebb came to prominence with *Flora, the Red Menace* (1965), *Cabaret* (1966), and *Zorbá* (1968); in the 1970s, they wrote *70, Girls, 70* (1971), *Chicago,* and *The Act* (1977); in the 1980s, *Woman of the Year* (1981) and *The Rink* (1984); in the 1990s *Kiss of the Spider Woman* and *Steel Pier* (1997); and at Ebb's death in 2004 they were actively preparing two new musicals for New York productions. Harnick's early musicals were *Fiorello!* (1959), *She Loves Me* (1963), *Fiddler on the Roof* (1964), and *The Apple Tree* (1966); in the 1970s, he did *The Rothschilds* (1970) and *Rex* (1976), and he has continued to work on new musicals and revivals of his shows. Strouse achieved his first successes with *Bye Bye Birdie* (1960), *All American* (1962), and *Golden Boy* (1964); in the 1970s, he wrote scores for *Applause* (1970) and *Annie* (1977); and in the 1990s, he worked with Laurents on *Nick and Nora* and also wrote *Annie Warbucks* (1993).

Certainly the most dominant figure of the last forty years in the American musical—and perhaps the most influential in the entire history of the form—is Stephen Sondheim. While he began by writing lyrics for *West Side Story* and *Gypsy* and in the 1960s wrote music and lyrics for *A Funny Thing Happened on the Way to the Forum* (1962) and *Anyone Can*

Whistle (1964), he reached new heights in the 1970s when he saw five ground-breaking shows produced during the decade: *Company* (1970), *Follies* (1971), *A Little Night Music* (1973), *Pacific Overtures,* and *Sweeney Todd.* In the 1980s, he wrote *Merrily We Roll Along* (1981) and *Sunday in the Park with George* (1984); in the 1990s *Assassins, Passion* (1994), and *Saturday Night* (1999); and in the last two years, *Bounce* and *The Frogs* (2004). He collaborated on many of these shows, especially in the 1960s and 1970s, with Harold Prince; more recently, he has worked with John Weidman and Susan Stroman. Sondheim has altered the nature of the musical forever and set a standard for all future practitioners. He is reluctant to talk about his work, and we feel very fortunate and grateful to have had the opportunity to interview him for this book. We are also grateful to others of the interviewees who spoke about him with us.

Among the latter are the several creators whose careers began in the last decades of the twentieth century. Although Tommy Tune began as a highly successful Broadway performer, he achieved his greatest successes as the director/choreographer of *The Best Little Whorehouse in Texas* (1978), *A Day in Hollywood/A Night in the Ukraine* (1980), *Nine* (1982), *My One and Only* (1983), *Grand Hotel* (1989), and *The Will Rogers Follies.* Lynn Ahrens and Stephen Flaherty, Susan Stroman, John Weidman, and George C. Wolfe all began their careers in the 1980s. Ahrens and Flaherty wrote the music and lyrics for *Lucky Stiff* (1988), *Once on This Island, My Favorite Year, Ragtime* (1998), and *A Man of No Importance* (2002); as this book goes to press, they are readying their new musical, *Dessa Rose* (about which they speak in their interview), for a New York production in early 2005. Stroman began as the choreographer of *Crazy for You* (1992), Prince's 1994 revival/reconception of *Show Boat, Big* (1996), and Kander and Ebb's *Steel Pier,* and then became the director/choreographer of *Contact, The Producers* (2001), *Thou Shalt Not* (2001), and *The Frogs,* as well as of a major revival of *The Music Man* (2000). After writing the book for Sondheim and Prince's *Pacific Overtures* in 1976, Weidman worked with Sondheim on *Assassins* and *Bounce* and with Stroman on *Big* and *Contact.* Wolfe's multifaceted career as a director, librettist, and playwright entered the musical theater arena with *Jelly's Last Jam* in 1991 and has continued with *Noise/Funk, The Wild Party, Harlem Song,* and *Caroline, or Change* (2004).

Our two youngest interviewees, Jason Robert Brown and Kathleen Marshall, both began their careers in the 1990s and certainly represent the American musical of the future. Brown, especially, talks extensively and candidly about what that future might look like. His first musical was *Songs for a New World* in 1995, and he subsequently wrote music for *Parade, The Last Five Years,* and *Urban Cowboy* (2003). Marshall, like Stroman and Tune, began as a choreographer, working on *Swinging on a Star*

(1995), *Violet* (1997), Sondheim's *Saturday Night,* and *Seussical,* as well as on revivals of *1776* (1997), *Kiss Me, Kate* (1999), and *Little Shop of Horrors* (2003). With the 2003 revival of *Wonderful Town,* she became a director/choreographer, a role she will undoubtedly continue to play in many future musical theater productions.

The fact that so many of our interviewees have worked together means that in this book their careers and personalities are illuminated not only by what they themselves say but also by what others say about them. As with the other books in this series, *The Playwright's Art* (1995) and *The Actor's Art* (2001), the interviews are a mix of questions that address specific aspects of the interviewee's life and work and those that deal in more general terms with the art of the American musical—with such matters as how a musical is put together, the history and future of the musical, what attracts creators to particular material, and the current state of criticism of the musical. These latter, generic questions have been asked of all the interviewees in the hope that the similarities and differences in their responses will be one of the rewards of reading this book in its entirety. Finally, it is worth noting that these theater artists speak not only about their greatest hits; they also talk candidly and sometimes at length about failures like Laurents and Strouse's *Nick and Nora,* Comden, Green, and Prince's *A Doll's Life* (1982), and Sondheim, Weidman, and Prince's *Bounce,* as well as many other unfamiliar shows. It is in the spirit of the intent of this book as an exploration of what the components of a musical are and how they interact that one can often learn as much when that collaborative process fails or falters as when it succeeds.

Seven of the interviews originated as programs in the Smithsonian Institution's Campus on the Mall series "Presenting . . . The American Musical Theatre!," which Jackson R. Bryer coordinated with Dwight Blocker Bowers of the Smithsonian in the fall of 1992. A few of those interviewees slightly updated their interviews when they were given the opportunity to look them over in 2004. Bryer is grateful to Bowers and to Binney Levine of the Smithsonian for their assistance and support in planning and supervising that series and to John Fuegi and Bonnie Nelson Schwartz for helping to defray the expenses of videotaping the programs. Michael Dale and Cynthia Freland of Maryland Secretarial Services aided in the transcription of the interviews. Our wives, Mary C. Hartig and Milena Davison, provided support and assistance at all stages of the project. Linda Stein assisted with our research. Leonard Fleischer helped put us in touch with interviewees. Once again, as with the earlier books in the series, we were extremely fortunate to have India Cooper as our expert copy editor and to have Leslie Mitchner and Marilyn Campbell at Rutgers University Press, who exhibited their unique mixture of patience, persistence, and encouragement. But, as always, our deepest debts of gratitude are to eighteen extraordinarily talented people who took the time from their busy schedules to participate in this project and to be so supportive of it. We hope the book justifies in some small measure their willingness and cooperation.

J.R.B., College Park, Maryland
R.A.D., Newark, Delaware
October 20, 2004

About the Interviews

Seven of the interviews originated as sessions in the series "Presenting . . . The American Musical Theatre!," which was sponsored by the Smithsonian Institution's Campus on the Mall and took place in Washington, D.C., in the fall of 1992 as follows:

The principal questioner for the interview with Betty Comden and Adolph Green was Bob Mondello, theater critic of the *City Paper* (Washington, D.C.) and frequent reviewer and commentator for National Public Radio's *All Things Considered.*

The principal questioner for the interview with Sheldon Harnick was Dwight Blocker Bowers, director of the Division of Museum Programs at the National Museum of American History and co-author of *Red Hot & Blue: A Smithsonian Salute to the American Musical* (1996).

The principal questioner for the interview with John Kander and Fred Ebb was Marc Pachter, director of the National Portrait Gallery.

The principal questioner for the interview with Burton Lane was Michael Feinstein, international performer and recording artist.

The principal questioner for the interview with Arthur Laurents was Ken Bloom, author of *American Song: The Complete Musical Theatre Companion, 1900–1984* (1985).

The principal questioner for the interview with Harold Prince was Hap Erstein, drama critic of the *Palm Beach* (Florida) *Post.*

The principal questioner for the interview with Charles Strouse was David Young, former producing director of the American College Theater Festival.

Additional questions were addressed to each of the guests in the Smithsonian series by members of the audience.

The other interviews in the volume were conducted by Jackson R. Bryer and Richard A. Davison and took place in the following circumstances:

The interview with Lynn Ahrens and Stephen Flaherty was conducted at Ms. Ahrens's New York City apartment.

The interview with Jason Robert Brown was conducted at Sarabeth's Kitchen restaurant in New York City.

The interview with Kathleen Marshall was conducted in her office in New York City.

The interview with Susan Stroman was conducted at the New 42nd Street Studios in New York City.

The interview with Stephen Sondheim was conducted at his New York City home.

The interview with Tommy Tune was conducted at his New York City apartment.

The interview with John Weidman was conducted at the offices of the Dramatists Guild in New York City.

The interview with George C. Wolfe was conducted in his office at the Public Theater in New York City.

The Art of the American Musical

Lynn Ahrens
and Stephen Flaherty

Photo by Joan Marcus

*Lynn Ahrens was born on October 1, 1948, in New York City. She was ed-
ucated at Syracuse University (B.A., 1970). She has worked as a librettist
and lyricist. She has written or co-written the books for the musicals* Lucky
Stiff *(1988),* Once on This Island *(1990),* A Christmas Carol *(1994), and*
Seussical *(2000). She has written the lyrics for the musicals* Lucky Stiff,
Once on This Island, My Favorite Year *(1992),* A Christmas Carol, *Ragtime (1998),* Seussical, *and* A Man of No Importance *(2002). She contributed the lyrics for the songs in the film* Anastasia *(1997). She received
the Tony Award for* Ragtime *(Best Score).*

*Stephen Flaherty was born on September 18, 1960, in Pittsburgh, Penn-
sylvania. He was educated at the University of Cincinnati (B.M. in composition, 1982). He has worked as a composer and librettist. He has written
the music for the musicals* Lucky Stiff *(1988),* Once on This Island *(1990),*
My Favorite Year *(1992),* Ragtime *(1998),* Seussical *(2000), and* A Man

of No Importance *(2002). He co-wrote the book for* Seussical. *He wrote the songs for the film* Anastasia *(1997). He received the Tony Award for* Ragtime *(Best Score).*

This interview took place on December 8, 2003.

• ———————————————————————————————— •

Interviewer: You are both relatively young and presumably did not see the original productions of the great American musicals of the 1940s, 1950s, and even perhaps the 1960s. Do you think that makes you more independent of that tradition and consequently more able to embrace newer ideas of what a musical can be?

Ahrens: I really have a great respect for the traditions of the form and its craft, but I'm also trying to find ways to break from the form. I feel that with each one of the shows we've written, we've broken some new ground, certainly for us in terms of our own writing process, and sometimes in terms of the form itself. I know, when we did *Ragtime*, we all felt that we had never heard or seen anything quite like it, which was great. But there is certainly a tradition that we feel part of, and a lot of the people who wrote those shows and established that tradition are still here. The first show I ever saw on Broadway was *Fiddler on the Roof*, and now I know Sheldon Harnick; I'm honored to know him. You learn a lot from the great creators of musical theater, and then you try to move forward and develop a voice and style of your own.

Interviewer: Musically speaking, Stephen, do you think that you are perhaps of a different generation?

Flaherty: As a writer for the theater, I think it's important to understand the traditions, to know where this art form came from. Obviously, being a contemporary writer, then you build upon the foundation that has been laid by the previous generations working in the medium. I have to say, though, when I first became aware of musicals, I wasn't familiar with what you would call "the classics." The first musical I ever saw was *Godspell*, in the early 1970s. It used pop influences and pop music. I got to know some of the more contemporary pieces before I found my way back to Rodgers and Hammerstein, and that's probably had some effect on what I write. As a composer, my personal music interests are quite wide and varied. My background is in classical composition, although I grew up in the 1960s and 1970s with the sounds of R&B and was influenced by the whole singer/songwriter period, which I think has affected the kind of music I write. Each of the pieces that Lynn and I have written together has its own unique musical vocabulary. *Once on This Island* is set on a fictitious Caribbean island, and in writing that piece, I was able to use a lot of contemporary world music sounds—Afro-Caribbean music, the sounds of Brazil—and combine them in a way that I think was fresh and theatrical at the same time. It's important to stay current, to keep your ears open to what musical influences there are today that are available; but at the same time, since we are writing for a theatrical medium, it's necessary to try to find a way to adapt these different musical influences in a theatrical way. You have to remember that we're first and foremost dramatists, and we choose music as the language in which we tell these stories.

Interviewer: Isn't *Rent* a recent show whose musical vocabulary seems to be completely different from that of any traditional musical theater sound?

Flaherty: It's interesting about *Rent*. If you talk to people in the pop world, they consider *Rent* Broadway show music; but if you talk to people in the Broadway world, they say, "That's not Broadway, that's pop." I think that show is a real tribute to what its composer, Jonathan Larson, was trying to do, in his career and in that piece, finding some way to bridge those two worlds. My feeling is that it's neither strictly pop nor strictly Broadway. It's a theatrical piece that uses a pop sound in an original way.

Ahrens: There are certain conventions and ways of telling a story that don't go away. A good story is a good story, and it needs to be told well. It needs to be told with drama and with heart and with characterizations. There are certain things that you learn to do with lyrics—for example, not to write imperfect rhymes if you can help it, because they pull the ear away and take the listener out of the story. But it's like a painter studying anatomy. Once certain basics are in your bones (and at this point they are for us), then you can free yourself to explore new techniques and break some rules.

Interviewer: Let's go back to the beginning. You met in a BMI workshop, didn't you? How did that happen?

Ahrens: He came after me!

Flaherty: I was in college in Cincinnati in the late 1970s and early 1980s, and that's where I first met Lehman Engel, the legendary Broadway musical director who founded the BMI Workshop. Lehman had come to the school to do a series of master classes on performance. While he was there, since he was an advocate of new writers, he asked if there were any student writers that had material. Luckily, at that particular time, I had a student production of mine in rehearsal, and I had a wonderful group of actors available to present my music. I presented it to Lehman and he said, "I want you to drop out of college now, follow me to New York, and become part of my workshop." Because I had been mostly self-taught musically up to that point, I was very much into finishing my education. I wanted to finish my studies in composition, orchestrating, and all of that—so I decided to complete my undergraduate degree, knowing that I would come to New York immediately following. The fall of 1982 was when I had planned to arrive in New York, but the week before that I read in *Newsweek* that Lehman Engel had passed away. So the person in my mind that would be my mentor was no longer there, but the workshop was still going ahead and happening. I came right off the bus and right into the workshop in a week, and I met Lynn the first month. We were both in the first-year workshop, and within six months we were working with one another. It probably took six months because when I arrived in New York I was writing music and lyrics myself. I had not had a lot of experience collaborating with another writer, and I thought that would be good for me. Also, there was something about how Lynn wrote that I found really interesting and also very different from my approach to writing.

Interviewer: Surely, for both of you, there were other people in the workshop that you could have collaborated with. What made you choose to work together?

Ahrens: Before the workshop, I had been a composer as well as a lyricist; for years I wrote music and lyrics for commercials, children's TV, and that sort of thing. But when I entered the workshop, I realized that I admired the form of theater enough to admit that I was not a trained composer and that my musical knowledge was very limited. So I applied and was accepted as a lyricist only. That first year, I worked with six or eight wonderful composers, but I always admired Stephen from afar. He was a self-contained entity who was writing his own lyrics as well as music. At the end of that first year, the last assignment was "two people singing a duet in different places." I was standing on the street corner talking to some of the other people from the class, and Stephen went running by. He skidded to a halt, turned around, and called over his shoulder, "Do you want to do that last assignment together?" I yelled back, "Sure." I was very flattered. We wrote a not-very-good song, but the moment he put his hands down on the keys—the way he understood the rhythms and nuances of the lyrics—I thought, "This is it." We've been working together ever since.

Interviewer: Stephen, why did you pick Lynn out to work with you?

Flaherty: I think anything good that ever happens in anyone's lifetime has to do with intuition, with a hunch. There was something about the way that Lynn wrote. She wrote very simple yet very direct and emotional lyrics. I was trying to be a serious composer; which meant I wore black and had a beard. When I wrote, I scored out every note as I went along on a piece of paper. I had a traditional, formal way of approaching music, as opposed to a looser approach. In terms of the yin and the yang of it, I felt that that would be a really interesting way to shake things up—and it was.

Ahrens: I would say, "Come on, let's just write something. Sit down, put your hands on the keys." I *am* a little bit more improvisational by nature, I think, than Stephen.

Interviewer: Has the collaboration made each of you more like the other?

Flaherty: We've met in the middle. In terms of my initial approach to writing, I think I'm looser now. I'm open to the happy accidents that oftentimes create the best musical moments in a song and in a show, those unexpected bursts of inspiration.

Ahrens: I tend to see the broad strokes, the general outline of where we're going. He tends to focus more on the fine points and small details within each moment. Over the years, working with Stephen, I think I've become much more specific and detail-oriented than I used to be.

Interviewer: How long after you got together in the workshop did you start working on *Bedazzled*, which was the first show you wrote?

Flaherty: That was within the first six months.

Ahrens: My husband actually thought of the idea; he said, "That would make a fun musical," and we both sparked to the idea.

Interviewer: Had you both seen the film?

Ahrens: Yes, but we rewatched it, of course.

Flaherty: The thing about that particular show is that it was—I don't want to say sketch comedy, but it had very self-contained sections. It was a good first project. The scenes that contained the songs were set pieces. If we had started out of the gate saying, "Let's write a fully composed, three-hour piece like *Ragtime*," that would have been very daunting and not the best way to get to know one another.

Interviewer: Did you realize that at the time, or are you saying that now in retrospect?

Ahrens: In retrospect. One of the things we've discovered—we've talked about this recently—is that every project that we've done has taken us to another level; each one has enabled us to stretch new muscles, as individuals and as a team. For some reason, we have an intuitive sense of what we would be good at doing at a particular moment in time. At that time, in 1983, we knew that what we should be doing and what we wanted to do was something fun and light and youthful and silly and comic.

Flaherty: Which was interesting, because the pieces that I had written on my own up to that point tended to be—as pieces by young writers often are—overly serious. They seemed to have been written by a young person that had a lot of technique but not necessarily a lot of life experience. A comedy right off the bat just seemed a really good idea, but I don't think that I would have done that on my own.

Interviewer: Did it not occur to you to worry about getting the rights to do *Bedazzled* as a musical?

Flaherty: Actually, we were trying actively to get the rights from the first day that we started writing it.

Interviewer: But not having them didn't stop you from writing, did it?

Ahrens: No. In hindsight, it was probably just as well, because who knows what would have happened with the show. Whether it was accepted or not doesn't really matter. It was important for us because it gave us an experience of collaborating. It also brought our work to the attention of the theatrical community; we made a lot of interesting friends. We presented it in various workshops—not to get noticed but to get some feedback on our work. There was a fantastic workshop at the Dramatists Guild at the time, where Stephen Sondheim and Richard Maltby and Sheldon Harnick and Peter Stone and John Kander and all these luminaries would sit on a panel and critique the work of young writers who had been accepted into the program. Their eyes started to glow as they spoke to all of us; they were so kind and helped us so much.

Flaherty: You can imagine how that was. You get off the bus from the Midwest, you find your writing partner in the first six months, you write the first draft of your first show in the next six months, and you're sitting in a room with Stephen Sondheim, John Kander, and Peter Stone—and they're giving you valuable feedback with a sense of excitement that obviously lights your fire as a young writer. That experience alone not only led us to be better writers and better collaborators, it also told us that our work as a team was really worth pursuing.

Interviewer: What came next, after you couldn't get the rights to *Bedazzled*?

Ahrens: We did an adaptation of *The Emperor's New Clothes*.

Interviewer: It was children's theater?

Ahrens: Yes, because we thought (a) no rights, (b) I can write the book for this one—I just feel like I want to try, and (c) we got a little commission for it, so we were pretty sure we would get produced. We knew we'd have all these new experiences. It was the first thing we ever had produced; it was an hour-long show at Town Hall with a thousand children in the audience. That was a whole learning experience in and of itself—how to read an audience, how to learn when they're engaged and when they're bored. When children are bored or when something isn't landing with them, they stand up, throw food, and run around in the aisles. If they're involved in the story, they're very quiet; they lean forward, they listen hard. They make their feelings very clear. Adults react with more subtlety, perhaps, but it's the same—either they're rapt or they're looking at their programs and their watches. We learned an enormous amount from that experience and moved on to our next show, *Lucky Stiff.*

Interviewer: You had had all that encouragement from a lot of people, so moving to *Lucky Stiff* was probably not that difficult after the disappointment of *Bedazzled,* was it? You just kept going, didn't you?

Flaherty: Yes. Actually, it was *Bedazzled* that led us to Playwrights Horizons and *Lucky Stiff.* They had been very interested in *Bedazzled* and in producing it. Even though that particular show didn't happen because of the rights situation, it began a wonderful relationship with André Bishop, the artistic director of Playwrights, and Ira Weitzman, the director of musical theater development at Playwrights. What was really key and very important is that they encouraged us as writers. They were very interested in supporting and encouraging our careers, not just in producing our individual shows. For example, *Lucky Stiff* got quite good reviews, although they weren't the kind of reviews that said, "You must see this show! This show needs to be playing the Winter Garden tomorrow!" They weren't those kinds of reviews, but at the same time we got some very encouraging notices, especially from the *New York Times,* which said, "Keep your eye on this team." The day after *Lucky Stiff* closed at Playwrights Horizons, André and Ira said, "We're interested in helping you develop your next piece." That led us to something very different in every way, *Once on This Island.* It was a very exuberant piece, but it was much meatier in terms of subject matter and certainly in terms of the emotional quality that I was able to delve into musically. It was a significant jump for both of us, in terms of our work as creative writers and in terms of our careers. It was the first show of ours that transferred to Broadway.

Interviewer: As I hear you talk, what comes to mind is that most musical theater artists today feel that it's harder to get into the field than it's ever been, because of economic factors principally. But in another way, it may be easier than it's ever been, because there is a network of people like yourselves looking to identify young talent. Early in your careers, you were very much the beneficiaries of that network, weren't you?

Flaherty: We began our work as writers in the Off-Broadway, not-for-profit environment, which was something, obviously, that didn't exist when Jerome Kern and Cole Porter were doing their shows. The whole Off-Broadway and Off-Off-Broadway movement developed in the 1960s; by the late 1970s, it helped redefine what the musical was or could be. I remember when I was in New York City on a trip with a college singing group that I was part of, I heard about the show *March of the Falsettos,* the William Finn piece that Playwrights Horizons had just opened the week before. I knew nothing about it, but I went and got tickets and saw it by myself. I was so excited, not only by the subject matter and by the energy of the piece, but also by the scale of the piece and by what this place called Playwrights Horizons was. I'd never been to an Off-Broadway theater before, and I found the environment very exciting. I think at that point I said to myself, "This is a place where I really want to work."

Interviewer: Do you think a young musical theater person today has a lot of that kind of opportunity?

Ahrens: Yes and no. We do a lot of work with young writers. Stephen and I co-chair the Dramatists Guild Jonathan Larson Fellows program, which provides young musical theater writers and playwrights with mentoring and master classes and a sense of community. There are more college programs and workshops available now than ever before, I think, for young writers to learn what they're doing. There are a number of places where they can go and study their craft. But there are fewer opportunities for actual production on and off Broadway, simply because of the economics. Either place, everybody's struggling, established writers and young ones alike.

Flaherty: But there are also shows that start way off Broadway, develop an audience, and ultimately demand that they be transferred.

Ahrens: That's right. But all of the not-for-profit theaters are having tremendous financial difficulties, particularly after September 11. Funding's been cut back, so on one level there are a lot of programs dedicated to trying to encourage new writers and new works. On the other hand, the actual deed of getting produced is quite difficult. You can get readings, you can get workshops; people are always willing to put a little money into those kinds of things. If you're good, if you're lucky, if you work really hard, if you do your rewrites and really work on your piece, your chances get better that you will get a production somewhere. But people write us letters and say, "I have a show and it's completely ready to go. I'd like to go to Broadway; it's got an all-black cast of twenty-nine." What can you say? The odds are so against that kind of thing ever happening. We started very small. We didn't think small artistically, but we thought small in practical ways—how big an orchestra, how big a cast would be viable for unknowns such as ourselves? And you know what? We still think that way.

You almost have to, because the larger you think, the more difficult financially it is going to be to find people willing and able to take the risk—and it's always a risk.

Interviewer: Let's say that, in the course of the year, you find *x* number of talented young people in the various workshops and master classes you do. What percentage of those people are likely to get some sort of production?

Flaherty: I would say, in general, that the cream always rises to the top, whether you're a performer, a writer, or whatever corner of the theater you're in; but it's difficult for anyone to get that full-fledged production.

Interviewer: You must know of very talented young people right now who have not been able to get a production.

Ahrens: Absolutely. Not twenty-five of them, but maybe three or four or five. They should be produced, they're pretty much ready, and they need their first production. That's the other thing we tend to forget: A young writer used to be able to do a production on Broadway and fail, and then somebody would put money into his next show and his next. People learned their craft by being produced. Now we learn it by being workshopped, and it's not the same.

Interviewer: When did George C. Wolfe come into your lives?

Ahrens: That was before *The Emperor's New Clothes.* After we did *Bedazzled* and didn't get the rights, we thought, "We're going to do something where we don't need the rights. We're going to do an original idea." We came up with *Antler,* which was based on a newspaper clipping that I had found about an elderly man in South Dakota who gave his land away to people in order to keep the town alive. We thought there might be a musical in it, and Ira Weitzman at Playwrights Horizons took us under his wing. He put us together with George, and the three of us tried to write this wacky little musical for I don't know how long—maybe eight months—and we decided that it was an idea in search of a real story. We couldn't make it good. We just couldn't figure it out, so we left it behind. I was so frustrated. That's when we decided to do something that was in the public domain, so we wouldn't have to worry about rights—and something where a real story already existed. That's how we came to do *The Emperor's New Clothes.*

Flaherty: I don't think *Antler* will ever be completed or produced, but what was good about it was that it was our first experience of working with a third writer. It happened in George's career right before his work as a playwright took off; it was just before *The Colored Museum* broke onto the scene. In our collaboration, Lynn has often written the book as well as the lyrics, but that was an early instance of working with a playwright. Since then, we've worked with two other playwrights.

Interviewer: How is that different? Lynn, do you give that up willingly or reluctantly?

Ahrens: I give it up completely willingly, because there are only certain kinds of librettos that I think I'm good at. Those are shows that are mostly sung through. I'm a very good structuralist, but until recently I've been uncomfortable writing dialogue. I always end up turning it into a lyric. In *Once on This Island,* there are maybe four or five tiny spoken sections. It happens that I am writing the book—and it's a bit of an experiment for me—for *Dessa Rose,* our new show next season at Lincoln Center Theater.[At press time, *Dessa Rose* was scheduled to open March 21, 2005.] There are very meaty book scenes; I feel as if I'm finally finding a way to make friends with the spoken word.

Flaherty: *Dessa Rose* is a real breakthrough for Lynn. It was her idea, and it's one of the rare examples of Lynn writing a lot of text before I approach it musically. Normally, when we begin writing, we bat ideas back and forth and discuss the musical structures and how they intersect with the ideas of the text. That usually happens in our collaboration together, whereas with this piece Lynn wrote virtually a complete first act, as if it were an opera libretto. The other thing to keep in mind is that when you go from show to show or project to project, not only are you looking for subject matter that will challenge you or bring out different musical ideas, it's also important to find new ways of working. This new piece is really a different way of working for us.

Interviewer: You've brought up how you work. Is it different when Lynn writes both book and lyrics from when you're working with another book-writer? When you work with a book-writer, do you have to wait until he has written the script, or do you work closely with him throughout the project?

Ahrens: We're all in the same room, and we talk about the moment that we want to do and about the structure. With *Ragtime,* we analyzed who the main characters and the secondary characters were and how the show would work, and we plotted it out to a certain extent. Terrence McNally, the librettist, would write a couple of pages and give them to us and we'd musicalize them; or sometimes we'd write a song that we felt needed to go into the show and he would write around that—so it was a very fluid process.

Interviewer: In that instance, then, you worked totally collaboratively, didn't you?

Flaherty: Yes. *Ragtime* was, for the most part, written chronologically. That was a smart way to work with that particular piece, because each step of the writing process informed not only the text but also the rules for the evening, the way the tale would be told. I don't think it would have been possible to start writing, say, the fifth scene without knowing the flavor and style of those initial moments.

Interviewer: What attracts you to a particular project? I assume that sometimes it's the people involved, but are there other factors?

Ahrens: I'm always in bookstores and in movies looking for stories. I look for a wonderful story that I can't put down, one that grabs me by the throat. I look for something that has a lyrical quality to it, which doesn't necessarily mean that it has to have beautiful language. The only way I can describe it is that when I read something, sometimes songs leap off the page and sometimes they don't. The very first lines of *Once on This Island* come directly out of the text of the novel. You look for characters with deep emotions, and you look for dramatic circumstances in the story. *Ragtime* has music built right into the title and woven throughout the piece; *Once on This Island* is Caribbean-inflected; and *Lucky Stiff* has an operettaish quality. If there's also a musical quality or style inherent, that's all for the good.

Flaherty: What I loved about *Lucky Stiff* was that it gave me an opportunity to send up so many different musical forms. I'd been a lover of musicals since childhood, and that show gave me the opportunity to celebrate and send up every aspect of musical theater within the structure of a musical farce. What we didn't realize starting the piece, which proved to be one of the most challenging aspects of writing that particular show, was that so much of the plot was told through the songs. In a certain way, the songs became the book, and just getting that amount of information and exposition across through song became quite a challenge.

Interviewer: Has Lynn ever come to you with a book project and you said, "It's not something that interests me"?

Flaherty: We've always had those discussions. It might not necessarily be something that doesn't interest me, but it's something that doesn't feel right for me at a particular time in terms of what I'm feeling.

Ahrens: With *Dessa Rose*, the show we're working on now, I first brought it to Stephen eight or nine years ago. I said, "I have this novel. You should read it." He read it and said, "I just don't relate to it." I said, "That's fine," and I put it in my file. Then, all these many years later, we were looking for new projects and I took it out and found it still very interesting, but Stephen still couldn't quite see it. That's why I said, "I feel like I have to do this, so I'm going to write something and I'll give it to you. If you still don't like it, fine." I wrote it, and once it took on a lyrical shape he did respond to it.

Flaherty: What's interesting is that when Lynn showed me *Dessa Rose* in 1993, it did lead me into thinking about American themes and American music. The novel is set in the Deep South in the mid-1800s, and in terms of my subconscious, it led me to think about the roots of American music. Then the opportunity to do *Ragtime* presented itself, and probably I was ready to do that show because I had been thinking about *Dessa Rose*.

Interviewer: Would you say that musically each of the shows you've done has presented interesting and different challenges?

Flaherty: Absolutely. If you look at our shows individually, you think, "How could these shows come from the same authors?" The styles of music that I use come from a wide palette, but a lot of the musical techniques and the way the music is used in terms of the storytelling are part of my musical style—even though the fabric that it's cut from is different.

Interviewer: Would you go back and do another musical in one of the styles you've already used? Would you revisit the Irish musical style you used in *A Man of No Importance,* for example?

Flaherty: *A Man of No Importance* is much more about Irish folk music and folk music in general. It's not a traditional "Broadway" score. I really feel that I made my statement in that musical style, so I don't think that I'd want to go back and revisit it. But down the way, there might be another interesting project that presents itself and I might realize that I haven't mined everything musically within that genre.

Interviewer: Do your shows change radically during the rehearsal and preview process?

Ahrens: In terms of the writing of the shows, they go through tremendous metamorphoses every time. You go into rehearsal with a draft that has been through a workshop or a reading and a workshop—some sort of developmental process to get it to the point where the producers say, "Okay. Let's go into production." You come from this lengthy developmental process, you get it as right as you can; you cast the show, you get into a rehearsal process—and that's when you always discover there's rewriting to be done. No matter how great and how final you feel the work is, there are always changes during rehearsals. The text changes along the way—and the music, too. The shape of any show shifts and adjusts somewhat as it gets on its feet.

Interviewer: Where does that come from? How big a role does the director play?

Ahrens: A lot of it comes from us, because we're our harshest critics. We know what's working and what's not working. And once you're on that production time clock, there's a limited amount of time before the show actually goes before the public, so it can be very intense. In terms of the director's input, as an example, Joe Mantello, who did *A Man of No Importance,* made some fine surgical contributions to that show. He was very astute when it came to text changes—what wasn't clear and what needed to be edited. He was wonderful, but then we've always been really lucky with our directors. At a certain point, any show becomes a collaboration between writers, designers, and actors—and you have to be sensitive to the ideas and needs of your fellow artists.

Flaherty: When Lynn talks about "what works," she doesn't mean "works" in a producerial way. For me, at least, the purpose of a workshop or reading is to allow the show to become itself. That's when I, as the composer, sit back and try to be as objective as I can and watch the piece and respond. What I mean by that is that I get a lot more information from hearing actors saying the lines than I do from us in our studio. Ultimately, when we go into any sort of reading or workshop, we generally have a very fleshed-out score, some sort of a completed draft. It's not like we throw little bits and pieces in the air and we see what happens. I like to do most of the vocal arranging and vocal composition on my shows in advance, but whenever I'm in a rehearsal room and I'm working with a group of, say, ten actors, all of a sudden I'm dealing with not only individual characters but also with individual performers playing those characters. I like to have a completed first draft with me when I go into that room; but when I hear how it sounds on these particular voices, I'm willing to throw everything away and reshape and rework based on what I hear from the actors—not just in terms of their ideas on character, but also from how the score sounds on those particular voices. I'm writing a very particular piece for a very particular set of instruments, these actors; so in terms of what works, it has to do with how the piece sits on a particular set of performers.

Ahrens: I'm looking at different things. He's looking at musical issues, and I'm looking at clarity and shape and structure and dramatic arc. We're trying to make the piece as whole and as communicative as we possibly can.

Flaherty: But it always comes from the writer, which is the good thing. It's not the producer saying, "We need this number."

Ahrens: We've never done that.

Interviewer: In the heyday of the American musical, Broadway music was the popular music of the day. Individual songs from musicals were hits. Today that's not the case. Why do you think that is?

Ahrens: Singer/songwriters. It used to be that famous singers would cover theater songs and sing them on the radio and on their albums. Theater music was the popular music of America. But singer/songwriters began to emerge; they wrote and performed their own material and had a very personal voice. That's what has become the norm for a number of reasons, not the least of which is that they keep their own royalties and their own copyrights.

Interviewer: That's certainly one explanation, but let me try two others and see if you agree. One is that it's hard now to take a song out of the context of the show, which often is a good thing, and the other is that Broadway show music today bears very little resemblance to the pop music played on the radio.

Ahrens: Book songs are much more integral to the plot in the contemporary evolution of the form, so yes, you're right, they're probably not as liftable as they used to be. But I also think that pop music doesn't make it dramatically on the stage for the most part. It's fabulous music, and we're getting a lot of compilation shows—of Billy Joel's songs and *Mamma Mia!,* for example—where they weave some kind of book idea around popular songs. But I think a large portion of the success of those compilation shows is that people know and love the songs ahead of time.

Flaherty: When you think of the musical, what is the function of the music? In the contemporary musical, the music carries the drama. The music is as important as the book scenes, and oftentimes the music *is* the book scene. That is very different from the early Rodgers and Hart shows. Somebody once asked why there were more Rodgers and Hart covers than Rodgers and Hammerstein covers. I think it's because almost all of the Rodgers and Hart songs were written to be taken out of context, while for Rodgers and Hammerstein it was mostly about the musical drama of the shows themselves. That's why the shows of Rodgers and Hammerstein are more revivable today than the shows of Rodgers and Hart.

Interviewer: What about the critics? Have you ever learned anything from them?

Flaherty: There are so few good critics writing right now. In the past, there were several critics that I enjoyed reading; it was part of my education in the theater. Reviews were placed in some sort of historical context; if they were talking about a particular play that opened, they would discuss how that play figured into the canon of that author's work or they would deal with it in terms of a trend in the theater. A lot of the current criticism is for me not helpful—amateurish and not usable as an educational tool. However, there are certain writers that I do respect and admire. John Lahr of the *New Yorker* is a wonderful writer. I think of him as a theater scholar more than a reviewer.

Interviewer: I would think that, as a composer, you must be particularly frustrated about theater reviewers and critics because none of them has any musical expertise at all. They may be competent to evaluate the book and lyrics, but how can they judge the music?

Flaherty: What always frustrates and astounds me at the same time is how little ink is devoted to the music of musicals, because most of the critics of musicals are theater critics rather than music critics. But even the music critics don't always understand the dramatic function of the music; they deal with music as a separate component, as opposed to seeing how it functions dramatically within the context of an opera or musical theater piece. I've found that the London critics generally have a lot more interesting stuff to say about music in general and my music in particular.

Ahrens: I really don't read reviews. I stopped reading them after *Lucky Stiff*, which was the first show we did that got reviewed. I said, "Never again." It can paralyze a writer—well, me, anyway—to read both the good *and* the bad. My husband reads them and once in a while he'll show me something that might have some good criticism in it that I might learn from. But for the most part, as Stephen knows, I don't read them. You know what the results of your show are without having to read what the reviewers say.

Flaherty: Within yourself as a writer, you know what your intentions were, and I think ultimately you know if you've hit the mark or not. Frankly, I've read reviews of a show of mine when I know I've absolutely hit the mark and achieved what it was that I set out to do and the critic might not understand even what it was that I was attempting—so for him or her that's a failure. I've also read reviews of shows where I know that I've not solved certain problems or what I had intended had not gotten across for whatever reason—and the review was absolutely glorious. They're both equally meaningless to me. Ultimately, it comes down to you as an artist sitting with yourself and being honest about what you're trying to achieve and whether you've achieved it or not—and if you haven't, how you can build upon that and learn from it.

Interviewer: Can you take us through one of your shows from beginning to end, in terms of your involvement with it?

Ahrens: Let's do *Ragtime*.

Interviewer: How did that show start?

Ahrens: In a nutshell, the genesis of the project was that Garth Drabinsky, the producer, had obtained the stage rights to the novel, and the first person that he went to was Terrence McNally. E. L. Doctorow had approval over the creative team, because apparently he was less than happy with the movie that was made from his novel; so he wanted to know who was going to be chosen and what their take on his work was. We all, in one form or another, had to do an audition. Terrence did an eighty-page treatment of the novel, and Doctorow liked the treatment very much—as did Garth. The next stage was that Garth took Terrence's treatment and gave it to eight or nine musical writing teams, Stephen and I being one of those teams. He said, "I'm giving you"—I forget whether it was fifteen hundred or a thousand dollars—"and you're going to deliver to me demos on tape of four songs based on the treatment and the novel." We never knew—and still don't know—who the other teams were and didn't want to know, because they were probably friends of ours. What was fantastic about Terrence's treatment was that it established the device of characters coming forward and speaking of themselves in the third person—"Mother did this" or "Father went there." We seized on that as being very interesting and decided that, if we were hired, we would keep that. We chose four moments: We wrote the opening number, the song "Till We Reach That Day" at the end of act one, the song "Gliding," and we wrote a little song for Evelyn Nesbit and Younger Brother. Three of those songs actually ended up staying in the show.

Interviewer: Had you worked with Terrence McNally before this?

Ahrens: No. We knew him slightly, but we'd never worked with him.

Flaherty: The great thing about Terrence is that, first of all, he's a very generous person with younger writers. When we had *Once on This Island* on Broadway, I received a note from Terrence—we'd not met—that said, "I've just seen your show. Congratulations," and he talked about how much he loved the score. I'd admired him for years, so I put that little note on my bulletin board, not knowing that just a few years later we'd be working on a piece together. A lot of people ask me what it was like auditioning for a piece, because Garth is a very unconventional producer and a writers' audition is a very unconventional method to hire writers. For me, I was very interested in writing the score of *Ragtime*, because at that time we had been looking at American ideas; but I don't think there was anything that Lynn and I had written up to that point that would have suggested we were the right writers for that particular show—so the opportunity to write four songs and be considered for the job was extraordinary. We chose four moments in the show that were wildly different and showed the complete canvas of what the music and the sound would be. We did the demos full out, with a large group of singers singing every vocal part.

Interviewer: Do you have any sense of what the vetting process was? Was McNally involved?

Ahrens: He was involved, along with Doctorow and Garth.

Flaherty: We delivered our little demo cassette on the opening night of Garth's production of *Show Boat*. It was as if we went to the theater and said, "Here's our cassette. Now, can we come in and see the show?"

Interviewer: How long after you submitted the demo did you find out that you'd been selected?

Flaherty: A couple of weeks. Those were really long days to go through.

Interviewer: Then what happened?

Ahrens: Garth hired us—and he told us he could fire us!

Flaherty: He said, "Congratulations, you have the job, and I have the right to fire you. I'm going to fire you if you don't come up to my level." Now it seems hilarious, but it didn't seem so at the time.

Ahrens: We sat down with Terrence and started discussing the show—how to handle so many characters and so many plots. We decided to simplify it by having the fictional characters be the leads and the historical characters be the secondary characters. Each of the fictional characters would have a historical character linked to him or her thematically in some way. Younger Brother would become a radical because of his contact with Emma Goldman; Father would identify with J. P. Morgan; and Mother would become the opposite of Evelyn Nesbit by becoming her own person.

Interviewer: And all that came from the three of you working together, rather than from Terrence McNally coming in and telling you what it was going to be?

Flaherty: We wrote those first four songs in August and September 1994. We found out soon after that that we had the job, and we began working in earnest with Terrence in January 1995. What Lynn just described to you—what is the story? who is the main character?—those questions are things that we agreed upon in our very first meeting with Terrence. Before we wrote a single note or a single word, we had to make sure that we were all in agreement about what the focus of the piece was. The writing, as I remember, was very fast; we began working that January, and by that summer we had the first draft of the complete show—which is incredible, considering the size of the piece. I think it was because we were absolutely on fire and excited and inspired. We loved writing it. We did a first reading six months later and we learned a lot from that reading about certain characters. Evelyn Nesbit was much more prominent in that first draft, and that didn't quite serve the piece, so we set out to rework Tateh and Evelyn primarily. We had a second reading about three months later.

At that point, some major numbers started emerging in the score. Three months after that, we had a workshop in Toronto for six weeks, which was really important in the creation of the show. Because we were writing new material constantly and reshaping it, putting the show up on its feet and seeing it hold the stage was crucial. Then, in the fall of 1996, we went into rehearsal for the world premiere in December 1996 in Toronto.

Interviewer: How was the casting done?

Ahrens: We cast it at the first reading, but it kept changing and evolving. Brian Stokes Mitchell and Audra McDonald were with us from the very beginning, but Donna Murphy was our first Mother, and Joel Grey was the first Tateh. We went through a lot of casting as we found our way with the characters.

Interviewer: When did you get a director?

Ahrens: Frank Galati came on board when we were fairly well into the writing process, when we kind of knew what we were doing.

Flaherty: I think we met Frank in February or March 1995.

Interviewer: Who selected him, Drabinsky?

Flaherty: No. We were all involved. I think the notion of Frank actually came from Terrence.

Interviewer: Had you seen his adaptation of *The Grapes of Wrath*?

Flaherty: Yes, and I think his work on that show was why he seemed like a good choice for *Ragtime*. One of the things that attracted us all to the piece was Doctorow's language; that's one of the reasons why Terrence had decided he wanted to do a lot of third-person narrative—so he could use the actual text of the novel. And that's what Frank did with *The Grapes of Wrath*. He takes works of classic literature and adapts them for a theatrical context. In terms of having a director who could deal with that type of language, he seemed like a natural collaborator, even though he had never done an original musical before. He'd done opera and a reworking of the musical *Lost in the Stars* in Chicago. It was a joy to watch Frank as new music would come in, because he had not had that experience in theater, where there's not a song one day and the next day there is.

Interviewer: What percentage of the songs that were in the first reading ended up in the show?

Ahrens: Quite a few did. There were certain areas of the show where we did a lot of rewriting, like the opening number.

Flaherty: With each reading or workshop, there was a new version of the opening number. We had always thought of it as being an overture of sorts, not only of musical themes but of ideas. As the musical themes changed, I would go back and make changes in the opening.

Ahrens: That opening number is an example, I think, of the fantastic collaboration of theater artists, and it's one that I'm personally very proud of. It's a ten-minute chunk that sets up every major musical theme in the show and every major character. Terrence is a very generous writer; he loves it when his best scenes and monologues become song. And Graciela Daniele's choreography for that number was so extraordinary. At the end of the number, the immigrants, the WASPs, and the African Americans formed three moving "clusters." These groups circled one another around the stage, and out of them came our main characters, thrust into direct confrontation—Mother, Coalhouse, Father, and Tateh—and then they were swirled back into their own groups again. It was choreographic genius, a perfect marriage of artists, actors, and material.

Flaherty: The strange thing is, you would assume that that moment would have been developed by the choreographer and a dance arranger; but in fact, that instrumental section Lynn described, where the different groups are swirling around one another, was on our original demo tape. It was part of the original composition, and Graciela responded to that composition. I believe there was one line that I wrote in the score, something like, "There is an altercation." She took that and created a fully choreographed sequence that not only mirrored beautifully what the music did but expanded on the idea of the music and the idea of what the show was about—assimilation.

Interviewer: To get back to the history of the show, when did *Ragtime* open in Toronto?

Ahrens: In December 1996. It got wonderful reviews and ran in Toronto for a year, while the Ford Center in New York was being renovated. That was Garth's tremendous contribution to New York City, to take these two old, decrepit theaters and combine them into one new, huge, state-of-the-art theater—and *Ragtime* was slated to open that theater. While the cast was up in Toronto freezing and waiting to come to New York, Garth opened a second company in Los Angeles.

Flaherty: We were flying weekly up to Toronto and putting new material into the show. We focused on several areas, writing new songs and new text; we did that throughout January and February 1997. When we opened in Toronto, the sequence in Atlantic City didn't quite work; it wasn't totally focused, so we wound up rewriting that. We threw out the original song that's on the concept album and wrote another one for Toronto. When we brought the show to L.A., we threw out the second song that had been written for Toronto and wrote a third song for Los Angeles.

Ahrens: You know what it was? We kept writing a song for these two characters, Evelyn Nesbit and Harry Houdini, to sing, but in fact, they didn't really merit a song. At that point, you just wanted the plot to keep going. Suddenly these two secondary characters had a whole stop-the-show number. It's a charming song; it's on the recording of the Toronto production, but it never got to New York.

Flaherty: Garth initially felt that we needed a lavish production number in Atlantic City, and Graciela, who's always about story, kept asking, "What is the story? What is the drama?" That's the primary focus of her work. It was a bit of a wrestling match, because she wanted to know, "What is the point that we're trying to make?" It was a delicate balance between giving the audience some sense of production value and at the same time really focusing on what the drama of the story was at that moment.

Interviewer: Did you make many additional changes specifically for the New York opening?

Flaherty: Very few. We added a short bridge to the song "Gliding" for Tateh, because the character of the mother is a presence in the novel and not in the musical and we felt that we needed to invoke her. So that was added, and some small bits of musical continuity.

Interviewer: You portrayed Garth Drabinsky at the beginning of the process as a terrifying and controlling person. Did he exert a great deal of influence during the evolution of the show or was he supportive all the way?

Ahrens: He was very supportive. Garth is a complex, passionate person. He *can* be terrifying, because he pulls no punches. He's loud; he can yell—and does. But I learned to yell back. I became very fond of him; I think he's a great, creative producer.

Flaherty: Throughout the development process and previews, obviously, we would have meetings to discuss what we had seen. Part of Garth's learning curve as a producer was that he had only produced one original musical prior to ours, *Kiss of the Spider Woman*, which was very much Hal Prince's production. I don't know that Garth was as involved on that show as he was on *Ragtime*. At the same time, I think what he needed to know was that he had hired three very strong writers and that while it was helpful to hear what his concerns were, it was not his job to write the show, rewrite the show, or find any of its solutions.

Ahrens: He learned that early on. We had a fight about it, because he tried to tell us what to do and I said, "You can tell us what you're unhappy with or any concerns you have, but we'll solve it. We'll figure out how to accommodate your questions or your confusions, but you will not come up with solutions." He was very respectful after that. When producers are putting millions of dollars into a show, they have a right to express their confusion and their questions. Garth really began to trust what we were coming up with, and he loved the material. Trust is an important thing, but you have to earn it.

Flaherty: We were very fortunate on *Ragtime* to have Bill Brohn as the orchestrator; he's absolutely brilliant. He and I had a phenomenal relationship on the show. Much of our time was spent not talking about instruments but talking about emotion, drama, and intent. We would often talk about colors and how they might transform themselves into sounds. In terms of the educational process, it was wonderful for me. Bill was brought in on the piece quite early; around the time that we were doing the second reading, he was already present and we were talking about the orchestrations. We got to do a concept album, which came out before the Toronto production opened—so we were able to hear what the arrangements would sound like and develop them much more slowly than you would in a typical Broadway show. I think that's why they have such amazing detail to them.

Interviewer: Often in a musical, it seems as if there's been a dominant figure among the creative team. It's a Fosse show, a Sondheim show, a Susan Stroman show, a Julie Taymor show, or a Jerome Robbins show. It sounds in your descriptions of your shows as if that hasn't been the case. Your shows seem to have been very much real collaborations. Is that so?

Ahrens: I would say that pretty much all of them have been. It's a funny thing, because there are certain theater artists who put a very specific stamp on their work. We tend to write differently from show to show; we try to become invisible and let the characters speak in their own voices. We want to create something in which the artistic team speaks with a unified voice. Sure, I'd like somebody to say it's an Ahrens and Flaherty show—and maybe they do. But I know whenever I hear "myself" coming out of a character's mouth, I rewrite.

Flaherty: I do have to say that *Ragtime* is probably, of everything I've done, the show-off piece. It was the chance to write in at least a dozen different styles of music.

Ahrens: But we always tend to humble ourselves to the material and to allow the piece to speak for itself in some odd way, to become what it needs to be and not impose a style on it. That's not to say we don't have a voice; I think we do.

Flaherty: What's really important to remember about *Ragtime* is that almost everybody that worked on the show had several talents. Lynn has written book as well as lyrics; Graciela is a director as well as a choreographer; Frank Galati is a playwright and adapter as well as a director; and

Santo Loquasto, who had so many great ideas that had nothing to do with costumes, is a scenic designer as well as a costume designer. When we had our meetings together as a creative team, the thing that was wonderful was that you could speak about anything, whether it was your particular department or not. There was so much cross-pollination with that particular group of people.

Interviewer: All your musicals have been adaptations. Do you think the American musical theater will ever have another *Music Man*, a show that is totally original, or are we always going to see adapted musicals now?

Flaherty: If there's a wonderful playwright out there who's got a great original idea, we'd certainly be open to it.

Ahrens: *Avenue Q* is an original idea; original ideas are happening even as we speak. But more often than not, adaptations happen, because musical theater writers are generally not playwrights. The blank page is scary for us. Someday I might try an original myself. In the meantime, it does happen from time to time. *Sunday in the Park with George* is as original as you can get. They took a painting and they wrote a whole story around it.

Jason Robert Brown

Jason Robert Brown was born on June 20, 1970, in Tarrytown, New York. He studied at the Eastman School of Music. He has worked as a composer, a lyricist, an orchestrator, an arranger, and a music director. The New York musicals for which he wrote the songs include Songs for a New World *(1995),* Parade *(1999),* The Last Five Years *(2002), and* Urban Cowboy *(2003). His work as an orchestrator and arranger includes* New York Rock *(1995),* john and jen *(1996),* A New Brain *(1998),* Love's Fire *(1998),* Dinah Was *(1999), and* Urban Cowboy. *He was music director for* The Petrified Prince *(1994),* When Pigs Fly *(1996), and* Urban Cowboy.

In 1996, he was the recipient of the Gilman and Gonzalez-Falla Foundation Award for Musical Theater; and he received the Tony Award for Parade *(Best Score). He also received the 2002 Kleban Award for Distinguished Lyrics.*

This interview took place on January 20, 2004.

Interviewer: Could we start with some information about your background? Where did you grow up?

Brown: I grew up in Rockland County. My folks are both from New York, so we lived just outside the city. When I was about ten years old, I demanded a piano in the house. I don't know why, but I said it needed to happen. Luckily, my grandfather had one in his basement in Brooklyn, so we brought it over to my house and I started playing. It was something I was bound and determined to do.

Interviewer: Do you have any idea what got you interested? Had you been to a musical? Had you had any experience with music?

Brown: My parents were lightly cultural. We came into the city, but I had never gone to the symphony or seen a concert or anything like that. When I was about seven, I went to my first show, *The Wiz*. The year after that there was a revival of *West Side Story* that Debbie Allen was in, and that was the next musical I saw. The piano thing came probably around the same time, but I can't say whether they were related. I think there was just a desire in me to make music.

Interviewer: Did you take lessons?

Brown: Reluctantly. I thought if you banged on the piano long enough it would start making sense, which was not necessarily true, so I did eventually take lessons. I wanted to be a rock star—Billy Joel or Elton John or Carole King—but, obviously, with shorter hair. There was that part of me, and then the other part of me loved the idea of being an actor; I wanted to be a kid on a TV show. Basically, I wanted any kind of attention I could get from anybody. Somehow, those two things, wanting to be an actor and wanting to be a rock star, are how I ended up writing for the musical theater. It was a place where I could get out my desire to be a performer, to invest myself dramatically in a piece of material, and at the same time it was musical and I could invest myself musically in creating a piece of material. My folks had a couple of cast albums in the house; *West Side Story* was one of them, and *Cabaret* was another. My mother was an English teacher and I used to make her go to her school library and get out the published libretti of any musicals that she could find. I remember she brought home *West Side Story,* and I would sit with the phonograph needle in my hand and read all the lines for Tony and Maria; then I'd put the needle down on the record at the point where a song was supposed to start. The song would go all the way through, and then I'd pick up the needle and read the next line of dialogue. I'd do the whole show that way. I did that with every show I could get a libretto and a record for. I probably spent most of my early teens doing that, trying to be everything in every musical that I could be a part of.

Interviewer: When you thought about your relationship to those shows at that time, was it as a performer or as a creator?

Brown: Probably both. I don't think I thought it was necessary at the time to make a distinction like that. I thought that you could be in them and write them. When I grew up in the 1970s, music was all made by singer/songwriters—Joni Mitchell, Paul McCartney, Billy Joel. They wrote and they sang their material, so I never made much of a distinction. It's still not a natural distinction for me to make; I tend to perform my own material. Most everything I write, I do thinking I'm going to sing it one of these days. I think that if it feels good for me to do it, then it will feel good for somebody else to sing it. I tailor my material first to me, and then I let it go out into the world and go to someone else.

Interviewer: After high school, what went into your decision to go to the Eastman School of Music?

Brown: I got very torn between the theater part of me and the music part of me and wasn't sure which way I wanted to go. I didn't like the idea of being a professional actor, because I felt like you could easily be a very small fish in an extremely large pond. I didn't like the odds. It didn't serve my need to get attention to be in a situation where I potentially wouldn't. I decided I didn't want to go to college. I didn't think there was a whole lot for me to do there, but my folks said, "We expect you to go to college. That's what nice Jewish boys do." I said, "All right, fine." I decided that, of the two, I would rather go more on the musical end; and once I had decided I was going to aim for a musical education, the question was: Do I go for a more commercial musical education or a more classical and conservative education? I don't know quite how I ended up with the idea that it was better to go with a conservatory, hard-edged, horn-rimmed glasses, pencil-behind-your-ear kind of musical life. I think I felt like I was capable of learning all the commercial tricks myself and that the things I couldn't learn by myself were the really hard things, like how to write twelve-tone music and how to orchestrate symphonically. I applied to Juilliard, Manhattan School of Music, Indiana, and Eastman; eventually, Eastman became the obvious choice and that's how I ended up there. The minute I walked in the door I thought, "This was a mistake. This isn't for me. I'm not designed for this life." I was always a terrible student, because I'm not good at the concept that a grade is a good motivator; it was never a good enough reason for me to get something done. Unless I was really interested in something, it was hard for me to do it. I'm still maybe one of the finest procrastinators I know. I took my first year at Eastman very seriously and tried very hard to get into the idea of what I was doing. I was learning a lot of things, but I wasn't doing well in my work.

Interviewer: What did you study?

Brown: I went in as a composition major. I studied with Samuel Adler, who was a very fine Germanic composer in the symphonic tradition. I also studied with a guy named Joe Schwantner, who was a Pulitzer Prize winner, also a symphonic composer. There were some wonderful people who were all doing contemporary classical music, which, as I said even then, was a great way to die poor. I learned a lot about more experimental musics, and I think that infiltrates my work now, even though what I do is considerably more accessible and commercial than anything I was being taught.

Interviewer: In what sense was going to Eastman a great mistake? As you describe it, it seems to make a lot of sense to learn the basics of classical technique.

Brown: It would have, had I been the kind of person who had the discipline to learn the basics of classical technique, but I wasn't.

Interviewer: You just didn't have the patience, did you?

Brown: No. And probably not even the internal intelligence to deal with the sort of intellectual structures that contemporary classical music is based on.

Interviewer: But aren't you also saying that, in retrospect, you did learn something?

Brown: Oh, absolutely. I was very curious about it and I was very interested in it, but the environment felt very sterile to me and very unencouraging of anything that smacked of commercialism or even popular music. At my first meeting with Sam Adler, he said, "What is it you want to do? What sort of ambitions do you have?" I said, "I think I'd like to maybe write for the musical theater." He said in his heaviest, most Germanic and disapproving tone, "Jason, if you want to write a musical, you sit down one afternoon and you write a musical—but it's not a life's work." I think that attitude was prevalent in that ivory-tower environment.

Interviewer: How long did you last there?

Brown: Two years. I did one real year, and then my second year I was just bouncing around waiting to get out.

Interviewer: What would you say is the greatest impact that your two years at Eastman have had on your work?

Brown: That time I spent in a very uptight conservatory served mostly to broaden my intellectual curiosity. I spent a lot of time in the library listening to music and reading. It was music that I would not have had access to otherwise. The music library at Eastman is substantial and fabulous. I spent probably twelve hours a day sitting there with my headphones on, listening to records that were long out of print or had only been pressed by one person and reading scores that I would never have been able to find here in New York or anywhere else. It broadened me as a musician and as a person thinking about music, so that when I hung out my shingle, I had a lot more exposure to different kinds of music than people who'd only ever done musical theater. I also had a lot more experience conducting very difficult, musically different, and adventurous work, orchestrating more difficult and musically adventurous work, and composing more difficult and musically adventurous work. I just have more tools in my toolbox, and they're not the same tools everyone else has. Most of the palette I draw from is pop music; I don't write contemporary symphonic music. Most of what I do still sounds in form like a pop song, but it would have been impossible to write *Parade,* a long-form show that accomplishes such a substantive arc, without a broad and eclectic musical vocabulary. Writing a two-and-a-half hour piece is very different from writing a three-minute piece. The most important things I got from Eastman were what all those tools were and learning how to use them. Even *The Last Five Years,* which seems to be discrete individual five- or seven-minute numbers, has a very long structural arc to it. It's a continuous eighty-minute piece of music. I was able to disguise that within the smaller song forms, but I think that the reason *The Last Five Years* falls together is that I have the tools to do a long-form work.

Interviewer: After you left Eastman, what did you do?

Brown: There was a high school for the performing arts in Miami that a friend of mine was attending as a student. They needed pianists and it was Miami, so it was going to be a nice climate change from Rochester. I went down, and very quickly they realized that I had an expertise in musical theater that they were lacking at the school. So I became an instructor at this high school within a month of having arrived in Miami. They were very keen on keeping me there, but after a year I said, "If there's any advantage on Broadway of having left college early, of being young, and of being new on the block, I should take advantage of that and go." I came to New York, and I started working in piano bars and cabarets and anyplace where I could get a job playing.

Interviewer: Were you composing at the same time?

Brown: Yes, I was writing. I had a million terrible ideas for shows, and I was working on all of them simultaneously; but then somebody would say,

"I have a cabaret act coming up and I need a closing number"—and I'd write a song. On one of my trips into the city from Miami, I had seen Richard Maltby and David Shire's show *Closer than Ever*. I said, "I could do something like that. I should do a revue, just a bunch of songs." So I was writing these songs for various cabaret acts and musicals with the thought that maybe I'd just put them all together and do a little club act. *Closer than Ever* had been developed in a cabaret called Eighty Eights, where I was playing piano bar downstairs. It's gone now, unfortunately, but I had started working there primarily because I knew that Richard and David had started their show there, and I thought, "I'm going to do this." I booked a couple of nights upstairs and I said, "I have an idea for a show." They all said, "Okay, sure, whatever." I called some of the girls who sang in the piano bar with me, and we did this show. I called it *The New World* partly because there were a couple of numbers from a show I was writing that was going to be a goofy revisionist American history. I had written a suite of songs about Christopher Columbus, and there was a song about Betsy Ross; but I stopped writing that show because I ran out of ideas very quickly. There's only so much American history that's any fun to play around with like that. I had gotten up to George Washington Carver and the peanut, and then I thought, "All right, I'm out." I had abandoned that project, but I still had these Christopher Columbus songs, the Betsy Ross song, and a bunch of other things; so I just threw them all together and called it *The New World*.

One of the girls who sang in it was friends with Daisy Prince. I didn't know who Daisy was, but she came to see the show, and she had a lot of great advice for me afterwards. So I said, "Do you want to direct my show?" She said, "Sure." We were going to do a reading and invite some people to see if we could get some money to take the show further. She said, while we were rehearsing for the reading, "We can do that up at my dad's house." When she said "my dad's house" was the first moment when it occurred to me that her dad was Hal Prince. Because of that, I ended up being sort of adopted by Hal and Judy and Daisy and their family. While Daisy and I were working on putting together what eventually became *Songs for a New World*, Hal took pity on me because I was a kid living in the Village with no income and offered me the chance to be the rehearsal pianist for *Kiss of the Spider Woman*, which had been in London and was coming to Broadway. That was an invaluable experience, because I got to see how a Broadway show got put together—and this wasn't a low-level Broadway show. This was people at the top of their game putting together a show that was at the top of its game. Just to be in the middle of that was thrilling and intoxicating, but at the same time I wanted so desperately to be in the middle of it more. I thought, "This is where I belong. I want to be with professionals who do what they do." When I had come into the city, I had thought that being younger than everybody might be an advantage—and in a way it was. But I wasn't particularly good at knowing my place, and a lot of people got bent out of shape at what they rightly considered my fairly presumptuous behavior. I really thought I knew what I was doing, even when I didn't know what I was doing, so there was a lot of having to tell me to cool down.

Interviewer: Were you that way with Hal Prince?

Brown: No. Being with Hal was the first time I felt like I didn't know more than everybody. It was the first time I was in a room where I felt like I was among betters.

Interviewer: That was a good thing!

Brown: It was a thrilling thing, a fascinating thing, and I was really excited about it; but it also made the other jobs I had, the survival jobs, that much tougher to swallow. I was like, "Hey, I've been in the big time!"—but I hadn't remotely paid my dues. From the moment my work on *Spider Woman* was finished, I was desperate to get back into a situation where I was with people whom I respected. I didn't respect Hal just because he was older than me or because he'd won Tony Awards; it was clear the minute you walked into a room with him that he knew what he was doing, he knew how to do it, and he knew what he wanted. The most exciting thing about working with Hal—and I know he's sensitive about this, but it's true—was that because he had been a very successful and very smart producer for a very long time, Hal was always thinking about what the audience was seeing and how we were taking care of them. He doesn't think about that in some sort of patronizing way—like how do we make sure they clap or how do we send them out happy. He wants to make sure that when they've spent their money they can see everything on the stage. Hal would sit in every seat in the house while the tech rehearsal was going on, just to make sure that none of the sight lines were bad. He was constantly moving people forward onto the stage because the Broadhurst (where *Spider Woman* played) was a wide stage and you could get lost. Everything that he did was always about making sure that everyone was going to feel like they got a total experience in the theater. The work that he was doing was never indulgent in an artistic way, and it never felt pretentious. It felt like we were all sharing this experience and we wanted to elevate it to the best that it could be, with the understanding that the audience was going to be pulled along with us for this ride.

Interviewer: How did working with him help you specifically as a composer/lyricist?

Brown: I can't even limit it to how it helped me as a composer/lyricist; it helped me as a man of the theater to understand that the work we do ultimately must relate always to what the audience's experience of that event is. We do not just happen to be putting things up on a stage. The commercial musical theater must ask of itself that the audience respond to and respect the work that we're doing in a way that more experimental theater does not have to do. The musical theater, in my view, cannot be separated from its commercial aspect. We know *Mame, Hello, Dolly!*, and *South Pacific* because they were commercially successful shows. You cannot judge *Juno*, which was a perfectly fine piece of musical theater, the same way you judge a more commercially successful show, because a commercially successful show is, by some definitions, a better work. It's hard to say that when I've written shows that were all financially unsuccessful, when none of the three shows I've done has been a hit. I don't pretend that the work I do doesn't have to hold itself to all of those standards. While I'm disappointed that my work is not financially successful and has not been commercially well received, that's still the standard to which I'm holding myself. I am still aiming for that.

Interviewer: How would you say that that aim manifests itself in your work?

Brown: It's hard to know. I have to be very conscious, while I'm writing, of how the audience is going to respond to everything I do. I can look back at *Parade*, which I'm enormously proud of on an artistic level, and see decisions we could have made that would have let the audience into the show more without compromising what we accomplished artistically. We didn't often enough ask ourselves, when we were writing *Parade*, if it met those standards. Maybe we thought we did, but in retrospect we really didn't. We very much were writing *Parade* in an ivory-tower place. It was my first show, but I think that Alfred Uhry, who wrote the book, and Hal Prince, the director, both thought that they had finally evolved as artists to the point where the audience was willing to go with them wherever they wanted to go. I wish that had been the case, but in point of fact the audience was clearly not ready to go with them, with us. I watched people file out of that theater every night through the entire first act of the show.

Interviewer: Can you be more specific about the kinds of changes you should have made?

Brown: I've been thinking about it a lot. I think that an audience for a musical comes in expecting to see a musical. I know that sounds reductive, but people who go to see a musical are expecting a certain kind of commercial entertainment. They're expecting a certain amount of base-level "we're here to entertain you" values in a piece of musical theater, and they get hostile when that's not delivered to them. The difference between a serious show like *South Pacific* and a serious show like *Parade* is that *South Pacific* has "Honey Bun," "I'm Gonna Wash That Man Right out of My Hair," a lot of very light and comic numbers, and a lot of conventions.

There's a younger couple, and the older couple are a more serious couple; there are exotic things; and there's a men's chorus that sings "There Is Nothing like a Dame." While it's a serious show that accomplishes a lot of things that no musical before it had accomplished, it does it by referencing backwards. There are only two moments in *Parade* where we do old-style entertainment. There's the trolley car number at the top of the show with the two kids, and there's Leo's number in the courtroom, "Come Up to My Office." I meet people to this day who, when they find out I wrote *Parade*, will say, "I loved that number in the courtroom." It's not a great number. Compositionally, it's two chords. I think there are some spectacular songs, some real musical and theatrical coups, in *Parade* that nobody mentions if they're people who want a musical to be what a "musical" is. I think we held ourselves above the necessity of referencing what that audience wanted. Even the "Come Up to My Office" number is put in a lot of quotation marks in the show; it's a lie, and you know it's a lie because all of a sudden it sounds like a musical.

Interviewer: But hasn't the American musical evolved beyond "Honey Bun"?

Brown: I would like to say yes. At the time I was writing *Parade,* I believed that it had; but let me say—and I'm probably going to be contradicted on this—there has not been a commercially successful musical in the last thirty years that does not significantly reference the traditional musical form. I certainly can't think of a blockbuster musical that doesn't. You could not have had *The Producers* if it did not specifically and identically reference traditional musical theater. Had we structured *Parade* slightly more in that direction, we would have earned a lot more goodwill from the audience. An audience feels that if they're paying seventy-five dollars, as it was then, they deserve to have the same experience for that seventy-five dollars as when they see *The Producers*.

Interviewer: And maybe you can sneak the other stuff in if you give them a little something of what they want.

Brown: It isn't even about sneaking it in. It's about acknowledging to them that you know the rules they want to play by. Once you tell them you know the rules and you're going to play by those rules, then they'll go with you. I think that once the audience is with you, they're with you, and you can do whatever you want. We never took the time in *Parade* to welcome them in that way. There are no breaks for applause in probably the first thirty-five minutes of *Parade*; it used to drive people insane. Hal and Alfred and I would say, "That's what we wanted. We wanted them to be so absorbed in the experience that they couldn't applaud; we wanted a relentless tug." It's a great idea, but the commercial musical theater is not a theoretical place. It has to work in practice. What we were getting from the audience—very clearly, not ambiguously, and not just from ninety-five-year-old people, but from everyone—was that they wanted to applaud. They wanted to embrace the show; they wanted to be let in, and we were saying, "No, no! You can't." I am obviously torn between the fact that we wrote the show we wanted to write, we did the show that we wanted to do, and we loved the result of what we wanted to create, and the fact that it did not meet our audience's desire for what they wanted it to be. When an audience comes in, they're perfectly willing to see whatever you put in front of them. They didn't come into *Parade* saying, "I hope this sucks"; they said, "What can we do to enjoy this more?" Not through some sort of perversion but through what we really thought was best for the show and best for the art form, we didn't give them what they wanted. I can't tell you the sort of ambivalence that I have toward saying this and putting it on the record, but I'm fairly sure that I'm right and that I cannot expect that if I only do things that turn me on artistically to the exclusion of the audience, they are going to be commercially successful.

Interviewer: Surely you knew then and know now how to write the kind of number that *Parade* didn't have but—as you're now saying—probably should have had?

Brown: I know better now how to write it than I did then, just because I'm older and I'm a lot more technically secure in the work that I do.

Interviewer: And wasn't *Parade* the sort of show it was because of Uhry and Prince's conception of it? It was the show that they wanted it to be, wasn't it, and didn't you buy into that conception?

Brown: It was not a question of my buying into it; I helped set that agenda. I very much thought we were ready to make art in the musical theater; that was what we wanted to do, uncompromisingly.

Interviewer: Would you say, then, talking generically about where the American musical is now, that that sort of show is impossible?

Brown: Certainly it's premature. But I don't even know that you can call it a "sort of show." With *Parade,* we were attempting very deliberately to do something new, something that nobody had seen before. I think that our intent to do something that was entirely new was the thing that stabbed us. It may be that after another twenty years, when people are more used to the way we were trying to tell a story, that *Parade* will then be seen as having been before its time and very progressive. People will come and see it, and because the storytelling conventions we were using will now be things they understand, they'll be able to sit and watch it and say, "I can't understand why this show wasn't a huge hit. It's the most wonderful, accessible piece of theater ever."

Interviewer: That assumes that there will be shows between now and then that will go part of the way there. In the musical theater world of *The Producers* and *Hairspray,* what chance is there that a show that somehow starts to go in that direction will ever get any further than *Parade* did?

Brown: I think a new generation of theater artists will inevitably bring their experiences, their influences, and their means of storytelling to the table. To an extent, it's already happening. As all of the people who tell musical theater stories the way they were told to do in the "golden age" die off, we can start telling stories the way we do. I can't tell you the hell we went through on *The Last Five Years.* I made a real challenge to the audience when I said, "I'm telling this story in two different directions time-wise." For an audience of my contemporaries, people who are in their twenties and early thirties and even in their forties, a show that moves chronologically in different directions is not an unusual idea. The audiences that came to *The Last Five Years* thinking they were going to go see a musical where there was tap dancing and girls with lots of teeth were baffled by why I would want to write a musical that went like that. Why didn't I just tell the story? But because my desire to tell the story involved telling it in a new way, the audience of my peers loved *The Last Five Years.* They have grasped on to that show as though it was their own. The response that I get when I perform that show or when I go see productions, or even the amount of times that it's done in colleges (there have been a hundred productions of the show this year), implies that there's an audience for musical theater that will eventually become the primary audience, as opposed to the older, more moneyed crowd that is now the primary audience. When that crowd is the primary audience, they will expect stories to be told differently, and the creators of those stories will be expecting to tell them differently. People of my generation think of musical theater as being a fuddy-duddy and corny art form. I don't think they even think of it as an art form. They think of it as a goofy thing that you go to and spend a great deal of money to do it. I have to believe that because musical theater can be so lucrative people will continue creating it. As they continue creating it, they will necessarily make it more fit their worldview, their view of what it should be.

Interviewer: Isn't *Avenue Q* an example of young creators who've done something different and been successful?

Brown: Exactly. It is one of the first places where we start to see the paradigm shifting. It's a very important show, regardless of how great it is, because it attracts a young crowd; the older audiences that come don't know what to make of it, but the younger crowds go over and over again and claim it as their own.

Interviewer: To get back to the problem of your musicals not being commercially successful, the CD of *The Last Five Years* seems to have been very successful and much written about. Do you think that's because when you listen to a CD the emphasis is on the music and not on the staging?

Brown: I think that the CD allows people to take their time. One of the hardest things about musicals, and the hardest thing about being a lyricist in the musical theater, is that the audience only has the amount of time that a character is onstage to understand what the character is saying. You can't pack a lyric too much or no one's going to catch it. *The Last Five Years* is an extremely dense piece of theater, musically and textually, and with the CD you can listen to it four times. You might put it on again because you like the music, but by the second time you start to catch a lot of things about the characters that you might not have been able to grab the first time they went by. With the CD, people are able to put their own imagery on top of it and time it out so that they can absorb it at their own speed. In the theater, you can't sit there with the booklet and read along with it. There were a lot of people who had problems with Daisy's production of *The Last Five Years,* with the way that it looked onstage. It was a very visually dense production; I loved it, and I thought it complemented what we were doing, but I think that the CD allows people to strip away that extra layer of visual density and say, "We're hearing things on these two levels instead of four."

Interviewer: What attracts you to material?

Brown: I have an instinctive sense of what makes a character sing; I know what I can do in order to have a character sing. If the material does not suggest people singing, if I don't hear the song when I'm reading it or thinking about it, then it's an easy pass for me. I remember there was a woman who sent me a play a couple of years ago. It had been fairly successful Off-Broadway. She said, "The author wants to adapt this into a musical. What do you think?" I read it, and it was a very contemporary piece of playwriting about people in various rooms in a hotel and all of their crises. Structurally I understood how to make it a musical, but their issues were so little and the stakes were so small that I knew that if they were singing about things like that, you wouldn't buy it as an audience member. You'd think we were putting too much weight on it. Singing, ultimately, magnifies everything you're feeling; when you sing it, it becomes epic. I knew immediately just reading it that it wasn't the sort of musical I know how to do.

Interviewer: What about the collaborative process? Is that something that attracts you to musicals? Is it something that sometimes can be an impediment? How do you regard it?

Brown: Over the years, I've come to embrace it very reluctantly. It's hard for me to give up the control over everything that I do, because at some point in any given process I feel that if everyone would just listen to me it would all be great. But I've come to realize that I am not always right and that on certain levels in certain departments there are things that I don't have a gift for. This is a thuddingly obvious thing to say, but I don't have the visual eye that Hal Prince has or that Daisy has; that's not what I do. To find somebody who can translate what I wrote into a stage picture is so thrilling and so far beyond anything that I could come up with on my own that when it's that kind of experience and when it's that caliber of creativity, I don't have a problem with the collaborative process. I have a problem with collaborators who aren't on my level, and it's hard to find the right people to work with. They're all very busy and very expensive and they've heard that I'm impossible or whatever. I go into collaboration very gingerly.

Interviewer: How do you know? Don't you sometimes find yourself in a situation where the material attracts you but the uncertainty of the collaborative circumstances makes it difficult to get involved?

Brown: I guess I have enough stature in the business that I can dictate the terms of my collaborations to a certain extent. I don't have to deal with people saying, "You don't really know what you're doing, so why don't you just work with this guy or that." I can be very emphatic that I'm not interested in a working relationship that isn't *x* or *y*. I want to trust that the people I'm sitting across the table from are as fast as I am and as committed as I am to the sort of work that I want to do.

Interviewer: Are you saying that, at this stage in your career, you can select your collaborators to some extent?

Brown: Sure. It's not going to make anybody happy if I have to work with someone I don't like or who I don't think is up to my level; it's a disaster for everybody. I have been in some situations where there's a person on the team—be it the book-writer or the director or the choreographer—who I don't feel is entirely with me. Because I've spent so much time as a music director, as an arranger, as an orchestrator, and doing the technical things on a show, I'm able to steer the collaboration in such a way that I don't put things into their hands that I don't trust they will be able to handle. I'm not 100 percent successful at that, but I deal with those liabilities as they come up.

Interviewer: Having worked in all those other capacities on musicals does afford you that luxury that you just described; but doesn't it also give you a capacity—and perhaps even a tendency—to second-guess that a lot of other composers and lyricists don't have? Do you always do your own orchestrations?

Brown: No. When we did *Parade,* (a) I knew that there wouldn't be enough time for me to do all of them, and (b) I always took *Parade* as a learning experience. From the day I was hired, I said, "This is a chance for me to learn everything I ever need to know, because I'll never work with this caliber of people again." I had hired two orchestrators for *Parade* because there were two different scores to the show. They work together, but there's the score for the people of the South, and then there's the score for Leo and Lucille, which is much more a chamber piece. I hired Don Sebesky to do the large stuff, because he had done this *Symphonic Sondheim* album with these unbelievably great symphonic transcriptions of Steve's music. He was so inventive and so gifted at understanding the orchestral instrument that I thought I would learn a lot from watching him orchestrate my music. Then I hired somebody else to do the chamber stuff, the smaller material. Sebesky's stuff started coming in, once we got in rehearsal, and I would look it over and say, "It's wonderful." The other guy's stuff would come in and I'd say, "This isn't what I want," and I'd send it back with notes. I don't think he was used to getting notes from a composer that were that specific, and he was very taken aback that I would second-guess him. When we got to the orchestra rehearsal, all of Sebesky's stuff was thrilling; but with the other guy's stuff, I had to stop a lot, go over the orchestra members' parts, cut things out of their parts, and change things. He got so offended that he walked out and left the show, which at that point seemed like the only solution to the problem. So I orchestrated the material myself. It was an incredible learning experience. It was a classic example of how you choose your collaborators and how, even in the best circumstances (the guy who left was someone whose work I very much respected), sometimes it isn't a good marriage. Since then, this guy's done some incredible work; we just didn't work well together. When it came to *The Last Five Years,* I wanted very much to orchestrate that by myself. I didn't want someone else putting their stamp on it, because inevitably they do. When an orchestrator takes on your material, it takes on the characteristics of that orchestrator's work.

Interviewer: Can you demystify the process of orchestrating a musical for us a bit? For example, how can you tell that Jonathan Tunick orchestrated most of Sondheim's musicals but somebody else did *Sunday in the Park with George?* What is the difference between having Sondheim sitting at the piano playing one of those melodies and having it played by a full orchestra?

Brown: Inevitably, the orchestrator is going to filter anything through his own aesthetic. If you hear Steve playing something and it sounds to you like there's a hint of maybe Ravel that he's digging up from, you say, "I choose to go toward that orchestrally." You need some palette to work from, so you say, "It feels like it's Ravel, so I'm going to go in that direction." Let's say that's Tunick; he orchestrates it and it sounds like Ravel. But in the same room at the same time, if another orchestrator was there, Ravel might not be the thing that jumps to his mind. He might say, "It sounds like a bossa nova. It has that feel to it. I can see that underneath it somewhere." So that's the palette he'll choose to work from. Even though the notes that Steve is playing are exactly the same, the choices that each orchestrator makes when he blows that up to a larger orchestral size— where he puts each of those notes and what he does around all of those notes—is very much informed by his own sense of what it sounds like to him. Steve can even say to them, "This feels like Ravel," and each orchestrator will have his own version of what he thinks Ravel is.

Interviewer: If your music is orchestrated by someone else, how close is the way it sounds in the theater to what you heard when you composed it?

Brown: It depends on what kind of composer you are, I guess, on how specific your writing is, and on how clear you are about what you want. Here's the tricky thing. Even I, when I orchestrate my own material, am not as gifted an orchestrator as Sebesky is. He's a master of working with an orchestra. He knows how to get every effect he wants. When I orchestrate something I've composed, I know that what I'm doing is going to sound like what I'm writing; but I only know what I know, and I may not be able to take my own work to the level that I want it to get to, because I'm not a full-time orchestrator who does this every day.

Interviewer: But you do know where you want it to get to, don't you?

Brown: I may know in an abstract way, but Sebesky has the technical, specific knowledge of how to do what he does. Hopefully, knock on wood, we so meld our minds and I can communicate it well enough that he says, "I know exactly what you want" and when I hear it I say, "That is exactly what I always dreamed it would sound like." I'd say that happens about half the time.

Interviewer: Does it ever sound better than you imagined it?

Brown: Yes. The funeral in *Parade* sounds much more fully and beautifully realized than I ever would have come up with. "Pretty Music" in *Parade* is supposed to sound like a parlor dance in 1916 or 1917. I could never have done with it what Sebesky did; he has an encyclopedic knowledge of how you arrange in that style. I would have faked it and said, "I think it's sort of this and sort of that," and 99.37 percent of the audience would not have thought, "He doesn't get it; he's just faking it." I'm so happy that now even that 0.63 percent of the audience that gets it hears Sebesky's version and knows exactly what he was trying to do.

Interviewer: Can you select one of your shows and trace your involvement with it from the beginning to the end?

Brown: I think I'll deal with *Parade*.

Interviewer: How did it start?

Brown: I wasn't there at the beginning. What I'm told happened was that Alfred [Uhry] and Hal [Prince] were having meetings. Hal wanted to do a musical about the life of Sammy Davis Jr. Alfred wasn't really interested in writing the show, but he met with Hal about it because it was Hal Prince and it was nice to have a meeting. While they were having a discussion, Alfred talked about the show he was writing, a play called *The Last Night of Ballyhoo* about very heavily assimilated Jews in the South. Hal said, "What is it about Jews in the South? Why is it that they have such trouble being Jews?" And Alfred said, "To be honest, I think it's because of the Leo Frank case." Hal said, "What's that?" and Alfred told him a short version of the Leo Frank case. What happened then is up to history to determine who's telling the truth. According to Alfred, Hal jumped up out of his chair and said, "That's it! That's the next musical I want to do." According to Hal, Alfred said, "I've always wanted to write a musical about that. Maybe we can do that instead of the Sammy Davis thing."

Regardless, they started working on it, and Hal called in Steve Sondheim, whom he hadn't worked with since *Merrily We Roll Along*, which was twelve or thirteen years ago at that point. Hal and Steve and Alfred would sit in a room together and try to figure out how to write the show. Steve, meanwhile, was doing *Passion*. *Passion* opened, got mixed reviews, and won the Tony for Best Musical; but it was clear that it wasn't going to be an enormous financial success for anybody. Steve said to Hal—again, I'm deep in the land of hearsay, so this could all be thrown out of court— "I don't want to write another dark show. This feels like a dark show. I want to write something lighter." So Steve left the project. At this very moment, I had been working with Daisy on *Songs for a New World*, so I was over at Hal's house all the time rehearsing. Every so often, Hal would pop his head in and listen, and we'd say, "What do you think?" and he'd say, "It sounds great." He asked me to come meet him in the park one day. While we were standing in the park, he said, "I want to talk to you about a show." *Songs for a New World* was about to get its first production, so I was as happy as a boy could be; but I really didn't know what was going to happen after that.

Interviewer: At this point, did you know about the show he was working on with Uhry?

Brown: I only knew that Alfred and Hal had been working on something with Steve that had fallen apart. I came to the office; Alfred and Hal were there, and Hal started talking about this project they wanted me to work on and asked if I would consider putting a couple of numbers together for it, entirely on spec, of course. So I wrote an opening number for the show. I knew it wasn't what would eventually be the opening number, but I wanted to compose something that would prove that my writing wasn't limited to the sort of stuff I was doing in *Songs for a New World*, which was a series of very narrative, self-enclosed pieces. I wanted to write something that felt like the opening of a longer-arc show. I wrote for every character in the show in that opening number; ultimately, the opening that we used had none of the characters in the show in it. I brought this ersatz opening to Hal and Alfred and they said, "That's not what this show is, but it's clear that you understand what we want, so why don't we just ask you to get on board with the show?" I went up to Alfred's house in Connecticut for a long weekend, and we hashed out what the central journey of the show was going to be: Leo and Lucille and how they were going to come together through this very traumatic and horrible event from having a very sterile marriage to having a truly understanding and loving marriage. Hal's input in that was equally important; that wasn't just something that Alfred showed up with one morning. We all hashed it out.

Having started with that, I went to Alfred's house and we worked out what the first twenty minutes of the show should feel like; it was just an outline. Then we gradually started chipping away at it. That was August, and I didn't write a note until the following March. I just wouldn't; I thought, "I don't know the show yet. I don't understand it yet." It was very clear that it was Alfred's story; he knew the Frank family and he knew the specifics of life in the South. I'd never been south of the Mason-Dixon line in my life. I spent one day a week, at least, in Alfred's apartment or at his house, just talking to him and writing down everything he said. He would talk about life in the South, about what it meant for southerners to lose the Civil War, about life before the Civil War. Those were all starting to feel like things that needed to be integrated into the fabric of the show. In March, I sat down to start writing the music.

Interviewer: What year was that?

Brown: March 1995. It was August 1994 that we started talking. In March, I wrote the opening number, "The Old Red Hills of Home," which was very much a distillation of hundreds of pages of notes and thoughts from Alfred. I played Alfred the first part of the song, and he was very excited about it; he said, "Why doesn't it now become that he turns into the older soldier and it's Confederate Memorial Day?" I said, "That's what I was thinking," and we then built in that transition. Then from the Confederate Memorial Day parade, we went right into Frankie and Mary's first scene, "The Picture Show." That was, I'd say, probably the beginning of April 1995, and we showed it to Hal, who said, "This is great. Let's keep going." So we kept chipping away and we got to the end of the first act by mid-December 1995. *Songs for a New World* happened in the middle of this, in October 1995, but we just kept working.

We took a shot at Lucille's first song, which eventually became "You Don't Know This Man," and that was the first time we walked into the office and Hal said, "You're off the mark." We said, "What do you mean? It's perfect!" He said, "No, it's not. Something's wrong." So we went back and tried to decipher what it was that Hal was feeling; because it was the first time that he'd had a response like that, we trusted that he actually was feeling something. We repointed the song and did a second version of it, but Hal said, "No, it's still not right," and he made a suggestion about how to fix it. We listened to Hal's suggestion, and then Alfred and I went to lunch. We were both feeling a little bummed out because we felt like we weren't getting it, trying to figure out how to make Hal's idea work. I said, "Let's not listen to his idea of how to make it work. Let's just listen to his instinct that it isn't working." So we threw out whatever Hal's idea was, and we started from scratch with a new idea that became "You Don't Know This Man." When we brought that in to Hal, with a new scene before it, he said, "Yes, perfect. We're great." That was essentially the way that the whole show was created.

In December, after we had written the first half of the show, Garth Drabinsky came in to listen to it. Garth was Hal's first choice of who to show it to, because Garth and his production company, Livent, had produced *Kiss of the Spider Woman* and he was doing *Show Boat* with Hal at that time. Hal felt comfortable that Garth was going to give the show the production it needed. Whatever else you could say about Garth, he was in the business as a producer for the right reasons; he had a lot of taste and he had a lot of integrity. Garth came in, and he liked what he heard of the first act and he said, "Yes, I'm interested in working on this. Keep going. Why don't we do a reading of the whole show in June in Philadelphia." We had now essentially four months to finish the rest of the show and get a cast so we could go into rehearsal at the end of May for the reading. I was writing a ballet at the same time; but, nonetheless, we very quickly wrote the second act in about three months. We pushed like crazy, but it was a hard act to write because there was so much event in the story and we had to compress it so heavily; it was hard to make sure we were choosing the right events. Finally, we started casting for the reading in Philadelphia. Garth highly recommended an actor from Canada for the lead role, a guy named Albert Schultz; and Hal was very keen on Carolee Carmello and wanted to work with her, so he asked Carolee to be Lucille. We auditioned for the rest of the parts. Some of the people we knew; some of them we didn't know, and they just came in and auditioned for us.

That was the first version of the show we did. After we saw it in Phila-delphia, we said to each other, "We feel like we're on the right track, but we haven't quite nailed Leo and Lucille as much as we want to." What we all felt that we had done well was getting the atmosphere of the South in 1913. What we didn't think we had was this relationship between Leo and Lucille that we had stated was the most important thing to get, so I had to find a new moment for Leo at the top of the show. In the original draft of the show, he didn't sing until "Come Up to My Office." We had made a very deliberate point of that, but at the same time having him be so enig-matic really worked against us ever getting particularly invested in him emotionally. So I came up with a new idea that eventually turned into a duet between Leo and Lucille, "What Am I Waiting For?" and "Leo at Work." Once we'd done that, we still felt like we hadn't done enough for Leo, which we found out after a workshop, and that's when I wrote "How Can I Call This Home?," which was the last song to go into the show. Af-ter Philadelphia, Garth said, "I want to do a workshop of the show, with four weeks of rehearsal in New York and three performances in front of an audience up in Toronto, where all my operations are based." We said, "Sure. That sounds fine." Logistically, it took about a year before that could happen, so we didn't do that workshop until September or Octo-ber 1997, and our process of working got dissipated in that time. We didn't get a lot of work done because we all had to do other projects. I wasn't get-ting paid while we were sitting around waiting to do the workshop, so I had to do a lot of music-directing and conducting jobs to pay the bills.

Finally, it was time, and we all agreed that Albert Schultz, who had done the reading in Philadelphia, didn't sing well enough to do the show. In June 1997, in preparation for the workshop, we did a reading of just the new material; we had Carolee come back and do it, but we had Matthew Broderick do the role of Leo. Garth was very excited about that because he was a big famous name; but Matthew had a lot of trouble with the ma-terial because he's a very subtle and quiet actor and Leo didn't really play to any of his instincts. He was a little lost and the music called for a sort of singing that was not stylistically comfortable for him. That was also the reading when Sebesky got on board and where I hired Eric Stern to music-direct the show. I had stated from the outset that I was going to do all the dance arrangements. Something that usually happens in a musical is that the choreographer works in a room separate from the actors and the director with a dance arranger figuring out how the dance arrange-ments are going to work. The composer often has nothing to do with all those twenty-minute dance sequences in a musical. They're based on things that he's written, but there's a pianist who arranges them, and he's sitting in the room with the choreographer. But I said, "I want to do them. There's not going to be that much dancing. I want to be a part of it. I want to do everything I can. I want this to feel like my show." I also did all the vocal arrangements myself, and I loved doing it; there was a lot of very complicated contrapuntal work in *Parade*, and I felt like no one else would understand what I wanted there.

We did the reading with Matthew Broderick, and now we had three months between that and the Toronto workshop, and it was clear that we didn't have a Leo yet. Hal had worked with Brent Carver on *Kiss of the Spider Woman* and had always said, "I want Brent to do this." Alfred and I had resisted because we thought Brent was too old, but Brent was very kind and agreed to audition because he wanted to be a part of it. His audition was an amazing thing; to see a brilliant actor take on your material was very seductive and intoxicating, and I thought, "Who cares if he's too old? He's going to bring something very special to the show." So Brent took over that role. I think we recast a couple of other small roles for the workshop, but by and large it was pretty much the same cast as the reading.

Now we really got to work—cut a whole bunch of sequences and changed a number of things. We had a choreographer we were working with, a modern dance choreographer who had done some thrilling things that we had seen on tape. We were all excited to work with him because we thought, "There's not that much dance in the show, but what there is now is going to be very new and very wild." We rehearsed in New York for four weeks, and then we did two more weeks of rehearsal up in Toronto; it was six weeks of concentrating on the material, with Garth looking over our shoulder, which drove everyone insane. Then we did those three performances for a lot of people. There were some invited audiences, but Garth had run a competition in a local newspaper to have people see the first version of a brand-new show, so there was an actual audience there as well as professional people. We learned an enormous amount about the show, not from the rehearsal process but from those three performances. I think we learned more from those three performances than we did in the entire rest of the process.

I'm not a fan of workshops or of readings, because I feel that what happens at the end of them is that a whole bunch of industry people come in with their own agendas and it's hard to get any sort of read on what they really think. When we did *The Last Five Years*, I felt I had been burned on *Parade* and on a couple of other shows I'd worked on by doing too many readings and too many workshops. The first time anyone saw *The Last Five Years* was its full production; that was possible with a show that only had two actors and where I had written the book, the lyrics, and the music and where it was such a simple physical production. You can't do that with a much larger show. It's just not safe, but it's my aim in the future to keep as close to that purity of intent as I can. Garth was a big believer in doing as many readings and workshops as you can; but the danger with that, I feel, is the longer you spend on a show, the further you get from your original artistic impulse. It's not like an opera, where it's just the composer sitting there scrawling on a piece of paper. It's a whole bunch of people, and they all keep having input and they all keep having ideas.

Interviewer: And that input is not always what's best for the art, is it?

Brown: Sometimes yes, sometimes no; but the impulse can disappear. Anyway, we did the Toronto workshop; we learned what we could from those audiences, and we said, "We know how we want to proceed with the show." Garth said, "We're going to do a tryout of the show in Boston and then come into New York." Meanwhile, the choreographer had taken a very long time in the workshop process to get his numbers done, and some of them were great and some of them were very not great. Garth said, "I want to take two weeks and have him do just a dance workshop. Tell him what your concerns were about what he did and let him come up with something new." That was an indulgence, and we said, "Great!" At this same time, Hal had fired the original set designer. He was a guy whose primary ideas were about projections and a very interesting playing space, but Hal felt like the show had gone away from that, so he was looking for a new designer. Hal and Alfred were not around for the choreographer's two-week workshop; but I came and watched it, and I saw something really interesting. The dancers wanted to kill him. We had the best dancers in New York working for two weeks with this guy, and they wanted to stab him in the heart. I thought, "Regardless of what he comes up with, I'm taking a lesson from the fact that everyone hates him." Then the work he did was not particularly good, so we all agreed that we were going to let him go. We hired Patty Birch, who had done *A Little Night Music* and *Pacific Overtures* with Hal; it was one of the best decisions we made. Because Hal wanted to work with new people, he did a competition for the new set designer. He worked with four different set designers at once; they would each bring in ideas and models and he was paying them a little bit of money just for the exposure of doing this work with him. Eventually, he picked Ricardo Hernandez, who works with George C. Wolfe all the time, and Ricardo did a beautiful job with our show. I don't know a lot of directors who would have taken the time to do that.

We were supposed to start in Boston in June; but, mysteriously, Garth didn't book the tryout. We didn't know what had happened. Meanwhile, Bernie Gersten, who runs Lincoln Center Theater, had come up to Toronto to see those three performances, and he had said to me at a Lincoln Center party where I was playing cocktail hour, "I loved your show. We would love to do it here." So the next meeting I had with Hal and Alfred after Garth hadn't booked the tryout, I said, "Bernie Gersten really wants to do our show." Hal said, "Since Garth seems to be punting on doing our show for this tryout thing he was talking about, why don't I see if he'll do it in collaboration with Lincoln Center?" Thank God, because no sooner had we made the agreement to do the show at Lincoln Center for their next season than Garth got in trouble with his board at Livent. On our first day of rehearsal at Lincoln Center, we found out that Garth had been fired from Livent entirely and was under indictment for corporate fraud. But Roy Furman, Garth's partner at Livent, came down and said, "Livent is still committed to the show. We still believe in it and we're still going to make it happen. Don't worry about it."

The agreement, as far as I was informed, was that Lincoln Center would pay for whatever Lincoln Center would usually pay to do a musical in their own theater and Livent would pay for anything over that that Hal asked for. Lincoln Center was doing their bit and advertising to their subscribers. So we got into the mindset that "we're just a subscription show at Lincoln Center like any other subscription show." We started previews and we were faced with Lincoln Center's audience, which is a very old subscription audience and a very stuck-in-the-mud audience. They started walking out about twelve minutes into the show, and by intermission a third of the audience would be gone, while the other two-thirds were enjoying it and would stay to the end. All of a sudden, RCA, which had said they were going to do the album, said, "We can't commit to doing the album. We're on the fence," so we started getting other record labels in to watch the show. We didn't change a lot during previews, which I was very grateful for at the time; but, as I said earlier, we weren't paying a lot of attention to the audience. We were doing the show we wanted to do, and we weren't hearing that the audience wasn't getting the show they wanted to see. The orchestrations were changing. As previews went by, we made a couple of changes. The biggest change that Hal asked us to make was about Leo's lawyer. A bunch of scenes in the first act had to change to accommodate the character of Leo's lawyer; he had been in the show, but Hal wanted him to be a much broader character.

When we opened the show in New York, the review in the *Times* was very dismissive. It said that the show was cold and academic. I hate carping about critics, but future history has shown that the critic on the *New York Times* [Ben Brantley] doesn't have a musical ear; he's sort of tone-deaf. Most of the emotional content of *Parade,* by design, is musical. It's subtextual; there's a lot bubbling under these characters. Many critics are not equipped to hear musicals that way. When these people walk in to see a musical, it's supposed to be very on-your-sleeve and obvious. Musicals are not noted for their intellectual subtlety, and in *Parade* we were saying, "People do things that they don't say and say things that they don't do. We're really going to try to push the envelope"—and some of the critics got it and loved it, and a lot of the critics didn't. There are different kinds of critics, and the one at the *Times* is the sort of critic who likes his musicals to be like "musicals." But I don't think that's any different from the majority of his readership, so it's hard to fault him for that. Without support from the *New York Times,* Livent pulled the plug on everything and left Lincoln Center holding the bag. Lincoln Center believed in the show, but they knew that without a positive *Times* review it was a hard sell. It also turns out that with a good *Times* review a show is a hard sell; it is not a guarantee of much of anything. But I didn't know that then.

Lincoln Center knew that they faced an uphill battle, because the critical word-of-mouth was not great and the word-of-mouth from their subscribers was not great. But we all loved the show and we all believed in it, so what do we do? Lincoln Center very courageously agreed to extend the show for another six weeks to see if we could sell more tickets; but the six weeks they happened to extend it were at the end of January and the beginning of February, when no one goes out. Our sales were not great, and my main concern at this point was that we had to record the show. I didn't want the show to go unrecorded while we still had this amazing cast and great orchestra, and so I worked with my record producer, who had done *Songs for a New World* and a couple of other projects with me. We determined that it would cost $300,000 to record the show. I said, "Fine. I have to raise $300,000." During the last six weeks of *Parade,* I was out trying to raise $300,000. Lincoln Center, God bless them, helped enormously; they tapped their board, and the board chipped in some money. Hal and Alfred and I all put in some, and then I raised a whole lot of cash by myself, and RCA very graciously said, "If you can make the album, we'll put it out. We'll market it. We'll do all the artwork and manufacturing. If you can pay for all the unions and all the other stuff, we'll do the rest of it." We knew that we would have to record it the day after the show closed, or else everyone was going to leave, but I didn't have all the money in place. Nonetheless, I booked the studio and paid for it out of my own pocket. I said, "I have to pretend we're going to have enough money to do it." We booked the studio for March 1; the show was to close on February 28.

We spent the last couple of weeks waiting the show out and seeing if it would sell, seeing if the word-of-mouth would improve, but it just didn't. People didn't come. We had a hardcore cult of people who came time and time again and would tell their friends. The *Times* didn't print just one bad review; after Brantley's review, [Vincent] Canby wrote a bad review of the show. And then after Canby's bad review, it was referred to about four times by other reviewers. They really enjoyed kicking us; there was something about what they perceived to be the intellectual pretension of the show that offended them. Eventually February 28 came, and we played the final show to a packed house of everyone who was a fan of the show and their families. Then we recorded the album the next day, and RCA put it out.

The vagaries of the season were such that there were only four full-scale musicals that opened that year: *Parade, Footloose, The Civil War,* and *Fosse.* There were a couple of other fringy sort of things, but those were the four big Broadway musicals, so we knew we would have a Tony nomination for Best Musical. We got thirteen Tony nominations, which sounds like a lot, but with so few musicals they had to give us a lot just to fill out the categories. The politics of it were that we had to get the cast album to all the Tony voters, because obviously not all of them had seen the show; even though they were all supposed to have, they didn't. So we got the CD of the show to them. *Fosse* didn't have a book, so the best book was a contest between *The Civil War, Footloose,* and *Parade,* so it was a foregone conclusion that Alfred was going home with a Tony. With my category, it was complicated because while nobody liked *The Civil War*—it got worse reviews than our show, if that was possible—(a) it was still running at the time, and (b) it was produced by a major touring organization, Pace. There's a block of Tony voters who are the producers of road tours, and *The Civil War* was clearly going to tour. It doesn't matter what Tony Awards a show gets, in terms of its publicity, as long as the road producers can advertise it as a "Tony Award–winning musical." So I felt like there was a very good chance that there was going to be a push for *The Civil War* to win the Tony for Best Score and I wouldn't have been surprised. *Parade* got the Best Score and Best Book Tonys, but it didn't get any other award.

Interviewer: Does the show have any future?

Brown: There's a guy named Chris Manos who does sort of middlebrow tours—but they're first-class productions—of shows like *Oklahoma!* or *West Side Story.* He has a little circuit of theaters, and his base of operations is the Fox Theatre in Atlanta. Because *Parade* is about Atlanta, Chris thought, "This show's a long shot, but I love it and I want to bring it to Atlanta as my gift to the city. I want to tour *Parade.*" More than a year after we closed in New York, in June 2000, we started a six-month tour that hit eight or nine cities. It was completely unexpected. I conducted that tour, because I needed the money, to be honest, but also because I loved the show and I wanted to say good-bye to it that way. I knew that that was going to be the last time anyone saw a first-class, top-of-the-line production of *Parade* for a long while. It was a tremendous experience—being outside of New York and having the show reviewed by people who were already familiar with it because they were able to listen to the record before they saw it. They could read about what had happened in New York and they knew it had won Tony Awards for best score and best book. Whatever that may have meant to me and to Alfred, to those out-of-town critics it was a sort of imprimatur. The reviews were night-and-day different from New York; all of a sudden, people were saying that the show was bold and emotional and heartbreaking and the music was transporting. It may also be that the critics are more easily swayed in other cities, just to play devil's advocate with myself.

Interviewer: Was the audience response better out of town?

Brown: The audience response was always better on opening night—the opening night audiences were always very enthusiastic—but the ticket sales were not great. If we had a three-week stand in a city, by the third week there were a lot of empty seats. Because it was a show about a lynching, regardless of the press it never sounded like a show they wanted to see; it sounded dark and upsetting.

Interviewer: So the misunderstanding that you had about audience response to *Parade* in New York was also applicable on the road, wasn't it?

Brown: The tour of *Parade* bore out all of my suspicions.

Interviewer: You could make the argument that in New York the reviews killed *Parade;* but you couldn't say that about the audience response on the road because the reviews were positive. There it was pure audience response.

Brown: The audiences were more evenly split, but there was very clearly a split. After the tour, the show got picked up after a lot of fighting by Music Theatre International, which is a licensing company. Because they've picked it up, it's gotten a couple of productions in colleges and high schools and things like that. *Songs for a New World* probably gets two hundred productions a year; *Parade* gets maybe ten, but it's a big show with a very ethnically diverse cast, which is hard to do. It's very complicated and very difficult, so I'm not surprised it hasn't been done more.

Interviewer: What are you working on now?

Brown: Not much. I have a couple of ideas that I'm thinking about whether I should do. I'm very wary of committing myself to what is essentially a very long process that is such a crap shoot. I'm not a guy who's able to dumb down my writing for a project. I don't think you should work at a level below your best work. I know shows that are very successful and are running right now that clearly represent less than the best work of their creators. Good for them that they're able to make money off of it, but I don't know how to do that. Check in with me in five years; I don't know how much longer people will hire me to be a musical director.

Interviewer: What effect does a music director have on a show? Are you an active part of the creative team? When you come in as the music director on a show written by someone else, what role do you play?

Brown: There are two things that the music director is most responsible for. One of them is a unity of tone, making sure that everybody is singing and playing and orchestrating and conducting the same show and that no matter how many varied styles there might be or how many different colors might be called upon, they all come from the same world and they're all done well. Especially in a situation where you've got a composer who's not technically on his game, a music director has to unify all of the elements and make sure the arrangers are all writing the same show. When all the dance arrangements get done, the music director sees to it that they all belong to the same piece. The music director, in conjunction with the composer, chooses that team. He says, "This is who should be orchestrating, and this is the color of the show." It's a technical job.

The second thing that the music director does is establish the pace of the show. He does this with the director, but it's very much a function of having the baton in your hand or having the piano under your fingers. You're going to determine how fast we get from one thing to another, the tempos at which those things get taken; and you will know, better than the composer will know, how the energy of the show runs from one end to the other, as opposed to from one end of a song to another. Where a conductor is invaluable is in his knowledge of the whole arc of the show, how it builds in terms of endurance and in terms of the emotional strength of what you're putting out there—because he's both a performer in the show and a technical member of the staff.

The music director is also very key in casting the show. Whereas a composer might say, "I love that voice," when it comes down to the chorus of a show and you've got twenty people that you have to cast, the music director knows what he needs in terms of how to balance out a choral sound. And he's got to fight with the choreographer over "I know you want this person because they dance well, but they sing like a goat; so I can't use them unless you're going to give me this other person who sings like a genius even though she only has one leg."

Interviewer: When you have all these people in a room protecting their aspect of a musical, how does anything ever get done? Here you are as the composer, the person you've described as knowing exactly how something should be done, and there's a music director telling you it isn't going to go that way.

Brown: It doesn't work that way. You only have that kind of power struggle if one of you is advocating something that's going to be a train wreck. All in all, the hierarchy is always very clear, though it differs on each project; but on the shows I write, when there's a conflict about the music, I'm going to win. Everyone involved knows that and respects it.

Interviewer: What about a show where you're the music director?

Brown: The composer wins. That's the hierarchy, and that's how it works best. I'd be a lousy music director if I didn't understand that. If I say to the writer, "We're stacking the chorus with too many sopranos and we don't have any altos," he'll say, "You tell me what we need." That's an area where clearly my expertise has to come into play. Composers know if they don't have the technical chops to do what I do; they're not foolish.

Interviewer: Don't you ever encounter a fool who thinks he knows?

Brown: Sure you do, but I don't work with those people. You're asking me, "What happens when you're the guy who's in the room with the idiot?" The idiot says, "I want all these people in the leading roles because they look right and I know you'll make them sound good." I know I can't make them sound good, so, as the music director, I've got two options. I can fight really hard right now and either I'll lose or I'll win—or I can leave the show. Me, personally, I probably leave the show. Not that it's easy to say no to a Broadway salary, but I've walked off of several shows. Regardless of everything else, it's just no fun if it doesn't sound good.

Betty Comden
and Adolph Green

Betty Comden was born on May 3, 1919, in New York City. She studied at New York University (B.S., 1938). Adolph Green was born on December 2, 1915; he died on October 24, 2002. They worked as lyricists, librettists, screenwriters, and performers. Their work as lyricists on New York musicals includes On the Town *(1944),* Billion Dollar Baby *(1945),* Two on the Aisle *(1951),* Wonderful Town *(1953),* Peter Pan *(1954),* Bells Are Ringing *(1956),* Say, Darling *(1958),* A Party with Betty Comden and Adolph Green *(1958),* Do Re Mi *(1960),* Subways Are for Sleeping *(1961),* Fade Out—Fade In *(1964),* Hallelujah, Baby! *(1967),* Lorelei *(1974),* Straws in the Wind *(1975),* On the Twentieth Century *(1978),* A Doll's Life *(1982), and* The Will Rogers Follies *(1991). They wrote the books for* On the Town, Billion Dollar Baby, Bells Are Ringing, Fade Out—Fade In, Applause *(1970),* On the Twentieth Century, A Doll's Life, *and* Singin' in the Rain *(1985).*

Their screenplays include Good News *(1947),* On the Town *(1949),* The Barkleys of Broadway *(1949),* Singin' in the Rain *(1952),* The Band Wagon *(1953),* It's Always Fair Weather *(1955),* Auntie Mame *(1958),* Bells Are Ringing *(1960), and* What a Way to Go! *(1964); and they wrote the lyrics for the songs in* On the Town, The Barkleys of Broadway, Singin' in the Rain, The Band Wagon, It's Always Fair Weather, Bells Are Ringing, *and* What a Way to Go! *They received Film Writers Guild Awards for* On the Town *and* Singin' in the Rain.

They received Tony Awards for Wonderful Town *(Best Musical),* Hallelujah, Baby! *(Best Lyricists and Best Musical),* Applause *(Best Musical),* On the Twentieth Century *(Best Score and Best Book), and* The Will Rogers Follies *(Best Score). They were elected to the Songwriters Hall of Fame in 1980 and inducted into the Theatre Hall of Fame in 1981. In 1990, they received the William Inge Award, and in 1991, the Kennedy Center Honors.*

Adolph Green was married in 1960 to actress Phyllis Newman. They have two children, Adam and Amanda Green. Phyllis Newman was in Comden and Green's Subways Are for Sleeping, *a performance for which she won a Tony Award.*

This interview took place on November 16, 1992.

• ———————————————————— •

Interviewer: Let's start by talking about the collaborative process—how you folks work together. Where do you work? I know how one lyricist might work, but how do two?

Comden: There's a lot of gloomy staring at each other across the room, which we've done, it seems to me, most of our lives. But we always feel if we hadn't put that time in staring gloomily and nothing happening, then the thing that eventually happens would never have happened. We usually meet at my house because, I guess, I have most of the records and the paper and the carbon and all that stuff. It's just easier. We meet almost every day.

Green: Sometimes we have fallow periods where we don't meet, but we usually do meet almost every day.

Comden: Of course, when we're in the middle of a project, if there's a show on that we're getting near to finishing, we could work at night, too, and all around the clock—or in Boston or Philadelphia or wherever we are.

Interviewer: This may sound like a very naïve question, but I simply don't know the answer. How is writing a lyric different from writing a poem?

Comden: I don't know how to answer that, because I think that some lyrics can be read as poetry—but not really. I think that a lyric is not really complete unless the music is there, because that's the purpose.

Green: And it wasn't intended to be anything that existed without the music.

Comden: A poet can take off and write any way he wants to—any length of line, rhyme, no rhyme—but music is a very stern taskmaster. It's very mathematical. When you write a lyric, it has to go to music, and there are lots of rules that go along with that. I think it's quite different from writing poetry.

Interviewer: When you write the lyrics preceding the music, do you have an idea of what the melody should be, and, if so, do you influence the composer?

Comden: Of course, a lyric is a rhythmic pattern, and sometimes we have what we call a dummy tune in mind.

Green: Which we don't usually tell the composer!

Comden: It's just to have a pattern for ourselves to write the lyric. Then when you hand it to the composer, it comes out completely differently. But yes, we have used sort of dummy ideas in our heads—so in a sense I guess we've influenced the music.

Interviewer: How did you both get started?

Comden: I went to NYU, where I majored in dramatic art, and somebody brought Adolph down to meet me when I was still a student. Then we kind of remet after I got out of school and started making the rounds of the offices. There was no television then—there was radio—so we used to go to producers' offices and agents' offices, and we never got a job. Never!

Green: Never! I was just an unemployed fellow who hoped he would get into the theater somewhere, and Betty and I met, as she just said, at NYU, and later I met her on my rounds looking for work in the theater. I had recently met a young girl of sixteen, Judy Holliday, just out of high school. She somehow got involved with a little Greenwich Village nightclub where the owner said, "Do you know any people who could put on a show here?" and she said, "Yes." She had met me, and I ran into Betty and I said, "Look, we can work. We can do a night's work in this place, the Village Vanguard. We'll get five dollars apiece, and no one will ever have to know about it!"

Comden: So I immediately left the audition line I was on, and we went down, and the Vanguard is where we started. We started a group, which eventually became an act called the Revuers. We didn't know quite what we were doing, but we couldn't afford to buy material. At first, we did other people's material. We had no money to pay royalties, so we started to write. We wrote little revues, numbers, and songs—and people began to discover us.

Green: Suddenly we caught on. We got several splendid reviews, and people started coming down like mad—distinguished people of the theater and letters and the arts—and I said, "My God, where did this come from?" We were discovered, but we were "too smart" for the average audiences. We went through long periods of unemployment. We stuck together for about five years, but then we ended up with Judy in Hollywood and us back in New York. We ran into Leonard Bernstein, who was already an old friend of mine and an old friend of Betty's. He'd suddenly become tremendously famous as the assistant conductor of the New York Philharmonic and had written the music for the ballet *Fancy Free,* choreographed by Jerry Robbins. He was asked to do a show based on the ballet, and Leonard suggested Betty and myself to do the book and lyrics.

Comden: Leonard brought the other people down to see us perform. We were at the Blue Angel at the time, as just an act of two, and Leonard got us the job to write the book and lyrics for *On the Town*—and that's how we began.

Interviewer: Why was *On the Town* changed so radically when it was made into a film?

Comden: At the time, MGM and Louis B. Mayer thought that the Bernstein score was too difficult. It wouldn't happen today, but they thought that the music was too symphonic and too classical and that audiences wouldn't understand it.

Green: We were under contract to MGM.

Comden: There wasn't much we could do about it. We were very unhappy about it. The only part of the movie we really liked is the opening, which is terrific—and wonderfully shot at the Brooklyn Navy Yard.

Green: Oddly enough, that's the only thing that critics and people ever remember from the score.

Comden: It's unfortunate. They should do that over again.

Interviewer: Bernstein was one of the first composers you worked with. I would imagine he was a fairly strict taskmaster. Did his music always come first?

Green: No. It could come first, and it did often, but a lot of the time he took off from the ideas we had.

Comden: We've worked all different ways with every composer. Sometimes we have an idea for a song and a title and then the composer will take that and write a phrase and continue. Sometimes there's a complete melody, that's true, which we then put words to if we find the right place in the show; and then other times we write a whole lyric and the composer sets that. That was true with Leonard or anybody we've worked with. When asked which comes first, the answer really is, in our case, the book. We haven't written just great popular songs that come from nowhere. We've always written in connection with a show or a movie, so the things that we write come out of situation and character. That's where you get the ideas from.

Green: You hope and pray that it'll be a hit, but that it'll be integrated and right and wonderful.

Interviewer: Is it different working with a different composer every time you do it? You had a long history with Jule Styne. Was it radically different working with him rather than working with Bernstein?

Green: Yes, they were very different kinds of talents.

Comden: So was Cy Coleman. They were all eccentric.

Green: In fact, they were all nuts!

Comden: They were all crazy. That was very stimulating.

Green: We've had great times with each one of those composers we've named. Our first was with Lenny, which was unique. Nothing can take the place of that.

Comden: As we said, he was already an old friend when we started to work with him, and yes, he was special. There isn't anybody and probably never will be anybody like him, so that was a unique experience—and fun.

Interviewer: Unique in what way?

Comden: Compare him to anybody else. You can't. He was so unique— one of the great minds of the century and so knowledgeable in every way and very playful and very brilliant and just terrific.

Green: At the same time, both really intellectual and playing at things, enjoying things as games.

Comden: He never thought about whether a thing was pop or serious, just whether it was good.

Interviewer: How did that affect the way that you wrote? When he came to you with music, let's say, or when you were working with him, in what way was it different from the way that you worked with Jule Styne?

Comden: Well, you're working on a show, and what's true of all composers is that they're dramatists. In the theater, the composer has to be a dramatist, because you're telling a story, and you have to write music that goes with the characters just as the lyrics do. I think they were all deeply involved in what the whole show was about, not just simply writing music. It's hard to say. They were very different people, different personalities.

Green: When we first got involved with Jule Styne, he represented everything that had never been a part of our lives. He was on the West Coast already and had been a tremendous success for years with Sammy Cahn, doing lyrics and writing just songs, not necessarily for any dramatic work, though sometimes it was for movies and there were scores. He represented success to us and scared us a little.

Comden: Out of ten hits on the weekly Hit Parade, he'd have six! It was terrifying to us. We didn't have that.

Green: But we hit it off when we got together, and we were very surprised and pleased. We found him to be, in his own way, a very creative musician and composer and dramatist.

Interviewer: I was looking at your songs that I am the very fondest of, and an awful lot of them are patter songs. Something I've noticed is that a lot of the people you've written for aren't natural singers: Rosalind Russell in *Wonderful Town,* Cyril Ritchard in *Peter Pan,* and Judy Holliday, of course. I wondered if perhaps the reason the songs are patter songs is that they were for those people?

Comden: They're for the characters, really. We wrote "Captain Hook's Waltz" because Captain Hook needed a great number to express his combination of villainy and elegance. We were writing for the character.

Green: With Rosalind, we had only four weeks to write the score in or we might lose her to some other commitments. She came to us one day and she said, "Listen, Leonard, listen, Betty and Adolph. I've got a voice with exactly four notes in it, and you've got to write for those four notes, and you better write some stuff that's pretty funny." Then she goes something like this: "da da da da da da, joke; da dee da da, joke."

Comden: So we took the information and fed it into a computer and we came up with "One Hundred Easy Ways to Lose a Man," which she did brilliantly. Sometimes stars really know what they need. She had good stuff to do in the show, but she said she needed one more song to really express her character in the situation—and the show needed it. We wrote "One Hundred Easy Ways" out of town, actually, in New Haven, and it was just right for the situation and for her.

Green: We wrote that number with Leonard. The three of us got together and we said, "Oh God, we've gotta do this—da da da da da da, joke." We wrote this number and came to perform it for Rosalind, and she was ill. We were in New Haven, and she was in bed with a terrible cold and a little flu; so a piano was dragged down the hall, and the three of us played the whole number for her. Rosalind was inside the bedroom with the doors open. She was lying there gasping, so we couldn't go inside.

Comden: We sang it to her from the hallway! It was the first time she heard it.

Green: She said hoarsely, "I think it's all right."

Comden: She gave a weak gesture of "okay."

Green: And it became a knockout. She was great.

Interviewer: It occurred to me when I was asking that question that there's a part of it that doesn't make any sense because a couple of the most lovely ballads that you ever wrote were written for a nonsinger, Judy Holliday. "Just in Time" is gorgeous and has all those long notes to hold. When you have a really superb singer and you know you're writing for John Cullum or Carol Lawrence, how does that affect the way that you craft a lyric—or does it?

Comden: It doesn't. If you have a great voice, sometimes it helps, but we never thought of Judy as a nonsinger. She sang "The Party's Over" better than anybody could. She was extraordinarily musical. She wasn't known mainly as a singer, that's true, but I would consider her a singer. John Cullum has a big voice, but we were writing that whole show—*On the Twentieth Century*—as a sort of comic opera.

Green: With a lot of bravura.

Comden: Yes, a lot of big singing. Everybody had to sing that way. Kevin Kline we sort of discovered for that show, and Madeline Kahn, who opened in it, had a beautiful voice, a big soprano; so we wrote knowing that these people could certainly carry those things.

Green: Each show has different needs and requirements; but with ballads, we rarely think in terms of nonsingers or singers.

Comden: Sometimes nonsingers are the best singers. Fred Astaire is the best singer of a ballad that you would want.

Interviewer: Is it odd when you see the material done by someone else after you've seen the first performance?

Comden: It happens all the time.

Green: You hope that someone understands.

Interviewer: I'm thinking in terms of your being performers yourselves. You really love it. Do you ever want to take it back and say, "No, no, no! You've gotta do it this way"?

Comden: No, we're very glad to have it done.

Green: But then sometimes we do take it back, because we do our *Party with Comden and Green* from time to time.

Comden: Whenever asked!

Interviewer: Does your being performers change the way that you do things?

Comden: I think it helps in the writing. We understand what works. You mentioned patter songs or comedy material; we're very experienced in performing it, and I think it helps us in our writing quite a bit.

Green: And as performers we have tremendous energy, and that often transmits itself into the scores of the shows that we write.

Comden: We often do demonstrate the score for the cast at the beginning. In Hollywood, we used to read the scripts for the people we were writing for.

Interviewer: As long as you've brought up movies, *Singin' in the Rain* is probably the greatest movie musical ever made.

Green: We like it.

Interviewer: It was turned into a Broadway musical a few years ago.

Green: Forget it! Forget it!

Comden: It's a subject we really don't want to talk about.

Green: It's a movie that we're terrifically proud of.

Comden: And we never thought it should be done onstage.

Green: Let's forget about it. Let's just talk about the movie. It's a great feeling that you don't always get in theater, because it's turned into one of those classic films that's performed all over the world. Anyplace we turn up, any country, anywhere, when *Singin' in the Rain* is mentioned, they go mad.

Comden: A movie lives; you can always see it, which is kind of marvelous. With the shows, they become memories.

Green: The only other part that's important was the owning part of it. We own none of it!

Interviewer: Are the characters in *Singin' in the Rain* based on real silent film actors and how they adapted to sound films?

Comden: Partially.

Green: We used the tragic end of John Gilbert. He was a big, big star in silent films, and his first talkie finished him off. It was a film in which he was a dashing kind of cavalier, and he said to the girl, "I love you! I love you! I love you!"—and the audience, who had been passionate about him, burst into wild, savage laughter, and that was the end of the poor man's career.

Comden: It was a tragedy. There were so many tragedies like that, but we decided to try to make the picture funny and have as many marvelously funny things happen as possible and get a different slant on it.

Green: And yet somehow have a real feeling of truth in it.

Interviewer: Is the reason you felt that it would not make a great stage musical that it was essentially film?

Comden: Yes. It was really a film. Stanley Donen and Gene Kelly did the most superb directing job possible. It is a film that is meant to be a film.

Green: It wasn't meant to be transcribed for the theater. If it were, it would have to be done flawlessly, brilliantly, and with the equivalent imagination. I will say nothing further.

Interviewer: Today we hear that in Hollywood the screenwriter is completely obliterated by the time a movie gets made. How did you get so much of what you wrote on the screen in *Singin' in the Rain*?

Green: We were writing at a time at MGM, the time of the Arthur Freed unit, when everything we wrote got filmed the second we stopped writing it.

Comden: It was a very unusual unit because Arthur Freed respected writers. He brought us out from New York, he brought Alan Lerner out, he brought all kinds of people out from the theater. We were very lucky.

Green: And Gene was there, Gene Kelly, an old friend of ours. Stanley Donen and Gene had just started directing pictures together, and they knew our work. We were friends, and they knew the eccentricities that we got into things. *Singin' in the Rain* was very difficult to write, but once we got it done, there was a lot of enthusiasm, and, astonishingly, it was filmed the way we wrote it.

Comden: It was because of our closeness and the fact that we were respected there; many times a writer is not. We were in this unit, and with both directors—with Gene and Stanley and with Vincente Minnelli on

The Band Wagon—we were lucky. Our scripts were actually put up on the screen.

Green: And there was a man named Roger Edens, who was Arthur Freed's associate producer and a wonderful musician and arranger. He sort of discovered Judy Garland and quite a number of others, and he was there all the time. So the proper fusion took place, and *Singin' in the Rain* was the result.

Comden: Gene and Stanley had seen our act, the Revuers. They knew all our bits; they knew the way our minds worked. If what was in the script had been handed to another director, he might have looked at it and said, "What is this? This is ridiculous." But they understood it; they thought it was funny the same way we thought it was funny. So it was a great short-hand that went on among us, and it was a very lucky and happy combination of people.

Interviewer: All right; we're agreed that *Singin' in the Rain* does not translate into musical theater. But let's talk about going the other way, about taking a movie and turning it into a musical.

Green: We haven't done that very often.

Comden: Just once—*On the Twentieth Century*. It was a play first and then a movie. When we started writing *On the Twentieth Century*, we didn't have the movie rights, come to think of it; so we had to go back to the original source, the play by Hecht and MacArthur. Later, when we got the rights to the movie, we didn't use it, because by that time we had written the show. What else have we done from a movie?

Interviewer: You worked on *Applause*, which was taken from *All about Eve*.

Green: For that we just wrote the book.

Comden: It's the first and only time we just wrote the book.

Interviewer: How did that happen?

Green: Lauren Bacall is a very good friend. We got excited by the idea, and then we were asked to do it.

Comden: We were asked to do the book because they had already signed Strouse and Adams, and they were having some trouble with the book that they did have, and they came to us. We came in late on the project, and we were delighted to do it. That's a movie that's so adored and revered that we thought we'd just be clobbered no matter what we did. It's the kind of film that people meet and they recite scenes out loud—they know every word of it; but actually we got wonderful reviews for the book. It was terrific. We're glad we did it.

Interviewer: You were also called in midway through a musical called *Peter Pan,* which is probably the best children's show ever written, and you had to make changes in it. I have this notion that all of you folks know all of you other folks who write musicals, so when you're asked in, is it an awkward situation?

Comden: It all depends on what the situation is. With *Peter Pan,* there were two young writers, Carolyn Leigh and Moose Charlap, who'd written the score, and they were very talented. It was their first show.

Green: And it wasn't quite a musical. It was much more a play with music.

Comden: We were called by the producer and by the director, Jerry Robbins, because it wasn't working. They were in San Francisco, and they were thinking of closing the show, and they asked whether we'd come up and look at it and give them some thoughts on the subject. We saw it, and we just knew it was *the* role for Mary Martin.

Green: Jerry said, "What do you think?" And we said, "We think it could work." He dragged us by the collar to Mary's dressing room and said, "Look, look, they think it can be solved!" And, indeed, we helped solve it.

Comden: We could have at that point, I think, taken over the whole show, done the whole score; but we didn't want to because it was the kids' first show.

Green: They had written some wonderful numbers, too.

Comden: Some of the things were good, so we kept all of their good things and then we wrote the rest of the score. We worked with Jerry on the book.

Green: We felt first of all—we worked with Jule Styne—that it needed a "motto song" that would give the whole spirit of the show at once, so we wrote "Never Land."

Comden: That has the spirit of J. M. Barrie and the whole sense of what *Peter Pan* is all about, and that was lacking in the score. They needed that, and then we knew that Mary Martin had great comic possibilities, that she had a coloratura voice, so we wrote a number called "Mysterious Lady" for her. And for Cyril Ritchard, we wrote "Captain Hook's Waltz"— to have a real motto song for Captain Hook.

Green: We turned the show into a musical comedy—which it always should have been—and it worked.

Comden: And it works every year all over the world!

Interviewer: When you came in on that show, how much time did you have?

Comden: Not much, because we were writing a movie, as a matter of fact. We were finishing a film called *It's Always Fair Weather,* and we went up to San Francisco. We worked in San Francisco, and then the show came down to L.A. It was about five weeks.

Interviewer: Was the pressure severe at that point? Everything was riding on you folks, wasn't it?

Green: The pressure wasn't severe because we were enjoying it.

Comden: And it worked! As long as the ending is happy, you forget how awful it was.

Interviewer: Most of the time you've been very lucky with that. Most of your shows have worked. When they finally get to Broadway, they have had extensive runs. I notice you taking a deep breath there. Is there something you remember that didn't?

Green: We've had some.

Interviewer: When you write both book and lyrics, do you like that best because it just makes things more graceful and it's easier?

Green: We like it best because it summons forth our creative drives — and if it's a successful show, then it makes us more money!

Comden: Twice as much. Don't forget, we have to divide everything.

Interviewer: Let's talk about two of your shows that didn't quite click the way one might have hoped. There was one in 1947 called *Bonanza Bound.*

Green: It closed in Philadelphia.

Comden: It closed in Philadelphia on New Year's Eve.

Green: Great show that New Year's Eve!

Comden: It was not a good show. It had some lovely things in the score, beautiful music by Saul Chaplin; but we just made too many mistakes, and it was a disaster. That was 1947, and about twenty years ago someone came over to me in the theater and he said, "I was in *Bonanza Bound*"—and I had this pang. I said, "I'm sorry." He said, "Do you remember that on closing night you and Mr. Green were so nice? You got up and performed for us for about an hour." We did it out of pure guilt; we entertained them, and then we said, "Now look, this show could be wonderful, and we're gonna work on it, we really are, and we're gonna save it somehow." That was in 1947; so twenty years ago, this guy came over to me and he said, "Is it all right if I take another job now?"

Interviewer: The other one is of more recent vintage, *A Doll's Life.* Hal Prince, who directed it, has said that he'd like to see that one come back.

Comden: We would, too. I'm glad he feels that way.

Interviewer: Why didn't that one work?

Comden: Again, I think it was just too many mistakes. There were a lot of reasons. I don't think they thought we had any right to do anything connected with Ibsen since we were just mere mummers from the jolly musical stage. I don't know. It was a feminist show, and it might have hit at a little time of reverse.

Green: Possibly it was a little overproduced, overdone, whatever.

Comden: And a little gloomier than it needed to be then; but it's a show we're proud of. I think if we could find a way, we'd love to see it done again, maybe on a small scale, have a chance to look at it. I used to sing a song from it in our *Party,* and in introducing it I'd always say that we had this show but if you didn't happen to be in New York that week you didn't see it. It ran a week in New York. That's a really horrendous experience because it is so hard to do a show. God knows, you don't set out to do a failure.

Green: And we basically believed in it. We knew that Hal was a great director, and we all went just a little bit awry, as can happen to anybody because you're not dealing in absolute things when you're dealing in theater. You're dealing in literature, and you're up for grabs every time.

Comden: It's not an exact science.

Green: That's the phrase I was looking for! We learn, but the secret is we never learn.

Comden: Each time you start from a standing position. You have a new idea, a new cast, a new group of collaborators often; and every time you start anew—so there are no rules for this particular combination, this particular idea. You can learn from experience, but you can continue to make terrible mistakes.

Green: Yes. And no matter how experienced you are, you're still a new-born babe every time you step into that world of a show, of a work of any kind that hasn't been done before.

Interviewer: You mentioned that *A Doll's Life* was a feminist musical, which is interesting because you have tackled a number of social issues in your shows. I'm thinking especially of *Hallelujah, Baby!,* which was a really rigorous study of racial issues in the 1960s. Is it your concern with these issues that causes you to write about them or does someone else suggest it to you? What was the driving force behind *Hallelujah, Baby!*?

Comden: We're alive today, and we're certainly interested in everything that goes on. That show actually was started by Arthur Laurents, who wrote the book. It was his idea, and we wrote the score with Jule Styne, and in many ways it was a wonderful show. It presented big difficulties. It was a very tough show to write, and the relationship between the races at that time was going through a great deal of change, day to day, so it was very hard for Arthur to find the right thing to leave at the end. The message, or whatever it was at the end of the show, was very hard to come by. We were going from integration through the militant movement and so forth, and it was very stimulating and exciting—but terribly hard.

Green: We all had a real basic respect for one another, and in some ways it came out very well.

Interviewer: Have you ever gotten up the day after a show opens and said to yourselves, "Oh, I wish we'd written that differently"?

Comden: We rewrite continually. We're always meeting and rewriting our shows.

Green: After *On the Town,* we resolved to quickly write another show because if we didn't try, we might never ever write again. So we wrote a show called *Billion Dollar Baby,* which was a look at the 1920s—which hadn't been done before. It was a terrific show, but it was off base in certain areas. In some ways it was quite remarkable. It was sardonic and tough. It ended with a girl, a ruthless kid from Staten Island who claws her way to the top, and at the end when she's about to marry the Billionaire, we have newsboys coming down the aisle yelling, "Depression! Stock Market Crash!" This person who was the Billionaire has been "wiped out," and the show ends with her throwing her jewelry around and him crawling around the floor trying to pick it up.

Comden: The audience was appalled. You have to realize that the Crash was in 1929 and this show was at the end of 1945. There were people in the audience who had had uncles who had jumped out of windows, because the time span between 1929 and 1945 was just too close for comfort. It was something that the audience wasn't ready for. It was the first look at the twenties, and it was not a very "Charlestony jazzy" look.

Green: That scared them somewhat.

Comden: But we also learned something. We killed off our most interesting character at the end of act one. Don't do it!

Green: We had him bumped off, rolling down a flight of stairs—and they never saw him again!

Comden: David Burns played that part. Brilliant. Just brilliant.

Interviewer: How about with a hit? Have you ever looked back after the fact and thought, "Oh, gee, I should have redone that"—or do you actually change them once the show is up?

Comden: Yes, sometimes you make some changes after you open—sometimes cuts or little changes. We've done that.

Interviewer: Do you get involved in the revivals of your shows when people do them? You came here to Washington to see the revival of *On the Town* at Arena Stage.

Comden: Yes, we came to see it.

Green: We were delighted with it. It was a wonderful production.

Comden: I do remember that they came to New York to talk to us and they asked, "When *On the Town* was done, did they play 'The Star-Spangled Banner' in the theater before the show?" We said yes—because it was during the war and before every show the audience stood for the national anthem. They wanted to do that, and I remember I said that, in this day and age, you cannot ask an audience to come in and then get up out of their seats and sing the national anthem. I felt it would hold the show up and would be terrible, but they used it and it was brilliant. I was so wrong! I was thrilled with it. They did it beautifully.

Interviewer: Because musicals have changed over the years, do you think your work is different now than it was fifteen or twenty years ago?

Green: Well, you can't help but write things differently.

Comden: We're older.

Green: We're older and the world's older, and at the same time you want to have a fresh look all the time. You don't want to live in the clichés of yesterday's behaviors in the theater, so you really look for something that will open you up as well as an audience.

Interviewer: On the recording of *A Party with Comden and Green* you say that there's a song in *Wonderful Town* that you might write a little differently today if you were doing it.

Comden: Oh, it's "One Hundred Easy Ways." It's just that that song has to do with relationships between men and women, and things are certainly different now since the women's movement. But the thing that we remind the audience of, if we say it anymore, is that those two characters, Ruth and Eileen, were living in the 1930s. The show was done in the 1950s, but they were living back when a girl was not supposed to be smart.

Interviewer: When you write a piece that is about a different era, when it has to capture a style of writing that is from many years earlier, is there anything in particular that you look for? Do you use models, some kind of song that's already there?

Comden: That is something that we avoided in *On the Twentieth Century,* because while it did take place in the thirties, we did not want to do a pastiche thirties score. Cy Coleman, who wrote the music, didn't want that either. Because the characters were so much bigger than life, this great big megalomaniac impresario and the equally megalomaniacal star, we felt that the music should be big and should be something like a comic opera—so the score does have that flavor and that bigness.

Green: It has nothing to do with the thirties at all.

Comden: And in *Wonderful Town,* which took place in the thirties, we used in background everything that spoke the thirties—swing music and the Eddie Duchin Band. All those things were from the thirties and we made many references in lyrics, of course, to things that were going on, in the conga number and "Swing," but the models for the songs were completely fresh. We didn't try to write thirties numbers.

Interviewer: Do performers affect the kinds of things that you write for them?

Comden: Of course. Anybody you write for, you certainly think about their strengths and their weaknesses.

Interviewer: What did you do when you had Phil Silvers in *Do Re Mi?*

Comden: We tried to be funny. That's the hardest thing in the world. He's such a brilliant comedian. We learned a lot from just listening to him.

Green: We've enjoyed writing for people who have a lot of fun in them and who have comic styles that can then be projected onstage.

Interviewer: Speaking of comic talents, what was Judy Holliday like, and how did *Bells Are Ringing* come to be?

Comden: She was very complex and brilliant, a brilliant girl and woman. We miss her so much. She was a voracious reader, very intelligent, not like Billie Dawn. She didn't want to be a performer at first. She wanted to direct, then she became this genius actress and performer. *Bells Are Ringing* started because we wanted to do a show for her. We wanted to get together again.

Green: We spent months trying to come up with a show for her, until finally we hit on this idea of a girl in an answering service, and we said, "Wow, that's it!"

Comden: Then we had a wonderful reunion.

Interviewer: Was Leslie Uggams a nightclub singer before she was in *Hallelujah, Baby!?*

Comden: Yes. In fact, she was in a club in Atlantic City, and we went to see her perform there. She was wonderful. That's how we signed her.

Interviewer: So in *Hallelujah, Baby!* you were creating her as an actress?

Comden: Well, she'd never done anything like that.

Interviewer: Is that an awkward situation, to take a person who hasn't ever done stage work before?

Comden: She was talented.

Green: If a person can't perform, that's awkward!

Interviewer: You've been collaborating for over forty years. Have you ever had a really knockdown, drag-out fight?

Green: Not really.

Comden: Not the kind you describe, really. We've fought, but here we are, rocking into the sunset together.

Interviewer: Considering all the composers you've worked with, is there one that you haven't worked with that you would have liked to work with? And considering how great your lyrics are, is there another lyricist whose words you admire?

Comden: Oh, both, a lot of them. Stephen Sondheim is brilliant. I guess we would have liked to have written with Beethoven.

Green: I was going to suggest Mozart, because Beethoven had a tough time with just one opera!

Comden: As far as composers, certainly Steve Sondheim. There are many lyricists we admire tremendously—Cole Porter, Ira Gershwin, Lorenz Hart. I loved the work of Carolyn Leigh, who worked with Cy Coleman and Dorothy Fields.

Interviewer: Forty years ago, if you got the assignment for a show, how long before it actually happened as compared to now?

Comden: Every show's been different. *On The Town* took about six months, which is insanely short. *Wonderful Town,* when we came in, they had been working on it and we did the score in four weeks. But I know what you mean. *The Will Rogers Follies* took years to get on—financial problems and people's availabilities.

Green: And a budget of about seven million dollars. Our first show, *On the Town,* was about a hundred and twenty thousand, at the most.

Comden: It's a very different world.

Interviewer: A lot of people say that the thing that would help Broadway a lot is strong producers of the sort that they used to have. Do you think that's true?

Comden: It would help. Sure.

Interviewer: Is it because it would narrow things down and it would be one person making the decisions?

Comden: In those days, there were people who were simply theater producers. There aren't that many who just do theater producing any more, who really understand it and know it and love it. There are some, but not very many.

Interviewer: Does the increased length of time it now takes to get a show on discourage you in any way?

Comden: No, I don't think so. If you have a goal and you know you want that show to happen, you are going to stay lively until you get it on. I think that we've been discouraged along the way. With *The Will Rogers Follies*, though, there *were* times when we thought, "This show will *never* get on."

Green: But we've thought that with almost every show we've been involved in. With *On the Town,* you say five months; it seemed like a dozen years at the time.

Comden: Because we couldn't raise the money for that either.

Interviewer: Was there ever one that just came together easily?

Comden: No, I can't think of any. There were those few weeks on *Wonderful Town.*

Green: Yes, that was exhilarating.

Comden: It was fun. In the first place, Lenny was available, so we started to work right away. And there was George Abbott, who was so great to work with. It was our second time working with this marvelous, marvelous man. Also, the other people connected with it couldn't criticize our work much because they were going to lose Rosalind Russell if it took too long. They were afraid to criticize, so we got our way.

Green: By the time they started criticizing and pulling it apart, it was too late; it was on.

Interviewer: Was the process different with *A Doll's Life* because the book was so much like a libretto?

Comden: We did actually give the composer, Larry Grossman, a lot of lyrics to set, come to think of it. I don't know if Larry ever came in with a melody that we used. A lot of things we worked out together, but we did give him a great deal of stuff that he set.

Green: It was a very difficult job, which he executed marvelously.

Interviewer: Did the three of you ever work together simultaneously?

Comden: Yes, very often we were in the same room and things happened simultaneously. It's like spontaneous combustion. The ideas are there and you set some words, and then he'd start to play something and a number would emerge. It happens that way sometimes.

Interviewer: Have you ever done things individually, or are there shows where one of you contributed much more than the other?

Comden: No, we've never done anything in the theater separately.

Interviewer: Is there a story behind your being Comden and Green as opposed to Green and Comden?

Comden: Because he's polite, he's a gentleman, and he let my name come first. Do you know the story about Lunt and Fontanne? A friend went to Alfred and said, "Alfred, it's really time. She's the woman. Make it Fontanne and Lunt." And he said, "This is the theater, not a goddamn lifeboat."

Interviewer: Do you write the songs together or does one of you give the other ideas?

Comden: We're usually in the same room at the same time and we write together. No rules.

Interviewer: Did you perform all the way along, or have you only done it since 1977?

Comden: When we did *On the Town*, we were in it. We wrote parts for ourselves—and we got the job. After that, we decided to concentrate on our writing and for many years we didn't perform. The first time we did was, I think, 1958; we did a version of *A Party*, and then we didn't again for years. We went back to writing, and somebody sort of talked us into doing it again. We did it again in 1977, and now we play at a lot of colleges and music centers. We love to perform.

Interviewer: Which of your songs are your favorites?

Comden: It's hard to pick a favorite. We love "Some Other Time" from *On the Town*.

Green: We like a lot of the material stuff. I think we have a lot of funny stuff in *Bells Are Ringing*, for instance.

Comden: Judy's last number, "I'm Going Back," and "Is It a Crime?"

Green: And the horse-racing number.

Interviewer: Did you ever write a song where you thought, "This one's going to be a hit"—and then it didn't do it?

Comden: We've been disappointed in songs a few times. We had a song in *On the Twentieth Century* called "Our Private World" we had a lot of faith in, and it didn't do anything.

Interviewer: Did you know the ones that did click?

Comden: Oh, no, you never know. You know when you think a song is good and it works.

Green: We had some real hits with Jule Styne—"Just in Time," "The Party's Over," "Make Someone Happy." In recent years, the score of *On the Town* is beginning to creep up. It thrills us every time it's played, especially "Lucky to Be Me" and "Some Other Time."

Comden: And "New York, New York."

Interviewer: I guess it's harder today because so much of pop music is rock and you're not writing songs that are easily adapted to rock.

Green: Now you tell us!

Comden: There is reinterest, I think, in show music among younger people, more than there was, say, in the 1960s or even the 1970s. I think that there's hope. I like rock.

Interviewer: How do you feel about critics out of town? Are they ever helpful? Do they ever suggest things that are useful?

Comden: There was a very good critic in Boston, Elliot Norton, who was very helpful. He used to come and see things several times out of town, and you'd meet with him sometimes and talk with him, and he was good. He was very sensible. You listen when you're out of town; you listen in general. You listen to the audience a lot. Unfortunately, today, it's very expensive to go out of town, and you don't do it that much. *The Will Rogers Follies* just opened on Broadway and played in that fishbowl. Everybody can see it from the first preview on, which I hate. You can learn a lot from being out of town.

Interviewer: What about negative reviews?

Green: *Variety* said about *On the Town,* when we opened, that it was a nothing show and it went over all right that night because we filled it up with friends and relatives.

Comden: We've one nice critic story. John Chapman, who was the reviewer for the *New York Daily News* at the time, saw *On the Town* opening night and wrote a very negative review of it.

Green: Which knocked us out!

Comden: We were just horrified, and so we called him up a few weeks later and asked him whether he'd come see the show again. I think we had dinner with him—or lunch.

Green: He said, "I don't know what was wrong. I wasn't drunk or anything. I just sat there. I didn't like it."

Comden: So we got him to come back and he saw it again, and the next day the headline was "Words Make Good Eating."

Green: It was a full page. And then he wrote a rave.

Comden: Critics don't usually admit they're wrong. It was nice.

Interviewer: Do reviews affect the way an audience sees a show?

Comden: The *New York Times* is extremely influential, but we have to be fair. No one liked *A Doll's Life.* It was a unanimous pan across the board. They just hated it, really rather violently. But reviews do affect the audience, of course. We thought we were in pretty good shape. The last few previews were wonderful. The audience loved it. And then it opened, the reviews were terrible, and that was it. That's how wrong you can be.

Interviewer: Can you think of any project that you've done that now you wish had somebody else's name on it?

Comden: We're not that ashamed! We've had failures—but it's okay. Adolph's very good about that. After *Bonanza Bound,* when we came back to New York, I felt very bad and kind of embarrassed and everything. Adolph walked right into Sardi's, and that's the way you should be. I admire that.

Green: I went up to somebody who said to me, "Well, what happened to the show?" I said, "It wasn't any good." That's about it. I felt a great halo over me.

Interviewer: When you have nothing that you're working on, do you sit and talk? Do you say words to each other?

Green: Yes, something like that. The case of *Bells Are Ringing* is a good strong one in point, because we spent months and months not being able to think of anything. We knew we wanted a couple of ideas for Judy, and finally one day it happened! We got so excited, we called Jule Styne in and described the idea, and he said, "They've got to fall down! This is it"—and we forged ahead.

Comden: But after all those days and weeks of meeting—I don't mean we only stared at each other; we talked occasionally—it's very discouraging. You go home after a day like that and you don't feel good, but finally something happens, something breaks through.

Green: And at that point you forget all those days because you know they were leading up to this. But sometimes they lead nowhere.

Interviewer: Is the process a messy process—paper crunched together and thrown all over the room? Or do you use a computer?

Comden: No, I don't know how to yet. I'm going to learn. I'm going to take it up. No, I use a typewriter; I used to just hold a pad on my lap and Adolph moved around a little bit more and I wrote things down. Now I sit at the typewriter and type things up. There's paper to throw away, but it's not like you see in the movies.

Green: It's still a messy process, because you're so filled with self-hatred.

Comden: The room is filled with self-hatred—and that's hard to sweep away.

Interviewer: Do you have a lot of trunk songs, songs that you haven't used?

Comden: I don't think we have. There were songs that were cut out of shows; we have some of those around, a few, but not a great thing that we can turn to and say, "Here's this gem that was never used."

Green: Composers can take a song that perished in one show and there's the melody and you can go on and on, but it's hard to use, "Griselda, I love you. / Even though your uncle hates me, I still love you." The words are not that easily movable.

Comden: Lyrics are specific, and music can be used in many different ways. We started a show with Leonard based on Thornton Wilder's play *The Skin of Our Teeth,* which never happened. At the end he was left with some gorgeous music which we're very happy he used in *The Chichester Psalms*—beautiful compositions—but we're left with a lot of songs about "save the human race!" It's hard to work that into your average show.

Interviewer: What do you see as the future of the Broadway musical?

Comden: We don't seem to have any theories. We're always so busy working ourselves. I guess we should look around and see what the trends are, but I think if you study trends and want to follow them, that way lies death—so we wouldn't do it for that reason. It's hard to say. It would be nice if the financial end of things loosened up so it wasn't that difficult and there could be more spontaneity again, which there used to be.

Interviewer: Considering how long you two have been writing together, what would you say is key to your partnership?

Comden: We always used to say that we stay together through sheer terror. I guess we're sort of on the same wavelength; we have the same sense of humor, the same sense of the ridiculous and the absurd.

Green: We have a basic respect for each other—or at least I have for her!

Comden: It couldn't work any other way.

Sheldon Harnick

Copyright Henry Grossman

Sheldon Harnick was born on April 30, 1924, in Chicago, Illinois. He earned a bachelor of music degree at Northwestern University. He wrote the lyrics for the Broadway musicals The Body Beautiful *(1958),* Fiorello! *(1959),* Tenderloin *(1960),* She Loves Me *(1963),* Fiddler on the Roof *(1964),* The Apple Tree *(1966),* The Rothschilds *(1970), and* Rex *(1976) and for the Off-Broadway musicals* Smiling, the Boy Fell Dead *(1961),* Man in the Moon *(1963),* Pinocchio *(1973), and* Alice in Wonderland *(1975). He also wrote the lyrics for* A Christmas Carol, Dragons, A Wonderful Life, *and* The Phantom Tollbooth, *musicals that have been performed around the country but have yet to be presented in New York.*

He received the Pulitzer Prize, the New York Drama Critics' Circle Award, and the Tony Award for Fiorello! *(Best Musical), a Grammy Award for* She Loves Me, *and two Tony Awards for* Fiddler on the Roof *(Best*

Lyrics and Best Musical). In 1993, he received the Marc Blitzstein Award for musical theater from the American Academy of Arts and Letters. This interview took place on November 9, 1992.

● ———————————————————————————————— ●

Interviewer: You have been quoted as saying, "Inspiration is the act of drawing up the chair to the writing desk." Would you say that that is how you have approached lyric-writing for the American musical theater?

Harnick: Actually, that's not my quote. I found that somewhere and I loved it, so I put it above the mantelpiece, along with a quote from Sean O'Casey, "Get on with the bloody job."

Interviewer: What is your writing process? How do you start, and how do you discipline yourself to do it? Is it hard or is it easy?

Harnick: Discipline has always been hard for me. I rationalize that by telling myself that the reason it's hard is that once I really get involved with a project, it takes over and everything else in my life suffers. I don't know whether that's a rationalization or not. It is true that once I get into it, it becomes obsessive. So I avoid it at all costs. I don't know if you've read that old essay by Bob Benchley on all the ways that writers can find to procrastinate: You sit down to write and suddenly you find that you must build a paper-clip chain that's four feet long, exactly four feet long. There are innumerable ways to keep from working. My discipline is saying, "Today I will work on it a half hour, and after a half hour I will quit; and tomorrow I will work on it an hour." Then, little by little, I put in more and more time, and then suddenly, as I say, it just takes over.

Interviewer: I'd like to go back to the beginning. How does a nice guy from Chicago find his way to a career in the American musical theater?

Harnick: I guess there are two answers. One is that I never found myself terribly articulate. When I spoke, especially in public, I tripped over my own tongue. It was very comforting to find that I could organize my thoughts quietly and in private and write something that I couldn't say. That was one of the ways that I drifted into writing. The other way was that my mother celebrated every occasion with a little piece of doggerel. Whether it was an anniversary or a birthday, she would write a little poem. So my older sister and I began to do the same thing. For some reason, my younger brother was spared this. My sister, Gloria, turned out to be a rather good poet, and in fact she won a Chicago citywide poetry contest, which was very impressive to me. I used to contribute things to our grammar school paper, silly things, and I guess because I didn't really have much confidence in myself as a poet I would try to make them funny. I would try to give them twists, try to make people laugh and disarm them. In high school, I met a young man named Stanley Orzey, who, along with his family, was in the little-theater movement in Chicago. Stanley wanted to write. Somebody introduced us because I had been writing these little verses for the school paper, and we began to write parodies at first just to entertain in school. We even sold some to Chicago comics, but much of that material bombed. Then we started to write some original stuff, mostly because of Stanley, who was very ambitious. In fact, Stanley got me into a play. I was in a play in Chicago that closed after two performances because of violations; we were closed down by the fire department, which was a good thing, because that was before the review came out.

Then I got drafted into World War II, and we had a volunteer special service outfit. I was down at Robins Field in Georgia. There was one summer when, with typical army efficiency, they lost my records. They sent five other men out in place of the team I was on. Every morning we would go out and they would say, "We don't know what to do with you." For ninety days, we were on our own. I soon discovered that there was a volunteer special service unit there. Whoever showed up on a Monday was in the show. The evenings were put together by a man named Sol Lerner, who had been an agent in New York and remembered all the sketches he had seen in Broadway revues. He would tell us the premise of a sketch and what the ending was, and we would go out and improvise. I was doing that, and I played violin; I was playing the two solos that I knew how to play. One was "Holiday for Strings," which was very effective, and the other wasn't. I was also writing songs that expressed what was happening in my particular outfit. I'm sure everyone remembers with great fondness "We're Members of the I.M.U."; that was one of my early hits. At least it was a hit at Robins Field, Georgia. I began to discover that when I wrote things that everybody knew about, that they identified with, the response was enormously gratifying. Sol Lerner's girlfriend came down to visit him, a very pretty blond lady who later married him, and the two of them said, "You have talent, and after this war is over, if you ever come to New York, look us up. If you want to go into this business, maybe we can help." Which is what I did. June, Sol's fiancée, it turned out, became June Taylor, who did all the choreography for the *Jackie Gleason Show*, so that didn't hurt either.

That's the short version of how I got from Chicago to New York. What also should be included is that I was a violinist, and it took therapy later in my life to discover that I was an extremely anxious violinist. This goes along with the inarticulateness, not much self-esteem, not much security. As a violinist, when I had to play in public, I would tense up. I had a job with a band at the Edgewater Beach Hotel in Chicago; they lowered microphones and three nights a week we would broadcast locally, and two nights a week we would broadcast coast to coast. I didn't know it, but when those mikes came down I started to tense up, and by the end of our engagement I could hardly play. I went to a doctor, and he said it was nerve and muscle exhaustion; he said, "Why don't you take off for a year? Maybe you'll recover"—which I never did entirely. I thought, "If I can't be a violinist, then let me see if I can follow out this budding career in writing lyrics." So I came to New York.

Interviewer: Didn't you have a very brief moment of fame with Xavier Cugat?

Harnick: Right. I had a reputation around Chicago for being a very good sight-reader, which I was. My name was in the union book, and I got a call from a man who had been hired to join Xavier Cugat's band; they were playing in Minneapolis. He said, "I can't make it. Will you go up there?" I thought, great, so I went up. I arrived about nine o'clock in the morning; the first show was at ten. The Cugat ensemble didn't arrive until a quarter to ten, and they gave me one of those shirts with all the ruffles and about a half inch of pancake makeup on the collar. Before the curtain went up, I was waiting to see the music. Cugat looked up and said, "Who the hell are you?" I said whatever his name was couldn't make it and he sent me. He said, "Do you have to play with those goddamn glasses?" I said, "Yes. I can't see without them." He said, "All right. The important thing is that when I play 'La Golondrina,' you three stand behind me; and when I sway to the left, you sway to the right." I thought, "I can do that." The problem came when I saw the music. It wasn't written out; it looked like a medieval manuscript with runes or something. The rest of the guys in the band knew what to do when they saw those things, but I didn't. There was nothing for me to read; so I put the violin down and I picked up the two sticks, the claves, and I started to play what I had played at Jewish weddings in Chicago, which was a rumba rhythm. I got a little way into it, and the drummer behind me tapped me on the shoulder. He said, "Would you mind? You're confusing the rhythm section." I was let go after the first performance. I came back to Chicago with my bow between my legs. The happy ending is that about three months later the Cugat band played the College Inn in Chicago, and I went to see who they had hired—and they hadn't hired anybody.

Interviewer: When you started writing, who were the lyricists that you listened to, that you admired?

Harnick: One of my first influences was W. S. Gilbert. As a violinist in high school, as I said, I was a good sight-reader and not a bad violinist. Some of us got requests to go fill in at places like the Goodman Theatre, where they would be doing Gilbert and Sullivan. I went to some of those and was just bowled over, especially by the patter songs. I suppose, like all young people, I was more impressed by technique than by emotional lyrics. I loved Gilbert; I was very impressed by him. I loved Yip Harburg; I loved Larry Hart, then a little later Frank Loesser, and, to a certain extent, Ira Gershwin. They were the witty ones. Mostly I think it was Harburg, more than anybody. When I got out of the army and I went to Northwestern, one of my classmates was a girl who had a career later under the name of Charlotte Rae. Charlotte had gone to New York; this was around 1947. She came back from New York and she said, "Sheldon, you've got to hear this album." It was *Finian's Rainbow*. I listened to it, and I thought it was extraordinary that a man could have such fun with words and yet be saying things that were important—that the lyrics could be playful and important at the same time. I kind of filed that in the back of my head—that that would be a career worth pursuing—although at the time I still thought I was going to be a violinist. I think those were the primary lyric influences.

Interviewer: Don't you have an anecdote about the tradition that propelled you at this time in your life, when things weren't quite there yet?

Harnick: When I came to New York, it was extremely difficult for about eight years. I would get depressed and think, "Is this ever going to work?" So I invented a tradition that guaranteed me my place in the musical theater. It was called the "HAR" tradition. I realized that there had been Otto Harbach and Larry Hart and Yip Harburg, and I thought. "Harnick has to be the next one in this 'HAR' tradition." On days when I really got depressed, I added Oscar Harmerstein to the list.

Interviewer: When you started writing for the commercial musical theater, you wrote for a form called the revue, which we essentially don't have anymore. Can you talk about that as a training ground—and do you lament its passing?

Harnick: I do lament its passing. I lament its passing particularly because so many of us were able to place songs in those early revues, on and off Broadway, and there's no way to learn quicker than seeing what you do in front of an audience—seeing what works, seeing what doesn't work. It's very difficult to get an entire show on, but it was not that difficult to get a song, or a couple of songs, on. When I came to New York, I looked up Sol Lerner, and he tried to help. In fact, he got me a job writing for—I think it was called the *Dupont Comedy Hour*, featuring an unknown named Jackie Gleason. I wrote a theme for them. Then I looked up Charlotte Rae. Charlotte knew Yip Harburg, and she introduced me to him. That was wonderful, paying homage to my god, and he was very encouraging. I went over, I played a lot of stuff for him—I had a pianist with me, because I don't play piano—and Yip said, "You're very gifted. I think you'll be a first-rate lyricist in about five years." Actually, he was off by three years; it was eight before something happened. Charlotte asked if I would write something for an act she was putting together. I felt that I owed it to her because I think it was Charlotte, perhaps more than anybody, who gave me the courage to come to New York. While I was still in Chicago, I had had a letter from her saying that in trying to put an act together she had met a lot of young writers, and she did not find nearly as much first-rate lyric talent as she thought she would in New York. She thought that if I came I could have a career, which was very important to me. So, although the furthest thing from my mind was to do special material, when Charlotte asked if I would do her number, I said yes.

I had no ideas for what to write for Charlotte, but one night I woke up about four o'clock in the morning with a song going through my head. I wrote down three stanzas, words and music, and I went back to sleep. The next morning I got up and I said, "I wrote a song last night. It's probably rotten. It's probably one of those four o'clock ideas which turns out to be absolute gibberish the next day." I looked at it and I thought, "My God, this is wonderful!" It needed a fourth stanza, but the fourth stanza was inherent in the way the first three were going. I called it "The Shape of Things." It was a Frankie-and-Johnny love story, but it was told in terms of geometrical shapes. I sold it to Charlotte; she loved it and used it. Eventually it was in a revue, and once it had been recorded, it turned out that it was then public property; anybody could use it. So she sold it back to me.

Charlotte was my entrée to the world of revue, because she was going to do a revue with Leonard Sillman. Originally it was to be *New Faces of 1950,* then *New Faces of 1951* when he couldn't raise the money. Somewhere along the line she was helping to do auditions, and she was going to do this song of mine, "The Shape of Things"; but it looked like Leonard would never raise the money, and Charlotte got an offer to do another show—I think it was *Three Wishes for Jamie*—so she left. And I had nothing in the show. But Leonard called and asked if I had anything else. I had started a song called "Boston Beguine"; I played what I had and he said, "Fine. This will be perfect for the girl who is replacing Charlotte, a wonderful performer named Alice Ghostley." I finished it, and "Boston Beguine" turned out to be a showstopper. It was 1952, and that was my entrée. After that, I managed to place songs in a couple of other Broadway revues, and then they began to disappear from Broadway. I had a few more in Off-Broadway revues.

Interviewer: How did you come to write "Boston Beguine"?

Harnick: That song came out of anger; some of the best things I've written have come out of anger, certainly my love songs. My wife at the time was in a show called *Top Banana,* which was playing in Boston, and I went to visit her. She was living in a women's residence that was across the Boston Common from the Shubert Theatre, and we would walk to the theater. At that time, there were a lot of very sleazy-looking characters who inhabited the Common. They would make ribald remarks, and, being the coward I was, I did nothing about it; we just hurried to get through the park. Also, the town just seemed gritty and sleazy. With this in mind, on my way back to New York on the bus, somebody next to me had a radio, and out of it I heard a song—I think it was Tony Martin—and the song was called "Johannesburg." I had no idea at the time that Johannesburg was a cosmopolitan city; I had this erroneous picture in my mind of a cluster of mud huts, and the song was very exotic. I just started to giggle to myself, and I thought, "I'm going to write a song about Boston like that," particularly because there had just been an article in the newspaper about an attempt on the part of the church to suppress a certain book, which made me very angry. That's why the song ends as it does, with this boy and girl, who have had no experience; if they had been able to read the proper books, they would have known what to do when they were alone together—but those books were suppressed, so their affair was hopeless.

Interviewer: In this revue period, you were writing both music and lyrics. When did you come to the decision to concentrate on writing lyrics?

Harnick: It started when I played for Yip Harburg. Yip said, "Right now you're writing your own music. Let me tell you as a piece of practical advice that there are more capable theater composers than there are theater lyricists, and you can facilitate your career by writing with other composers besides yourself." I took that seriously. I had a song in a revue featuring your and my favorite musical comedy performer, Bette Davis. My song was not sung by Bette; it was sung by somebody else equally tone-deaf. That's not fair; Bette had a sense of melody, she just had no musicality to her voice. The conductor for that show was a man by the name of Milton Rosenstock, and Milton was very ambitious; he wanted to produce a musical. He had hired as his rehearsal pianist a wonderful musician, now dead, David Baker. He put David and me together and he said, "I'd love you to do something. I'd love to produce." I had tried to put together a revue at one point, with my own material. I needed revue sketches, and I had read several hilarious books by a man named Ira Wallach. They were books of literary parodies; the most successful one was called *Hopalong-Freud*. And there was a sequel, *Hopalong-Freud Rides Again,* and another book called *How to Pick a Wedlock: Five Thousand Years of Foreplay*. I got in touch with Ira and asked if he would do sketches for this revue. It never materialized; but we became friends, and Ira had an idea for a musical. He wanted to do a satire on the rags-to-riches stories of Horatio Alger—so we did one. David Baker wrote the music. Before that, David and I had placed some songs in Off-Broadway revues, but never on Broadway. So we wrote this show. It went through several metamorphoses; it was originally called *Fair-Haired Boy,* then *Horatio,* and finally *Smiling, the Boy Fell Dead.*

Interviewer: That's a great title!

Harnick: That was Ira's title. Eventually we got it on, in Dallas in 1954 at Margo Jones's theater, which was just in time because I was about to turn thirty. I had yet to realize my dream and I thought, "If I don't do it by the time I'm thirty, I'll never do it. I'll go back to Chicago and be a violinist again." It was one of those pieces of luck where, because of somebody else's misfortune I got lucky. The misfortune fell on a friend of mine, a writer named Michael Brown, who also wrote for *New Faces of 1952*; he did the Lizzie Borden number—"You can't chop your papa up in Massa-chusetts." Michael was supposed to have a show done by Margo Jones, and he came down with either hepatitis or mononucleosis, and he just couldn't work. He knew that I had a show that was almost done, so he put me in touch with Margo. I sent her the script and the score of what we had and she said, "This just fits our company, so please come down," and we did. We were a big hit in Dallas; but we were not a hit when we came back to New York. We had an impossible time raising money. Eventually it got on in 1961 Off-Off-Broadway, and it was not successful.

Interviewer: But later came a long and prosperous collaboration with Jerry Bock. How did that happen?

Harnick: While I was trying to stay solvent, I envied pianists because they could work as rehearsal pianists; they could accompany people. I didn't have that, so I was trying not to take a day job. I was trying to devote my-self as much as possible to writing. There were enough musicals then so that there were musicals in trouble out of town, and I got calls to go help them if I could. My father, by the way, had been a dentist, and when he died I inherited a little black medical bag of his. Even though my rhyming dictionary and my thesaurus didn't fit very well in it, I used it. I figured, "If I'm going to be a show doctor, I'll use a doctor's bag." With one of the shows that I was asked to help, the lyrics were by two very capable men, Jerome Lawrence and Bob Lee. But they had already committed to do the book for the musical *Mame*. They were in trouble with this other show, *Shangri-La.* They were on the road longer than they had expected to be and they had to leave, so I was called in to replace them. One of the people in the company was Jack Cassidy, and we became friends. Jack wanted me to meet a young composer friend of his, Jerry Bock, so when I got back to New York, after one of the rehearsals I met Jerry. I was very envious of him because he had done a book show, *Mr. Wonderful.* For rea-sons I never fully understood, he had a falling out with the collaborator he had worked with regularly up until then, Larry Holofcener, so Jerry was minus a lyricist. We were introduced, and not too long after that, through Tommy Valando, my then publisher, we were put together as a team on a show.

Interviewer: That first show together was *The Body Beautiful,* which was not very successful; but your second show, *Fiorello!,* won the Pulitzer Prize, Tonys, and all sorts of citations.

Harnick: It made up for the first show.

Interviewer: When you went into *Fiorello!,* did you realize the potential that was in this story?

Harnick: No.

Interviewer: Did it feel right? Did it feel musical to you?

Harnick: Yes, it felt musical because as I read about Fiorello La Guardia, he was such a colorful character, so emotional a character, that there did seem to be music inherent in the man. I didn't know much about his life. One of the things, by the way, that I had learned from the failure of *The Body Beautiful* was that, in that show, I had tried to write my idea of what hit songs were and what a successful show was. I was not writing enough out of what I felt, out of what I wanted to say; so by the time I got to *Fiorello!,* thank God, I had had this flop—because now I knew I had to say what I felt. One of the reasons I got hired was that I was not a New Yorker; the producers, Hal Prince and his partner Bobby Griffith, didn't want it to be a show that was so detailed about the New York aspects of Fiorello that only New Yorkers would understand it. I did my research, I read a number of books. I fell in love with La Guardia—with his honesty and his genuine concern for the oppressed. I had another semimystic experience, which was that when I would be writing a lyric I had the feeling that he was leaning over my shoulder and in his high-pitched voice he was saying, "That's not good enough! You've got to do better!"

When we went into rehearsal, all I knew was that it was a lot of fun— and that George Abbott was not the man I expected. I thought that George Abbott would be a man who only knew how to direct comedy and that everything would be gimmicks; of course, I was dead wrong. In his own way, he came right out of the Stanislavsky school; everything had to be honest. I remember a rehearsal when Tom Bosley ad-libbed something and we all fell on the floor laughing, including Abbott, who roared. When the laughter stopped, he turned to Tom and he said, "Tom, in that situation, would Fiorello La Guardia have actually said that?" Tom thought for a long time and he said, "No." Abbott said, "Then we can't say it either, can we?"—and Tom agreed. While we were on the road, one of the actors came to him and said, "Mr. Abbott, I lost the laugh in such and such a place. I don't know why. I've tried everything, but I can't get the laugh back." Abbott said, "Don't worry about the laugh. I don't care if you never get back the laugh. But you're not playing the scene. Stop worrying about the laugh and play the honesty of that scene. If the laugh comes back, fine. If it doesn't, don't worry about it." He was just interested in truth, and he also had a lovely sense of humor. His basic thrust was in the truth of scenes and the economy of scenes. Our conductor, Hal Hastings, while we were in New Haven, I think, said, "I've never been with a show where there's been less trouble." We did have book trouble in the second act; big hunks of things had to be redone. Nevertheless, there was never any panic. Everything got done, we came into New York, and we were a hit. All I had known was a flop, so it was very gratifying. Within the year, we heard that we'd won the Pulitzer Price—which meant, if I remember right, we each got a check for five hundred dollars. George Abbott suggested that we each give our five hundred dollars to some charity. I said, "Not on your life! This is the first time I've been solvent in eight years!"

Interviewer: You followed *Fiorello!* with a musical that is much loved but was not a commercial success, *Tenderloin*. If you had to do that show over again, what would you do differently?

Harnick: Take more time is one thing. All of us were so euphoric about the way *Fiorello!* was going—Jerry Bock and myself and Jerome Weidman, and George Abbott and Hal Prince and Bobby Griffith—that even before *Fiorello!* opened we had started working on *Tenderloin*. We were going to do it all over again. It was based on a novel. We worked too fast. One of the things that sunk us out of town and sunk the construction of the show was that a star had been hired, Maurice Evans; and when you really look at the novel, you realize that the role that the star was playing was really a small role that had been inflated out of all proportion to serve a star. Once we got on the road, we discovered that *Tenderloin* really is about a street kid with almost no sense of morality who wants to make good but also is a kid who needs a father. He meets a crusading minister and the minister becomes a father figure to him; the minister is trying to change him. The kid gets put in a situation where either he can frame the minister and thereby advance his own career or he can do the right thing and suffer for it. Eventually he does the right thing, but it's very difficult. In the novel, the minister is almost peripheral; he's just a figure, and you understand his purpose. In our show, most of the fun was when people were doing naughty things, when they were going to the Tenderloin; that was where it was colorful. There was nothing really evil about it; it was a musical comedy version of bawdiness. But every time the church came onstage, every time the minister came on, the fun was over. As much as we tried to make the minister human and a fun-loving man, it never quite worked—and we were stuck.

If I were ever to go back and try to do that show again, which I won't, the first thing would be to rewrite the book in such a way that the minister is a small role. Where everything got into trouble was in the second act; and as one finds out in this business, second-act problems usually start on page one of the first act. *Tenderloin* was a wonderful turning point for me in a different way. We had a meeting, in I guess it was George Abbott's hotel suite, right after opening night in New Haven. We had not had a good opening. Up until that time in my life, with the two musicals I had done, I thought my job was to read the script, to be told where the song should go, or to discover places on my own where the songs should go, and write the lyrics with the composer. On opening night of *Tenderloin*, George Abbott, who was the soul of candor, faced us all and said, "Well, gentlemen, I had a concept for this show, and it doesn't work. Any suggestions?" All I could think of was "Don't look at me. What do I know about book?" But I resolved right then and there that in my next show, whatever it was, I would really study the book, try to anticipate where the weaknesses were, try to be able to know the book so well that I could make contributions in one way or another. It really changed my professional life.

Interviewer: What effect, if any, have original cast members had on the final score of a show? Did something ever happen in a rehearsal that spawned a particular scene or number?

Harnick: Almost nothing in my experience. The one place where I can remember specifically that we wrote something for a performer was for Zero Mostel. When I knew that Zero was going to be playing Tevye, then I purposely included in "If I Were a Rich Man" a chance for him to cross his eyes and to make animal noises and so forth. Aside from that, quite the contrary. What happens often is that an actor will ad-lib, and you laugh because it's so unexpected; you say, "Leave it in." Then you see it before an audience and you realize it shouldn't be there. Once in a while, an actor will ad-lib something that's terrific and you leave it in, but more often than not it works the other way—you're fooled because of the surprise element, when somebody springs something on you. I did a version of *A Christmas Carol* with Michel Legrand, and we had a wonderful actor, Gary Beach, playing Scrooge's nephew. At the end of the show, when Scrooge, who is a changed man, comes into his nephew Fred's parlor, Gary looked at him and under his breath, very quietly, he said, "Oh my God." In context, it was just the right thing to say, terribly funny and terribly dear, so I added that. But that doesn't happen very often.

Interviewer: Another show of yours that deserved a far better run initially was *She Loves Me,* which is now regarded as one of the most exquisitely crafted American musicals, with a wonderful interplay between the way the dialogue moves into song and back again. What was the working relationship between you and Jerry Bock and librettist Joe Masteroff in developing this so beautifully?

Harnick: Joe Masteroff had never done a musical, so Jerry Bock and I simply told him, "Why don't you write your adaptation first." It was based on a Hungarian play that I don't think to this day has ever been done in this country, *Parfumerie* by a man named Laszlo. We had the rights to the

Ernst Lubitsch film, *The Shop around the Corner*, so Joe absorbed all that material and then sat down to write his own version. We said, "Why don't you write something that's only about an hour and leave room; we will then supply the songs. If you have any ideas for songs, put them in, but otherwise we will find the places for them and for the dances." And that's what he did. That story is just so drenched with emotion that our problem was being selective, not writing too much music. In fact, when we opened out of town, we found that we had about forty-five minutes too much music, which had to be cut. Probably if we were writing that show today, we would try to follow the Andrew Lloyd Webber route and do it as wall-to-wall music; but we didn't think in those terms then, so we did it as a musical that was just filled with music.

It was not just Joe and Jerry and myself; we needed a director. We first tried to get Gower Champion, but he was already committed to another show; so we asked Hal Prince—and he accepted. Then we got the call from Gower Champion that the other show had fallen through and he was available, which was quite a problem, but we opted to go with Hal—and I'm glad we did. Hal was stimulating, wonderful to work with; we had a terrific choreographer, Carol Haney, and we had a wonderful cast. We loved the villain, who was played by Jack Cassidy. I loved everything about that show.

When we opened, we got nice reviews, and we thought, "Good. We're here for two or three years." Then, little by little, business fell off, which we didn't understand. And I still don't understand. It just went downhill. I asked Margery Gray, who is now my wife and who I think has second sight, "How long will we run? Tell me that we'll hit at least three hundred performances, because otherwise it will be just too disastrous." She said, "It will run about three hundred and two, three hundred and four performances"—which is exactly what we ran. We closed and it was very depressing for about a year, because there was no activity in summer stock or amateur; we thought it was dead. I couldn't understand it—this show in which I had invested such affection. In fact, I missed out on a good thing. I didn't go to the Grammy Awards, because I thought it would be another disappointment—and we won. Then, about a year later, there was a production, I can't remember where, it might have been Bucks County, and Jerry Bock and I got a surprising letter from the company. It said, "We don't understand why the show closed, because it's absolutely delightful and our audiences love it." We began to get more of those letters. It took a while, but we discovered it had become a cult show, which was nice. From that, it's graduated into the ranks of shows which are regularly done in all size theatres. It's certainly one of my favorite shows.

Interviewer: That brings us to *Fiddler on the Roof*, the show that really put your name in everybody's life. What was the gestation period of that, and what attracted you to the project initially?

Harnick: A friend, I can't remember who it was, had recommended as the basis for a musical a novel by Sholom Aleichem called *Wandering Star*. It actually was done, I just discovered, as a Soviet movie, not a successful movie for the same reasons that we found problems with it. It's one of these stories that's epic. It covers about twenty years in time and wanders all over Russia; it's about a theatrical troupe, and it had too many people in it. Jerry Bock and I read it and brought it to Joe Stein and said, "What do you think?" He said, "It would be just too difficult to compress this into the two hours that we need for a stage musical. But since we love Sholom Aleichem, let's read some more." So we did, and we found the *Tevye's Daughters* stories, loved them, and thought, "If we can realize the beauty of these stories, maybe we'll get a year's run if we do our job right." It was the first experience I'd had where *we* went to the publisher and *we* got the rights; there was no producer involved at the beginning. I never read Sholom Aleichem in the original Yiddish because I don't read Yiddish, but Joe Stein did. We started around 1961, I think, but there were interruptions. It's hard to say how long it actually took, because in the midst of writing it—there was no deadline, because there was no producer—Jerry and I had the chance to write *She Loves Me*, which we accepted. We took time off, and Joe Stein did a play, *Enter Laughing* I think it was; then we came back to it, worked on it, and Jerome Robbins came on board. We were having auditions in the theater. Beatrice Arthur had just auditioned; and Fred Coe, who was at that time our co-producer, came rushing in with a little radio and he said, "Kennedy has just been shot!" We all laughed and said, "Yeah, sure. We're having auditions." He said, "No, I'm not kidding." They sent Bea home, everything stopped, and the whole show got put on hold for a while. Eventually we went into rehearsal in 1964, so the gestation period covered from 1961 to 1964, but a lot of that time was spent doing other things.

Jerry Robbins accepted the show because he loved the source material, and also he had a personal interest in it. As you may know, Sholom Aleichem's real name was Solomon Rabinowitz, and Jerry Robbins's name was Rabinowitz. Also, Robbins said that when he was about six he had been taken to Poland to where his family had come from and that he always remembered that as being a tremendously moving experience. Realizing that shtetls in that area of the world had been wiped out during World War II, what he wanted to do was to put that shtetl culture onstage and give it an additional twenty-five years of stage life. That was Jerry's motivation; he felt fierce about it. When we started working together, a number of things happened. One was that Jerry allowed himself at least six months of preproduction meetings because he knew, as we all have found out, that once a show goes into rehearsal, it's a toboggan slide and there's not enough time. So we had six months of preproduction meetings, and every time we met his question was "What is this show about?" We would always answer, "It's about this dairyman in prerevolutionary Russia, and he has five daughters," and Jerry would say, "No, that's not what it's about. That's part of the plot. But what is it about?" We didn't understand that he was talking about the subtext. For months we would have these meetings. We would talk about other aspects of the show; he had us rewrite a great deal. I think about nine songs were thrown out and new ones were put in. But we kept coming back to "What is this show about?" Then at one meeting, one of us—I'd like to think it was me, but I don't know—said, after reading and rereading the *Tevye's Daughters* stories, "All these stories are about the changing of a way of life. That's what happens in these stories—pre-Revolution, post-Revolution—the changing of a whole way of life." Robbins's eyes lit up and he said, "If that's what's happening, then we have to have an opening number about the traditions that are going to change. And I know how it should look. I know how to begin the show now, and I know how to end the show. I'm going to begin it with a circle and end it with the breaking up of a circle." And that's what he did.

The job became to do a song about tradition, which actually didn't get thoroughly put together until we were in rehearsal. Watching Jerome Robbins assemble all the elements was like watching a Rodin or somebody just take the clay—my lyrics, Jerry's music, the script, the actors, the movement—and put it all together into an opening number. In fact, there's one piece of it we never wrote; Jerry did. It's towards the end; there's an argument about a horse, a mule, a horse, a mule. That was Jerry's lead-in to the final statement. Something else happened in that show, which I'll mention now, out of sequence. In the wedding scene, toward the end of the first act, the master of ceremonies, Mordcha, gets up and he has everybody sing a little. Then he stops them so that they can all have a community grieve; but he started to sing what I assume is some old authentic Yiddish song—I never did learn the lyrics—and the cast would sing and he'd cut it off after about two bars. Through the years that has become part of the show, and now they sing about eight to ten bars. It just goes on and on; it's like Topsy, it just growed. It's there—and nobody ever wrote it!

Robbins, because he was so concerned about not having enough time, persuaded Hal Prince, who by this time I think was the sole producer (Bobby Griffith had died, and Fred Coe was undergoing some kind of emotional problem in his own life, so he had bowed out) to give us eight weeks out of town instead of the usual two. We started in Detroit, and we were all scared, because it seemed like a dangerous show to be doing—a show about this Jewish community, with maybe not a tragic ending, but certainly a poignant ending, a dark ending. As a matter of fact, doing the backers' auditions, especially for the ladies who run theater parties, Jerry Bock and I as usual would do a good part of the score, describing the book that linked the score together. Then at the end Hal Prince would have to get up and give a real pitch about how "It's got humor. We have Zero Mostel, and there's going to be a lot of comedy," because a lot of these women were Jewish and they would just stare at us, thinking, "What are you telling us here? We're not going to be able to sell theater party tickets." We were all quite worried, and Hal, for reasons I don't know, chose to go to Detroit, but they wouldn't give us a five-week subscription. We only had three and a half weeks of subscribers, so we knew that we were okay for three and a half weeks—but we also knew that the show could die in the third and fourth weeks. We could die right in Detroit.

And we were doubly horrified when we got to Detroit to find there was a newspaper strike and we didn't get reviewed. Jerry Bock and I went on a couple of radio programs; we all did. But I guess the key to what happened was in a story Joe Stein told. At intermission, he went to call his wife, who had not come with him, and he was waiting behind some woman who was on the phone, and she was saying, "Harry, Harry! I told you that you should have come tonight. Would you believe that at the end of the first act there's a pogrom right onstage! It's wonderful!" When we opened, we were very long; the curtain came down close to midnight, and I thought, "We're going to lose lots of people"—but we didn't. We lost a few people, but even those were people who obviously were reluctant to go; they went up the aisle looking at the stage, trying to get in their last-minute peek before they had to leave. We didn't get reviews, so we had to wait. I had an experience that I remember vividly, because I didn't even know how anxious I was, how terrified I was. After the opening, I went to a restaurant that I think was right across the street from the Fisher Theatre, and near the entrance was a group of our cast, and they said, "Sit down." So I sat down with them, and after about two minutes I said, "Excuse me," and I got up and I went to the men's room. I went into one of the stalls, and I thought, "Either I'm going to be physically sick or I'm going to faint, I don't know which," and I sat down on the john and began to perspire. Water just poured out of me. I was in there for what seemed like ten minutes—I suppose it was four or five minutes—but by the end of that time I was soaking wet. For the first time I realized how scared I had been. I went back out and joined them and dried off.

Word-of-mouth was good. We got a dreadful review in *Variety*—so much for reviews. A classmate of mine from Northwestern, who was theater critic Claudia Cassidy's assistant on the *Chicago Tribune*, had come to Detroit, and we were supposed to have lunch, but he never showed up. When I read his review, I understood why. He just didn't understand the show. He said it was a rehash of Stravinsky's *Soldier's Tale* because there was a violin in it. By the time we got to the third and fourth weeks, we were doing about 95 percent capacity, which was good, and then we went to Washington. And I had another mystic experience, of which I've had so few. I was in my apartment in New York, and in the middle of the night there was a crash in the other room. I got a weapon of some sort and I said, "You have time to leave"—and there was no answer. I turned on all the lights, and what had happened was a picture had fallen off the wall and the glass had broken. It was a print that I had bought not too long before that, by a Soviet artist who had done a series about Sholom Aleichem. There were some prints about Tevye and his family. I had this one of Tevye talking to Sholom Aleichem, and it had fallen off the wall and broken. I thought, "Oh my God! Oh my God!" And I went to Washington. I told somebody about this and said, "Oh God, I've had such an awful omen. It's going to be a disaster." He said, "No, no, no! You're misinterpreting. Smash!"

When I arrived in Washington, I had the very rare experience of seeing big lines at the box office; so people had been phoning their relatives and saying, "There's a pogrom here!" Then the same thing happened in New York; there were long lines in advance of the opening. It's one of the few times when I felt we didn't have to worry about the reviews. It's a good thing that we didn't, because the reviews were not smash reviews. They were quite mixed. One of them, I don't remember which one, said, "What a nice show this could have been if they hadn't spoiled everything with that pogrom at the end of act one." One review that really disturbed me was by Irving Howe, a very knowledgeable man, who wrote in I think it was the Jewish publication *Commentary* that if you didn't understand Yiddish, there was no way you could possibly understand what Sholom Aleichem had created. I thought, "He is robbing us of the show's universality." I don't read Yiddish. As Joe Stein put it in an interview once, "This is a show about people who happen to be Jewish; but it's about people." We worked very hard at making the show universal. The reward for me was when, at our first Actors' Fund benefit, I was standing in the back and Florence Henderson came racing up the aisle and said, "Sheldon, this is about my Irish grandmother."

Somewhere during the time when we were putting the show together, I had gone to a New York nightclub to see Lenny Bruce. I had heard a lot about him, and I had heard about the obscenities that he included in his act, so I was curious. The obscenities were used in such a way that they didn't bother me at all. What did bother me was that every so often he would use a Yiddish word, and there were little groups of people who would laugh, and I thought, "That's cheap, that is so inside." So when we did the show, we thought, "Let's just for salt and pepper use a few Yiddish words, but if they get laughs they come out immediately." So there are only a couple of words: *l'chaim*—and I took great pains to be sure that you can't miss that it means "to life"—and *mazeltov*, which I think is done in a way where the meaning becomes clear. There's another word that I can't remember. Nobody ever laughs, so they stayed in. If the audience had laughed, they would have come right out.

Interviewer: What were the sources you drew on for the lyrics in *Fiddler on the Roof*, say, for "Sunrise, Sunset" and "Do You Love Me?"

Harnick: I can only tell you that I was steeped in the Sholom Aleichem stories, and also a wonderful book which we used as much as Sholom Aleichem, if not more—a book by two anthropologists called *Life Is with People*. I can't remember the two people who wrote it, but it was written, I believe, at the suggestion of an anthropologist, Ruth Montgomery, toward the beginning of World War II. She was aware that these cultures, these communities, were going to be wiped out, and so these two anthropologists interviewed every immigrant they could. They thought that what they were going to find was different Jewish cultures in the different countries. What they found was that the cultures were basically similar, with local differences. That book was just a treasure trove of information which I used, and it allowed us to make the show more authentic. People who had lived through the experience asked me, "How can you, a young middle-class Jewish boy, know these things?" I said, "It's because it's in those books." I was so steeped in everything, I imagine, that phrases were very close to the surface. For Jerry Bock and me, 50 percent of the time the music came first, and 50 percent of the time the lyric came first.

In the case of "Sunrise, Sunset," it crystallized because of the melody Jerry had written. Suddenly I found myself singing, "Sunrise, sunset, sunrise, sunset," and the lyric just poured out; we finished it very quickly. We were very pleased with the song, and we called upstairs to Jerry's wife, Patty, and said, "Come down. We want to play you something." So I sang it and, as I always do, I didn't look at the person that I was singing to, I just looked over her head. When I finished, I looked at Patty and she was crying. I thought, "Oh my God, what do we have here?" Then the same thing happened when I played it for my sister. We really didn't know what we had written. I say we wrote it very quickly. We didn't; we had a *version* very quickly. But Jerry Robbins kept saying, "You've got to do something more specific for those people on the stage at the end of the second chorus." I think I finished the final lyric about two weeks before we opened.

"Do You Love Me?" I remember because, before we went out on the road, from reading the book and knowing the people, it had struck me very funny if Tevye were to say to Golde, "Do you love me?" It was so remote from the reasons they got married, the way they thought, that she had to reply to him, "Do I *what?*" We had been trying to write another song for that spot. I think it was along the lines of talking about these two fledgling kids that were going to get married; it was called "Baby Birds." If I'm not mistaken, we didn't have the song, but when we needed to have a title for the program in Detroit, we said, "Put 'Baby Birds.'" The song never got written. Once we got there, I thought, "I'm going to try to develop that idea of 'Do you love me?'" I remember taking long walks every day; it took about a week, and I would get maybe four lines by the end of the day. It was very difficult, trying to write what these people might be thinking and how this song might develop in that culture at that time, and I couldn't make it come out as a compressed song. Finally when I had a draft of something, I gave it to Jerry and I said, "I know it doesn't look like a lyric, but do what you can with it, and I'll rewrite whatever I have to." He set it as I gave it to him, which was a big surprise to me. I think I was proudest of the song when I saw it in the film and realized that it was a scene, it wasn't a song. It played just as a wonderful scene. I did not write the ending to get a laugh, and I was astonished when it did get a laugh—for the right reasons. When it was finished, we played it for Hal and for Jerry Robbins and they said, "It's charming. Put it in." We showed it to Zero and to Maria Karnilova; they loved it and learned it in a day. The next night it was orchestrated and they put it in. They were a little insecure, but it worked, and then each night it got more secure and it got better and more touching and funnier. About the fourth time that I went to see it, I was watching it and I suddenly started sobbing. I was standing in the back, and I had to leave the theater. I went out thinking, "Why am I crying?" I thought about it for a long time, and I finally realized it was because it was a scene that I wished I had seen my mother and father play—but they never did. They had the fights, but they didn't have the tenderness that was in that song.

Interviewer: What about the line "Would it spoil some vast, eternal plan" from "If I Were a Rich Man"?

Harnick: Well, there are not too many rhymes for *man*. I don't recall if there was any specific spur. It just seemed a characteristic line; it seemed very Jewish to ask questions, rather than to make statements, in that song. It's a line that has to be sung with hunched shoulders. I will say one other thing, though. Running scared as I was, just before we went out of town I suggested that we truncate the song a little and end it on a high comic moment. And Zero Mostel yelled at me; he was absolutely right. He said, "You don't understand this man. This is not about jokes. This is not about the comedy. This is about a man who is deeply religious and who wishes he had the opportunity to go to synagogue and really have a good seat by the eastern wall but he can't afford it. He's exhausted every evening, but he comes home and he tries to read a little of the Bible, and he falls asleep. That's this man, so you mustn't change the ending of it." So we didn't.

Interviewer: What was it like to work with Zero Mostel? Was he difficult?

Harnick: I really didn't work with him; I found him too intimidating. My first meeting with Zero was in the fifties. A friend of mine directed a revue Off-Broadway that Zero was in, and he invited me to a run-through.

Zero was doing a pantomime; the first part of it was cruel but hilarious. Zero did a pantomime of a man who was sitting home at night, reading a newspaper, and there's a knock on the door. He goes to answer the door, he looks, there's nobody there; he looks at his feet and there's a baby that's been left on the doorstep. He looks around, there's nobody to be seen. He picks up the baby, cradles it tenderly, doesn't know what to do with it, puts it back on the doorstep, and punts it out the door. But then the pantomime went on, and it lost me. I went backstage afterwards and my friend introduced me to Zero. I still had my winter coat on, and my friend said, "Tell Zero what you thought about the pantomime." Zero started to help me off with my coat, and I said, "The beginning is just brilliant"—by this time, my coat was about halfway down my arm—"but after that I got lost." Suddenly I wasn't wearing a coat, I was wearing a straitjacket. Zero just put his face right next to mine, and I don't remember what he was saying. I was just so embarrassed I couldn't bear it; I couldn't get out of the coat, I couldn't move. So I was intimidated by Zero. Also, Zero sometimes could be very cruel in ways that to him were funny. He would come to me and say, and I won't try to quote what he actually said because it was probably funnier, "So where is the lyric for 'Sunrise, Sunset' that Jerry Robbins wants?" But he would say it in a way that I couldn't deal with, so I stayed out of his way. Once he and his wife gave a big party for the company after we had opened in Washington. It was interesting to watch Zero, because he entertained us for about a half hour, and it was brilliant, inventive, and hilarious. Then we all wanted to go talk to each other, have some food, and he wouldn't stop. He wouldn't let us fraternize; he had to be the center of attention. It just went on and on, and finally his wife stopped it. She couldn't bear it anymore.

It took a Jerry Robbins to work with him, because he trusted Robbins. I think he was a little intimated by Robbins. They had their own political problems; but, nevertheless, Zero did what Jerry wanted. As long as Jerry was around, Zero was controlled. I remember asking Jerry, after we opened, "How often will you come around and check on the show?" He said, "I rarely do. Once a show opens, I want to go on to the next one. With this show, I can tell you I'm not coming around, because I guarantee you that, two months from the time we open, I don't want to see what Zero's doing." Ninety-nine percent of the audience adored whatever he did, so I can't complain. But people that I would give my house seats to would call me and say, "The show's wonderful, but did you know that Zero was doing this, or that." I'll give you an example. This was while Robbins was still with us. In Detroit, he had staged "If I Were a Rich Man" so that Zero would raise his arms to heaven and sigh. Then, when he dropped his arms, one arm would go into a pail. When it came out, the sleeve was covered with milk. It was nice, because it was one more awful thing that happened to this victim. He would wring out the sleeve and go on with the song.

Within three days, it was no longer a song about "if I had money"; it was a song about "what does a man do when he gets his sleeve covered with milk?" He made about four minutes out of it—including, of course, putting some of the milk behind his ears, putting some on the hub of the wagon to make it run more smoothly. The song went right out the window. It was funny, because Zero was brilliant. I think at the fifth performance, Zero sighed, dropped his arm, took his arm out of the pail, and there was no milk on it. The pail was empty. That was Robbins's way of coping.

Interviewer: One of the shows you did after *Fiddler on the Roof* was *The Rothschilds*. Some people have said that the first act of that musical was more successful than the second act. Do you have any thoughts about that?

Harnick: There are two reasons for that. One was, I think, either a failure of nerve or of imagination on our part. The first act was about the five boys and the father, and that's a love story. We were thinking traditionally, so we thought, "We've got to have a love story in it." So Sherman Yellen, who wrote the book, with all of our agreement wrote a love story in the second act for one of the sons, Nathan Rothschild, who goes to England. In real life, he did meet Hannah, they fell in love, and they got married. It wasn't until after we had opened that Jerry Bock and I were in a taxicab with Jerry's twelve-year-old son and he said, "You guys really blew it." We said, "What do you mean?" He said, "The love story is about the father and the five sons, not about Nathan and Hannah." And he was right. We didn't blow it; the show was good. We ran about fourteen months. But it's true that the second act, instead of remaining about those five boys, got overshadowed by Nathan. Also, what we discovered on the road was that the strongest character in the show was the father. He was played by a remarkable actor, Hal Linden, who won a Tony. The audience adored him, and we had him die about halfway through the second act—as he did in real life. We took the liberty—it was a musical!—of keeping him alive longer. But we were not able to keep him alive until the end of the show.

After the show closed in New York, we had a chance to do it in California. Michael Kidd, who was our director, said, "This show needs a lot of pruning." We had never gotten around to doing that on the road. We spoke to Sherman Yellen, and he was busy doing other things, so he gave Michael and me carte blanche to trim the show. We went through it ruthlessly. When we opened in California, it was a better show; it was a tighter show, and we were a big hit there. I suspect, because of the nature of the show, it wasn't produced as much as we would have liked; but about two years ago, there was a revival at the American Jewish Theatre. The man who runs it called me and said, "What's the minimum cast you can do this show with?" I went back and looked at my program, and, in terms of theater today, I was astonished to find that in 1970 we had a cast of forty. I went through it and thought that I could get it down to about eighteen, if everybody doubled and tripled, but not less than that. I called him back, and he said, "That's too many for our tiny theater." Then a friend of mine called and said, "I see it's being done at the American Jewish Theatre." I called the producer and said, "How did you find a way to do it with fewer than eighteen people?" He said, "You'll have to call the director Lonny Price; it's his idea." I called Lonny and he said, "You may not remember this, but I was one of the children in the original tour in California, and I've always wanted to do this show again. I suddenly realized if the five boys played all the male roles, when they weren't playing the brothers, except for two roles who go throughout the show, then it could be done with fifteen people." That's the way they did it, and the critics were ecstatic, including some who had been lukewarm to it originally. We also trimmed it some more. I found that if I took about a minute and a half out of a scene between Nathan and Hannah, it helped minimize the fact that it was too much about Nathan and not enough about the other brothers. It was the best version we had had, in this tiny little theater, and it was moved. We went to the Circle in the Square Downtown, and again we ran for fourteen months Off-Broadway. I think that that production has given the show a new lease on life, and we're beginning to get productions.

Interviewer: More recently, you worked with Joe Reposo on a musical version of the film *It's a Wonderful Life*. How did that happen?

Harnick: Jerry Bock and I had had a falling-out during *The Rothschilds* because of some aspects of the way the show was done. As a matter of fact, I did ask Jerry to do the show, but he said no. I thought that I would like somebody who can write a nice simple tune but who also has a legitimate background and can do complex stuff, because I wanted to do some complicated things in the show. I knew that Joe Raposo had studied in Paris with Nadia Boulanger and had lived in her home as a protégé of hers, so I asked Joe and he said yes. I don't know whether Joe was intimidated by me, but he never gave me any music first. I love to work to music as well as writing lyrics first, but in this show, for whatever reasons, all of the lyrics came first. I feel that Joe did a superb job; I love the score. One of the reasons that I wanted to do it when I was asked was that the film has always made me weep, and there are aspects of the movie that I thought were never realized. There are a lot of close-ups where you look at Jimmy Stewart's face and you don't really know what he's thinking; you think you know what he's thinking, but I thought I would like to say what I think he's thinking. Also, the show was about something that's very close to me, and that's the sense of failure, the sense of time being wasted. I've been there, I've experienced that; I wanted to say things about it.

The other reason is that I thought the role of George Bailey was a great role. I felt that it was wrong to confine it or restrict it to one man who happened to be the one cast in the movie; it should be played by a lot of people. That's why we did it. When we did it at Arena Stage in Washington, I personally was thrilled by the production. I used to circulate during intermission and at the end of the show, and most of the comment that I heard was wonderful. When I looked around at the end of the show, I found people weeping. I felt it was very successful, and I was quite startled to read the two reviews in Washington. The *Post's* was mixed, but the *Washington Times* review was dreadful, which I didn't understand at all because the night before, at our first performance, we had a standing ovation. We had standing ovations, or partial standing ovations, at least every other night. And it has had a good life since in other productions.

John Kander and Fred Ebb

John Kander was born on March 18, 1927, in Kansas City, Missouri. He studied at Oberlin College (B.A., 1951) and Columbia University (M.A., 1954). He has worked as a composer, director, conductor, and musician. He has written the music for the musicals A Family Affair *(1962),* Never Too Late *(1962),* Flora, the Red Menace *(1965),* Cabaret *(1966),* The Happy Time *(1968),* Zorbá *(1968),* 70, Girls, 70 *(1971),* Chicago *(1975),* The Act *(1977),* Woman of the Year *(1981),* The Rink *(1984),* Kiss of the Spider Woman *(1992),* Steel Pier *(1997),* Over & Over *(1999), and* The Visit *(2001).*

His film scores include Something for Everyone *(1969),* Cabaret *(1972),* Funny Lady *(1975),* Lucky Lady *(1975),* New York, New York *(1977),* French Postcards *(1979),* Kramer vs. Kramer *(1979),* Still of the Night *(1982),* Blue Skies Again *(1983),* Places in the Heart *(1984), and* I Want to Go Home *(1989).*

He received Tony Awards for Cabaret (*Best Composer and Best Musical*),
Woman of the Year (*Best Score*), and Kiss of the Spider Woman (*Best
Score*). He was elected to the Songwriters Hall of Fame in l983 and the
Theatre Hall of Fame in 1990. In 1998, he received the Kennedy Center
Honors, and in 2002, the William Inge Award.

Fred Ebb was born on April 8, 1928, in New York City. He studied
at New York University (B.A.) and Columbia University (M.A.). He worked
as a lyricist, writer, director, and producer. He wrote the lyrics for the
musicals Morning Sun (1963), Flora, the Red Menace (1965), Cabaret
(1966), The Happy Time (1968), Zorbá (1968), 70, Girls, 70 (1971), Chicago (also librettist with Bob Fosse) (1975), The Act (1977), Woman of the
Year (1981), The Rink (1984), Kiss of the Spider Woman (1992), Steel
Pier (1997), Over & Over (1999), and The Visit (2001).

His film credits include lyrics for Cabaret (1972), Funny Lady (1975),
Lucky Lady (1975), New York, New York (1977), and French Postcards
(1979).

He received Tony Awards for Cabaret (*Best Lyricist and Best Musical*),
Woman of the Year (*Best Score*), and Kiss of the Spider Woman (*Best
Score*). He was elected to the Song Writers Hall of Fame in 1983 and the
Theatre Hall of Fame in 1990. In 1998, he received the Kennedy Center
Honors, and in 2002, the William Inge Award. He died on September 11,
2004.

This interview took place on December 14, 1992.

● ———————————————————————— ●

Interviewer: I want to start biographically, by asking each of you in turn
about the time that led to your collaboration. I want to ask it in the form
of the classic theater question: When did you get the bug, how did you get
it, and did you think you were going to be working in the theater from the
beginning? May I ask that of you, Fred, first?

Ebb: I think I always had the bug. I had no idea of a way in which I could
function in the theater, and I didn't know I was talented. I still am not sure
about that. I met a girl who knew a professional songwriter. At that time,
I had considered that maybe writing lyrics was something I could do. I'd
already gone to school as much as you can go to school, which was a delaying tactic so I wouldn't have to face life.

Interviewer: It wasn't much of a delaying tactic. You had a master's degree by the time you were eighteen, didn't you?

Ebb: Yes. Then there wasn't much else I could think of to do scholasti-
cally. This professional songwriter had written a couple of hits, "Santa

Baby" and "Moonlight Gambler," songs I'd heard of—so I was wildly impressed. I went to see him. I had never written anything. On the way over, on a matchbook, I wrote what I thought was a lyric; it was called "Four-Eyes." He played a song for me. I tried very hard and I came up with a lyric. I've never written that way again. I handed it to him, and he thought I was promising, I guess. He said that if I would work with him every day from nine to five, regular office hours, he would literally teach me how to write songs—and so I did.

Interviewer: I think we owe it to posterity to know who your teacher was.

Ebb: His name was Philip Springer. I started to write with him, and in about a year he got a paying job with a music publisher, to be a staff writer, which they had then. We're talking years ago. I found another fellow to write with, and we got signed by a publisher. This is the *Reader's Digest* version! That publisher also had under contract a writer named John Kander, who he thought I ought to meet.

Interviewer: That brings us to John. I gather that you never felt that it was inevitably going to be your destiny to be in the musical theater, that in fact it was a series of chance opportunities. Is that accurate?

Kander: I always knew that somehow or another I was going to be involved in music. I grew up in Kansas City, Missouri. There was a piano in our house, and I found the piano when I was about four. I fell in love with it. My parents let me study when I was about six. Everybody in our house loved music, or loved to make music. Nobody was professional and some of them were tone-deaf, but there was a lot of enthusiasm. I think when I was in second grade during arithmetic class the teacher asked me a question that I couldn't answer, and she said, "What are you doing?" I said, "I'm writing a Christmas carol." She thought that was obviously a lie, so she came and looked, and there were these great big notes on the pages. I had written a Christmas carol. They sang it at the assembly that Christmas. I only found out years later that she had called my parents, very perturbed because we were a Jewish family, and asked if it was all right for me to be writing Christmas carols. They allowed that it was. Anyway, I guess I was always writing and always playing. I was more interested in classical music, but I was always interested in show music as well. On my bureau, I had a picture of Gertrude Lawrence on one end and a picture of Lotte Lehmann on the other. I knew that if I ever ran away from home I would run away to one of those two women! After the war, I went to Oberlin and to Columbia. The head of the music department at Columbia, Douglas Moore, who was a composer and a great friend of mine, one drunken evening said that if he had it to do over again he would write for Broadway. That was sort of my blessing. From then on, I directed myself in that way.

Interviewer: Does the fact that you felt you needed Moore's blessing in order to write for Broadway indicate that it might have been perceived by either you or others at the time as not quite legitimate, as not serious music?

Kander: I think it was perceived by me that way. I think I was the snob. I was busy writing the worst chamber music you'd ever heard, but on the side I was writing songs and shows in college. When Douglas told me that, it was a big relief. While I was at Columbia, I had an assistantship in the opera workshop, where I was coaching singers; and I went from there to working in stock, then conducting, and then doing dance arrangements for Broadway shows. Then I had a show on Broadway that was a big flop, *A Family Affair,* with James and William Goldman. Then my publisher said, "I'd like you to meet Fred Ebb. I think you two guys would like each other." That's literally what he said.

Interviewer: That was a good guess.

Kander: That was a very good guess.

Interviewer: I think people are just as interested in great partnerships as they are in marriages that last a long time, as though there's some sort of secret. Did your partnership seem to click instantly or did it build?

Kander: Instantly. Why was that?

Ebb: I have no idea. It wasn't anything specific.

Kander: We're very different.

Ebb: I think what happened was the work. Hal Prince, who we love and quote from all the time, had a play on called *Take Her, She's Mine.* We didn't know exactly what you do when you get together after we were introduced by this publisher. I assumed maybe we had to write pop songs, so we started to try to write. Then what is it you write about? We brought that problem to our publisher, who said, "Why don't you write a song called 'Take Her, She's Mine.' Maybe Hal will use it in his play." We wrote the song, which Hal did not use, but it was the beginning. The ease with which the song came, the fun it was to write it, and the pleasure we both took in it, despite the fact that it didn't go anywhere, were the clues. A couple of weeks later, we wrote "My Coloring Book," which was a big clue that maybe we should stick together because we'd be lucky.

Kander: I think that the thing Freddy said about us, about the pleasure of writing, is what really has sustained us all these years. We've been writing together a long time, and we've done a lot of shows. Some of the shows have been hits and some of the shows have been flops. We've written a lot of stuff that we're proud of and a lot of stuff that is really rotten. But the one thing that's consistent—and Freddy would bear me out on this—is that we've always had a good time writing. Everything else connected with this business can be horrifying, but the one thing that has always been a pleasure to us is just the sheer process of writing.

Ebb: I think you sense that when you meet somebody who you're going to marry.

Interviewer: Have you ever had violent disagreements, screaming matches?

Kander: No. We disagree; we can disagree about anything.

Ebb: But it's not our temperaments to yell.

Interviewer: Have you ever had those kinds of encounters with your collaborators?

Ebb: I don't remember anything being horrible. I remember it being unpleasant, but I don't remember screaming matches or anybody walking out of rooms—the kind of legendary stories you hear about other musicals and other people. I don't, unless I've forgotten something. I do tend to forget the bad stuff, but I don't remember anything being that bad.

Kander: I have an instinct—which Fred has always partly envied and partly accused me of—of being able to sense when things are going to get really terrible and knowing when to leave the room.

Ebb: That's a fact.

Kander: I've ceased being embarrassed by it, and I've learned to cultivate it.

Ebb: There was one scene in particular that was horrible. It happened during *Chicago,* but he wasn't there; he just happened to have left three minutes before it all started. But we weren't really involved in that; it wasn't about us. It was watching two other people go at it, with me in the middle. I didn't say anything; I just ducked. John was gone. We had written a song called "Nowadays," and we played it for Chita Rivera and Gwen Verdon, the stars of the show, and for Bob Fosse, the director, all at the same time. Gwen said, "I want to sing that song by myself." Bobby said, "No, I think you ought to sing it with Chita." It turned into a terrific ruckus. That's when he left.

Kander: I was sitting at the piano with the music in front of me, and I kept getting lower and lower so I didn't have to witness this. Chita was standing behind Bobby and Gwen, and she was crying.

Ebb: She kept writing me notes: "Give it to her! Give it to her!"

Kander: I finally managed to get out of there. The interesting thing about that is that it ended up being a duet between Chita and Gwen, just as we had written it.

Ebb: When we went backstage the night the song went in the show—it had been very successful—and congratulated Gwen, her words to us were "You see, if you only stand up to him, you'll get exactly what you want."

Kander: The fact is that she did it exactly the way he wanted!

Interviewer: To go back to the early part of your career, what was your first book musical?

Kander: Our first book musical was a show called *Golden Gate*, which was one of those "almost" stories.

Ebb: We decided we would try to do a full musical, and we knew a fellow who had written a libretto. It took place three or four days after Jeanette MacDonald came back to set things right in San Francisco during the rebuilding of the city. It had a fairly decent score, and it was okay. At least it was a full work; and we somehow knew enough to know that if anybody was going to audition us, it wouldn't do to sit down and play a random bunch of songs. We knew that it might help us if we did a completed piece with character development serving a narrative. So when George Abbott was going to do *Flora, the Red Menace*, although that was set in the thirties and the Depression in New York City and *Golden Gate* was 1906 San Francisco, we played it for him. It was a wild audition because we thought that one had nothing to do with the other, but he saw something in us and gave us our first show, *Flora, the Red Menace*.

Kander: That was courtesy of Hal Prince, by the way, who was producing the show.

Interviewer: Of course, you performed the same "courtesy" for Liza Minnelli, because that was her first Broadway show, too. Was she initially involved with it?

Kander: No. While we were writing *Flora*, a friend of Fred's asked us to meet this girl that she thought was very talented. She was playing Lili in *Carnival* somewhere in New Jersey. We were working over at Fred's house, and a seventeen-year-old girl arrived on the doorstep.

Ebb: A ragamuffin named Liza Minnelli.

Kander: And we've been together ever since. She came in, looked at the things we were writing for Flora, and immediately sang them gorgeously.

Interviewer: You were convinced, but Abbott wasn't, was he?

Ebb: Not at all. I was sitting next to him when she came to audition. She had done the revival of *Best Foot Forward*, which Abbott had directed in its original production, at an Off-Broadway theater, and he had hated that—and I think he hated her; I *know* he hated her. The stage manager came out, as they do at auditions, and said, "Liza Minnelli." Abbott turned to me and said, "Well, this is a waste of time." Liza was just crossing the stage to come center to sing, and I saw her falter. You knew she'd heard him. It was hard not to hear Abbott. She sang despite that, which I thought was remarkable of her, but he didn't think much of her.

Interviewer: If this were a movie, he would have signed her on the spot.

Ebb: It's not a movie!

Interviewer: Life is not a movie; so how did she end up getting the role?

Ebb: Abbott wanted Eydie Gorme, which we thought was a nifty choice, but she stood him up one night. He made a dinner date with her and she didn't come, and Abbott got really p.o.'d. He came in the next morning and said he was going to Florida for a while, because casting this show had become like the search for Scarlett O'Hara. While he was gone, we worked on Hal to come to our side to proselytize for Liza—and finally Hal agreed. He said, "Let's give him a call and I'll bring it up again." We all listened on extensions in Hal's office. He said, "Mr. Abbott." No, he called him George, actually, which was very impressive. He said, "George, we have looked and we've all thought about it, and we really think we ought to go with the Minnelli girl." To which Mr. Abbott said, "Okay, fine. Sign her."

Interviewer: After all that?

Ebb: End.

Kander: The final result of that is that I have never seen anybody so smitten so quickly as Mr. Abbott was with Liza. She had her birthday during rehearsal and he came waltzing in with a big birthday cake. He thought she was the most talented thing that he had ever seen.

Interviewer: When did you start writing material for her nightclub act and TV shows?

Ebb: Right after *Flora* closed, her agents wanted to send her on a nightclub tour, so she asked me to write the act for her. That's when we started writing special material for her. She played the Shoreham Hotel. We were both twelve; we knew nothing about what you did when people stood up when she was finished. Liza thought they were leaving, and so did I. Then we suddenly noticed that they were also applauding—and they were not putting on their coats. It was the first standing ovation I ever saw. Now I don't know that she ever doesn't get one, but it was an amazing thing. She sat down on the stage, she got so scared of it all. That was our first experience, and from then on we just kept writing, and she got more and more successful.

Kander: One of the nice things about writing for Liza is that you don't have to write for Liza, because she can do anything. You know that whatever you do write, she's going to deliver it exactly the way you intended it. It's really the same with Chita Rivera, the other woman in our lives. Both of them are wonderfully disciplined performers. We write and they sing.

Interviewer: Getting back to your work in the theater, how did you make the leap from *Flora, the Red Menace,* which was not a great success, to *Cabaret,* which certainly was?

Kander: I'll always remember this. At least a week before we opened with *Flora,* Hal, who had always really wanted to direct it and was kicking himself that he hadn't, said, "Whatever happens to *Flora,* the morning after it opens let's meet at my house and go to work on the next project." Literally he said that. That project was a show that eventually became *Cabaret.*

Interviewer: Was there some hesitation about doing a show that had a strong dose of Nazism, even on its own terms? Surely somebody must have said, "Is this going to work on Broadway?"

Ebb: Oh, lots of people, including my collaborator—not John, but the book-writer. He snuck up on me during previews and said, "You realize, of course, that this is a big flop." I hadn't realized that. He said, "It's a succès d'estime. The critics will like it because it's brave, but the audience will hate it." There was a lot of evidence of that. The first preview in New York (let this be a lesson) was a hundred dollars a seat—this is a long time ago, so that was a lot of money—for some charity. Intermission came and that place nearly emptied out. They just left in droves. All you could hear outside was frantic screaming, "Taxi! Get me out of here!" They just really hated it. Then when we got very good reviews, it all turned around. It says something not so hot, I guess, about the American theatergoing public. They were fighting to get in. We ran three years, but you could have never known that. What he whispered in my ear seemed very logical. I didn't know that we'd be a flop, but it seemed to me that we were a dicey proposition all along. But the fact that it was a risk show had nothing to do with it.

Kander: I don't think we ever considered that.

Ebb: We were working; that was the thing.

Kander: I don't think either of us has a sense of what will or will not be successful. We have a show running now in London that just won a big award, *Kiss of the Spider Woman;* it's about torture, homosexuality, and death. If that's going to attract the *Me and My Girl* crowd, we'll see.

Interviewer: If you don't think in those terms, what does get you started on a musical? Is it just a matter of what interests you?

Kander: Absolutely.

Ebb: And I have something to add to this—which is how I felt about *Kiss of the Spider Woman.* I don't ever remember telling anybody that I thought *Kiss of the Spider Woman* would be a good musical who agreed with me, except Johnny. I just thought it would and I called him. I said, "What do you think about doing *Kiss of the Spider Woman?*" and he said, "Oh, good!" Then I thought maybe he knew something. Everybody else said it was an awful idea. A couple of the critics did, too. Hal was the next one we called. I said, "I'll just give you a title, and you say yes or no, and I'll hang up." I said, *"Kiss of the Spider Woman,"* he said yes, and I hung up. That's really how that started. The fact is there was something about that material that inspired me. I felt that it was really interesting; it was very daring, it was bold, it was essentially terrifically romantic, and it offered a great contrast between the harsh reality of prison and the wonderful fantasy of a man's imagination. If I had to sit down and parse it for you, that's what I would say attracted me.

Kander: We both feel that as far as writing is concerned, since this is what you spend your life at, you want to spend your life doing something for which you feel a passion. We've been very lucky in that most of the time that's what we've been able to do, whether the show has been a success or not.

Ebb: In writing, I think, you're forgiven your flops. When you say "Kander and Ebb" years from now—and I hope you will—you'll think of *Cabaret* or something that we did that was very successful and forgive us or not quite remember the shows that we did that were not as successful as that or as well chosen.

Kander: There's a quote from Oscar Hammerstein that says basically, "It's hard enough to write a musical that you love. If you don't love it, it's impossible."

Ebb: And you shouldn't be doing it.

Interviewer: With *Cabaret,* what sort of research did you do? How did you find the melodic mood? How did you find the right historical sense of the time?

Ebb: For John, there were a lot of recordings that he could listen to in terms of the musical sound. I of course had Isherwood; I could always read

Isherwood's stories. For most of our shows that weren't original, there's been an author. For *Spider Woman,* I bought the complete work of Manuel Puig. I also bought Manuel Puig; he was around.

Kander: We had Puig with us, very strongly, until he died.

Ebb: If you match the lyric of the song to the dialogue you've been handed and it sounds like the same person, then you know you've done well.

Interviewer: I'm not expert enough to characterize it precisely, but the music in *Cabaret* certainly does suggest a sense of Germany at that time. It's a kind of jazz, but it's not a familiar jazz. John, how did you find that sound?

Kander: I listened to a lot of German jazz and a lot of German vaudeville songs of the twenties; there are a lot of recordings. I listened and listened, then put it all away and just forgot about it. I've done that since. I did it with *Zorbá* and with *Kiss of the Spider Woman,* in terms of a particular flavor. If you listen enough, eventually it sort of seeps into your own style as you're dealing with it. The greatest compliment that I ever had about the score of *Cabaret*—and I will always remember it—was when Lotte Lenya came to me after I had gotten some review that called the score watered-down Kurt Weill.

Ebb: "More wail than Weill" is what it said. I remember it!

Kander: Lenya said, "No, no, it's not Kurt. It's Berlin. When I'm out there on that stage singing your songs, I feel that I am in Berlin." I thought, "If she feels that way, the hell with the rest of them!"

Ebb: The fact is that when Lenya agreed to do the show, by walking out on the stage she validated the whole project. We could never be accused of slipping up if she was around to keep us honest.

Interviewer: Liza Minnelli has become so identified with *Cabaret* because of the film, but she was not in the stage version. Was she ever considered for the role?

Ebb: She auditioned, but Hal turned her down this time.

Interviewer: How did that turn around when it came to the Hollywood version?

Kander: Because Fosse was directing the movie.

Ebb: It was Hal's notion that the girl absolutely had to be British and the boy had to be American. Bobby, on the other hand, felt the girl could be American and the fellow be British. By making that seemingly very small change, it allowed Liza to be perfectly right for it. We coached her to audition for the stage version, and she came and sang it with a cockney accent for Hal, who just thought she was dead wrong. His comment was

"She's as American as apple pie." At the time, we said, "Well, why not make the girl American and the guy British?"—but he just didn't see it. It's a very collaborative art; the director is going to tell you what's going to be. The way he felt this piece should go was that she be British, and he was immovable about that.

Interviewer: When it became a Hollywood musical, did you have to re-think the music and presentation in terms of this other medium? What changes did you make?

Kander: We didn't have all that much to do with the film. The rights were bought, and Bobby had his own ideas about the direction it should take, which involved altering the story a great deal. When there were new musical moments to be written, we were required to supply them. Our sole contribution really was to write the new songs for the movie.

Ebb: It was like answering a quiz. Bobby said, "I need a new opening number for Liza. I want it to be more bombastic." So "Mein Herr" came to be where "Don't Tell Mama" was. Then he wanted Joel Grey and Liza to do a number together. He liked the idea of "The Money Song," but "The Money Song" in the play is just done by Joel and a group of show-girls. He wanted it to be a duet, so we wrote a new "Money Song." He liked the idea of Liza having a solo; he said, "It will be about all the other times I was really unlucky." About fifteen years before that, we'd written a song called "Maybe This Time." We went to the trunk, took out the song, played it for him, and he loved it. I don't think he ever knew that it was an old song.

Interviewer: Do you consider the film and the stage version as two different musicals?

Kander: The first time we saw the film was at a special screening. They put us in a room and showed it to us. Everybody was very excited about it. When it was over, we didn't know what to say, because we had both just hated it.

Ebb: I thought it was just awful. Everything they had told us, we forgot. "This is a rough cut, so there will be black lines going across the screen." At the end, I said, "Why were all those black lines on it?" They had said, "You'll see a hand and the hand will put on a recording; the recording will be of 'Married,' but you won't hear that on this track, because we haven't done it yet." I said, "She puts her hand on a phonograph and then nothing comes out." I forgot everything I was told!

Kander: I think even more than that, we sat down remembering the show that we had written as it had been on the stage—and what was in front of us was something altogether different

Ebb: It didn't have Lenya; it didn't have Jack Gilford.

Kander: The second time I saw it I thought it was brilliant.

Interviewer: After *Cabaret* came *The Happy Time,* which I gather was not maybe the happiest time in terms of the kind of research you did. I've read that you didn't think you had gotten the French Canadian world absolutely down pat.

Ebb: I didn't think we got that show right altogether, and we made a lot of very serious errors. We opened in Los Angeles, where you get positively the worst conceivable advice you can get on how you can fix a show. Bob Goulet was playing a sort of rake, a rainmaker character, a fraud. The first comment we got from the Hollywood know-it-alls was that he was too attractive to be a failure. There is no story unless he's a failure. That was the kind of advice Gower Champion, our director, was getting—and listening to! We were, unfortunately for us—I don't mean that in a bad way—a big hit. The show was an enormous success out there, and it's hard to change things when the audience is telling you you're right by clapping a lot. Gower made that one fix, and that one fix led to another fix; then, before you knew it, it was not the show that we started out to write. We were writing a small musical, and it became enormous. It was the biggest musical I ever saw. It had back projections and all sorts of things that we hadn't counted on. I think we just didn't know enough to fix it.

Kander: While we were there having a not very good time, we got a call from Hal Prince, who said, "Would you take a look at *Zorbá* and tell me what you think of it as a musical?" We called him back and said that it was not a good idea. In five minutes, he had us wound up to do it, and we had a wonderful time on that.

Ebb: It almost made up for *The Happy Time.*

Interviewer: *Zorbá* was revived later with Anthony Quinn re-creating onstage the role he'd played in the film. What did you think of that production?

Ebb: For a number of years, no one saw the virtue of doing that show again; but suddenly Quinn made it a really good idea. The director was Michael Cacoyannis, who decided he would not use one single notion that Hal Prince had in the original production. Hal is extremely conceptual; he built the show around a bouzouki circle and a leader of the chorus, a girl who took you through all of the adventures of Zorbá. Cacoyannis cut that. The girl existed, but there was no reason for her; she was never explained. We never knew who she was, whereas Hal, of course, made it very plain. A lot of our songs were dependent upon that concept—her talking to the audience or talking to musicians who were always with her, who guided you through the story: "Watch this!" or "Now this will happen." He cut all that.

Interviewer: It must be heartbreaking for you to see something like that happen to a show you care for so much.

Kander: Let's just say the revival of *Zorbá* was not an improvement.

Ebb: The only thing that gave us joy was the box office receipts, because Quinn was some powerful draw. And he was really wonderful; he is Zorbá, and everybody associated him with the role. At the end when he came out to bow, he could have started a war; they just went nuts. That never happened in the original show, but something very vital was lost. What was gained was Tony Quinn—and our bank accounts!

Interviewer: With one of your next shows, *The Act,* you had quite bad reviews out of town, didn't you?

Ebb: The worst, and very well publicized in New York: "The stinker of your dreams is coming to town."

Interviewer: Were you daunted?

Ebb: I'll say! Chita Rivera came to see it wherever we were playing, San Francisco or someplace. The curtain came down and she turned to me— she really loves me, I truly believe—and she said, "Freddy, this is the worst musical I have ever seen." I said, "I know, but can you tell me how to fix it?" She said, "No, I don't have a clue. It's just awful." For Chita to say that meant it was really bad. I knew it was bad, except we didn't know any way in the world to fix it—but eventually we did.

Kander: What fixed it was the same person who had destroyed *The Happy Time,* Gower Champion. Gower came in and with a very clear vision started putting the house in order, and by the time we came to New York, it was respectable.

Ebb: We got pretty good reviews in New York. It was reverse snobbery, I think. The show had been so blasted in the gossip columns, which were keeping everybody abreast of how awful we were along the way. When we finally got to New York, Gower had worked on it, polished it, and made it a very professional-looking show. The content was still kind of pukey, but it looked good. Liza looked good; she finally wore Halston clothes, which is what they expected. We gave them what they had come for, which was to hear her sing a couple of good tunes. "Arthur in the Afternoon" was in there and "My Own Space," some nice stuff that we were proud of. It looked okay. The *Times* critic loved the show, so we got a big *Times* review and a lot of good reviews. We sold out for about eight months; we'd still be running if Liza had stayed with it, which she didn't care to do.

Kander: Fred's right about the reverse snobbery. The fact that it had gotten bad reviews in the West helped us. I remember the first line of one of the reviews basically said, "It's remarkable. No matter what you've heard, this show isn't nearly as bad as what you've been reading about in the paper."

Interviewer: After that came a show that I really would enjoy hearing about that was based on the notion of two women associated with a roller-skating rink. I've heard both of you talk about *The Rink* in interviews, and you said very opposite things. Fred, what you said is that it was your greatest disappointment, although it may have been because the reviews were bad; and John, you said it was the most complete realization of what your intentions were of any production you've done.

Kander: That's absolutely true.

Ebb: I don't disagree with that.

Interviewer: So what was disappointing for you, Fred—that the public didn't see what you wanted them to see?

Ebb: Yes, that it wasn't appreciated.

Kander: I think, of everything we've ever done, that was the most satisfying experience I've ever had.

Interviewer: What made it so satisfying?

Ebb: Every single element of it was exactly as we imagined, which is a situation you hardly ever get. The sets were wonderful, exactly what we would have hoped for; the performances were brilliant. There were only seven people in it and a kid, and they were all wonderful. The costumes were wonderful; the lighting was wonderful; and I thought Terrence McNally's book was wonderful.

Kander: This sounds really phony, but I mean it. I thought that it was the most emotionally honest work we had ever done. I found myself moved by it when I saw it, and I am very proud of it.

Ebb: I thought the show was very touching, and I seldom get carried away by my own work. That show used to make me cry. When I watched the final scene, I saw the invention with which the director treated it and the respect that he had for the material. There up on the stage were two of my best friends, Liza and Chita. It was an overwhelming experience; and when they weren't treated well, it was as if we had gotten attacked on the street by some drunk who started to maul them—and I had to defend them. It just hurt. That show hurt me more than any show I've ever written. Certainly we had had failures before, but that one hurt really badly. I felt that I had let them down.

Kander: The audience response was really quite strong. The critics were particularly savage to Terrence and the book. They also did not want to see Liza that way. Interestingly enough, Liza asked to be in it, because the part she played was really the second lead. The leading role was Chita Rivera. Over the phone Liza said, "I want to do this part because there's not one sequin in it." She played a dumpy, shlumpy, fat girl; she had one costume. She was fabulous, but the audience did not want to see her be that way. They wanted to see her be Liza Minnelli—and the critics did, too.

Ebb: There was a mad moment because of that. Liza went to Halston, who whipped up two red dresses, and during the curtain calls the two girls ran off—it was one of the most embarrassing moments of my life—and put on those dresses. When they came out to bow, they were in those red dresses, and the audience went nuts. They cheered and screamed and thought that was nifty. I said, "What am I missing here? Why don't they just accept what we were doing? Why is this necessary?" Cooler heads prevailed, and we only used those dresses for about five performances. Even Liza said, "It's cheap, isn't it?" And I said yes—so we stopped. But her instinct was correct. They were rejecting the Liza we were giving them. They would not separate the persona from the actress.

Interviewer: Do you think perhaps the musical would have worked had she not been in it?

Ebb: Yes.

Kander: But I don't think anybody could have played it any better than she did.

Ebb: That's right, but the power of that name and the strength of that personality, I think, hurt us very much. She was what gave the audience a false expectation.

Kander: She was really dismissed by the critics, particularly in the *Times*. She was crying backstage the next night when Terrence went in to see her. She said, "They dismissed me in one sentence!" and Terrence said, "You're lucky. They dismissed me in two paragraphs!"

Interviewer: Something I've always been curious about is the relationship between the music composed for the singers and that composed for the dancers in a musical. John, your music has been interpreted by some great choreographers and dancers. Can you talk a bit about the creative relationship between the choreographer and the composer? Does one suggest things to the other? Have you ever done any composing with a specific choreographer in mind?

Kander: The answer to that is complicated. I've been the dance arranger on several shows, and on my own shows there has been a dance arranger. There's a lot of talk. The main thing about any collaboration in a musical is that you have to talk and talk and talk endlessly. If you're in a good collaboration—and sometimes we have been, fortunately—there's a lot of conversation between the choreographer and the composer, as well as the general conversation, particularly in terms of what the style is going to be. If it's my own show and I'm not doing the dance arrangements on it, I will come in and supervise them and maybe rewrite them, though I've worked with some of the best people in the world as dance arrangers. More often than not, you give a choreographer his or her freedom to go ahead and do what he wants. If what he's doing doesn't fit with the style of the piece, then all the collaborators will try to explain that to the choreographer and prevent that direction from being taken.

Interviewer: To follow up on that, and speaking of working with choreographers and dancers, one show of yours we've only mentioned briefly is *Chicago,* where you collaborated with one of the greatest choreographer/directors, Bob Fosse, and two of the great dancer/actresses, Gwen Verdon and Chita Rivera. We've spoken a bit about Chita Rivera, and you told a story about Fosse and Verdon. But could you talk a little more about what it was like working with Fosse and Gwen Verdon?

Ebb: They were both geniuses, I think. They were both difficult, as we mentioned earlier. You got your money's worth for what you put up with. They were very abrasive people. Bobby was especially; he was a difficult man. I think what you have to keep remembering is that that is offensive only when there's no talent behind it. It never really bothered me a lot. I had co-written the book with him, and everything was going terrifically until we had a couple of difficult scenes in Chicago. He would invariably take out his frustration on whoever was handiest, which was me a couple of times.

Kander: As I told you, I always knew when to leave the room.

Ebb: At the end of it all, when he was ill, and I think putting together *All That Jazz,* he called me on the phone. He said, "I guess you'd like to know why I picked on you?"—and I can't define Bobby in any better way than this—and I said, "Yes, I did kind of wonder. I always loved you so. Why did you pick on me?" His answer was "Because you were vulnerable." That's who that complicated man was. It was an enormous loss to the theater. Gwen and he were going through a rough time maritally when we worked together. As a matter of fact, *Chicago* was his divorce gift to her. Hoping it would be a hit, he gave her an enormous percentage of the show. That was his divorce settlement to Gwen in terms of cash, the royalties from that show. It was left to her in his will as well. So, as you can see, it was a complicated arrangement, which we found out about little by little. We were dealing with two of the most complicated people in the world. Despite it all, I have to say I loved them.

Kander: We were fortunate in that we also had Chita Rivera.

Ebb: To make us laugh.

Kander: The three of us held each other up a lot during that time.

Burton Lane

Photo by Roddy McDowall, copyright 1991 Harlequin Entertainment Ltd.

Burton Lane was born in New York City on February 2, 1912. He was a student at the High School of Commerce and studied piano with Simon Bucharoff. He began his career writing the music for songs in Broadway musical shows including Three's a Crowd *(1930),* The Third Little Show *(1931),* Singin' the Blues *(1931), and* Americana *(1932). He composed the entire score of* Earl Carroll's Vanities of 1931 *(1931),* Hold On to Your Hats *(1940),* Laffing Room Only *(1944),* Finian's Rainbow *(1947),* On a Clear Day You Can See Forever *(1965), and* Carmelina *(1979).*

He composed music for films including Dancing Lady *(1933),* Bottoms Up *(1934),* A Wicked Woman *(1934),* Here Comes the Band *(1935),* Artists and Models *(1937),* Spawn of the North *(1938),* St. Louis Blues *(1939),* She Married a Cop *(1939),* Dancing on a Dime *(1940),* Las Vegas Nights *(1941),* Babes on Broadway *(1941),* Ship Ahoy *(1942),* Rainbow

Island (*1944*), Royal Wedding (*1951*), Give a Girl a Break (*1953*), Jupiter's Darling (*1955*), *and* Heidi's Song (*1982*).

He received the Mercer Lifetime Achievement Award and the Richard Rodgers Lifetime Achievement Award in 1992 and was elected to the Theatre Hall of Fame in 1993. He died on January 5, 1997.

This interview took place on November 23, 1992.

• ⎯⎯⎯⎯⎯⎯⎯⎯⎯⎯⎯⎯⎯⎯⎯⎯⎯⎯⎯ •

Interviewer: You've had an incredible career. You wrote your first songs in the 1920s, and you're still writing songs. We're going to concentrate on your work in musical theater, but I think we should start by talking about your background. How did you get involved with music?

Lane: I remember we had, in our small apartment, an upright piano that you pumped with your feet, and we had piano rolls—and I could pump. I thought I was going to turn out to be a dancer, because when I was about five or six years old, my brother would be pumping and I would be dancing around the room. I just loved music, and my father was a great enthusiast of the popular songs. I started to take piano lessons when I was about seven or eight, but my aunts and uncles thought I was too young. They prevailed upon my father to postpone it, and I was disappointed, cried a lot, and didn't resume until I was about ten years old.

Interviewer: Did you continue to fiddle at the piano during that time?

Lane: I always fiddled, but I had no way of knowing what I was doing. Then, when I started taking lessons, I took to that very quickly. My father came home one night with the sheet music of a hit of the day. I was just learning how to read music. In trying to play this music, I played a wrong chord—and it sounded good to me! Then I struck something else that was a wrong chord, and that led me to something else, and all I can say is those two mistakes led to my first song. I wasn't writing anything; I was fumbling. But it was a nice experience; I enjoyed doing that. I had no idea what I was doing, but that's how I came to write. That's what led me to a career. But at that time, I had no idea of a career or anything else.

Interviewer: Then your brother introduced you to a lyric-writer with whom you wrote a song?

Lane: I had started to write melodies, but it was a game. I enjoyed the experience of putting notes together that sounded good to me. My brother was going to college, and he introduced me to a friend of his who was studying law but who wanted to write lyrics. He was my first collaborator.

Interviewer: Your first published song was called "Broken Butterfly," but I know that you don't like to have it mentioned.

Lane: I don't like to think about it. It's kind of a long story. Friends of my family heard me and introduced me to somebody they knew, a very successful professional lyric-writer, Joe Young. Joe Young wrote lyrics with another fellow, Sam Lewis. They used to write songs, special material for acts that were playing in vaudeville. They wrote some songs with Harry Warren. I was now fifteen years old. This friend spoke to Joe Young, who said, "Sam and I just finished a lyric. Give it to your friend and see what he does with it." So this friend brought the lyric over to me, I looked at it, and in five minutes I had a melody. He said, "Gee, let's go and play it for Joe Young," which we did. Joe Young immediately took me to the head of the Remick Music Publishing Company, and I was signed to a contract. I was fifteen years old. I was going to school, and this was my first contract. Up to that point, I had no idea there was a career in this. I was just doing it because it was fun.

Interviewer: It must have felt amazing, at that age, suddenly to have a contract and to be a professional songwriter.

Lane: It did—and it led to some nice experiences. In those days, publishing firms used to have very tiny offices just large enough for an upright piano, and the acts would come in from all over the country to hear the new songs that were being published by this publisher. I met Fats Waller. He and I used to sit at one piano and play four-handed. I'd come down after school, meet some of these acts, and play the songs for them—and that was great fun. In fact, music has always been fun for me, and I think that's a very important part of making a career for yourself. If you can do something that you really adore doing, that's the most ideal thing. I've been lucky in doing that.

Interviewer: There's a lot of humor in your music, too. You've said that Yip Harburg talked about that with respect to George Gershwin's music.

Lane: I met George and Ira when I was seventeen years old. It was Ira who introduced me to Yip Harburg. Yip had gotten out of college and had gone into the electrical appliance business, of all things. He knew Ira very well; they had been in school together. Ira invited Yip to sit with him and George when they were working on a score. Yip wanted to write lyrics, but he had gotten himself into this electrical business. Yip used to say that luckily the Depression hit and he went broke. Capitalism forced him into doing the one thing that he loved, which was writing lyrics. George Gershwin was my idol. Every time my father took me to a musical show, it was George Gershwin's music that electrified me. I remember sitting in the theater trembling before the overture started and just being excited by it. But I also liked operettas—Sigmund Romberg, who wrote music that was very reminiscent of other composers but had great craftsmanship, and Rudolf Friml. I was writing music then, aimed at trying to imitate Gershwin and Kern and also the operettas. It was Yip, when I met him, who pointed out that one of the things that made George so great was his humor, the marvelous surprises he would come up with. And that stuck with me.

Interviewer: What are your earliest memories of musical theater? What was the first show you saw? Did your parents go to a lot of shows?

Lane: My father loved the musical theater, and every Friday, because the next day was not a school day, he took the family—my brother and my stepmother and me—to a musical show. The first musical I ever saw was *Dearest Enemy,* which was Rodgers and Hart's first show. There were some lovely songs that came out of it—"Here in My Arms," wonderful melody, lovely lyrics. That was the beginning of my romance with the musical theater.

Interviewer: Then you got a contract to write some songs for a Shubert show, but something happened with an issue of plagiarism where, at a very early age, you discovered that the Lord giveth and people taketh away.

Lane: You couldn't say it any better. I was signed when I was, I think, sixteen or seventeen, to write a *Greenwich Village Follies,* starring James Barton. Barton became ill, and the show was called off. I did not know how to make piano parts. I would write the music and I would remember it. I didn't notate at all. So J. J. Shubert, who was going to be the producer of this revue, assigned a fellow by the name of Maurie Rubens, who wrote some music for some shows, was in charge of music in other shows, and worked all the time for the Shuberts, to make piano parts. I remember sitting at the piano and playing forty or fifty tunes, and he would just notate them. The show was called off. Fade out. A couple of years later, I was the rehearsal pianist for *Three's a Crowd,* starring Fred Allen, Libby Holman, and Clifton Webb. We were in Philadelphia; the show had just opened there. I had written a couple of songs with Howard Dietz. I think I was about nineteen years old at this point, eighteen or nineteen. I got a call from my father. Shows in those days used to open out of town—in Newark, in Brooklyn—so it was easy for my dad to go to these openings. He had gone to a show in Newark with music by Maurie Rubens. Three-quarters of the score were the tunes I had turned in! A show opened in Brooklyn with Jeanette MacDonald; three-quarters of the score were my tunes! There were four shows involved. My father threatened a lawsuit, and Shubert agreed to the terms of an agreement. He was going to give me, I think, fifty dollars a week per show, but he never lived up to it. So my father started a suit, and four shows closed in one week—because the Shuberts refused to pay—but I think the shows weren't doing so well.

Interviewer: So you started by writing songs that were interpolated into musical revues?

Lane: That's right. That's how young writers got their starts. I think it was then dawning on me that this was going to be my life, writing songs. When I got through with the Remick contract, I was then meeting other music publishers, and I met Jack Robbins of the Robbins Music Company. He sent me over to play some tunes for Earl Carroll, who then signed me. At that time also I met Harold Adamson, who had just graduated from Harvard, and he and I teamed up to write the score for the ninth edition of *Earl Carroll's Vanities* in 1931.

Interviewer: The whole score?

Lane: The whole score. At that time, I had two songs in *The Third Little Show,* two songs in *Three's a Crowd,* one in *Singin' the Blues,* and one in another show. I had songs in four shows playing at one time when I was seventeen years old.

Interviewer: That's extraordinary.

Lane: No hits. Not one hit.

Interviewer: How did you learn about theatricality, about the devices used in theater? You must have learned from the performers, from the choreographers, from the director, from the producers; because eventually you started writing book shows. I'm curious to know how you gained the knowledge of the craft.

Lane: When I wrote two songs with Howard Dietz for *Three's a Crowd,* I was a kid. Max Gordon was the producer; Dietz was really the working producer of the show—he was putting it together—but it was "Max Gordon presents." Because I was a kid, they invited me to their production meetings. I loved that, because I was there learning. I learned how a show is put together, all the steps that had to be taken. I was absorbing all this; it was a real schooling for me, and I took advantage of it. I loved being invited into these meetings because these were really talented people— Howard Dietz and Arthur Schwartz, marvelous composer, and Max Gordon, who had many big hits playing on Broadway.

Interviewer: And, of course, you continued to write Tin Pan Alley songs.

Lane: Not really, not as much. I wrote some songs. A couple made some noise—the first American rumba, called "Tony's Wife."

Interviewer: Paul Whiteman and "Ramona."

Lane: That's right; that was a big hit record. But mainly the kind of tunes I was writing was show tunes. Publishers, when I would play a new song for them, would say, "Oh, that would be good for a show!"— but they wouldn't take it. Early in 1933, the Irving Berlin firm signed Harold Adamson and me and sent us to California on a six-week contract to see if we could write songs for films. That led to my spending twenty-two years in California, writing music for movies, although interspersed with that were a couple of Broadway shows that I wrote.

Interviewer: Your first major hit song was "Everything I Have Is Yours."

Lane: That was my first movie—and my first hit.

Interviewer: The movie was *Dancing Lady*.

Lane: With Joan Crawford.

Interviewer: And Fred Astaire.

Lane: Fred Astaire's first picture. Clark Gable and Franchot Tone—a big, big musical.

Interviewer: Was it extraordinary to see the workings of Hollywood with hundreds of people and a huge orchestra?

Lane: It was a fairyland. One week I'm in New York, and the next I'm in California—and it all happened accidentally. I called a friend of my brother's, Leonard Spigelgass, a writer who lived in California, not knowing that he and my brother were on the outs. Leonard very politely but guardedly—I remember his voice on the phone not being as welcoming as I had known him to be in New York—said, "I'm having a dinner party tomorrow night. Why don't you and your friend"—he meant Harold Adamson—"come over after dinner." So we did. We had only been in California three or four days. At that dinner party was a writer, Allen Rivkin, who was a co-writer of the screenplay of *Dancing Lady*. He said, after I had played some songs after dinner, "By the way, do you fellows have a ballad? We're desperately in need of a ballad. The picture is shooting." I said, "We started a song in New York just before we came out, but it's not finished yet. The song's called 'Everything I Have Is Yours.'" He said, "When can you have it finished?" I said, "When do you want it?" He said, "Immediately. We're desperate." So I said, "All right, we'll have it finished by tonight. We'll go home and finish it"—and we did. We were only in California for three or four days, and I found myself the next day in Joan Crawford's dressing room, playing this ballad for her, with David Selznick sitting there.

The change was so sudden that I didn't really react to it until weeks later. I'd never moved in such circles. As I said, it turned out to be Fred Astaire's first film. David Selznick said, "Do you have any other tunes that we could hear?" We had a couple of others, and they bought them; they were the songs that Fred Astaire did with Joan Crawford. One song was called "Let's Go Bavarian"; the other was called "Heigh-Ho, the Gang's All Here." The film starts in America, goes on a flying carpet to Bavaria; on the set there must have been two thousand people—dancers, singers, orchestra, I never saw so many people on a stage—and they were doing my songs! It was really an incredible experience. And then it turned out that L. B. Mayer, who was the head of the studio, was having a fiftieth birthday party, and Harold and I were invited. Not only all the stars of MGM went to this party, but all the stars from every studio were there—and Harold and I were called on to entertain them. It was really a whirlwind experience for us.

Interviewer: Then, of course, you were signed to an MGM contract. And not too long after that, you helped launch the career of one of Hollywood's greatest stars.

Lane: I went to the Paramount Theatre in downtown Los Angeles to see a film, and the theater also had stage shows, just the way the Paramount in New York had. On the bill was a sister act called the Gumm Sisters. It was two women about eighteen or nineteen or twenty years old, and for their finale they brought out their kid sister, who was eleven years old. I was so impressed with the young girl that I went out into the lobby of the theater and called the head of the music department of the studio at his home. He said, "If you think so much of her, go backstage and see if you can arrange an audition." I went backstage and met the Gumms' father. I told him I was under contract at Metro, that I was very impressed with the young daughter—her name was Frances Gumm—and arranged to have her brought out to the studio the following week. I played her audition. It started at about nine o'clock in the morning and lasted until six o'clock at night. First, the head of the music department, the man I had called, heard her. He called L. B. Mayer, the head of the studio, who came down with an entourage of people. When he heard her, he said, "I want every director and every producer on the lot to hear this kid." Well, Judy Garland—and she was some find.

Interviewer: And you found her.

Lane: The sad thing was, many years later, my wife and I went to California, and we were sitting in a restaurant when I saw Judy come in with some people. I said to my wife, "You haven't met Judy, have you?" She said, "No." Judy had been through rough times. When kids become stars as quickly as she did, the way they're treated at a studio can just destroy your character. You have to be so strong to withstand the overwhelming praise; the pressures are tremendous on anybody, but how a child can take them—it's many times more than they can bear. After dinner, I took my wife over and I introduced her to Judy. Judy got up and kissed me, embraced me, looked at my wife, and said, "I owe everything to your husband. He started everything that meant something to me, my career." When we left the restaurant, I said to my wife, "I hope she's not blaming me for all the bad things"—because by this time she was in bad shape. It was sad.

Interviewer: You worked with her later on, on *Babes on Broadway*, didn't you?

Lane: Yes, that's right.

Interviewer: In 1940, you wrote your first book show for Broadway, *Hold On to Your Hats*, with Al Jolson, Ruby Keeler, Martha Raye, and Jack Whiting. How did you get back to Broadway? During the time in California, did you have a longing to go back to the musical theater? You had a lot of commercial success with films; you wrote hit songs, you met incredible people—like Jerome Kern and Frank Loesser.

Lane: In 1937 and 1938, I was under contract to Paramount. That's when I, in quotes, "found Frank Loesser." He was brought to my office by an agent. He had never worked in Hollywood and needed a job desperately. He was working with a composer, Manning Sherwin, who had had one hit in his life. He wrote lovely tunes, in the style of Dick Rodgers but not as strong.

Interviewer: Didn't he write "A Nightingale Sang in Berkeley Square"?

Lane: Yes. I didn't know at that time that Frank and Manning were not getting along very well; but I was so impressed with Frank Loesser's lyrics that I went up to the head of the studio, who I knew very well, and said, "You must hear this fellow's lyrics. This guy is really something." And they ended up signing him. I worked with Frank Loesser, but at the end of two years—they gave you yearly contracts, and there were things happening at the studio—I was let go. I was going through really rough times, because I had to earn a living—I had a child—and musicals were on their way out. They had made a lot of bad musicals, they hadn't done well, and Hollywood stopped making them for a while. So I tried to put an orchestra together. I was in Chicago.

Interviewer: As a bandleader?

Lane: Yes, as a bandleader. I was desperate to do something to earn a living, and I was in Chicago because I had some contacts there—and I was just about to sign up a band. I was a day away from that, had made the decision that was what I was going to do, when I got a phone call from a Broadway producer, Alex Aarons of Aarons and Freedley. He used to produce all the George and Ira Gershwin shows. He said, "I have a musical

I'd like you to do." I said, "I'll do it." I didn't ask what it was. I borrowed some money and flew to New York. It turned out that it was Yip Harburg who was going to do the lyrics. Although Yip and I had written a couple of songs after I met him at the Gershwins', we never had worked together professionally. Yip had asked for me, and we did this show. That was the beginning of writing for Broadway, I mean really writing a book show for Broadway.

Interviewer: This show was not a pleasant experience, was it, because of Jolson?

Lane: Jolson was sensational when he was on the stage but not a nice person off. He treated people badly, and I didn't like to see that. The show opened in Detroit for one week and went to Chicago and then was going to Philadelphia and New York. I left the show in Chicago and went back to California. I never saw Jolson play the show in New York. I just couldn't stand the cruelty that he displayed to other people; it was too much.

Interviewer: That was Jolson's last Broadway show, wasn't it?

Lane: Yes.

Interviewer: Didn't he leave the show abruptly, even though it was doing quite well?

Lane: Yes, he did.

Interviewer: And it closed.

Lane: He had been married to Ruby Keeler, and she was originally in the show. They hadn't been divorced yet; they were separated. Jolson, a big egomaniac, said, "She's never worked with me on the stage. When she does, she'll come back to me." What happened in Chicago was something that I don't think anybody had ever seen before. Jolson was playing a scene with Ruby Keeler, and it led to a song. He sang the song, and the music was continuing under the dialogue, when suddenly he said, "You know, Ruby"—and he's now using her real name—"we'd still be together if your mother hadn't walked into the kitchen that day." Ruby's eyes opened and a look came on her face—I've never seen anything like this—she turned around, walked off the stage, and never came back. He understood; he finished the performance. She left the show. When Jolson recovered the money he had invested—there was standing room only in New York—he closed the show, claiming he was sick, and disappeared. One of the co-producers had him tracked down at a racetrack in Florida, got pictures of him, went to court, and claimed that Jolson was not sick. He was forced to reopen the show, but by the time it was ready the steam had gone out of it and it didn't work.

Interviewer: There are a couple of questions that come to mind. One is the experience of writing for a star. The other is, that was 1940, and supposedly *Oklahoma!* was the turning point in Broadway as far as integrated books in musicals. I assume this show was essentially a showcase for Jolson, so how important was the book?

Lane: I thought the book was terrible. But it was terrible compared to what followed. It was in the old tradition of an excuse to do numbers. The plot made no sense at all, but it was the kind of show that had worked in the twenties and early thirties. When books started to have more meaning and take on more weight, the scores became better because the books demanded better music.

Interviewer: Did you feel that coming? Were you aware of that at the time?

Lane: No, not at the time when this book had to be created, The score got very good reviews. Three songs started to become very big hits, but we ran into the BMI-ASCAP fight. What happened was that BMI was not around yet. Broadcasters were complaining that they didn't want to pay for the use of music; so one minute after midnight, one minute into 1940, all ASCAP music was off the radio. All you heard was public domain works; ASCAP for one solid year was off the air. Just before that happened, three songs from *Hold On to Your Hats* started to become hits: "There's a Great Day Coming Mañana," "The World Is in My Arms," and "Don't Let It Get You Down." The three songs started to become hits, but one minute after twelve in 1940, all were off the air for a solid year. That was the year that BMI was formed by the broadcasters. They formed what is really to this day a company-owned performing rights society. The writers and the publishers have no voice in the running of that organization, where ASCAP is run by the writers and publishers. That's a major difference.

Interview: Weren't you having a problem with Jolson always wanting to sing his old hits at some point in the show?

Lane: Yes. Here's what happened: *Hold On to Your Hats* was originally written with Jack Haley in mind. As I said, I was broke when I first started to do the show, and we wrote it very quickly. Jack Haley came in finally, listened to the score, listened to the book, raved about it, and left the apartment where we had auditioned it for him. I took my wife out to a marvelous steakhouse to celebrate; we were going ahead with the show, for Jack Haley. We were sitting at a front table in the restaurant that night, enjoying this wonderful steak, when who walked in but Jack Haley. He came up to me and he said, "Burt, that's a hell of a score you guys have written, marvelous. But I'm not going to be in the show." I said, "Why? What happened?" He said, "The producers haven't any money. They're going to use my name." This is how shows were financed, but he resented that. So again I borrowed some money and went back to California. One day, about a month and a half, two months later, I got a call that Al Jolson was interested, and would I go to New York and play the score for him. I met Yip that night and I said, "Yip, we don't have a real Jolson song in this show. We've got to do something." Yip came up with a brilliant idea, and we wrote it that night. It was the opening of the show. In the show, Jolson played a guy who was a big star on the stage who was suddenly forced to give up the stage and become a radio actor. He became the Lone Ranger on radio. Yip came up with an opening song that was called "Walkin' Along Mindin' My Business." It began, "I was walkin' along mindin' my business, singing a song—'When whippoorwills call, and evening. . . .'" We got the medley of his old songs in the first number! I was so thrilled with this, because Jolson at the end of every show would undo his tie, say, "All right, guys, close the curtain," come out and say, "Folks, you ain't heard nothing yet!" and he would destroy the new score by singing all his old hits. We did this in the opening song, and he stopped the show cold. Came the end of the show, he undid his tie and did the same songs. He did all the hits, and our songs hadn't started yet to become hits. But that was Jolson.

Interviewer: You went back to Broadway, didn't you, in 1944, to write songs for the Olsen and Johnson revue *Laffing Room Only?*

Lane: Yes. Again I was in financial difficulty, struggling to earn a living. The way Hollywood operated was if a great musical came out, then every studio started to make musicals. If a gangster picture came out that was a hit, they all started to make gangster pictures. Musicals were on the way out.

Interviewer: But you were at MGM, and they were making musicals on a regular basis—and you had had hits.

Lane: Once in a while, they would do something with an Irving Berlin— a special kind of a show. But at this time I was freelancing; I wasn't with Metro. For *Laffing Room Only*—L-A-F-F-I-N-G, because it was Olsen and Johnson—they signed Al Dubin and me to do the score. Al Dubin was the great Al Dubin; Dubin and Warren did all those wonderful songs at Warner Brothers.

Interviewer: "Lullaby of Broadway," "I Only Have Eyes for You," "Lulu's Back in Town," "About a Quarter to Nine."

Lane: A ton of hits. But at this point in his life, he was having trouble and he was a sick man. I could see that something wasn't right here, but I was afraid of losing this job.

Interviewer: He was an alcoholic, wasn't he?

Lane: Yes, he was an alcoholic.

Interviewer: And he was also, what, about three hundred or three hundred and fifty pounds?

Lane: He was a heavy man, he was an alcoholic, and he kept disappearing; and it's painful to see that when you're working with a man that you have such respect for. He gave me one title, "Feudin' and Fightin'." It was supposed to be the finale of the first act—the Hatfields and the Mc-Coys—and he came up with this title. I wrote this tune, but he never wrote a lyric. I started to fool around with lyrics. I had always contributed lines to lyrics, but I had never really tried to write lyrics. I didn't think I was good enough—and I still don't think I'm good enough, although once in a while I come up with a good line. But I needed this job desperately, so I wrote a couple of lyrics to my melodies. Sure enough, Al Dubin disappeared, and he was found dead. I had protected myself by writing a couple of songs. Olsen and Johnson said, "Why don't you just go ahead and finish the score." One reason I took on that responsibility is that with an Olsen and Johnson show, lyrics meant nothing. It was strictly low-down fast-moving routines, full of vaudeville gadgets and gimmicks—and the score would mean nothing.

Interviewer: You wrote the whole score, music and lyrics?

Lane: That's right.

Interviewer: How long did it take you? Were you scared?

Lane: I was. I should have been more scared, but, as I say, I knew that the songs wouldn't mean anything in this kind of a show—and they didn't. It was making a living.

Interviewer: The thing that's ironic, of course, is that "Feudin' and Fightin'" became a big hit song, didn't it?

Lane: Not until after the show closed. You run into these kinds of things that happen. The Shuberts suddenly decided they wanted to put ASCAP out of business. I had placed the score with good publishers who had published a lot of hit songs and were very well established. They loved the score and were very hopeful that it was going to be a hit, when they got a letter from the Shuberts threatening a lawsuit. They were already in print, but the publisher said, "Burt, we're going to give you the score back. We can't take a risk of being in the lawsuit." So for three years until 1947, after *Finian's Rainbow* opened, nobody heard of "Feudin' and Fightin'." I got a call from ASCAP one day; they had had a request from somebody. Would I give permission for them to do "Feudin' and Fightin'" on the radio? I called my lawyer and I said, "What should I do about this? The Shuberts stopped me three years ago." He said, "Go ahead and give them permission." And I did. I never heard the song on the radio at this time; but one morning, three or four months later, I got a call from a music publisher, someone I had known many years ago, who was making conversation: "Burt, how are you?" And he told me that calls were coming in from all over the country for this song, "Feudin' and Fightin'." I finally had Chappell set up a firm for me and we published it. It came out the year I had "How Are Things in Glocca Morra?," "Old Devil Moon," and "When I'm Not Near the Girl I Love"; but it was the biggest hit I ever had in royalties. It was incredible.

Interviewer: Speaking of that year, why don't we get to *Finian's Rainbow.* How did that happen?

Lane: Yip came to me with a first draft of the show.

Interviewer: You were in Hollywood?

Lane: I was living in California.

Interviewer: Was he there, too?

Lane: He was living there. So was Fred Saidy, who collaborated with Yip on the book. When I read this first draft of the first act, I said, "Yip, this is the best script that's ever been written for a musical. But I don't think you want me." He said, "What do you mean?" I said, "You want George Gershwin. You want somebody who really has the craft, the experience, and the genius to do this kind of show. This calls for the greatest. It's the most wonderful script I've ever read." Well, Yip, thank God, didn't agree with me. I never had the kind of real musical training that I wanted. I studied the piano, I had a minimum study of harmony; but I never had the kind of training that I wish I had had. I wanted to go to a school like Damrosch or Curtis; I wanted a real thorough education. My father was not, I guess you'd say, a highly educated person; he said, "It's so much better that you can do it without studying." I never understood the logic of that. I remember George Gershwin wanted me to be the rehearsal pianist for *Of Thee I Sing.* At that time, I was about seventeen and I was going to school. I said, "I'd like to do this." He said, "I don't think you should." I said, "Why not?" He said, "I don't think you should work for another songwriter." That was the kind of education that I needed, and I finally got it with *Three's a Crowd.*

When Yip came to me with *Finian's,* he wanted me to do the modern songs, and he was thinking of Earl Robinson, who wrote "Ballad for Americans," to do the American folk songs. I didn't think this could work, because I knew Earl's work, which was good but it wasn't theatrical. I had never heard anything of his that had the quality that would belong on the stage; but I didn't say anything to Yip about this. I just went along, When

Yip persuaded me he wanted me to do it, I started to do it. One of the great things that I would advise every young writer who's working on a play to do is to workshop it the way we did. I am sure the idea came from Yip. He would invite people to his home, twenty to thirty people. I remember the first time we did this we had three songs. Fred said he would read the book, and where the songs came, Yip and I would do them. We learned a lot from the reactions of these people. In fact, we learned so much—we must have had a dozen of this kind of readings, as the show was progressing, as the book was developing, as the score was developing—that when we went into rehearsal and opened, not one note had to be changed. Not one word of lyric had to be changed. The book was 98 percent perfect. It was an amazing experience to go through. And it's something that I've always believed in: that you do all your preparation before you go into rehearsal. Your rehearsal should be a rehearsal of what you have approved of up to that moment. My other experiences were not so happy, where we went into rehearsal not prepared.

Interviewer: Do you mean with *On a Clear Day*?

Lane: Yes, with *On a Clear Day* and *Carmelina*. It's a whole different world you're in.

Interviewer: *Finian's* was almost like a magical or charmed experience, wasn't it? Very few people in musical theater have had the experience of not having suddenly to write a song out of town or suddenly come up with a new scene.

Lane: I know it's a very rare thing. I want to get back to Earl Robinson. The first reading that Yip had, we had three songs, and Earl Robinson was there. When we got all through, after everybody had left, Earl took Yip aside and he said, "What you and Burt are doing is just right, and I can't do that. You'd be destroying the score." So he bowed out on his own.

Interviewer: By that time, you felt comfortable that you could write the score?

Lane: I didn't feel comfortable anytime until three or four years after *Finian's* opened. I was a very insecure guy. I'll tell you how insecure I was. This went on with Yip through *Hold On to Your Hats* and through *Finian's*. I never wrote a melody and sat down at the piano and said, "Yip, I just wrote a melody for this." I would wait until he was talking to somebody else and I would quietly underscore to see if I could get his attention. I was that insecure. He would be talking to Fred Saidy and I'd be quietly playing. He'd say, "What's that you're playing?" I'd say, "Oh, it's nothing." I was so frightened. That kind of insecurity is terrible to go through. But he got accustomed to it: "What's that you're playing?"

Interviewer: You have said that you were not out to write hits for that show, and yet it produced a lot of hit songs.

Lane: Eight standards out of eleven songs.

Interviewer: That's extraordinary, and you did not set out to write hit songs.

Lane: I didn't, that's right. I was so in love with what *Finian's* was about. I loved the characters, and if I was going to do it, I wanted to write something that was absolutely true to the subject and to the characters. When I was working on *Earl Carroll's Vanities* or *Hold On to Your Hats*, it was a whole different kind of attitude. You try to write a hit and sometimes it works, if you're a writer like Vincent Youmans. Vincent Youmans used to say, "You must have at least a hit in the first act and a hit in the second act"—and he would write them; he was a marvelous songwriter. Irving Berlin would do that. It wasn't until shows like *Oklahoma!* and *Carousel* came along that scores started to take on a different weight. Although I hadn't seen *Carousel* or *Oklahoma!*, I had heard the scores. All I knew was that I loved what Yip had written with Fred Saidy and I wanted to have it come to life when the music was there. I never believed in what they used to call throwaway songs. I once started a show—this was after *Finian's*— with Dorothy Fields and Herbert Fields; it was a musical based on a play, *The Pursuit of Happiness*. I remember looking at a scene—I didn't like the way the book was going—and in one spot a scene ends and Herbert puts down "Song." I said to him, "What's happening?" He said, "We're changing the scenery." I said, "You can't write a song about changing the scenery. You're in the Revolutionary War period. What are we going to write about?" I always knew that if a scene had a purpose, that purpose or some aspect of it should be caught in the musical number. It shouldn't be just a song to fill in some space.

Interviewer: Why have you written so few Broadway shows? You've turned down a lot of things. You turned down *Pajama Game*, didn't you?

Lane: Yes, I turned down *Pajama Game*. I was living in California. Hal Prince was in New York, and he sent me the book, the novel from which it was written. I didn't like the novel, but I said, "Show this to Yip. I'd like to get an opinion from Yip on this, because if I do a show I'd like to do it with somebody I've worked with before. I feel much more secure in that." Yip turned it down, and I never pressed it. It happened on that occasion and one other. I can't remember the other show that I turned down, but it was something I was not sure about.

Interviewer: You started to work on *Flahooley* with Yip, didn't you?

Lane: I started to work on *Flahooley* with Yip and didn't like the book, so I resigned from it. Actually I started to work on it with Fred Saidy and Yip, after I had told them what was bothering me. They said they would rewrite it. That first week, I wrote three melodies, which I liked a lot. Yip wrote a lyric to one of the songs, "Who Said There Ain't No Santa Claus?" I was working also with Yip on a score for Metro, *Huckleberry Finn*, and Fred and Yip were doing *Flahooley* at the same time. I had written three tunes when they said they would rewrite the show. Three or four or five days later, Yip and I were working when Fred Saidy came over to my house, and Yip looked at him and said, "What time is your train leaving?" I said, "Fred, where are you going?" He said, "I'm going home." He lived on Long Island. I said, "What about the rewrites?" He said, "We're not going to rewrite the show just to please one person." I said, "Okay, you're now looking for another composer"—and that was the end of it. Three weeks they played.

Interviewer: To go back to *Finian's*, when did you discover Ella Logan? How did she come into the picture?

Lane: Yip had discovered Ella Logan. I knew her work and thought she was wonderful. But it was Yip who said, "I think she'd be good for Sharon in *Finian's*."

Interviewer: So you didn't write anything specifically for her?

Lane: I did. I wrote songs that I thought would be right for the show and right for her. That came to be the same thing; she was a Sharon and she was good. When you work on a show, you can be trying to write three or four songs at one time. One of the songs that was painful for me was the first song that Ella Logan was to sing. My favorite Irish ballad is "Danny Boy"; when that song is done the way it should be done, I cry. I was trying to write a song for this opening number in the show, and I couldn't please myself. I said to Yip one day, "Give me a dummy title. It will give me something to focus on." So he gives me a title, "There's a Glen in Glocca Morra." It's not a good title, but it was a meter. I had a book of manuscript paper, and over a period of about two or three weeks, I filled it. Each staff was the start of another melody. Yip and I were finishing up "That Great Come and Get It Day" at my house; we got through and he said, "What about the ballad?" I was so frustrated with myself; I didn't like anything I had written. I took the manuscript book and threw it on the floor. I said, "I've got fifty ideas in there, and I don't like any of them." He said, "Let me hear something." I was really going to punish him, so I said, "I'm going to start with the first one and go through the fifty!" I started to play the first one—"There's a glen in Glocca Morra"—and, as I played it, I saw his eyes light up, and I said to myself, "He looks like he likes it!" I didn't have a whole refrain; I just had eight bars or sixteen bars, or something like that. He said, "Play it again." And when I started to play it, he said, "How are things in Glocca Morra?"—and the minute he said "how are things" and it became personal, I loved it. The whole thing changed for me. It shows that sometimes you can struggle so hard to get what you already have. You get so close to it you don't hear it. Of course, "There's a glen in Glocca Morra" wouldn't make any tune sound good. It was just a way of getting started. The minute he said, "How are things in Glocca Morra?" I knew we were home.

Interviewer: He was your favorite lyricist, wasn't he?

Lane: He was my favorite because my tunes always sounded better with his lyrics.

Interviewer: I want to jump to *On a Clear Day*. That was not a happy experience for you, partially because of problems with Alan Jay Lerner, who wrote the book and lyrics. But you were never satisfied with the show, were you?

Lane: No. Alan started the show with Dick Rodgers, and that didn't work out, so he called me. When he called me, he described one scene that made me say yes before I heard everything else. It was a scene in which Daisy Gamble finds out that this doctor who's been treating her under hypnosis has fallen in love with her as she was in the past. This led to what I think is a great lyric of Alan's, "What Did I Have That I Don't Have." It was funny and touching at the same time. I thought the premise of the show was wonderful. A girl, a kind of a nothing of a character, who comes from some little town, Mahwah, New Jersey, has exceptional talent. She makes flowers; she talks to her flowers, and they grow fast. She can find lost objects; she reaches for the phone before it rings, and then it rings. She has extrasensory perception. I thought it was a marvelous premise, very imaginative and with a very fairyland kind of quality to it. I adored it. But I didn't like when he went into the past; I didn't like the story of the past. I thought he was taking it too seriously. I thought he should have been much lighter, and have fun with it. I threw out an idea, which I didn't think he would take seriously; I said it should be something like, there wouldn't have been the United States of America if there hadn't been Daisy Gamble, she had done something that was extraordinary, that nobody knew about—and treat that with great fun and exuberance. But I never could sell him on that. So there were things wrong with the book, despite the fact that there were wonderful things in the show.

Interviewer: Looking back, do you know now how you would have fixed it? You've had a long time to think about it.

Lane: A couple of years ago, we called in another writer who did some rewrites, and we did make some changes in it—not substantially the way I wanted it, but we did improve it——and the show worked a lot better. It was a big hit in California. Feuer and Martin produced it out there.

Interviewer: There's a story about the famous title song from that show, isn't there?

Lane: Alan had started the show, as I said before, with Dick Rodgers. It was then called "I Picked a Daisy." When he began to work with me, he said, "I think we ought to have another title." One day, he came in with the title "On a Clear Day You Can See Forever." I had lived in California for twenty-two years, and the cliché phrase out there was "on a clear day you can see Catalina Island"—because of the smog. I was not excited about the title, but then, one night, I was home and I was thinking about it. I said, "There's something about this title that is attractive, but I don't know what it means." I thought that if Alan could write a lyric that would make sense of that title, it would work. I sat down and wrote half a tune, and the next day I played it for him—and he liked it. Alan wrote, literally, nine lyrics. Every time he brought one in, I'd say, "I don't get it" or "It isn't right." In some cases, I thought the person who wrote it had never held a pencil in his hand; it was so off the face of the earth, I didn't know what it was. Then, one day, Alan came in with the lyric that we used— and the song became a big hit.

Interviewer: That's a great story. Finally, I want to ask you about musical theater today.

Lane: Does it exist?

Interviewer: Do you feel that people leave now humming the scenery and the special effects?

Lane: I like wall-to-wall carpeting where it's right to have it, but I don't like wall-to-wall music just to fill in spaces. I want to feel something. I want to feel it when *I* write it and to feel it when somebody else writes it. Writers like Jule Styne and Dick Rodgers and Berlin and Gershwin and Kern, so many others of the really great writers, have made me feel something. Andrew Lloyd Webber is a very good musician; what he does has marvelous craftsmanship involved in it, and I couldn't do it. I respect that. But I would like to hear a melody that really moves me and touches me, and I don't hear it.

Arthur Laurents

Arthur Laurents was born on July 14, 1917, in Brooklyn, New York. He was educated at Cornell University (B.A., 1937). He has worked as a playwright, librettist, director, screenwriter, and novelist. His books for New York musicals include West Side Story (1957), Gypsy (1959), Anyone Can Whistle (1964), Do I Hear a Waltz? (1965), Hallelujah, Baby! (1967, 2004), The Madwoman of Central Park West (1979), and Nick and Nora (1991). He directed the New York musicals I Can Get It for You Wholesale (1962), Anyone Can Whistle, The Madwoman of Central Park West, La Cage aux Folles (1983), Birds of Paradise (1987), Nick and Nora, and two revivals of Gypsy (1974, 1989).

His plays include Home of the Brave (1945), Heartsong (1946), The Bird Cage (1950), The Time of the Cuckoo (1952), A Clearing in the Woods (1957), Invitation to a March (1960), The Enclave (1973), Scream (1978), The Radical Mystique (1995), Jolson Sings Again (1995), My Good Name (1996), Claudia Lazlo (2001), 2 Lives (2002), Venecia

(2002), The Vibrator (2003), *and* Attacks on the Heart (2003). *He directed* Invitation to a March, The Enclave, Venecia, *and* So What Are We Going to Do Now? (1982).

Among his screenplays are Rope (1948), The Snake Pit (1948), Caught (1949), Anna Lucasta (1949), Anastasia (1956), The Seventh Sin (1957), Bonjour Tristesse (1958), The Way We Were (1973), *and* The Turning Point (1977). *He co-produced* The Turning Point. *His two novels are* The Way We Were (1972) *and* The Turning Point (1977). *In 2000, he published* Original Story By: A Memoir of Broadway and Hollywood. *He received Tony Awards for* Hallelujah, Baby! *(Best Book) and* La Cage aux Folles *(Best Director); he was awarded the Writers Guild Award and the Golden Globe Award for* The Turning Point. *He was elected to the Theatre Hall of Fame in 1981 and received the William Inge Award in 2004.*

This interview took place on October 26, 1992; Arthur Laurents made additions to it in July 2004.

• ———————————————————————————— •

Interviewer: Why don't you start with how you got involved in the theater.

Laurents: I'm from Brooklyn, and there was a stock company, believe it or not, near where I lived. My cousins and I would go every Saturday afternoon. I don't know what kind of a stock company it was, but it was thrilling. One day I came home and my mother said, "What did you see, dear?" I said, "*Rain*"—and I never went again! That was my introduction to the theater. I think it was also my introduction to musicals, because I saw their version of *No! No! Nanette!*, and it was an enchantment. I think one of the reasons I began doing musicals is because I don't think there is anything more exciting than walking down the aisle of a theater when the overture to a musical is playing. It's not as exciting as it used to be, because they don't use curtains so much anymore—which I'm totally against. The theater should take you into another world, and I want to not be in that world until the play or the musical begins. And that's when the curtain rises. But when I walk in and I see the scenery under some flat worklight and it looks pretty dreary, it hurts. It hurts the impact of being transported.

Interviewer: They don't use overtures anymore either. As a matter of fact, they don't use opening numbers anymore, and they don't seem to use choreography much anymore. True?

Laurents: Fairly true. I think it's economics. There are a couple of good choreographers, but I think the nature of the musical has changed. I wrote an article on musicals years ago for the *New York Times Magazine*, and the title of it was "Look, Girls, Here Comes the Man with Our Tap

Shoes." That was a line from a Pulitzer Prize–winning musical called *Fiorello!* The girls were standing around the stage, and one of them said, "Look, girls, here comes the man with our tap shoes"—and they put their tap shoes on and began to tap. You couldn't get away with that today. I think that's a big reason there are fewer dances in musicals. You need a reason now.

Interviewer: Do you think there is more cynicism on Broadway? Do you think audiences are more sophisticated?

Laurents: I think audiences are less sophisticated. I think entertainment has almost killed off the theatergoing audience, along with the excessively high price of tickets. People go on their anniversaries or a birthday. They've saved up. It's an event, but it doesn't make them want to go see theater. There's no illumination; there's no emotion. They're going to see this great big slobbering, whopping hit. I don't think that's theater, and I think it's why people stay away. In New York, the audience that we have goes Off-Broadway, where you can't do a musical unless you only have one and a half chorus girls.

Interviewer: I think what has replaced emotion in musicals is volume. They think that if they turn the sound system up and make the show louder, then it is a more emotional moment. It saves the writers a lot of work. Everything is lowest common denominator and is made simple for the ten-year-old. It seems like a sophisticated musical just does not have a place anymore.

Laurents: I'm an eternal optimist. I think it has to be better than it used to be; if it is really good enough, they will come see it. Maybe not as many as you would like; but if something is really good enough, it will find an audience.

Interviewer: Do you think that the theater community itself is more cynical?

Laurents: Oh, the theater community is beastly! They are mean-spirited. They pray for your failure every time anyone does a show. It's foolish, because there is an adage that is absolutely true: Nothing builds audiences like a hit. I do want to differentiate between success and what is good. I certainly think you try to have both, but if something is really good and it is a success, I think you know. You walk out of the theater and you think, "God, I had a good time. I want to go see something else." But if you see something that you feel you paid too much for and it's the same old junk, you don't go back.

Interviewer: A lot of your shows have been artistic successes, if not financial successes, and at least tried to expand the form—*Hallelujah, Baby!,* for example. What attracts you to certain types of shows?

Laurents: *Hallelujah, Baby!* is a strange show to bring up. I wrote *Hallelujah, Baby!* for an extremely good friend of mine named Lena Horne. This was at the period when civil rights was just taking hold, and someone got to her. She never read a word of the book, never heard a note of the score, and said she should not do any musical written by whites. I knew her terribly well and I really wrote it for her. The character was kind of glitteringly angry and sexual, all the things she is, or was at that time. She was a great star—this can show you what can happen in the theater—and she walked out. With her went the producer and the director and the money. But the show was written. What we should have done was abandon the show. It is one of the things in the theater that people don't do. There's a certain moment when you should say, "It's not going to work. Give it up." Instead it was rewritten for a woman who is one of the nicest women I have ever met in the theater, Leslie Uggams—and, God knows, she has a beautiful voice. She is a wonderful woman and she was good, but it wasn't that original show. The show lost its edge, and I must say I lost interest in it. We went on with it, and we shouldn't have. I've recently done a radical revision of the script and restored the best song—which was cut from the original show just before opening night in one of those moments of insane panic that are normal in the theater. Many lyrics have been polished and altered by Amanda Green, Adolph's very talented daughter. We go into rehearsal in September 2004 with me directing, and I'm excited. Again. As I said, I'm an optimist.

Interviewer: Another show of yours that was much more successful, *West Side Story,* also changed drastically, didn't it, between its inception and what ended up on the stage? It didn't start to be about Puerto Ricans and Anglos, did it?

Laurents: No. Jerry Robbins wanted to do a fifties version of *Romeo and Juliet* with the boy Jewish and the girl Catholic. I said it was *Abie's Irish Rose* and I didn't want to be involved in that. He kept pushing, but nothing happened. Then Lenny Bernstein and I happened to be in Hollywood at the same time when there were juvenile delinquent gangs and there were rivalries between so-called Anglos and Chicanos. Suddenly, there it was. You could do it in New York with Puerto Ricans and blacks and the supposedly Americans. That is when we took off.

Interviewer: Can you talk a little about collaboration and how it differs from show to show?

Laurents: The *West Side Story* collaboration was absolutely marvelous. We wanted to do what we called lyric theater, for want of a better term. I thought the show would run three months and be a flop, but I didn't care. None of us really did, and we got along marvelously until opening night, when Lenny and Steve and I didn't speak to Jerry Robbins. But that is backstage stuff after the fact. The creation of the show was wonderful.

Steve Sondheim is the best collaborator in the world, and every time I have worked with him we have had a wonderful time. I guided the writing on *La Cage aux Folles,* but I didn't write it, and I had a wonderful time with Jerry Herman and Harvey Fierstein; we just enjoyed ourselves. That's what the theater should be. It should be exciting and fun, but you should care about what you are doing and you should enjoy the collaboration. There were other shows that were problems.

Interviewer: Let's talk about one of the problem shows, *Nick and Nora.*

Laurents: I don't want to go into all the problems, but I'll mention three crucial mistakes that I made, because they might help somebody in the future. The first one was the reason that I did it. I had what I thought was a friend of mine. He was the best production stage manager on Broadway. He had done three shows for me, and he wanted to be a producer. He came to me with the idea of doing *The Thin Man,* and I said, "Good. It could be a fun musical." Not my kind, but I thought, "Okay." He couldn't get the rights, so I agreed to direct it, and then he got the rights. Mistake: Never do anything just for a friend; that's not professional in any kind of business. It ruins the friendship finally. He ended up not producing the show; he couldn't raise the money. The second mistake was the collaborators. None of us collaborated with the other. In any combination that you could think of, we were wrong for each other. The mistake that I made—and, mind you, by that time I was writing it as well as directing it—was that I realized that a year before it went into rehearsal. Why didn't I pull out? Well, my friend at that time was still the producer. The other thing is—and this sounds sort of admirable, but I'll give the other side of it—I am very tenacious. I won't quit. I refuse to admit that I can't bring it off. It was stupid. That collaboration was never going to work, and it didn't work. The third thing is the most important of all. I didn't care deeply about the material, and if you don't care about anything that you're doing creatively, you're a fool to go on with it. It takes so much time and so much hard work that if in the end it fails, you have to be able to say, "I don't care. I'm proud of it." I was glad when *Nick and Nora* closed. It was an awful experience. A fourth mistake, which might help deter someone from doing a musical adaptation of a movie with inimitable stars: Much too late I realized that Nick and Nora Charles might exist in the novel *The Thin Man,* but for audiences they were William Powell and Myrna Loy. Any actors had to be unsuccessful impostors.

Interviewer: What attracts you to a project? It seems that often in your musicals and your plays your lead characters need a sense of belonging. Somehow they are misfits or see themselves as misfits, and they are trying to find their place in the world. Whether it is *Hallelujah, Baby!, La Cage aux Folles,* or *The Time of the Cuckoo,* where they are going may not be where they think they want to be. Do you buy that?

Laurents: Yes, but I don't think it's conscious on my part. I am always surprised when I write something and find out that basically it is about someone who has to accept himself or herself for what he or she is. It's this
need for recognition that everybody has. I think that theme is particularly
strong in *Gypsy*, which is beyond just mother and daughters.

Interviewer: Do you want to talk a little bit about producers, since
you mentioned the person who tried to raise the money for *Hallelujah,
Baby!*? It seems like there aren't any producers on Broadway in the old-
style sense of a David Merrick, who could force anybody to do anything
he wanted done.

Laurents: Merrick was sui generis.

Interviewer: So what happens when you do a big show like *Nick and
Nora*? There's got to be some person who gets everybody together and set-
tles the differences.

Laurents: We didn't have one. We had an executive producer. She fed
malicious lies to the *New York Times* gossip column about the show. She
didn't realize that anything bad about any of us was hurting the show, but
she did it.

Interviewer: Speaking of the *New York Times*, do you want to talk a little
bit about the situation with theater critics in New York?

Laurents: As long as I've been in the theater, everybody has bitched
about the critic of the *New York Times*. I don't have any beef against any
of them. When I came into the theater, the *Times* critic was Brooks Atkin-
son, who was very nice to me. The trouble is there's only the *Times*. There
was one period when there was the *New York Herald Tribune* and Walter
Kerr was the critic on that. We had two critics, and that helped the theater a lot. I'm just used to the *Times*; they behave like the Republicans in
Washington. They think they have a right; they think they're imperial. It's
the royal family and we're all peasants—so I accept it.

Interviewer: Another problem is that the audience doesn't want to make
up its own mind. People don't want to read a variety of critics or just go to
the theater just for the sake of going to the theater. It's an event now.

Laurents: Years ago—this is absolutely true—I saw a play called *The
Happy Time*. I've never forgotten this. It was a comedy and it got rave reviews. I went the second or third night; the curtain went up, there was nobody onstage, and the audience howled. They had been told it was funny.
When you go to the theater in New York, any line that a *Times* reviewer
says is funny, the audience laughs like Pavlov's dog. They have been told.
I did a show with Steve Sondheim called *Anyone Can Whistle*. I think we
played nine performances. The *Times* killed it. A couple of papers liked it.

But I think that even if it had gotten good reviews, it wouldn't have run too long. It was too far out for that period.

Interviewer: Many of your shows have had revival productions. *Gypsy* especially has had major revivals. How do you feel about these revivals? How true do you think they have to be to the original production?

Laurents: That's one of my complaints about revivals. When I did a production of *Gypsy* with Tyne Daly, it was very, very different from the original—because times have changed. She's a terrific actress, and you can use that and play relationships that you couldn't have done earlier with Ethel Merman, who was only a buddy to a man. With Tyne, it was very sexual, and that made it interesting.

Interviewer: What about shows that have stars? With *Gypsy*, having Ethel Merman threw the weight of the show completely on her. It's called *Gypsy*, and Rose should only be a part of the story. With Merman, Rose became the focus of the show, didn't she?

Laurents: No, Merman wasn't the reason. They had asked me to do *Gypsy*, but I turned it down three times because I wasn't interested in the story of a woman who became the striptease queen of America. One of the producers, Leland Hayward, kept after me. I live most of the time at the beach in Quogue, and in those days we drank a lot; AA wasn't in the ascendancy then. A lot of people dropped by, and one time, everybody was talking for some reason about their first lover, and this girl said, "My first lover was Gypsy Rose Lee's mother." That was interesting. Then she told me what that woman was like, and it was fascinating. She was sort of like a Renoir, very soft, very feminine. There is a scene in *Gypsy* where Rose yells "Rape!" to the hotel manager; in real life she pushed him out the window and almost killed him. That kind of a woman with all that charm and that murderous instinct—I thought, "Let's do her."

Interviewer: And you made it an entertaining musical, even though Rose practically suffers a nervous breakdown at the end.

Laurents: That show can go in so many directions depending on how you play Rose, because she affects everybody else. My objection to most revivals is that they try to do a carbon copy, and I don't see why. You don't do a carbon copy—and I'm not comparing them to *Gypsy*—of Chekhov or Shakespeare. If the show is good, you should look at it with the eyes of the period in which you are living.

Interviewer: How true to the actual facts was *Gypsy*?

Laurents: Gypsy Rose Lee once said to me, "God, I wish I'd thought of Herbie for my autobiography." The only insistence she had was that it had to be called *Gypsy*. She didn't give a damn what I did with it. Some of it was based on fact. It was very hard. I said to her, "Where did you get the name?" She said, "Oh, I've given fourteen versions of it, darling. Make up your own." I said, "Give me one." She wouldn't tell me—so I had to make it up, which wasn't easy. I knew that she loved animals, so we have the lamb. My suspicion is that in burlesque those little girls were nude. That's a suspicion, but it's vaguely connected to the truth.

Interviewer: Can you compare and contrast some of the actresses who've played Rose: Angela Lansbury, Ethel Merman, Tyne Daly, and the next person who is going to be doing it?

Laurents: Merman had this glorious voice. She was also not very smart—I'm censoring myself—and she was naïve and sexless. When they said Ethel Merman was going to play the mother, I said, "I'd better meet her." I said to her, "This woman is a monster. How far are you willing to go?" She said, "I'll do anything you want"—and she did. She was wonderful to work with. She was also common, and Rose is common as dirt. Angela Lansbury is a terrific woman, she sings up a storm, and she is a marvelous actress; but she couldn't be common. Her Rose was middle class, and that was off. With Tyne, I'm just mad about her; but it was hell in the beginning of rehearsals. We fought like cats and dogs. Every actress always wants to cry, no matter what. At the end of the first act of *Gypsy*, Rose is really having a nervous breakdown in a railway station. She says something about "this one walked out on her and I cried, and the next one walked out and I cried, but this time I'm not crying." Ethel, Angie, and Tyne got to that, and when they said, "This time I'm not going to be crying anymore," they were in tears. So you have to stop them. They don't want to stop; they want to cry. It's hell to stop them. The only time that Rose finally—and it's the point of the whole piece—reveals her vulnerability is at the very end. Gypsy says to her, "Why did you do it?" She says, "I wanted to be noticed." And the daughter says, "Like I wanted you to notice me." She realizes that the daughter is saying, "You never loved me." That makes her cry, as it damn well should, but that's the only moment. But Tyne Daly is a terrific actress, and I loved working with her.

Interviewer: And who is going to do it next?

Laurents: Bette Midler is going to do it. It was done as a movie, and it was one of the worst movies ever made. Rosalind Russell in black-and-white shoes is all I remember. They wanted to do it again as a movie, and I fought hard to stop it from being made, because on the stage, everything is illusion. A woman can go bonkers, can have a nervous breakdown on-stage in a railway station, and start to sing to a twenty-six-piece orchestra—and you accept it. In the movies, they've got a real train, a real station, and where the hell is that orchestra coming from? This woman is *really* sick. What we are doing with Bette Midler is filming the show as a show, and it will be done on television. It's a dream come true; I think she will be wonderful. She's got all the qualities, all the talent; I think she's brilliant. We can keep the illusion part of it because it begins in a theater, and it doesn't have to be rewritten for the screen—as I think it would be if you were going to do it as a movie.

[Added in July 2004:] I was completely wrong. The TV show was a dud. The director and the producers didn't shoot it as we discussed, so illusion went out the waiting-room window. The sets were absurd and the performances—dear reader, we discreetly draw a curtain. But in 2003, there was a new Rose alive on Broadway: Bernadette Peters! Brilliant, original, totally unlike any of the others. Well, each of the four was unlike the others. Unfortunately, the physical production in 2003 was misconceived and hurt the show more than people realized.

Interviewer: Did you ever consider Liza Minnelli for the role of Rose?

Laurents: No. I think Liza Minnelli is a wonderful performer, but I don't think she's right for Rose. Liza Minnelli begs you to like her—and Rose doesn't give a shit.

Interviewer: How about the various actors who've played Herbie in *Gypsy*?

Laurents: In the original production, Jack Klugman walked in and he was just wonderful. Ethel respected him as an actor, which helped a lot, because she would go on automatic pilot if you let her. He kept her sort of alive. With Angela Lansbury, it was a man named Rex Robbins, who was a very good actor; but she didn't like him—and what do you do? With Tyne, we were desperate, and an actor from Washington named Jonathan Hadary came in. He sang "April Showers," and I cried. He was so touching and so period and so right. Then, because of Jonathan, I had Herbie sing a lot more. I broke up songs; they became duets, which helped the relationship. When Ethel sang "Small World," she just bellowed it at this man; but when Tyne and Jonathan did it, you could build a relationship. "Small World" is not a ballad. It's a very witty song, which you wouldn't have known before. If you listen to that lyric—"you're a man who likes children, I'm a woman with children, small world, isn't it?"—she's conning the hell out of him. In that production, you could get it. Jonathan was wonderful. One of the virtues of *Gypsy* is that there are roles, besides Rose, that can be played very differently. John Dossett, who was Herbie for Bernadette, was utterly unlike Jonathan but excellent in his own right. Tammy Blanchard, who played Louise/Gypsy with Bernadette, was ravishing and electrifying but again, unlike Crista Moore, who played the part with Tyne and who I thought could never be equaled.

Interviewer: When you speak about making changes for revivals, aren't there some directors now who take too much liberty with shows that, after all, are under copyright, in an effort to update them and make them more "relevant"?

Laurents: I wasn't clear. I don't think that you update. I didn't change any of the lines or any of the songs in *Gypsy;* I changed the attitudes of the people. Take *West Side Story.* In the fifties, you couldn't say a four-letter word onstage. If you start putting them in now, then what do you do about the lyrics? You have to begin changing the whole show. A couple of years ago, I redirected a touring English production before it came into London. The only thing that could be called updating was cutting the length of the skirts and throwing out the boys' jackets. In the main, what made the show seem surprisingly contemporary was that I made it extremely sexual every place possible—Tony and Maria almost devoured each other in the balcony scene—and I gave the company subtext to play through, even during the dances. If you are going to do *West Side Story* today, I would cast it as young as possible. I would have them thirteen, fourteen, if I could. You don't put Chekhov in the communist state. You can't remove a piece from the period in which it was written, but you can induce a kind of sophistication in the attitude. But I didn't change the material; I changed the attitudes of the actors. For example, in *Gypsy,* with the first scene where the man and the woman meet: The way I did it this time is I said to them, "Instantly, they want to go to bed together." And that was very clear in the way they played it. You couldn't have done that in the fifties. People didn't go to bed; they had twin beds. I think if you did *La Cage aux Folles* today, you would have to do it very differently. As a matter of fact, the gay community wasn't so mad about *La Cage* in 1983; they thought it was very old hat.

Interviewer: Speaking of *La Cage,* how was Gene Barry chosen to be in the original production?

Laurents: That was the hardest part to cast. It's a very hard part to play, because we don't have old vaudevillians anymore—and that is what that character's style is. Gene came in and auditioned, and he really did an old vaudeville routine. It's very hard for straight actors—and this was not a problem for Gene—unless they are very sure of their sexuality, to play a gay character onstage. When you see a play where there's an actor playing a gay man, if you look at the program you will find out how many children he has and how he was on the football and hockey teams. You don't see that unless an actor's playing a gay man.

Interviewer: With *La Cage,* were there worries in 1983 about how it would be received because of the subject matter?

Laurents: I wasn't worried at all. I had decided on the way for it to work— I hate to use that word, because it makes everything seem so calculated, but you do want a show to work. It's like everything else; you have to decide what line you won't cross. I thought the show's best chance was to make it asexual, not to have any sexual relationships. Nevertheless, that was the first time on the Broadway stage that one man sang a love song to another and touched him and kissed him. We were in Boston before coming to New York, and we didn't know how the audience was going to react—and they went through the roof. Every morning I would meet with Jerry and Harvey for breakfast and they would give me their notes. Finally they didn't have anything, except I had the two men literally dancing off into the sunset at the end, and Harvey said, "I wish you would change the ending." I said, "What would you like?" He said, "I would like for them to kiss." I said, "Well, in France they kiss on the cheeks. It doesn't mean anything." Jerry said, "I hate it that they even touch." We left it the way it was, but I was very careful about the sexuality. Putting homophobia aside, I think the thing that makes people nervous about anything concerning gay men or lesbians is facing the fact that there are sexual relations; that begins to make people uptight. You don't want to throw it in their faces. On the other hand, that show opened with twelve people seemingly in drag. Actually, there were ten; two were girls. After it got to Broadway, the theater parties came, and at the beginning the men would sit with their heads in their hands, eyes averted; but at the end of the show, they stood up. They stood up because it was a very moral show. It's about honoring your parents and the family. True, the mother was a man, but that's what it's about. They played "The Best of Times" from that show at the Republican convention; they didn't know they were subverting themselves!

Interviewer: Let's have some free association. I'll give you a name and you respond. Jerry Herman?

Laurents: He's one of the sweetest men ever, one of the sweetest people in the theater. He's tough in a good way. I wish he were tougher. This is an example. We did *La Cage aux Folles* in London. I went over to look at the theaters, and the producers lied to me. There was a theater in London called Her Majesty's that would have been perfect for *La Cage; West Side Story* had played there. It's small, and the producers said, "The scenery can't fit on the stage." So they took me to the Palladium, which is huge, and, foolishly, I agreed to it. I called Jerry and he said, "Oh, no, it's too big." I said, "Well, it's this and that and the other." He said okay. He should have said no to me. He really should have. Sometimes I frighten people. It was wonderful working with him. I would like to do another show with him. Collaborators are so important.

Interviewer: Speaking of frightening people, Jerome Robbins?

Laurents: He was the most brilliantly talented choreographer and stager, I think, in American musicals. He was not an easy man to work with. We had a wonderful time on *West Side Story*. There's a joke about him in *Gypsy*. One of the things I had in my contract for *Gypsy* was that we all had to have equal billing. I didn't care what color, what size, but it all had to be equal. We were ready to go into rehearsal, and the producer, David Merrick, called and said, "You lost out." I said, "What's the matter?" He said, "Jerry wants his name in a box." I said, "He can't have it unless you put all our names in a box, and it's going to look stupid." He said, "He won't put the show into rehearsal, and you're too professional to let that happen." I said, "You work it out. I don't care." It went on like that for what seemed like forever—but it wasn't—and finally I said, "Okay, I will give in, but on one condition," and I asked for some percentage additional, and Merrick said, "Fine, it's yours." It came out of Leland Hayward, so he didn't care. In *Gypsy*, there's a line in the burlesque-house scene when they're booked there; Herbie comes in, and Louise, who is Gypsy, says, "I'll bet we got top billing." He says, "Actually, they kind of had us lost in the middle," but then he adds, "I'm making them put a box around it." Typical of Jerry, he made no objections.

Interviewer: Harold Rome, with whom you did *I Can Get It for You Wholesale?*

Laurents: I had a fine time with him and Jerry Weidman, up to a point. I don't think anybody's very interested in *I Can Get It for You Wholesale*, so I'm not going to go into much detail, except to tell you that the show opened in Philadelphia and it was called anti-Semitic, which I think it was. I was the director, and Weidman had written the book; but he had hit a sort of dry spell, so I rewrote it. We opened in Boston, and the show got terrific reviews. The authors sent for me, and Harold said, "We want everything put back the way it was." I said, "My God, what's the matter here?" Jerry said, "Merrick"—he produced the show—"told us that you said the show was a piece of shit, but you could put your mark on it and save it." I said, "I never said that." He said, "Well, we want everything put back"—at which point David Merrick came into the room. I said, "Jerry, would you repeat what you just said?" He said, "David, I said that you told us that Arthur said the show wasn't so good and he would save it." I said, "No, no, no. You said that I said it was a piece of shit." Merrick said, "You're a fucking liar, Weidman, and I will repeat the four-letter word, liar." Jerry Weidman said, "True." It gets crazy, but this shows what the theater is. Then Merrick said, "However, I'm a signatory of the Dramatists Guild contract, which says the authors have total control of the material. If they want everything put back, you have to do it." I said okay, and I started to walk over to the theater. And I thought I couldn't do it; the company morale was so high. So I called from the theater and I said, "David, I'm leaving the show." He said, "Okay." I thought, "Oh my God, rejected." I felt terrible. "I mean I'm leaving; I'm going back to New York." He said,

"I know. I'll come over and say good-bye." I felt like hell, and he came over to the theater beaming. This is the kind of producer he was. He had said to Harold and Jerry, "He's leaving. Do you think you can get anybody else to come in on this turkey?" They looked at him and he said, "You've got to do it his way or I'm closing the show." That's how he got them to agree to what had been done. And it worked. The changes were mostly in the book; one or two of the musical numbers I did differently. But every night I got a poison pen letter slipped under my door from Harold Rome, who wrote the songs and lyrics, not from Jerry Weidman. You explain it to me; I haven't figured it out yet.

Interviewer: While we're talking about *I Can Get It for You Wholesale,* how about Barbra Streisand, who made her Broadway debut in that show?

Laurents: Barbra came in off the street, as it were, to audition. She was unknown. She started to sing and I thought I was in heaven. I just kept her singing and singing; I'd never heard a voice like that. She asked for a chair, and she took her chewing gum and put it under the chair. After she auditioned, I said to my assistant, "Go up and look at the chair. I'll bet there's no chewing gum." There wasn't. She knew not only what she was doing, she knew then she was going to be Barbra Streisand. No two ways about it. There was no part for her in the show. There was a part for a fifty-year-old spinster, and I said to Jerry and Harold, "Let's have her do it. What's the difference?" They agreed, and we began building up the part. She was tough. She knew. It's only recently that she has softened. She's a tremendous talent, and I think she's finally come to some kind of terms, which makes her much easier.

Interviewer: Richard Rodgers?

Laurents: A beast. He and Steve Sondheim and I did *Do I Hear a Waltz?* It was understandable because Oscar Hammerstein was sort of a foster father to Steve, and Dick knew him from when he was this pubescent kid running around using long words and making them rhyme. Dick treated Steve terribly. The worst—and it was typical—was when we were in New Haven. Dick had written a new song; the company was onstage, and Steve brought the lyric in. Dick put it on the piano and said, "Do you think I can give this piece of shit to *my* actors?" Terrible.

Interviewer: With *Do I Hear a Waltz?,* I've heard that Anne Bancroft, Gwen Verdon, and Mary Martin were considered for the lead before Elizabeth Allen got the role. What did you think of Elizabeth Allen's performance, and do you wish you'd cast one of the others?

Laurents: I didn't want Elizabeth Allen in it. I thought she was cold. Mary Martin wanted to do it. Dick and I thought she was too old; we were wrong. The other two were never mentioned, but it should have been someone else anyway. That show had another thing to avoid in the musical theater. Dick Rodgers was the producer as well as the composer, so he had final say over everything

Interviewer: Jule Styne?

Laurents: I loved him. He was an original. He was one of the dearest men I've ever met in my life, in or out of the theater. He had the most marvelous attitude. In *Gypsy*, sometimes I said, "Jule, I don't think that song is so good." "Why?" I'd tell him why and he'd say, "Okay." He'd come up with about a hundred ideas; ninety-five of them were terrible, but five were brilliant.

Interviewer: Musical ideas or theatrical ideas?

Laurents: Anything. Ideas for everybody. There's a Jerry Robbins story with Jule. We were in Philadelphia with *Gypsy*, and there was really no opportunity for Jerry to do what Jerry does best. So he was trying to build up "Mr. Goldstone," which is a song that gets nowhere at great length. In this hotel he had jugglers and tumblers and all sorts of people coming in; and he cut "Little Lamb," which was necessary for the character of Louise. He wouldn't put it back. That day, Jule arrived at the theater and he came onstage. He was a very natty dresser—hat and coat and attaché case—and he said, "Mr. Robbins, I have notified my lawyer that if that song is not in the show tonight, I am withdrawing my entire score. Good night." And it went back in the show! On opening night in New York, he almost threw Jerry in the pit. The pit at the Broadway Theatre is very low, and he was promised stools for the musicians, and they didn't arrive. He was furious, and he blamed Jerry. I don't know why. Anyway, they got the stools.

Interviewer: Leonard Bernstein?

Laurents: Wonderful, wonderful collaborator. We had the best time on *West Side Story*. Then he and I started another show, and he kept pushing it to be an opera. I'd go up to his house to meet with him, and I was so high I'd kind of fly up. But when I left, I was wearing the heaviest shoes in the world. We were going in different directions, so we quit.

Interviewer: What was the subject of the show?

Laurents: It was an original. It was about what it means to be free.

Interviewer: Was he going to do the lyrics, or was there another lyricist?

Laurents: He and I were going to do the lyrics. That was not bright.

Interviewer: What are some other projects that you've started that haven't come off?

Laurents: There was my first experience with Jerry Robbins, before *West Side Story*. He came to me—I was in the army when we met—and he wanted to do a musical about the ballet, so I thought of doing a musical about him, a kid from Jersey City and so forth. I did an outline, and I had a title, *Look, Ma, I'm Dancin'!* At the time, I was going to a Freudian analyst whose best friend was the playwright Arthur Schnitzler; the analyst's name was Theodor Reik. He had a son named Arthur, who disappointed him, so I was going to be that son. He said to me, "It's not versatile to do musicals. It's vulgar, and you mustn't do it." So I walked out, which was terrible of me. I signed everything away, and Jerry did it with somebody else. I don't think it was very successful. Then Lenny and I started to do one based on the James M. Cain novel *Serenade,* and we asked Jerry to do that. That was about the same time that the whole Chicano thing happened in California. That brings to mind a mistake that I think people who write musicals often make. They look for a character who sings in his or her professional life or who plays an instrument or who is a performer. It's so wrong, because if that person sings professionally, how do you differentiate in the book? In *Gypsy,* there are these kiddy acts; but otherwise, Rose is no singer. As a matter of fact, the whole point is that she's lousy, which was one of the reasons Tyne Daly was so good in "Rose's Turn." She made no effort to say, "I could have been"—because her Rose couldn't have been.

Interviewer: What are some projects that you turned down that became successes? Did you regret any?

Laurents: No. With *1776*, I said, "I'm no good with knee britches." They wanted me to write and direct. Another one was *Pippin*. That was these long fur robes; I couldn't do that either. Those are about the only ones. I don't flirt with projects. Either I'm going to do them or not; it's amazing how many terrible ideas are flying around. It really is. It's why collaboration is so important. The theater is essentially collaboration, and the epitome of it is the musical. It's so important to have the right people, and very hard to find.

Interviewer: Is it more difficult for a collaboration when you're the director and the librettist?

Laurents: I think so. I didn't until *Nick and Nora*. If I had been one or the other, I would have walked. Being both, I felt a responsibility.

Interviewer: Do you lose any perspective from one point of view or the other?

Laurents: I probably don't serve the writer as well as I should. I'm rather ruthless with myself as the writer. Sometimes I get too practical that way. If it doesn't work, cut it, change it, throw it out. I do that too fast when it's my own work.

Interviewer: What are your feelings about musicals in recent times that have very little libretto, that are sung through?

Laurents: They have the same amount of libretto as a musical with dialogue. The thing is that they're sung. The reason for that is that people don't hear very much that's sung. When *Dreamgirls* originally opened in Boston, a lot of it was spoken; Michael Bennett was smart enough to know that if we sing it, they won't hear it. And it's true. Even with Steve Sondheim, whose lyrics are so brilliant that he almost makes you listen, you don't hear it all. I know a lot of people are very devoted to *Les Misérables,* but if you heard those lyrics said, you would throw up: "Jean Valjean, you stole some bread. Jean Valjean, you should be dead." What is that? And that's one of the biggest hits in ninety million years. It's discouraging. Years ago, people like Steve and me would get angry about that. I think he still does. I don't anymore. I think, "Oh well, there they go again." Don't people really want to test their imaginations, to use their brains, to hear, to listen, to be excited, inspired?

Interviewer: How do you feel about some of the supposedly great musicals of the last twenty or thirty years that you didn't write or direct? What did you think of *A Chorus Line?*

Laurents: *A Chorus Line* was a hell of a show; it really was. The people who did that show cared so much, and I thought that came through. But I question the point. I think what that show said to the audience was "Each and every one of you is special"—and I think each and every one of us *is* special. But it also said, "Each and every one of you on the assembly line is special anyway." I'm not so sure about that. It's making you content with being on the assembly line or the chorus line.

Interviewer: What about some of Sondheim's recent shows, say, *Into the Woods, Assassins,* and *Sunday in the Park with George?*

Laurents: I think the first act of *Sunday in the Park* is brilliant. The second act did not work for me, although it has a lovely, lovely song in it called "Children and Art." *Into the Woods* has too many stories for me. Anything Steve Sondheim does is worth seeing, anything. I think the point of *Assassins* is disgusting. I really do. I'm serious about that, and I told Steve that. I mean, take a shot at a president and be a celebrity? I saw that in a workshop, and I spent a lot of time with Steve and John Weidman talking about what I felt was wrong; but that's what they wanted. I think it has some of his best songs in it and it has some wonderful moments, but finally comes the point. On the one hand, it's trivial. On the other, to glorify the assassination of a president I find horrifying and antihuman. It's like saying to all these kids, "Go out and shoot; you'll be famous." Suppose that show were done in the ghetto. What is it saying to those kids? Go out and kill. That's horrendous, and I think it's irresponsible.

Interviewer: A lesser-known musical of yours that we haven't discussed is *The Madwoman of Central Park West,* which was a one-woman revue in

1979 that starred Phyllis Newman. Do you want to say anything about that show?

Laurents: Phyllis is a wonderful woman and a wonderful performer. It was a small show. That showed the power of the *Times*. At that time, the *Times* had a critic named Richard Eder. What he said about the show—and I remember this because it was unfair—was that it was Phyllis Newman helped by her friends. That's mean, and it has nothing to do with the show. That's an example of where they kill you in an awful way; but I had a great time working with her. We did that show originally Off-Off-Broadway, for the Hudson Guild, and had a wonderful time.

Interviewer: Have you seen any musicals recently that you liked?

Laurents: There's a musical in New York called *Jelly's Last Jam,* which I liked enormously. The man who wrote and directed it, George C. Wolfe, was a student in a seminar in musical theater that I did at NYU for one year. I wrote him a note telling him how much I liked his work, and then I put a P.S. I said the first book of a musical I wrote was *West Side Story;* I didn't get a Tony, and the show didn't get a Tony. The second was *Gypsy.* The show didn't get a Tony; Ethel Merman didn't get a Tony. I just thought I should prepare him. He didn't get a Tony—and he should have. There is no comparison between the excellence and adventurousness of that show and *Crazy for You*—and the theater needs *Jelly's Last Jam.*

Interviewer: Can you talk a bit about your creative process? Do you disappear for a while? Do you develop the essence of an idea and work around it? Do you get very excited? Do you get disgusted?

Laurents: I've just finished a play. My age is no secret; I've been in the theater a long time. I've written this play differently than I've written any other. I don't understand these writers who say, "It's so awful. You're alone. It's agony." I love writing. I'm enormously happy when I'm writing. When I do a musical, I usually do an outline and then sit down with my collaborators. We discuss it, and then I write ahead. Steve Sondheim does what he calls robbing the dialogue for the lyrics. He's the only lyricist who can slip into the skin of any character presented to him and write from the heart and mind of that character. When I write a musical, I'm always writing ahead of the composer and lyricist. When I wrote this play, *Jolson Sings Again,* a thing happened that I had always heard about. I didn't have an outline. It's a play about the witch hunt; suddenly the characters took on a life of their own. I always thought that was nonsense, but it happened. They took over and began doing things that I didn't see coming. It was thrilling, and I had a wonderful time. I'm sure that's very discouraging to hear!

Interviewer: Earlier, you referred to the high costs of producing and seeing a show. Where are we headed when standing room is twenty or thirty dollars?

Laurents: To answer that you have go into the producing end of theater. I've been at it so long and, fortunately, have had enough success at it that I just do it. That's my job. The theater itself is in a terrible state. I think one of the things that was helpful in the theater is disappearing, regional theater. The regional theater, it seems to me, is too busy trying to find something that they can move to Broadway and make money on. That's not allowing people to experiment and develop. But it's like that Thornton Wilder play, *The Skin of Our Teeth*; it will work. It's got to—I hope.

Interviewer: How does the theater balance the demands of the marketplace against artistic innovation and quality? Many of the most innovative musicals of the last few years, including several of Sondheim's, have been commercial failures, while the shows that have been successful are often the least adventurous.

Laurents: That's the decision everybody has to make who does anything creative. In my experience, you make a mistake when you write down, because it's no good. I haven't done all that many movies, but every movie I've done was a success. The reason, I think, is that I don't have much respect for movies. I don't call them films; I think there are only about two or three films. The rest are movies, and they're meant to reach millions of people. They must because someone is putting millions of bucks into them. So I think I owe it to that person to try to write something that will appeal to more people. In the theater, you have to go all out to do what you want, what you believe in. That's what the theater is for, and when you write down, you're kidding yourself. First of all, it's a kind of contempt for the audience. You think, "I know they want this." You don't know what they want; nobody knows what they want. I think the only thing the audience wants is something good, and you have to try to reach that. If you were able to say, "I'm going to have a popular success," we wouldn't have any flops. I think most flops result from people saying, "This is what's going to work!"—and it doesn't.

𝒦athleen 𝒮Marshall

Kathleen Marshall was born on September 28, 1962, in Madison, Wisconsin. She was educated at Smith College (B.A., 1984). She has worked as a choreographer, director, and performer. The musicals she has choreographed include Swinging on a Star *(1995),* Violet *(1997),* 1776 *(1997),* As Thousands Cheer *(1998),* Kiss Me, Kate *(1999),* Saturday Night *(2000),* Seussical *(2000),* Follies *(2001),* Little Shop of Horrors *(2003), and* Wonderful Town *(2003). She has directed the musicals* Saturday Night *and* Wonderful Town; *and she has choreographed the play* Ring 'Round the Moon *(1999). She received the Tony Award for* Wonderful Town *(Best Choreography).*

This interview took place on January 27, 2004.

Interviewer: Can you start by talking about your background and how you became interested in theater?

Marshall: Like a lot of people, I was a theater fan before I ever thought it was something I could do as a career. Growing up in Pittsburgh, my parents took my brother, my sister, and me to see everything—musicals, plays, Shakespeare, operas, ballets—and we loved it all. We especially responded to the musicals and the great cast albums that we had at home. I didn't start taking dance classes until I was thirteen, which was kind of late. When I started dancing, I felt as if somehow dance fit me, and I was able to plunge right into it.

Interviewer: How did you choose dance? You could have become a singer or an actor, couldn't you?

Marshall: I started taking gymnastics lessons—I think it was back in the Olga Korbut days—and I was horrible. I didn't have flexibility in my back; I didn't have that kind of strength. The only things that I could do well in the gymnastics class were the dance moves; that fit me very well, and I started taking dance.

Interviewer: Did you ever think of yourself as a potential singer or actor?

Marshall: My brother, Rob, my sister, Maura, and I performed in local shows in Pittsburgh while we were still amateurs. We all performed with the Pittsburgh Civic Light Opera, which is the local professional summer stock company. They were doing *The Sound of Music,* and we saw an ad in the paper and we wanted to go down to audition. My parents said, "You're kids who like to do plays at school and sing and dance around the living room. You're amateurs. You've never had any lessons. But," they said, "we'll take you down to audition." And we all three got in and did *The Sound of Music* that summer.

Interviewer: You were three of the children?

Marshall: We were three of the von Trapp children, from one family. It was one of those summer theaters where they do six musicals a season, so while we were rehearsing *The Sound of Music,* next door the singers and dancers in the ensemble were rehearsing the rest of the season. We used to go over on our breaks and watch, and I think that sparked the first interest in dance and choreography—watching a rehearsal and watching a show being put together. We were fascinated with that, and eventually we wanted to do it.

Interviewer: Did you take dance lessons all the way through high school? Did you also dance semiprofessionally?

Marshall: In high school I danced in a semiprofessional ballet company in Pittsburgh with a crazy Russian guy. I also was dancing then with Don Brockett, who was mostly known as a local impresario/producer with his comic partner, Barbara Russell. They were the Nichols and May of Pittsburgh; they did comedy improvisations. He was also Chef Brockett on *Mr. Rogers' Neighborhood,* so a lot of people know him from that. He produced local musical revues and industrials. I started doing musical revues for him on the weekends when I was in high school. When I was eighteen, I got my Equity card. Interestingly enough, both my brother and I, when we were in college, at separate times in different years, got our Equity cards back at Civic Light Opera. We became those dancers in the ensemble whom we had watched and were in awe of when we were in *The Sound of Music.*

Interviewer: Where did you go to college?

Marshall: I went to Smith College in Massachusetts. I wanted to go to a liberal arts college, and at the time, also, there was a woman on the faculty there named Gemze de Lappe. It's amazing that she was there, because she comes from the Broadway and classical world. She was one of Agnes de Mille's main dancers; she was in the original *King and I* and the original *Paint Your Wagon.* She stages *Oklahoma!* and *Carousel* and *Brigadoon* with the de Mille choreography around the world. She was one of the founders of the American Dance Machine, but she also danced with American Ballet Theatre. It was marvelous because she was a wonderful ballet technique teacher but also taught courses in choreography and musical theater dance. We danced the *Carousel* ballet as part of a dance concert when I was in college, so learning from her was incredible.

Interviewer: While you were at Smith, then, you came back to Pittsburgh in the summers?

Marshall: Yes. In the summers I came back to Pittsburgh, lived at home, and did shows at Civic Light Opera. I got my Equity card working with Susan Schulman, who was the resident director there at the time. I don't know how they did it, but they did six shows a season back-to-back. It was great. It was like a graduate course in musical comedy because you did everything. You did *West Side Story* one week, *Once upon a Mattress* the next, an operetta the week after that, and *Fiddler on the Roof* the week after that. You did all of these shows and learned so much about them; I eventually became a dance captain and assistant to the choreographer. I learned a lot from Susan, from watching her put the shows together.

Interviewer: Did you at that early stage see yourself as primarily a dancer or as someone who wanted to learn about all the elements of dance and musical theater with the idea of possibly becoming a choreographer and director?

Marshall: I was interested in everything. Susan Schulman said I was always aware of what was happening in the whole room—and I liked that. A lot of the dancers didn't even read the script of the show; they came in to learn just what they were taught. I wanted to listen to the music and get the script and learn everything about it before I even started. It's interesting because at that point I didn't think that choreography was something that was an option for me. When I became a dance captain and assistant to the choreographer, my mom actually asked me, "Do you think you would ever see yourself becoming a director?" I said, "I don't know if I want to do that. Maybe I could be a stage manager." And Mom said, "That's like saying you could be a nurse but not a doctor"—which was a great thing to say, to say, "Why not?" But at that point I was still concentrating on dance and saw myself as maybe an assistant down the line or a dance captain, not as the person in charge.

Interviewer: You were concentrating on being a performer?

Marshall: Yes. Almost all choreographers have gone up through the ranks. There are certainly a lot of directors who were actors first, but there are some who never were actors and basically went into directing right away. But almost all choreographers—because, I think, choreography is an apprenticeship art—were dancers in an ensemble, became a dance captain, became an assistant, and got jobs on their own.

Interviewer: Why do you think choreography is an apprenticeship art? Why is it different from being a director?

Marshall: The only way choreography can happen is in the room. I don't know how you can learn choreography in a classroom. You learn a lot by watching and reading and all that kind of research. But I think I've learned so much assisting my brother; and he assisted Graciela Daniele, and she assisted Michael Bennett and Bob Fosse, and Fosse was supervised by Jerome Robbins on his first Broadway show. The lineage goes back and back. Certainly directing happens in the room as well, but a choreographer is an author to a degree. When you start a dance rehearsal and the dancers come in, there's a blank page ahead of them. When you're working as a director, you have a script, a playwright, and actors. When a director comes in, there's words on a page; you have somewhere to start. When you start choreography, you're starting from ether.

Interviewer: Do you think it's also partially the physical angle of it? Obviously, acting is physical, too, but the sheer physical knowledge of understanding firsthand what the body is capable of must be invaluable to a choreographer.

Marshall: I think so. When I choreograph, I like to be able to dance it. If you have an idea, you need to be able to dance it to see if it feels right. My assistants and I will map something out and we'll go back and try it. When we do it in context and up to speed, we'll say, "Wait a minute, this doesn't feel right" or "this does feel right" or "this could be smoother," because, besides the effect you're trying to create, you also want it to be danceable. There certainly are a lot of directors who were not really good actors, whereas most choreographers have had some career as dancers.

Interviewer: Let's pick up after you graduated from Smith. What happened then?

Marshall: I moved to New York and was sort of doing the audition thing. I toured with a show for a little bit, but I never danced in a Broadway show. I moved to New York in 1986, and four or five years later I basically had stopped dancing. What happened is that as I was still touring, my brother, Robby, started choreographing, and I began assisting him. I assisted him on the tour of *The Mystery of Edwin Drood,* which I was also in, and a couple of other things. I was touring in *Cats,* of all things, when I got a call from Robby saying that he had been asked to come in on *Kiss of the Spider Woman,* which at that point was in Toronto before heading to London and Broadway. They wanted him to come in and do some additional choreography and change some choreography for Chita Rivera. It was a dream phone call: "Do you want to come work on a show with Hal Prince, Kander and Ebb, Terrence McNally, and Chita Rivera?" That was a no-brainer! I ended up working on the show for the next couple of years in all its incarnations, tours and the national company.

Interviewer: So you were pretty well attached to *Spider Woman* for that period of time?

Marshall: Yes, but I also worked with Robby on his next couple of Broadway shows. *Spider Woman* overlapped with *She Loves Me,* his second Broadway show, and *Damn Yankees* followed pretty much on the heels of that. We did those three shows back-to-back. I was assisting him, and when things were overlapping, we'd trade off. There was a point when *She Loves Me* was in rehearsal in New York and *Kiss of the Spider Woman* was about to open on Broadway. They were having simultaneous rehearsals, so we were shuffling back and forth between them.

Interviewer: How did you go from being your brother's assistant to getting some work on your own?

Marshall: It was actually through John Kander. A friend of his, Michael Leeds, was directing a little revue called *Swinging on a Star* at a theater in New Jersey called the George Street Playhouse. It was a revue of Johnny

Burke's music; he was the lyricist who wrote "Pennies from Heaven," "Misty," "Imagination," and many others. They were looking for a choreographer, and Michael Leeds asked his friend John Kander if he could recommend somebody. John Kander knew me from *Kiss of the Spider Woman* and recommended me. That was really a stroke of good fortune, because that little show ended up going to the Goodspeed Opera House and eventually to New York. Even though it lasted only less than four months in New York, it was my first Broadway show, and I got a Drama Desk nomination.

Interviewer: What happened after that?

Marshall: Before *Swinging on a Star* opened in New York, between its Goodspeed incarnation and coming to Broadway, I got a call to come do one dance for *Call Me Madam* in the City Center Encores! series. It was just the second season of Encores!, and I hadn't seen any of the shows the first season, so I didn't know much about what the format was and kind of learned as we went. *Call Me Madam* was originally choreographed by Jerome Robbins, and there was a number at the top of the second act called "Something to Dance About." It's a funny story. It's an Irving Berlin score, and Ethel Merman starred in it. They needed a production number at the top of the second act; they had something out of town that wasn't working, and they needed a new song. Irving Berlin said to Jerome Robbins, "What do you want me to write?" and Jerry Robbins supposedly said, "I don't know. Just give me something to dance about"—so Berlin wrote a song called "Something to Dance About." It was a brilliant arrangement and brilliant orchestration that went through jazz and waltz and tango and blues. Tyne Daly starred in the Encores! version, and I had three couples, six great dancers, and we put together this number to the original orchestration. That was the first thing I did in New York. Thank goodness I didn't know that it was going to be reviewed by the *New York Times* and be this kind of big industry event, because I ended up getting a paragraph in the *Times* just about my number.

Interviewer: Did that ultimately lead to the Encores! connection?

Marshall: That was my first job with Encores! The next year I choreographed *Du Barry Was a Lady* for them. That was the season of *Chicago*, and Walter Bobbie, the artistic director of Encores!, was stepping down to transfer *Chicago* to Broadway. I got a call from Rob Fisher, who had been the music director of Encores! since its beginning, asking if I'd be interested in taking over as artistic director. I was flabbergasted. Why me? It's funny, because I didn't realize that I'd been accumulating all of this knowledge, but I had. I realized I'd been a student of musical theater my whole life and knew a lot about the history of it. I think they were looking for somebody from inside the family to take over. I called my brother and I said, "I can't believe it"— because I was just getting myself established as a choreographer, having just done my first Broadway show and wanting to do more shows on Broadway. This seemed like a slight left turn, but Robby said, "If this is something you ever thought you'd be interested in down the line, running a company, you should take this plunge because it's a great opportunity." I did; I did it for four years, and I loved it. So many people I know now that I work with all the time—actors, musicians, designers—are people I first started working with at Encores! They were also wonderful about allowing me to go off and do other things.

Interviewer: Wouldn't it have been a bit confining if Encores! had been the only thing you could do? Also, isn't it a slightly unreal experience? It's a lot easier to get Tyne Daly or Nathan Lane for one week of rehearsal and five performances than it is to get them to commit to a full show, isn't it?

Marshall: You do get spoiled because you get a bigger cast, a bigger orchestra, and more stars than you get on a Broadway show. We did *Do Re Mi* with Nathan Lane and Randy Graff, and the secondary couple was Brian Stokes Mitchell and Heather Headley. No Broadway producer could afford all those people at one time on the stage. But eventually, as much as I loved it, I also felt that I had other projects, especially in the spring, when Encores! happens, and I didn't want to strain that bond too much by not being as available as I needed to be. As much as I learned about dealing with estates and publishing houses and lawyers and things that you never do as a director or a choreographer (it opened up my eyes to the administrative and the producing side of theater, which is very helpful), I realized I was happiest in rehearsals and not as happy in an office on my own. They needed somebody who could devote themselves more fully to it, so I stepped down after four years.

Interviewer: Didn't working with Encores! also spoil you about material? Here you were dealing with famous musicals of the past, some of which don't have great books but have tremendous scores. When somebody comes to you with a new musical, do you have to adjust your standards a bit?

Marshall: It's a very different kind of thing. I directed *Saturday Night,* Stephen Sondheim's first musical, [Off-Broadway] at Second Stage. That was the New York premiere of a musical that he wrote when he was twenty-three. It had never been produced in New York; it had been done in London and Chicago, but this was a different production. Rob Fisher worked on that with me, too. At Encores! the mission is always the score. The scores are usually pretty great, maybe not perfect. We don't do *Guys and Dolls* and *Oklahoma!* and *My Fair Lady* at Encores!; we're exploring the lesser-known shows of some of the great composers.

Interviewer: They are also shows that you realize, after you've seen them there, that Encores! was the perfect venue in which to do them, because one could never do a full-scale production due to the weakness of the book.

Marshall: Yes. Encores! has a very intelligent and forgiving audience who understands that you're saying, "Come back with us. We're going to take you back to a Cole Porter show in 1938, and each song is going to have ten verses—because that's the way Cole Porter wrote it—and we're going to do all ten verses. That's why we're here." That's okay, because that's the venue at that point. When we were doing *Saturday Night,* it was not a new musical. It was a new musical, but it wasn't a classic musical because people didn't know it. Sondheim didn't want to tinker with the score too much because, he said, "This was written by me as a twenty-three-year-old, and I don't want me now forty years later to change it." There is actually a tape I have of him when he was twenty-three doing a backers' audition and singing the whole score himself. We wanted to maintain the show as it had originally been written, but the harder thing to figure out was what the intent of the production was. It was not an Encores! presentation at all because it was being done as a full production in an Off-Broadway house, but, as I said, Sondheim didn't want to tinker with it too much. He didn't want to go in, fix, update, and change. He changed one lyric, he allowed us to make some cuts that he suggested in the score, and we worked together on cutting the book down. But it was not an Encores! experience; we had to get in there and mess around with it a little bit more. Nonetheless, you're right. It was still a very different approach from when you do a new musical.

Interviewer: With *Seussical,* you were dealing with a brand-new musical that had no track record. That's very different, isn't it?

Marshall: Yes, it's a very different experience because you're trying to figure out what the show is and how it needs to behave. If you're the choreographer on a new show, you're trying to figure out where the dance should be and why, who should dance and why and when. In a revival, usually those decisions have already been arrived at and you can go along with them or not. In *Kiss Me, Kate,* everywhere there was dance in the original production, we had dance. It was all different arrangements and all different choreography, and a lot of it was even a different scenario of why the dancing was happening—but where the dance happened was the same. With a new musical, you're finding out where it should open up and where it shouldn't. *Seussical* was fun to work on because the music was so beautiful, so rhythmic, and so danceable. Even though there weren't a lot of long instrumental dance breaks per se, the music was so joyous and had such great grooves to it that it made you want to choreograph to it and to create.

Interviewer: Talk a little bit about your role as a choreographer as you experience it in the collaborative process where there's a director, a composer, a lyricist, designers, and performers. I'm thinking primarily in terms of the new musicals that you've done. How does the choreographer operate within that complex of creative people and personalities?

Marshall: It really depends on the show and on your director. There are some shows that want to dance more than others. It depends on the score to lead you to that. There are times when even if people want to have more dance, you end up trimming it down because it's getting in the way. I choreographed *Violet* by Jeanine Tesori and Brian Crawley Off-Broadway, which Susan Schulman directed. It's a beautiful score, but the tricky thing is that most of it takes place on a bus. It's about a girl who's traveling across country to see a preacher who she thinks can heal her childhood scar. Susan Schulman and I worked very much together on how the whole show would look, how it would move—it was written almost like a screenplay—and how we were going to get from one location to another in transitions. None of that was built into the original script. A lot of it took place on the bus, and we ended up breaking it up and putting things in a waiting room, or changing the angle of the bus when you were looking at it. That was very collaborative; we were all in the room figuring out those problems together.

Interviewer: Were you involved in the whole conception of that show from very early in the process?

Marshall: There had been several readings of it before I got involved.

Interviewer: But once a production was contemplated, as the choreographer you were in on it right from the beginning?

Marshall: Yes.

Interviewer: When you choose a project as a choreographer, do you select it based on that and on the opportunities to put dance into the project? If someone comes to you with a project that you like but it doesn't seem to be one where you as a choreographer would grow or have opportunities, is that a major criterion affecting your decision?

Marshall: It depends. I don't choose a project just to show off as a choreographer. *Little Shop of Horrors* doesn't have a big dance ensemble or big breakout dance numbers, but I wanted to do it because I loved the show so much. I think it's a brilliant score, and that's really why I wanted to do it. I think that it again depends on the show. With *Violet,* the story moved me, I thought the music was beautiful, and I loved working with Susan Schulman; all that combined made it something I was excited to do.

Interviewer: What are your reasons for not doing a show that you're offered?

Marshall: If it's a project that doesn't have breakout dancing, that doesn't have a dance ensemble and big dance opportunities, then there has to be something that draws me to it other than that. There are projects that I have chosen not to do because they didn't have breakout dancing or an opportunity for a choreographer to flex his or her muscles. At the same time, if I wasn't drawn to the story or the music, then maybe there's not a good reason to do it. For a choreographer and a director, all we get is the process right up to opening night. You go over to visit the shows, and it's so much fun backstage; they're back there having a great time. They hang out in the dressing room. They go through a year or a season together. They celebrate birthdays and holidays, and they support each other. I don't get that; as soon as it opens I'm out of there. All we have is the process of putting it together, and if you're going to be in a relationship with a show for the next six months or year of your life, you have to choose carefully—if you have the luxury to choose. You also can't choose projects based on what you think is going to be commercially or critically successful. If we had any formula to know what that is, everything would be a huge success. Since we don't have any formula to know what's going to be a hit, you'd better like the piece and you'd better be happy working on it.

Interviewer: To get back to the collaborative process, it's one of the intriguing things about musicals to outsiders. There are so many egos involved, when a musical is successful we wonder how it ever happens. Can you think of some examples when the collaborative process and your part in it worked particularly well?

Marshall: Two of the smoothest experiences I've had were *Kiss Me, Kate* and *Wonderful Town* in terms of no bumps. Everybody seemed to be on the same page right from the beginning and right on through.

Interviewer: Would you say that, in most musicals, there's a dominant force in the room? With *A Chorus Line,* it was Michael Bennett; with *Annie,* it was Mike Nichols who really turned that show around. I assume that with a Sondheim show, he has a great deal more clout than another composer would have.

Marshall: He's also very collaborative. He will—and it was very shocking for me to hear him—humbly say, "I defer to the director on that." He really does trust his collaborators in that way. But he's also a workaholic, so he's there constantly involved and constantly giving his input. I found that ultimately he allowed the production to be what the director's vision was. He is gentlemanly and old-school in that way.

Interviewer: You're saying, then, that the collaborative process varies tremendously from production to production?

Marshall: Absolutely. There have been plenty of times when there are a bunch of very smart people in a room and it quite obviously doesn't work.

Why is that? How could all those smart people not have been successful? Then there are times when people stumble onto things and you think, "How did that ever happen?" Look at *Avenue Q*. Where did those guys come from? Here they are, and they've got this successful Broadway show that they probably thought up in their living room. They never dreamed a few years ago that they would be on Broadway and be this successful. You never know, and that's the nature of theater; with each project, you never know from one second to the next.

Interviewer: As an audience member, do you sometimes see a show and say to yourself, "How could they not have known that this wouldn't work?"

Marshall: There's a very basic level on which musicals work or don't work. They can sweep you up and bring you along in their wake. It can be a story that compels you, a performance that galvanizes you, or a production that is so artfully and beautifully designed, staged, and choreographed that it just washes over you. I think that a lot of times when there's something strong at the core like that, you forgive a lot of little things. Sometimes it's a star like Ethel Merman. You were so happy to see Ethel Merman that the little flaws of the show would wash away because she took you along for a great ride. There are shows that do that as well. The problem is that if you don't have something like that at the core—a great score, a great performance, a compelling story, something that people hook onto—you can do all the fixing and putzing around the outside and it's not going to help. You're rearranging deck chairs on the *Titanic*. When there's something missing at the core that's not compelling and not connecting to an audience, that's the hardest thing to admit.

Interviewer: Regarding the creative process, I read somewhere that the Encores! productions used the original dance arrangements. What does that mean? How does that affect your creative process?

Marshall: Most people don't know that the composer writes the songs and then usually the dance arranger and the choreographer go in a room and create the dance arrangements. The composer doesn't necessarily write all the dance music. Sometimes they do. Leonard Bernstein in *Wonderful Town* wrote all his own dance music. Richard Rodgers did a couple of times; I think he did in *Babes in Arms,* but later on other people wrote the extended dance music. Then an orchestrator takes what the dance arranger has written and creates an orchestration for the full orchestra. At Encores! you create to existing music scores just as you would if you were choreographing a classical piece for the City Ballet and you were going to use a Bach concerto. There it is; there's the Bach concerto. You might be able to work with your musical director to get the tempos exactly where you want them, but the music is what it is and you need to create to that music. When I did *Li'l Abner* at Encores!—it has a seven-minute

Sadie Hawkins ballet in it, and we did the whole thing. I remember we listened to the original dance for a couple of weeks before we started rehearsals; we played through all the music. I heard all the music with the whole orchestration, which was brilliant. It was cartoony and fun and wild; then I had to sit down and basically write a libretto to go with that music. I'd say, "What is that music telling me to do? That sounds like the sneaky section. That sounds like the frantic section." I created little scenarios and story lines to match the music. It was a challenge that was very different from when you as a choreographer go into a room with a dance arranger to start from scratch and create something for a new musical.

Interviewer: Do you do a lot of research? If so, what kind do you do?

Marshall: Oh, yes. It depends on when the show takes place, its era. If I'm doing a show that takes place in the 1930s or 1940s, the Lincoln Center Library has a great dance archive; you can look at original swing dancing or social dancing or movies from the time.

Interviewer: Can you give us an example of research you did for a specific show?

Marshall: *Kiss Me, Kate* takes place in the 1940s, so I watched a lot of the great movie musicals of the 1940s and 1950s that were backstage musicals—*The Band Wagon, The Barkleys of Broadway, Summer Stock, White Christmas.* I watched those musicals because they're the MGM version of a Broadway show in rehearsal. It's not exactly a Broadway show in rehearsal, it's the MGM version of a Broadway show in rehearsal. I looked at the style of those, how they looked, and at the movie version of a chorine. It was fun. For Bill Calhoun, I based all his movement on a kind of Gene Kellyesque style, because he's very athletic and very gymnastic. For Lois Lane, who's a little vixen, I based a lot of her movement on Jack Cole's choreography for Marilyn Monroe. "Always True to You (In My Fashion)" was based on the little, contained Jack Cole movements that he did for Marilyn in *Gentlemen Prefer Blondes.*

Interviewer: Of course—and I don't say this in any derogatory way— only one out of a thousand people who sees the show will know that you're doing that. You do that for yourself really, don't you?

Marshall: It's an homage to that kind of style because I grew up watching movies, especially the *That's Entertainment* series. When those movies came out in the 1970s, they were a huge influence, seeing all the dancers, all those styles, and all that choreography. It's like the Seurat painting that you have to get up close to to see that it's made of little dots of blue, red, and green; from far away, you see a hat. All of that research is hopefully for us to create a canvas that has some life and depth to it. It's not necessary for you to get all the little relationships that I create between actors and ensemble. It's important to have an ensemble of real people and individuals and to give them little stories of who they are and what's going on—so that they can feel connected.

Interviewer: Can you give an example of that, of the bits of business that you've given to members of the ensemble to create personalities and stories for them?

Marshall: The opening number in *Wonderful Town* is "Christopher Street." It's this group of tourists that have come down to explore the bohemian West Village and run into a bunch of artists; so we created personas for the artists. We have some modern dancers who are Martha Graham–style dancers; we have a wild painter with Jackson Pollock–like big moves; we have a writer who is a Quentin Crisp type; and we have an actor and actress who are obviously very Method and into their moves. Once we created these personas for the artists, sometimes they did a movement in unison and other times they all did individual things. After we created the parameters of each character—their style and how they move—then we allowed the dancers to find their own poses, but with a flourish because these artists are all a little over-the-top. I love finding a character-based reason and then allowing the actors to develop their own movements and poses. You're always in charge of the overall design, but I find that when actors are involved in the process like that, it will mean more when they do it, because they are constantly developing themselves. I like finding that kind of detail.

Interviewer: Let's talk a little about the transition you made to becoming a director/choreographer from being just a choreographer. How did that happen, and what are the differences for you?

Marshall: The first things that I directed and choreographed on my own were in Encores! at City Center. I was the artistic director at the time, so I guess I hired myself. But it was after consulting with everybody, saying, "Do you think I'm ready for this?" I think it's natural for choreographers to become director/choreographers because you're basically doing all the same things in terms of dealing with actors, dealing with writers, and dealing with designers. A lot of times in a musical the choreographer, depending on the director, is in charge every time there's music. Whether it's a ballad, a duet, a transition, or a big dance number, with a lot of directors, if there's music, the choreographer is in charge.

Interviewer: Is the director, then, only responsible for the non-musical moments of the show?

Marshall: Sometimes, but also, of course, for the overall concept and design and look. There are some directors who will stage musical numbers and some who will stage only ballads but won't touch a rhythmic number.

It's natural for choreographers to become directors, because they've done all the things that a director has done. But as a choreographer, you always have this shield of the director, and believe me, you feel that—and often in a good way, especially in a big musical. You have this other person above you who has more responsibility than you. It's a little scary when that shield is gone and you realize, "Oh my God, it's all on me!"—including the hard things like having to go up to an actor and say, "We're going to cut your song" or "You're going off in the wrong direction and you need to change."

Interviewer: Would you never do that as a choreographer?

Marshall: It depends. My brother and I have a joke about it; we say that as a choreographer you can step back a little and say, "Boy, she's really over-the-top in that scene. I hope that gets calmed down" and then you might be able to say on the sly to the director, "Don't you think she's going a little far there?" And the director is the one who has to go and give the bad news. When you're the director/choreographer, you realize, "That person's me. I'm the one who has to go tell the costume designer that we don't like that dress and that it needs to be replaced. I'm the one who has to go tell the composer that we need to change that song or we need to cut it." You're getting it from everybody—from the producers and from the designers.

Interviewer: As a choreographer, you're insulated.

Marshall: A bit. You get pressure, but not quite as much as the director. When a show is in previews and you're called in for the notes from the producers, a lot of times the director will go and get the notes from the producers and then come back and filter out to everybody which of those notes he or she thinks you should concentrate on. But as the director, it was me, and I had to go to the principal's office.

Interviewer: And you have to do the filtering, don't you? You've got to decide which of the criticisms you want to pass on and how.

Marshall: A lot of times what you do is filter things from other people and get them to the right people at the right time in the right manner. Sometimes you say, "The producers would like this to change," but other times you need to make it seem like it's your own idea or your own concern and not necessarily one coming from someone else. I think directing basically is disseminating information; it's deciding who to tell what when. Even when you're in rehearsals, you may have an idea for where a particular performance should go; but you can't necessarily give it all at once, because sometimes if you overwhelm people, they get defensive and they feel that nothing they're doing is right. You have to gently guide and herd everybody into a cohesive whole, even if as you're going you change your vision of what that whole is. You may think you have an idea of what it is, but you have to be ready to see where everybody else is guiding you.

Interviewer: Don't you also have to know a lot about each performer? Don't some performers need time on their own, while others need to be guided?

Marshall: Yes. Some performers say, "Tell me right away. Give me my medicine straight. If you don't like what I'm doing, tell me, because I don't want to waste anybody's time." There are other performers who need you to give them a little freedom; they need to at least try something before you decide. With some performers, you need to make sure that they're constantly given positive support, three compliments before you give them one note.

Interviewer: You started directing at Encores! How did that lead to doing other shows?

Marshall: I got the call to do *Saturday Night* at Second Stage after I directed *Babes in Arms* at Encores! *Wonderful Town* is my first Broadway show as a director. We did *Wonderful Town* at Encores! when I was artistic director, and I chose to direct it myself. It was successful enough that commercial producers wanted to transfer it to Broadway, which took us some time to do. Thank goodness the producers were persistent and stayed with us—and three years later we opened on Broadway.

Interviewer: Do you see yourself now as going forward as a director/ choreographer? If somebody said, "Choreograph my show," would that be a step back for you or not?

Marshall: I would never say, "I'm not going to just choreograph again." It would depend on the project. It would depend on the director, and it would depend on whether it was a dance-driven show. I don't think I'd be interested in choreographing a show that just had enhanced musical staging. I'd want to have something where I could have a little more authorship of it.

Interviewer: What about directing and not choreographing? Can you see yourself working with another choreographer?

Marshall: Well, as you get older, it takes longer and longer to warm up! That's a tricky thing. Rob Ashford is a great pal of mine who assisted me on *Kiss Me, Kate;* now he's the Tony Award–winning choreographer of *Thoroughly Modern Millie.* I feel like I'd love to work with him again; but I wonder whether I could back off enough and not be proprietary about it and want to hover and have control over everything. That's a good question.

Interviewer: I would think it would be very hard to give that up, because as a director/choreographer, you see the total show in terms of its movement, and to relinquish the responsibility for the movement would be very difficult.

Marshall: If I was doing something that had a very specific specialized movement that I don't do—say, a hip-hop musical—I could learn about it and figure it out; but if I could find somebody who really had the skills in that particular area, I'd probably use them. I'm not a great tap dancer, and if there was a big tap-dance musical, I might work with someone on that.

Interviewer: What do you think the future of the American musical is? The success of *Hairspray* and *The Producers* seems to indicate the continuing popularity of traditional musicals, but *Avenue Q* might be pointing us in a new direction, toward a younger audience with different expectations.

Marshall: Broadway always has been and I think always will consist of a lot of different flavors. I don't think that there's any single flavor that is going to dominate over everything. *Little Shop of Horrors* has families and kids and teenagers in the audience all the time loving it, and they're going to come back to see other musicals and not just revivals. Broadway also has always had very strong family musicals—*The Lion King, Beauty and the Beast,* and now *Hairspray*—and those kinds of shows are creating audiences. I was eleven years old when I saw my first Broadway musical in New York and fell in love with it, and I'm sure there are a lot of kids who are being taken to see those shows who will buy tickets on their own in twenty years. There are a lot of musicals now like *Avenue Q* and *Hairspray* that are attracting a younger audience and a new audience. In the glory days of the musicals of the 1940s and 1950s, it was a relatively new form. In the past twenty-five years, musicals have developed their shape. Here we are in the twenty-first century and we have basically seventy-five to eighty years' worth of American musical heritage to keep exploring. Nobody in England says, "Oh God, another *Hamlet*" or "Oh God, another Pinter play"; the fact that new generations want to see and explore classic plays is not seen as not moving forward. A new production of a classic show is fresh, it's exciting to see, and it's important to do. Nobody at the opera says, "Oh God, another *Carmen*" or "Oh God, another *La Bohème.*" It shouldn't be fifty years until the next Broadway production of *Wonderful Town*; I hope I get to see another one in my lifetime. The deriding of Broadway revivals makes me a little crazy, because I think they are very important.

At the same time, progress is happening. I'm excited to see *Caroline, or Change* reach Broadway. This year alone, we have *Avenue Q, Wicked,* and *Caroline, or Change,* three very different and new kinds of shows, and it's thrilling. With all of this bemoaning of the state of Broadway, you still can't get a theater for a Broadway musical. There are planes circling looking for a place to land because all the big houses for musicals are booked and unavailable. Yes, we hope that new writers come along, but it's harder today. Rodgers and Hart wrote a musical a year, sometimes two a year; they were produced, and they kept coming in every year. There's the economics of it now; it can't happen in six weeks. You can't expect a composing team to have a musical on Broadway every year. It's exciting when there are new writers, and you hope that everything keeps pushing the envelope, but that doesn't mean that we're going to burst through the envelope and never look back. Broadway is always going to have a lot of different things going on, because Broadway basically is entertainment. I don't mean that in a negative way, that it's fluff and mindless. It means that it has to be smartly done and has to be compelling. Let's face it, our greatest writers of musical theater have been showmen at heart—Irving Berlin and Cole Porter and Rodgers and Hammerstein and Sondheim. They know how to construct a show that draws you in, moves you, entertains you, delights you, and uplifts you; but they also are aware that they have an audience that they are trying to please. That doesn't necessarily mean that they're trying to factor it down to the most common denominator and make things mindless, but you do have to be aware that audiences want to be amused.

Interviewer: You've mentioned the fifty-year gap between Broadway productions of *Wonderful Town*. What were some of the specific differences between doing *Wonderful Town* in 1953 and doing it in 2003, with regard to style, with regard to a sense of a different audience? How did you stay honest to the piece while simultaneously being aware of the fifty-year gap between your production and the original?

Marshall: Because you have contemporary actors playing this, either they all have a great sense of style or a great sense of the kind of period comedy this is, and they naturally infuse it with energy. I think that our pace in 2004 is a faster pace. We're used to getting information faster, getting more of it, and processing it faster; so we trimmed the book down a bit, and in that way the tempo of the piece moved more. I feel that when you're doing a revival like this, you don't have to impose any kind of modern political correctness on top of it such as modern feminist ideals, because you know Donna Murphy playing Ruth Sherwood and Jennifer Westfeldt playing Eileen are such strong, vibrant, and wonderful women. They bring a contemporary edge to it naturally just because of who they are and their own strength as women and as actresses. In that way, I feel like it naturally gives it a new spin. I also think that because of the way we designed this production, it was not as literal. We didn't have full sets and fourth wall; everything was more representational, which gave it more modernity, too. Also, we cut down some of the transition music because obviously we were getting faster from one thing to another than they did originally.

Interviewer: Isn't the audience at a show like *Wonderful Town* watching it with two simultaneous awarenesses? They know that they are watching an older show and they also know they're watching a new version of it?

Marshall: They're forgiving in that way. There's a line in the show when Wreck says to his future mother-in-law, "What are you lookin' at, you old bat?" and I couldn't believe it, the audience laughed every time! I just shrugged my shoulders and said, "I don't get it"—but they laughed. Also, *Wonderful Town* isn't a new old show. It's truly vintage, so it's authentic in that it was written by very smart writers. It's based on a hit play and has a brilliant score and lyrics by two of the best comic lyricists Broadway has ever produced. I think that authenticity shows through. It's harder when you try to do a new musical that feels like an old musical.

Interviewer: Isn't it fatal to try to update a show like that?

Marshall: Yes. With *Kiss Me, Kate,* I had no problem knowing that this musical was written fifty years ago and that it was based on a play that was written five hundred years ago. What's amazing is how much still resonates as opposed to what doesn't work. One thing that Encores! has taught me is to allow the material and the performers to shine.

Interviewer: It's interesting that you talk about trusting the material, because so often today, both with plays and musicals, one sees directors who want to add their "stamp" because they apparently don't trust the material.

Marshall: Quite honestly, I feel that sometimes what you've got to do is get out of the way. Your hand is there in getting everybody into the room, but once you've gotten them in the room, let 'em go. Broadway musical performers are like thoroughbreds. When they are at the top of their game, there is nothing like it. There is nothing more thrilling than seeing a Broadway musical performer, in a role that fits them, giving 100 percent; so you just have to set up the craft and let 'em loose, let 'em run. That energy created in the theater is why live theater will always be vital, because you can't get that experience at a movie, in your living room, on a videotape, or on a computer.

Harold Prince

Harold Prince was born on January 30, 1928, in New York City. He was educated at the University of Pennsylvania (B.A., 1948). He has worked as a director, producer, and playwright. The musicals he has directed and produced include She Loves Me (1963), It's a Bird . . . It's a Plane . . . It's Superman (1966), Cabaret (1966), Zorbá (1968), Company (1970), Follies (1971), A Little Night Music (1973), Candide (1974), Pacific Overtures (1976), On the Twentieth Century (1978), Sweeney Todd (1979), Evita (1979), Merrily We Roll Along (1981), A Doll's Life (1982), Grind (1985), and Bounce (2003). He has directed the musicals A Family Affair (1962), Baker Street (1965), On the Twentieth Century (1978), Evita (1979), Roza (1987), The Phantom of the Opera (1988), Kiss of the Spider Woman (1993), The Petrified Prince (1994), Show Boat (1994), and Parade (1998).

He produced the musicals The Pajama Game *(1954)*, Damn Yankees *(1955)*, New Girl in Town *(1957)*, West Side Story *(1957)*, Fiorello! *(1959)*, Tenderloin *(1960)*, A Funny Thing Happened on the Way to the Forum *(1962)*, Fiddler on the Roof *(1964)*, *and* Flora, the Red Menace *(1965)*. *He wrote the play* Grandchild of Kings *(1991)*. *He has directed the films* Something for Everyone *(1970)*, A Little Night Music *(1977)*, *and* Sweeney Todd *(1982)*.

He has won Tony Awards for The Pajama Game *(Best Musical)*, Damn Yankees *(Best Musical)*, Fiorello! *(Best Musical)*, A Funny Thing Happened on the Way to the Forum *(Best Musical and Best Producer of a Musical)*, Fiddler on the Roof *(Best Musical and Best Producer of a Musical)*, Cabaret *(Best Musical and Best Director)*, Company *(Best Musical and Best Director)*, Follies *(Best Director)*, Fiddler on the Roof *(Special Award)*, A Little Night Music *(Best Musical)*, Candide *(Best Director and Special Award)*, Sweeney Todd *(Best Director)*, Evita *(Best Director)*, The Phantom of the Opera *(Best Director)*, *and* Show Boat *(Best Director)*. *He was elected to the Theatre Hall of Fame in 1982. In 1994, he received the Kennedy Center Honors; in 2000, he was awarded the National Medal of the Arts.*

This interview took place on November 2, 1992. Harold Prince made additions to it in September 2004.

•────────────────────────────────•

Interviewer: In general, are you optimistic or pessimistic about the future of the American musical?

Prince: Let me answer that with a story. Some years ago, I had a show at the Kennedy Center called *End of the World* by Arthur Kopit, which I loved. I was sitting around talking with the cast; I was telling anecdotes, and suddenly a little light went off, saying, "God, don't start doing anecdotes. You've been around thirty years. You're going to get into that thing where you don't direct any more and all you do is tell anecdotes. Then they'll tell other people that's what you do. I've heard that all my life about older directors; just stop right now." So in the middle of talking about the good old days, I suddenly stopped myself and chastised myself in front of the company—whereupon the youngest member of the company, a young girl, raised her hand and said something very sad. She said, "We know what you're saying. Don't stop. But we also want you to know something else. We all know that it indeed *was* better in those days." I suspect that that's the first time that was ever true, and that's very sad. I think it *was* better. I think it will always have been better, and the question I ask myself is "Could anyone today have the career I've been lucky enough to have in the theater since 1954?" Sadly, I think the answer is no. Now you can have a wonderful life in the theater, but you can't have the kind of life I've had, which is the kind of life Sondheim has had. Unfortunately, I think that kind of life is over.

Interviewer: On that happy note, let me take you back to the good old days. In 1948, you went to work for the legendary director/playwright/producer George Abbott as, in a sense, an intern. What were some of the things that you learned from this incredible master of the musical theater that you have kept in mind throughout your career?

Prince: He was the most disciplined, no-nonsense man I ever knew. He didn't think the theater was a crazy, self-indulgent arena where we can be late, can indulge our emotions, and can panic publicly. We all panic, but you go somewhere and panic on your own time quietly. He was totally disciplined and respectful of all the people he was working with and respectful of the process. He was incredibly honest. This was a man who had a reputation for inventing the American farce where the doors slam all the time, but I never heard him or saw him direct anyone to slam a door if it wasn't valid in terms of the character and the situation. Over the years, there's been something called "the Abbott touch," and I've gone to theaters often and seen people slam doors to no effect, because it was funny or "Wouldn't it be fun there to make a noise and leave the room?" It doesn't work, because of course it all must come from some deep basic prevailing honesty; that informed all his work. And there's one other thing. He told me that the best thing you could do if you wanted a long life in the theater was to be sure that you had an appointment at ten o'clock the next morning after an opening to work on another show. You can figure that one out. If the reviews are bad, it certainly is a good idea to know you're still working. If the reviews are good, you can say, "I wish I'd stayed in bed," but still it's exhilarating to move on. It also is a metaphor for not looking back—and I never knew him to look back. I never knew him to tell any anecdotes in all the years I knew him, so I didn't listen to him on that score.

Interviewer: Is that sort of mentoring that you had from Abbott happening today? Where does a young person go to learn how to direct musical theater?

Prince: That method, no, of course not, but it works in my office. I have had apprentices all the way back for twenty-five years, and some of them are doing quite well. But there aren't many offices like mine, and there aren't many people who've been around that long. The process of handing the baton along used to be standard. Remember, there was not a lot of regional theater; there was summer stock. We didn't learn a hell of a lot in summer stock except what a nice thing it would be to meet a star on Sunday who was going to be in the show the following week and bring him coffee; you didn't learn about making good theater that way. All the experience you got was confined essentially to the New York area, from which the road companies went across the country. In those days, there were twenty or thirty expert, respected directors, just as many composers and lyricists, and twenty or thirty active producers who turned out at least one new production every year. If they were great successes, those Rodgers and Hart musicals ran a season, not from September to June but from November to May, and yet those are some of the biggest hits from that team. If you closed in May, you had to have another show ready the following season if you were going to keep going. That's what they all did; they wrote a show every single year. No one would think of doing that anymore, because you wouldn't get it on. No money. So—finally!—the answer to your question is that, today, you must go and work in the regional theater. The problem is that there aren't many musicals done in regional theaters. Also, regional theaters can't usually provide the composers, the book-writer, and the director with all the accoutrements that often go with musicals—which is to say full orchestras. Sondheim very sadly said to me when *Assassins* originally opened at Playwrights Horizons, "Is this it? Am I reduced to writing shows for three instruments for the rest of my life?" That from Steve Sondheim! I think he's feeling a little sorrier for himself than he should, but it's not an out-of-order question at all. What we need is to fill that gap with regional theaters that can cater to the musical form, be it small or large.

Interviewer: So frequently through the years, you have pushed the bounds of musical theater. Did you ever consciously go out intending to be innovative?

Prince: No, not in the least. I'm just serving my own taste. Most of the shows that I was lucky enough to produce were not the sort of shows that I could have directed. *West Side Story* is an example of something I would love to have directed, but I couldn't have. It was so predominantly choreographic that I couldn't have gone near it and accomplished it. Most of those shows were the work of another artist, and I was there to serve him.

Interviewer: You don't think, then, in terms of what is risky or what the audience is likely to like?

Prince: No, not remotely. If I had, I wouldn't have done some of these things for a minute. One of the main shows my career's identified with, *Follies*, lost all of the money invested in it, and yet my success as a director is identified with shows like it. That's the irony. It's a wonderful circumstance to be in. I was never encouraged to worry about whether a show was going to make money or not. The shows that I didn't direct were all blockbusters at the box office. The very first show I directed from scratch was *She Loves Me,* and it was a lovely show that lost all its money for the investors. The next one also lost all its money, and the third one did so as well, so by the time I got to the next one, though it was exactly what I wanted to do, I decided that if that did not make its money I was never going to be able to raise the scratch required to put on a musical, which in those days was all of $250,000. That next show turned out to be *Cabaret,* so I was encouraged to go on.

Interviewer: But when you brought *Cabaret* back after twenty years, you said, "Here are some additions that we thought originally were a little too risky." What sort of censoring process did you go through on that show when you first did it?

Prince: Remember, at that time, we were phasing out one kind of traditional musical into something else. The whole shape of that show was very different from other shows and influenced a dozen subsequent musicals. It didn't even occur to us to deal more overtly with the homosexuality. Look at all the musicals that preceded that one. Almost every one had two serious leads and two comic leads—and that includes *Carousel, Oklahoma!, The Pajama Game, Damn Yankees, Fiorello!,* and so on. We were not even in that frame of mind. I was much more interested at that point in breaking the shape of a musical. That was the first time in my life—and thank God for it, because it was almost happenstance—where I flew blind and thought, "I've never seen this before. What the hell!" It was very frightening, but when it worked it was very encouraging.

Interviewer: Then, twenty years later, what did you do differently?

Prince: Twenty years later, we said, "What did we do wrong?" We understood that twenty years later there was a whole other mindset, and we realized that we had not dealt with the homosexuality at all and that it was intrinsic to the story and to the initial source material. So we decided to deal with it—and we did. There were numbers in the original production that were conventional love songs between people. We examined cutting all of them or some of them out. A very chastened director found me in London two weeks ago backstage at *Kiss of the Spider Woman* and said, "I'm not sure I should be telling you this. I'm directing *Cabaret* in Nottingham, and we've taken all the book scenes out of the show. We've diminished the love story, and it seems like it's going to be a powerhouse." I said, "You've done everything we should have done, but we got there too early. I'm sure it will be simply wonderful that way."

Interviewer: Can you think of any other shows you have done that, were you to revive them today, you might consider being more daring or pushing the bounds more?

Prince: Yes. There is a show that Comden and Green and I did together called *A Doll's Life* that I have enormous respect for. We didn't get it right, but we got a lot of it right. I don't think I want to go back and get the rest of it right—I just did that with *Spider Woman*—but that's a show that somebody should take, roll up his sleeves, and remove the treacle and all the diversion. Mind you, we didn't sit down and say, "Let's divert the audience." Comden and Green came up with a very serious notion for a musical, and the best of it was that part. The weaknesses were the parts where they went back to what they knew had served them well over their careers. That's something that I struggle with all the time, the difference between expressing yourself and repeating yourself. Sometimes it's very hard to find that distinction. Sometimes you repeat yourself because you've done it before and it works and you know it. But sometimes you say, "I mustn't do that. That's rather like something I did before." If a great artist said, "I've painted that before," he'd have painted six paintings, not six hundred paintings. You have to know that it's an expression of your vision of things, your politics, your priorities, and your style, rather than just a feeding off something you did earlier. Sometimes it's very hard to define.

Interviewer: I know you're very fond of the original production of *Follies.* Can you see that being revived? If so, would you make changes in that show?

Prince: There may be some thought of a revival of *Follies,* but it wouldn't be mine. I think I persuaded Steve Sondheim that that's a bad idea. I've never worked so close to the bone on material. I thought we were all working as if we were on fire—Michael Bennett, me, Steve, Jim Goldman, the performers. I don't think we could ever duplicate it. Without saying it's my favorite show, I do think very highly of it. I did see the London production and it was a very, very painful experience for me, because Steve had been talked into throwing out some of the numbers and putting in surrogate numbers that weren't as good. The whole show was done totally realistically, with tables, chairs, and a party. There was no magic at all. I was proprietary, so I was ill-humored about it. There was going to be a movie version, and I was going to do it at MGM. My idea was to make it about movies and about the last night of MGM, because you could see that that was actually happening. I said, "Why don't we get every movie star in Hollywood to come for this party? I'll give the party, and we'll talk to the stars about theater." Joan Crawford wanted to sing "Broadway Baby," and Bette Davis wanted to sing "I'm Still Here." We had all that lined up and I said, "If all the other people, the Lana Turners and the Dorothy Lamours, come, we'll pay them a stipend and give all the money to charity." All of that was put in the pipeline, and MGM did *That's Entertainment* instead because it was cheaper.

Interviewer: As long as you've brought up the subject of movies, relatively few of the musicals you've directed have been made into films. Is there any reason for that?

Prince: Hollywood made movies of the first two shows I produced, *The Pajama Game* and *Damn Yankees,* and they were almost identical to the originals. At that point, totally coincidentally, the movie musical no longer was popular. That was the end of the great MGM years. From then on, very few musicals were done. *On a Clear Day* was done with Barbra Streisand, but very few others. *West Side Story,* of course, was a great success, but there were not any others that I can think of. *Hello, Dolly!* was a major film, but it was not a gigantic success. *Fiddler on the Roof* was made and did wonderfully well at the box office, though I didn't think it was equal to the stage production, and then *Cabaret* was a big hit. So, in fact, they *were* made periodically, but the interest in making them doesn't exist any more. I think as the musical gets more and more a matter for black boxes, it gets to be more dependent on what there is about the stage that's unique to the stage. What is there about the stage that you can't put on television and you can't put on film? And those are the musicals that are most successful now; look at *A Chorus Line* and *Phantom of the Opera.* The movie of *A Chorus Line* is a perfect example; they "opened it up," but to what end? It was awful.

Interviewer: But *Cabaret* was very stage-specific and yet made a very good film, didn't it?

Prince: I think that the stage production and the film were two totally different entities. There was a lot of spoken dialogue added to the film version of *Cabaret,* which gave it guts. And they went with the original story of homosexuality, so they made many right choices. But they ignored the trajectory of the Emcee from pathetic entertainer to fascist, a metaphor for Germany after the Depression. I regret that.

Interviewer: To get back to the stage musicals, what about *Company*? That's a show that seems very much of its time, the early 1970s. Could it be revived, and if so, would there be changes you would make?

Prince: Musicals age faster than straight plays, and you never know when they're going to seem to have aged or why. There's a hump in the middle where they don't work as contemporary musicals and they haven't yet worked as a piece of history. I don't know where *Company* is, but I'm going to have a sense of it very soon. They're putting the original cast of *Company* together for a concert in Long Beach, California, next January. They've got absolutely everybody but one poor fellow who died and Merle Louise, who's in *Spider Woman* in London, but everyone else will be there—including Dean Jones. It will be very interesting to try to see in my head whether it would still seem fresh or whether some of it's dated.

Interviewer: What is it that you look for in a show? What does it take for you to want to spend what could be years of your life on a musical?

Prince: It's very often an instant reaction. I used to say blithely, "What do I want to see? I'll go work on something I'd like to see, because I'm tired of seeing the same old thing." To some extent that's true. Certainly, with *Phantom of the Opera,* what I wouldn't do to go to a theater and have a romantic, theatrical experience and lose myself in another place and time with a lot of incense and drapery. It's something, of course, I'd never gone near before, and this was the time for that. In another case, Comden and Green asked, "What do you suppose happened after Nora slammed the door in *A Doll's House?*" That's very intriguing for me: "What *did* happen to her?" *Company* was a series of seven one-act plays, and Steve Sondheim said, "A friend of mine wrote these, and Kim Stanley's going to play in them. Will you read them? Something is wrong with this project." I read them and they were of varying lengths, and I had a vision of Kim Stanley, who was one of the greatest American actresses I've ever seen, offstage changing costumes and putting on wigs rather than onstage playing the seven plays. I thought, "She's going to be exhausted doing this thing—and it's a trick. Of course they're worried about it. Of course George Furth thinks this isn't quite right." Then I said, "I think it's a musical." "About what?" "About marriage." Both Steve and George were stunned, but then we started to meet and go from there. Many times, it's an almost whimsical blurting out of "This would make a musical," and sometimes that blurting gets you into terrible trouble. It has with me.

Interviewer: I find it interesting that you want audiences to think, and perhaps even to think politically, at your musicals. Don't audiences want to go to a musical just to be entertained?

Prince: There are certainly some audiences who do. They go to see *42nd Street* and make somebody wealthy. I went to see *42nd Street* and I admired the craft and scratched my head and didn't know why I was there; I appreciated the craft but not the show. But the years change a person; when I saw the revival of *42nd Street* a couple of years ago, I was enchanted. We're talking about what I want to see when I go to the theater. Too often when I go to the theater, I don't see what I want to see.

Interviewer: In your book *Contradictions,* when you talk about the need for motivation for you in a musical, you say that if you had directed *Bye Bye Birdie* you would have screwed it up.

Prince: I would have screwed up *Hello, Dolly!* I was offered *Hello, Dolly!* I had just done a very good production of *The Matchmaker,* the Thornton Wilder play on which the musical was based, that was touring New York State, and that's why the producer, David Merrick, offered *Hello, Dolly!* to me. He had the composer, Jerry Herman, come to my office. He started to play the score, and I said to him very patronizingly (I was much more patronizing thirty years ago than I dare be now), "'Hello, Dolly, it's so nice to have you back where you belong.' Did you read the play? She was never there. The idea is that this is a whole new life that she's grabbing before it's too late. What are you talking about?" He just gently folded his music and left the office. Gower Champion did it and that's that. Did I ever regret it? No, of course not. I went to see the show and I appreciated it, but it was not something I would have done. Mine would have been a much more depressing version.

Interviewer: How would you have made *Bye Bye Birdie* depressing?

Prince: I don't know, but I would have found a way!

Interviewer: In the 1970s, your career gradually changed from producing to directing. Many people feel that one of the biggest lacks in the musical theater today is the absence of producers with vision. Do you agree?

Prince: Thoroughly. For years you'd read in the newspapers that the Shubert organization or the Nederlander organization would say, "There's nothing wrong with the theater that more product wouldn't solve." You see the word *product* and you know they're all wrong. There's plenty of product, but it needs nurturing, it needs love, and it needs money to get it on. The truth is that what we most lack is producers, because if we had the producers, the directors who are so talented would have more chance to stretch and get experience and do shows in front of audiences. So, indeed, would the composers and lyricists and book-writers. The first show that Steve Sondheim wrote was a flop. The first show that Kander and Ebb wrote was a flop. The first show that Bock and Harnick wrote was a flop. The first show I directed was a flop. But we all went right back to the same arena, the most difficult arena, the Broadway theater, and did our second show. In almost every instance, the second show worked—not in my case, but in theirs. There's a lot to be said for all the trappings that professional productions give you: the best scenery if your taste is good, the best designers, the most talented performers, and a large audience. One of the things that is inhibiting the musical form is that wonderfully talented people are forced to work in hundred-seat theaters. That will work for certain material, but I wouldn't want to see *Phantom of the Opera* in a workshop.

Interviewer: If you see a lack of producers with vision as a major problem, why aren't you producing?

Prince: Because I never liked it in the first place. I never wanted to do it, but you don't look a gift horse named George Abbott in the mouth. I wanted to be a playwright and I wasn't good enough, so the nearest thing to it was directing. I never wanted to perform; I don't know the first thing about it. Directing was it, and directing is juicy and terrific and, in fact, ultimately more enjoyable for me than playwriting would have been, because I don't like the solitary business. I love the whole elaborate, complicated collaboration. When I do a play that doesn't have music, dance, and an orchestra, I feel cheated. I keep waiting for the overture, but it's not there.

Interviewer: Were the years of producing, then, a matter of learning the business?

Prince: Yes, learning the business, because I had to; I had to be awfully good as a producer the first time out, and I was. What I learned quickly was that what I didn't know I could cover by saying no: "Don't spend the money. Get the money back to the investors." Also, since I did turn out to be a director, I had taste. Ruth Mitchell, my assistant for thirty-five years, asked me when I started directing the shows I was producing, "Do you remember how you used to say no to Jerry Robbins and then sometimes you said yes? What did you use to define the reply?" I said, "I used to put it into the artistic head and ask whether he was indulging himself or this was artistically valuable." I was judging him, but I did have the purse strings. She became that with me. For all the years that I was producing as well as directing, the minute I asked for something, she'd come and repeat the Jerry Robbins question. Then I'd have to put on that other hat temporarily and often say, "No, you're right. Forget it."

Interviewer: I believe you say in your book that *Follies* didn't make any money because it cost too much. Was that producer Hal Prince not being tough enough on director Hal Prince?

Prince: No. It was the most elaborate musical probably ever done, certainly the most elaborate that I've seen. It had hundreds of Ziegfeld Follies costumes and the most elaborate scenery; it cost $800,000 to do. Any other producer at that time would have spent double that to do it, although no other producer would have had it to spend. We watched it very carefully, and then we lost the whole $800,000.

Interviewer: You've been very closely associated with two of the most important composers of the musical theater today, Stephen Sondheim and Andrew Lloyd Webber. In what ways would you say they are similar and different to work with?

Prince: They share one similarity. They both have terrific theatrical heads; they have an instinct about theater. They do anything to serve that, and they get excited about it. They're totally professional; it's as if they worked for George Abbott. They're totally disciplined, and I have never had a scene with them or seen them have a scene with someone else. There's never been an indulgent, histrionic moment from either of them in my presence. Where do they differ? They're as different as their work, and it's astonishingly different. The fact that Steve writes his own lyrics gives him a freedom that Andrew doesn't have. Andrew writes in England, where the musical theater tradition is not as solidly based as here, so it became very difficult for him to find lyricists. That's why I think so many of his shows have been sung through. When you take the operatic tradition and do *recitativo,* you don't have to rhyme and the listening is different. I don't think people listen to lyrics the way they listen to spoken dialogue. They sit down, the music washes over them, and soon they're not quite listening. That's why reprises are so popular and why simple lyrics are so prevalent.

Interviewer: Isn't it the director's challenge to get the audience to listen more carefully?

Prince: It certainly is. I just opened *Kiss of the Spider Woman* last Tuesday night in London, and with that show I vividly remember saying, "No, no, no. Don't musicalize that. Let's save Terrence McNally's scene and have them say that. People will listen more carefully." Everybody nodded and appreciated that, and it stayed that way.

Interviewer: By opening *Spider Woman* in London, you've benefited from the fact that theater in England is government-subsidized. Do you think that American theater should or could have a similar sort of system?

Prince: It's never going to happen here. Do I think it's a good idea for this country? No, not until many other ideas are exhausted first, because I think that an awful lot of valuable money is wasted on the wrong priorities. I would rather it be out there. I've spent all my life saying that being in the marketplace is not a dirty word. All the artists we admire came out of the marketplace. I hate all that high-falutin', talking-down-your-nose stuff that has emerged with the phrase *not for profit,* the self-congratulatory thing that's out there. That's the part I don't admire. You have to know one thing: There is money to be made in the musical form. I don't know so much about the drama, but certainly with the musical, if you come up with something good—and it doesn't have to be treacle; it can indeed be *Cabaret, West Side Story,* or *Fiddler on the Roof*—you can make money. Those shows would be successful today.

Interviewer: *Spider Woman* started as part of a project you originated to foster the development of new musicals. Can you tell us about it? How did it start? Why didn't it work? What, in retrospect, might you have done differently?

Prince: I was not part of the administration of that project. I was just a fellow goading other people by saying, "Somebody somewhere give us a theater where we can do new musicals experimentally and keep the critics out, sort of glorified workshops." The only thing that made them different from workshops is that workshops have no scenery and no costumes and are generally turned into nothing more than backers' auditions—and backers don't understand a show without all the trappings. I said, "Let's go somewhere and do that," and a fellow named Marty Bell said, "I want to do that badly. I will find the money." He went right out and got ABC, some theater owners, and others to put up money. The deal was that there would be no critics. We found a theater at the State University of New York at Purchase, about an hour and thirty minutes away from Manhattan, and we went about our business to do *Spider Woman*. The other thing I counted on was that there were eleven new musicals aside from ours, half a dozen of which had already been picked, that would go through that same process, three a season, for the next four years. I said, "The one thing wrong with this project is that Terrence McNally, John Kander, Fred Ebb, and Hal Prince don't need this. We can get a show produced. This is for those other people." They said, "We can't get the money for those other people without opening with your show."

So we opened *Spider Woman,* and the critics immediately said, "We never said we wouldn't come." I could never adjudicate who was telling the truth. We went hat in hand to the *New York Times* and said, "Don't do this. There's a show following this one called *The Secret Garden* and another one following that called *My Favorite Year*. These are shows that are actually going to happen, and they will be jeopardized if you come and go sour on the project." I can't prove it, but I think there's an agenda in New York that if you can put it on a stage the size of, say, Playwrights Horizons, you can then blow it up and put it on the stage of the Winter Garden; but you can't, because the material makes different requirements of you. It doesn't work that way. Anyway, they came, and the show was clearly not right. Actually, one of the reasons we so quickly acquiesced and agreed to be the first show was that we knew it wasn't right and we didn't know what was wrong with it. What wasn't right became very clear and what was right also became clear. What happened then was that we discovered that the money for the other eleven shows was not in hand but was based on additional payments after the success of the first show. We had no idea that was the case. Everybody just backed away and the project went dead. At that point, speaking for my collaborators and me, it was, next to *Merrily We Roll Along,* the lowest point in my life in the theater. In this instance, I felt betrayed. With *Merrily* I just felt I did a bad job, so that's a different thing.

Interviewer: Betrayed by whom—the critics?

Prince: Betrayed perhaps by the backers of the project, and certainly by the critics. The *New York Times* looked us in the eye and said, "You're news. That's why we have to come. We're not coming because it's theater; we're coming because you're news. When you do something, we have to be there." I thought, "Why? Who said? What's news? Everything's news now; the most trivial thing is news." Anyway, we felt betrayed on all sides and felt that we had betrayed the actors, who had committed themselves to it for no reviews and no money. No one was getting regular salaries. They were all traveling an hour and a half, twice a day, to do this show. The good part of the story is that after a year, during which I couldn't talk anybody in our country into letting us do *Spider Woman* again, I was able to talk a Canadian, Garth Drabinsky, into financing a brand-new production, providing that we reworked the material. There's about 40 percent new music in the show, some of the best stuff. We reworked the book totally and recast and redesigned the show. Garth read what we were doing and committed himself to it. We went to Toronto, opened there, and had a very welcoming experience. We went to London, where the reviews were mostly wonderful. We seem to be the first show in five years that's actually going to make it in the West End, and that's exciting. And now we're coming to Broadway in April. What's interesting about all this is that we proved our point, but there are no new musicals left for anybody to benefit from it. What I'm hoping is that somebody will analyze it and say, "See, they were right after all" and re-create a new-musicals project farther from New York and open it with less than the likes of us.

Interviewer: So is the new plan to save money international tryouts?

Prince: No, that was *this* plan. I think it's a very dangerous thing. We are the first American, actually Canadian, musical with mostly an American cast to open in London before it played here. That's unique. Is that a game plan? Not remotely.

Interviewer: In the end, was the decision to do the show in Canada originally more about avoiding the New York critics or about the finances?

Prince: There are critics in Canada, and they can be very difficult; they can be the like of any critics in our own country. I've seen that, not with *Spider Woman* but with *Phantom.* The truth is that we went there because there was a man there willing to give our show a first-class production, to love it, and not to worry about what happened in America. All the American producers, as I said, wouldn't go near it; it's like gambling on a horse race. Too much of the commercial theater is seen as win or lose—which is no way to create theater.

Interviewer: Let's talk about some other developmental possibilities. You've said that you don't really care for the workshopping process.

Prince: It's almost dead. I'd like to say, "I told you so," because I knew it in the beginning. I knew that what was going to happen was that these fat cats with millions of dollars would come in with checkbooks and they wouldn't make out the checks. They would leave saying, "It's not good enough." There have been a few exceptions—*Nine* is one—but not many.

Interviewer: *A Chorus Line* certainly comes to mind.

Prince: *A Chorus Line* is not an exception, because it's a totally different thing. *A Chorus Line*, oddly enough, did exactly the same thing we did years earlier with *Candide*. It opened in a prestigious Off-Broadway theater, the critics came and loved it, and it moved to Broadway. It was a wonderful show, but the workshop element of it had to do with it being written by the very people who performed it.

Interviewer: Isn't that a true workshop, as opposed to the backers' audition sort of thing you mentioned?

Prince: That *is* a true workshop, but when you come in with a book and music and lyrics and you say we're going to workshop a show, I think you'd better get the promise that you're going to have the scenery, the costumes, the orchestra, the orchestrations, and the choreographer.

Interviewer: We mentioned regional theater briefly earlier. You've been wary about developing musicals in the regional theater, but you did do a show there called *Roza*.

Prince: I didn't want to come to New York with that show. It was terrific in the regional theater, where it just kept getting extended, and it would have been a very valuable copyright for the authors if they hadn't insisted on coming to New York. I said, "Don't come to New York with this. They'll slaughter us." But they wanted to—and we were slaughtered.

Interviewer: Is that a comment on what people outside New York, in the so-called hinterlands, will accept?

Prince: No. As a matter of fact, regional theater audiences are frequently much more open and often more discerning. There can be a very codified thing that happens in New York. I'll give you an example. Is London the hinterlands? Let's say it is. If London is the hinterlands, *Phantom of the Opera*, had it opened originally in New York, would have been perhaps one-tenth the success that it is—and it certainly, as far as I'm concerned, represents the greatest box office success that I'll ever be attached to and perhaps that anyone will ever be attached to. But it had to open in London first, in that hinterland. Why *Roza* worked is that it was a single set show with no moving parts and one set of costumes for everyone. It could have just as easily have opened at Playwrights Horizons and played to ninety-nine people. The reason that I find I can't work in the regional theater is that there is no place where, for example, I could have done *Kiss of the Spider Woman*. It's very complex scenically.

Interviewer: How has *Spider Woman* changed from its original incarnation at the theater in Purchase?

Prince: In Purchase, it was as if we were doing a late-1940s MGM musical. Half, if not more than half, of the show was concerned with a Rita

Hayworth clone doing a forties musical. It seemed to be much more concerned with escape than with the subject at hand. Now Terrence McNally and Kander and Ebb are dealing with the subject at hand. The show is now another 25 percent different from what it was in Toronto. Toward the end of the summer, Kander and Ebb put in new numbers and we added new scenery and new costumes.

Interviewer: How important are stars to the success of a show?

Prince: They are important only if they are the most appropriate people for their specific roles. I've been around so long; I saw Ethel Merman on the stage in too many flops not to know that the greatest star of the musical stage could be in a show that didn't work. That has always been so. Stars may get you an advance, but the minute that the iron door closes on the show the audience evaporates. The ideal star is Angela Lansbury, because she's a brilliant actress and a star. What could be nicer? She also is the kind of performer who looks like she studied with George Abbott, because she, too, is thoroughly disciplined.

Interviewer: As a director, you've been described—and I think it was meant as a compliment!—as a control freak. Is that a good definition of what's necessary to run a major musical?

Prince: I do like to oversee a whole lot, but I don't think I'm a control freak at all. The implication of the term *control freak* is that I'm not open to collaborators' opinions; I would say that I am as open as anyone I've ever known who does this. Collaboration is regenerative; when I hit a stone wall, the answer is out there, and not necessarily with me. The generalship thing is fun, but it's not as much fun as being in a small room with five actors and having them be so good that you go in in the morning thinking, "This is the way it's going to work. This is what the dynamic of the scene will be"—and then you have an Angela Lansbury try something else, which just switches everything around. That's a gift.

Interviewer: I do think of your staging as being very exact, with great attention to detail. Is that your intention?

Prince: I think that in the best shows I've done, that detail has been augmented by the scenery. I anguish over the scenery for a year or eighteen months; I start working on it when the show isn't even written yet, because it will affect the completion of the writing of the show. When I go to see a show of mine that someone else does, it's invariably in a smaller venue, and invariably the critics say that it's far better than the production I did originally. There's a little bitterness in this fellow every once in a while if you just listen carefully! I rarely go to see those shows, but when I have, they've usually been very close in motor energy and blueprint to the one that I did. I think I trapped them in the production somehow or other, and they don't try to get away from it. If you take a show like *Evita,* it's awfully hard to get away from that show when you do it again—and I've not seen anybody do that yet.

Interviewer: The term *concept musical* is one that you don't hear much anymore. I wonder whether it's gone the way of workshopping, or have we just assimilated it into what we do in the musical theater? What is a concept musical?

Prince: It's what somebody named something that Steve and I were doing on our first or second show. It's nonsense. If I'm going to take the term seriously, what is it? It means the guys doing the show knew the beginning, the middle, the end, and the whole trajectory of the piece before they went into rehearsal. It sounds naïve, but there are some wonderful directors around who can give you the most beautiful, sensitive reading of a scene but don't know the beginning, the middle, and the end—and they get into deep trouble. If you know where you're headed and there's an arc over the whole evening, that then feeds the scenery, the costumes, and the motor. I'm very concerned about the motor of a musical. What is its style—smooth and seamless or abrasive and abrupt?

Interviewer: Would you agree that your production of *Phantom of the Opera* is a prime example of that principle at work? There were people who loved the staging of that show but had difficulties with its book.

Prince: Yes. With that show, I thought that it was very important that we got all the senses working. I wanted the audience to think they smelled incense even though we didn't have it on the stage—and people did. Yes, that is where the term *concept musical* may well be applicable. I wanted the mood of the piece to saturate everything.

Interviewer: You've said that your shows are subject to harsher criticism just because they're your shows. Do you really think that is so?

Prince: It must be true. It sounds as if there's a tinge of paranoia, but looking away from me at other people—at Steve Sondheim, other people—if you've been around a long time and you have a body of work, then your work is subject to comparison with what preceded it. If you're a new boy in town, it's much easier. My father-in-law is a composer and was a good friend of Cole Porter. He and Porter were having dinner one night toward the end of Porter's life and Porter said, "Until *Kiss Me, Kate,* I had thirty years of reading reviews that said, 'Not up to his usual standard.' I thought my usual standard was so bad by then that I could get by with it, but no."

Interviewer: You're about to do a revival of *Show Boat.* Why is Hal Prince interested in a revival of *Show Boat?*

Prince: Because I don't think it's a revival. I was very intrigued by the multicassette version of all the songs that were cut out of *Show Boat* and the other songs that were in various versions. You could take ten songs out and put ten other songs in; they're all there. Also, I've seen *Show Boat* and I've never liked all of it. I've always liked the first act but had trouble with the second, because it seemed to go awry. There are many reasons why it went awry. The opening of the second act of *Show Boat* takes place at the Chicago World's Fair, and it has nothing to do with the leading characters in this very tight story. Why? Because it's the only book show that Florenz Ziegfeld produced, and he said naggingly, "Unless I get some Ziegfeld Girls somewhere in this evening, I'm not going to go on with this thing." So they gave him the Chicago World's Fair, and some nearly naked girls came out and danced. After that scene, they went on with the story. I was asked whether I'd be interested in a revival of it, and I decided that it would not have to be a recycled revival. I talked to Bill Hammerstein—who represented the rights and is an old friend or he never would have listened to me—and said, "I would like to redo this book. I would like to tell the second act in a much straighter line, stay with the people, and replot a little. It's not a big rewriting job, but I'd like to be allowed to do that. Then I would like to put in songs." "What songs?" "The gambling song, 'Mis'ry's Comin' 'Round.'" "Why do you want to put in 'Mis'ry's Comin' 'Round'? That's so depressing, Hal. That's why they took it out." "Because it won't be depressing anymore. That was 1927; this will be 1993." He said, "All right. Do it all. But how are we going to know?" I said, "I'll take actors and we'll sit in a room for a week and I'll do a workshop for you. They won't stand on their feet. They'll just sit around and we'll do the whole show. They will sing all the music and they'll speak all the lines." We got Bobby Morse to play Cap'n Andy; he was thrilling and will be thrilling again. We did a first-class workshop, and Billy said, "I didn't believe it. I believe it. Go for it." And that's the show.

Interviewer: You've mentioned that *Merrily We Roll Along*, the last show you've done with Sondheim, was one of the low points of your career. It was originally cast with teenagers—it takes place over many years of the characters' lives—but subsequent productions have used adult actors. What are your feelings about that show? What went wrong?

Prince: I didn't do any of the versions that followed the original. I considered it the worst work I'd ever done. One of the reasons is that I never had a view of what it should look like. Here it is twelve years later and I still don't know, so I guess I don't know. By the way, I think it's one of Sondheim's best scores, so it's a tragedy that it isn't there to be seen. They have now done it three times that I know of, once outside of London, with actors of varying ages. Generally, they do it with young middle-aged actors, so they're spanning the youthful scenes and the older scenes. It has arguably worked a bit better; and each time it works, they think it's going to come to the West End or to Broadway, but it never does. I would maintain—and it's a little unfair of me because I haven't seen these versions—

that the problem is in the structure of the piece and in the book, which was full of wonderful scenes but was difficult. I didn't know how to solve it and wouldn't know now.

Interviewer: One of your shows that we've mentioned but haven't really talked about is *Fiddler on the Roof.* What was it like being in on the creation of that classic of the American musical theater?

Prince: I didn't create it, and that's really hard. I actually was asked to direct it by Bock and Harnick. I said, "Though I'm Jewish, I don't know the whole shtetl thing. I don't understand it and I don't feel it, so I shouldn't. Do you know who should? It needs universality. It needs one person. It needs a choreographer/director, and that one person is Jerry Robbins." I'd been through *West Side* with him, but Jerry was unavailable. So Bock and Harnick said, "We have another show," and they gave me that; it turned out to be *She Loves Me.* Years went by and Jerry became available. He decided to do the show to honor his father, who came from just such a community. I then came back into it and produced it. I adored it, but I could never have directed it. While it was being done, my responsibility was limited to making Jerry Robbins go into rehearsal, which he kept putting off, putting off, and putting off as it cost me more and more money. Finally one day he went into rehearsal because I made him. We won't go into the details of that, but it required the suggestion of litigation. Of course, he wanted to be pushed, because he got pushed and he gloriously went through it. Then I pushed him again some weeks later. He insisted on an eight-week rehearsal period because he was doing both the book and the dances. We got to the seventh week and there wasn't a single dance staged, so I began to get nervous again. I pushed again and there was this miracle: The dances all got done in a week and a half. The bottle dance was done in three hours of an afternoon when we were waiting to do a tech rehearsal. He put the time where he felt he needed it. But I can't take any credit artistically for that show except for helping to nurture it.

Interviewer: Are you always somewhat amazed when a show comes together?

Prince: A little, sure. There's a day in the life of every show when it looks like the biggest mistake you ever made. It's usually during the early tech rehearsals, and for twenty-five years I panicked. When I was a producer, I panicked because I wasn't the director so I had no control over fixing anything. Then I became the director and the producer and I panicked, and when I panicked I would absent myself for the hours it took to get over that. Now I don't panic much anymore. But now I know that on the day when the run-through has been its absolute best, a little voice will say, "It's going to be terrible sometime between now and the first preview." And that little voice never lets me down!

Interviewer: What about the prospects for finding new talent in the American musical? There seems to be a dearth of new composers, lyricists, and librettists—or are there just no places for them to get produced?

Prince: They're there, and their work comes to my desk often. I see a new musical every week if I choose to. Two-thirds of them are not very good, but one-third have merit—and that's a lot. How do they get nurtured? Who's going to do what I did for all those years and what I still do? I have a new musical that we haven't talked about; it's a new composer, new lyricist, and new book-writer. I'm the only old party involved in it. We've been at it for three years and the guys are saying, "When is it going to happen?" It's going to happen next year maybe, or maybe a little later than that, but it's going to happen when it happens. The fact is, that's what a musical deserves. Most of the musicals I've done have taken a minimum of two years to do, or, in the case of *Spider Woman,* going on five. You need somebody to do that. People need a little seed money. We're able to give a composer fifteen hundred dollars—five hundred now, five hundred when the score is finished, and five hundred the first day of rehearsal. In 1955, fifteen hundred dollars was useful; today it's of no use whatsoever. It pays one month's rent. It's costing so much money to support these projects, and most of the people with the money are not equipped to be valuably supportive.

Interviewer: What can you tell us about this new musical?

Prince: It's called *The Petrified Prince.* It's based on a film that Ingmar Bergman wrote that was never made. It was purchased by Warner Brothers. A friend of mine found it and sent me the script, and I said, "There's a hell of a musical in this." It's a very black comedy, but a busy black comedy in the style of *Candide.* It also fed a need I have to work with new people—and I knew exactly who I wanted to work with. We called Warner Brothers and they said, "We don't know anything about it." I said, "You spent a lot of money to purchase it." They said, "We'll look it up." They called back and said, "We found the file card, but we can't find the script, so send us the script." We said, "No. Once we own the rights, we'll send you the script." So we made a deal with these guys and then everybody got very friendly and nice. They read the script and they said, "We'll read you what it says on the card. On the card it says, 'Isn't it time someone told Ingmar Bergman to retire?'"

Interviewer: Well, I guess after all this talk about how much more difficult it is to survive in the musical theater world than it once was, the ultimate question is if someone wanted to be a producer today, how would one go about it?

Prince: That's tough. I think there's a real place for somebody who understands the form, is patient enough, and has taste enough to find composers and lyricists and do the nurturing. Then you have to take the project to one of the money boys or to a regional theater that is looking for new musicals. It has always seemed naïve to me that the guys with the money, be they theater owners or just millionaires, didn't hire younger versions of me to put together shows for them. Give them a salary for a year and a little seed money for the various writers. There used to be something called the Freed Unit at MGM, where all those great musicals came from. They gave them an office and they worked on projects. If anybody would take that to heart today, the musical theater would have a great shot of adrenaline.

Stephen Sondheim

Stephen Sondheim was born on March 22, 1930, in New York City. He was educated at Williams College (B.A., 1950). He has worked as a composer, lyricist, and playwright. He wrote the lyrics for the musicals West Side Story *(1957),* Gypsy *(1959),* Do I Hear a Waltz? *(1965), and contributed lyrics to* Candide *(1973). The musicals for which he has written both music and lyrics include* A Funny Thing Happened on the Way to the Forum *(1962),* Anyone Can Whistle *(1964),* Company *(1970),* Follies *(1971),* A Little Night Music *(1973),* Pacific Overtures *(1976),* Sweeney Todd *(1979),* Merrily We Roll Along *(1981),* Sunday in the Park with George *(1984),* Into the Woods *(1987),* Assassins *(1991),* Passion *(1994),* Saturday Night *(1999),* Bounce *(2003), and* The Frogs *(2004). He has co-authored with George Furth the play* Getting Away with Murder *(1996).*

He provided incidental music for the plays The Girls of Summer *(1956),* Invitation to a March *(1961),* Twigs *(1971), and* The Enclave *(1973). For films, he co-wrote* The Last of Sheila *(1973), composed the score of* Stavisky *(1974), co-composed* Reds *(1981), and wrote the songs for* Dick Tracy *(1990).*

He has won Tony Awards for Company *(Best Score and Best Lyrics),* Follies *(Best Score),* A Little Night Music *(Best Score),* Sweeney Todd *(Best Score),* Into the Woods *(Best Score), and* Passion *(Best Score). From 1973 to 1981, he was president of the Dramatists Guild. In 1981, he was elected to the Theatre Hall of Fame; in 1983, to the American Academy of Arts and Letters. He received the Academy Award in 1990 for the song "Sooner or Later (I Always Get My Man)" from* Dick Tracy, *the Kennedy Center Honors in 1993, the Pulitzer Prize in 1995 for* Sunday in the Park with George, *the National Medal of Arts in 1996, and the William Inge Award in 1998.*

This interview took place on June 15, 2004.

• ——————————————————————————— •

Interviewer: Before you met Oscar Hammerstein II and his family, had you had much experience with theater and with musicals?

Sondheim: No, very little. My father was in the dress business, so he used to go to musicals because he would take buyers to them. He was a big fan of musicals and he played the piano amateurwise, so I was taken to a few musicals when I was six, seven, or eight years old. The first one I saw was called *White Horse Inn,* an operetta starring Kitty Carlisle, as she was then known. The first musical I saw on Broadway was *The Boys from Syracuse* and then *Very Warm for May;* those are the only two musicals I remember seeing before I became involved with the Hammersteins when I was eleven. I saw a couple of straight plays like *Arsenic and Old Lace,* but I didn't go to the theater very much, mostly because in those days you didn't stay up past seven or eight o'clock when you were six, seven, or eight years old.

Interviewer: Do you remember what you thought about theater at that age? Was it something that fascinated you?

Sondheim: No, not particularly. It was fun, but movies were my thing. I do remember the opening moment of *Very Warm for May.* It was about summer stock, and it took place in a large, elegant house. There was this grand piano on the stage, and the curtain went up and the butler came out; he took a cloth and he wiped the keys from the base to the treble, *rrrruuuppp,* and I would have thought, "I think I'm going to have an orgasm!" if I'd known what an orgasm was. I thought it was the most exciting thing I had ever seen in my life. I don't remember anything else about the show, but I do remember that. I thought, "I can't wait to go home and try it."

Interviewer: Were you taking piano lessons?

Sondheim: Yes. All nice Jewish boys on Central Park West took piano lessons, and I took mine. I was seven years old, I know, when I gave recitals at the teacher's house with all the other little boys and girls. My father and mother used to drag me out in my pajamas when they had guests over for cocktails to play "The Flight of the Bumblebee," which was very showy because it has that very fast right hand.

Interviewer: Did you have a fast right hand?

Sondheim: I had a fast right hand.

Interviewer: Did you have any interest in composing at that point?

Sondheim: No. I was just doing what my parents told me to do. I don't even remember having fun particularly. I remember I liked to sit next to my father when he would pick out show tunes by ear from shows he had seen, and that was fun. I would put my hand on his right hand and pick the melody out with him and he would play the chords. I liked to listen to recordings of songs, and I was very precocious. Before I could read, I could look at the label and see by the length of the words that it was "Ain't Misbehavin'" by Fats Waller.

Interviewer: What did the friendship with the Hammersteins mean to you? Did it get you interested in theater?

Sondheim: Oh, sure, of course. I just wanted to be what Oscar was. He became a surrogate father, and I wanted to follow in his footsteps. As I've said many times, if he'd been a geologist, I would have wanted to be a geologist. The subject that interested me was math. I would have been a mathematician if I hadn't met Oscar.

Interviewer: Were you a math major for a while at Williams?

Sondheim: No. I deliberately didn't take any math courses, because I was afraid that if I did I wouldn't do anything else. I was good at plane geometry but terrible at spatial geometry. I was very good with numbers.

Interviewer: Do you think there's a relationship between math and music?

Sondheim: Sure. During the war, Milton Babbitt taught higher math at Princeton. He was the beautiful mind.

Interviewer: Do you see your interest in music coming from the same part of your brain as your skill at math?

Sondheim: Absolutely.

Interviewer: They're both about solving problems, aren't they?

Sondheim: It's not only that. It's the relationship of the chords, the relationship between a fourth and a fifth or a sixth and a seventh and the proportion of the sound. It all absolutely is related.

Interviewer: But wasn't it a music course at Williams with Robert Barrow that really got you interested in music?

Sondheim: It did. I had already started to fiddle with the piano and write stuff, because in prep school at the George School I wrote a musical, *By George,* but there was no such thing as composition or anything like that. I took the music course as an elective in college, and Barrow's attitude was in the best sense so scientific and analytical, as opposed to romantic, that it hit the math part of my brain.

Interviewer: In your mind, when that clicked, did you associate it with writing musicals?

Sondheim: Only because of Hammerstein. If I hadn't met Oscar, maybe I would have ended up trying to write so-called serious music or maybe I wouldn't have. I was being groomed for a concert career as a piano player when I was in prep school. When I say groomed, I mean that the music teacher there had high hopes. I used to give recitals for other schools in Pennsylvania. As I said, I have a very fleet right hand, but I have a terrible left hand. I am extremely right-handed. I can hardly feed myself with my left hand, I am so uncoordinated and weak. It's fine for performing songs, but not when you have to play fugal entrances with the left hand. But I was fairly impressive with the right hand. I had an epiphany when I was doing a recital at some school in Pennsylvania and I was playing a Chopin piece with an ABA form. I was on automatic pilot with the A, and I got to the end of the A and realized I had no idea of what came next, how the B section began; so I suddenly went back to the beginning of the A and played it to the coda at the end. And nobody knew the difference. They all applauded. I thought, "That's the end of concert performing for me. If they don't know the difference, I'm not going to tell them."

Interviewer: How old were you then?

Sondheim: Fifteen, maybe fourteen.

Interviewer: So it was because of Hammerstein that you got interested in writing music for the theater?

Sondheim: I got interested in shows and writing songs because of Hammerstein, although at that point I had no musical training except piano playing. But piano playing, when you're writing songs, is in its own sense a compositional process, because when you play a lot of Kern or a lot of Gershwin, you pick up by osmosis what's going on. I couldn't analyze them, but I could pick them up, and I got to know their chord progressions and use them in the songs I wrote for the teenage show at George School. So I was writing songs, but what Barrow did was give me the tools to write my own kind of stuff instead of just imitating, which is what Oscar had told me to do. Oscar told me to write what I felt, not what he felt. I had been writing about nature. He said, "You don't care about trees and larks. I do. Write what *you* feel." Then he said the smart thing; he said, "If you do that, you'll be 90 percent ahead of everybody else." Once he made it competitive, being a teenager, the floodgates opened for me.

Interviewer: Were you writing lyrics, too, then?

Sondheim: I did some lyrics with one of the girls at George School for *By George.* We wrote lyrics, not together but alternately. I did about two-thirds of the show and she did one-third, and there was another guy who wrote the book with us; so she and I did the lyrics, I wrote the music, and the three of us wrote the book.

Interviewer: Was it about this time that you also got interested in crossword puzzles?

Sondheim: Yes, simultaneously, as a matter of fact. I think I got it from Oscar. He introduced me to the puns and anagrams in the *New York Times,* and in fact I sent in a crossword puzzle to the *Times* when I was fourteen or fifteen. They sent it back to me with a letter when they found out how old I was—maybe I'd told them in my letter—and they said, "You are very precocious." I had to look up the word *precocious!*

Interviewer: You have said that solving crossword puzzles is not unlike writing lyrics. What did you mean?

Sondheim: Working words out to the pattern of music and making them sound and land where they're supposed to is puzzle work. It's manipulative work. It's like certain kinds of positional puzzles, where you move blocks around to free up another block. It's positioning work; it's that kind of puzzle.

Interviewer: While you were at Williams, you wrote two musicals, *Phinney's Rainbow* and *All That Glitters.* What were they like?

Sondheim: That was all satire. I was imitating musical styles in both of those shows. *All That Glitters,* which I did my junior year, was an adaptation of *Beggar on Horseback,* the Kaufman and Connelly play. Of course, I was starting to learn something about the technique of putting a musical together, but they were essentially "musical comedy of the year." There were little moments of my own voice starting to come through, though.

Interviewer: Those shows were written after Hammerstein told you to write in your own voice, weren't they?

Sondheim: Oh, yes. What Oscar started me on begins with *All That Glitters.*

Interviewer: You were having fun, weren't you? You were enjoying yourself.

Sondheim: Yes, absolutely, but I was really doing it as part of Oscar's set program for me. My junior year I wrote *All That Glitters,* and then I wrote a musical version of Maxwell Anderson's play *High Tor,* but Anderson wouldn't give me permission to put it on—so it was an exercise. Then I started a musical based on the Mary Poppins novels, but I didn't finish it, because I couldn't solve the problem of disparate short stories—so I only did about one-half of that. And then, in my senior year, I started work on an original musical, *Climb High.*

Interviewer: Between Williams and *West Side Story,* what did you do?

Sondheim: I worked for a living. First of all, I got a scholarship called the Hubbard Hutchinson Prize, which was—I don't know if it still is—given at Williams. It was a stipend of three thousand dollars a year for study over two years; the idea was they gave you the first three thousand dollars and if you went and bought a car then you were not likely to get the second, but if you studied, as I did with Milton Babbitt, they gave you the second year. The first two years out of college I lived at my father's apartment, so I didn't have to pay rent. The minute the scholarship ran out, I ran out. I got a job writing a television series called *Topper* and went out to the West Coast and saved up; I worked for five months and quit. I wanted to save up enough money to rent an apartment in New York and be on my own, and that's what I did.

Interviewer: Is that when they came to you about *West Side Story?*

Sondheim: No. The first thing that happened was that I got a job writing a show called *Saturday Night,* which I got through a producer named Lemuel Ayers, who had produced *Kiss Me, Kate* and was a leading Broadway set designer. He'd optioned this play that Julius and Philip Epstein had written about their third brother and about their childhood and young manhood, and Lem wanted it to be turned into a musical. I think he had offered it to Frank Loesser, who had turned it down. I met Lem at a wedding where I was an usher. He asked to hear my stuff, and I played him what I'd written. He asked if I would like to write a few songs on spec for the project, and I said fine. I wrote three songs for a hundred bucks, and Julius Epstein flew in from the West Coast and heard them, and I got the job. Then Lem went out to California to design a movie called *Girl Rush*, and he and his wife rented a house, and I went out and stayed with them for three or four months, writing the score for *Saturday Night*. When he finished the movie, we came back to New York and had backers' auditions. We raised about half the capitalization over a period of eight backers' auditions—and then Lem died. Unbeknownst to me, he had leukemia. The rights then passed to his widow, who was really nuts, so it never got anywhere; but now I had a professional portfolio of songs.

George Oppenheimer, the head writer on *Topper,* brought me to see two producers who were going to do a musical version of James M. Cain's novel *Serenade*. It was going to have a score by Leonard Bernstein, with a book by Arthur Laurents, and Jerome Robbins was directing. I don't know who was going to do the lyrics, but Bernstein and Robbins had dropped out, so they were looking for a composer. I went up and played for them, but then the project was dropped about two months later, because Warner Brothers had announced that they were going to do a film of *Serenade*. Months went by, and I ran into Arthur at a party and I asked him what he was doing, and he said he was working on this project called *Romeo and Juliet,* with Bernstein writing the music. I just idly asked who was doing the lyrics and he said, "Oh, I never thought of you. We're looking, because Betty [Comden] and Adolph [Green] were supposed to do it, but they can't get out of their Hollywood contract. We have to know immediately and we've been trying to think who else might write the lyrics if they can't do it. I really liked your lyrics to *Saturday Night*. I didn't like the music much." I wasn't really interested in doing lyrics, but I was interested in meeting Leonard Bernstein, so the next day I went and played some songs for him. He said, "I'll know in a week and I'll let you know." I didn't think I'd hear from him, but, sure enough, he called a week later and I said, "I'm very flattered. Let me call you back." I didn't want to do just lyrics, but I spoke to Oscar and he said, "I think you should do it because these are extremely gifted professionals—Robbins, Bernstein, and Laurents—and you can always write music later. And it's a job."

Interviewer: Was doing just lyrics for *West Side Story* and then *Gypsy* an easier way to get into the world of musical theater than if you'd had to write both music and lyrics immediately?

Sondheim: No, not at all. I wanted to write music. Lyrics have always been very, very difficult for me to write.

Interviewer: Is it more difficult if you're not writing for your own music?

Sondheim: Sure, because you make compromises and you have to state your case to your collaborator. It was different with Lenny because he fancied himself a lyricist. In fact, he was going to do the lyrics for *West Side Story*. Then we were going to do them as co-lyricists, but I ended up doing them all, all but one or two lines. When we got to Washington, I was not even mentioned in the reviews, and he knew that I was upset and he said, "Look, the lyrics are yours. I'm happy to take my name off."

Interviewer: Was it billed as lyrics by both of you before the show got to New York?

Sondheim: The original show music said that. It also said it on the marquee in Washington. By the time we got to Philadelphia, it was just me. In a momentous moment, Lenny said, "Of course, we'll readjust the royalties," and I said, "Oh, I don't care." If only someone had stopped me from saying that! If I told you the amount of money that single sentence has cost me, your hair would stand on end!

Interviewer: To go back for a minute, as a teenager, hadn't you been a gofer on some of Hammerstein's musicals?

Sondheim: Only on *Allegro*. *Allegro* went into rehearsal at the beginning of the summer, so I could do it because I was at the end of my freshman year. I could afford to take the summer, work for Oscar, and be back in school by the time they opened in Boston.

Interviewer: It's kind of fortuitous, then, isn't it, that the one show you worked on was Rodgers and Hammerstein's most experimental musical?

Sondheim: Yes, it was experimental. That's the most significant thing. It's a show Oscar always wanted to fix. I don't think he could have fixed it, because the theatrical sophistication and the imagination in the experimental aspect of *Allegro* are so much greater than his writing ability. The writing is simplistic, and nothing could ever really fix that show. Even the point of what he was trying to say never came across. I knew what he was trying to say, because he told me.

Interviewer: The cliché has always been that *Allegro* was unsuccessful because it was ahead of its time.

Sondheim: It was ahead of its time in terms of theatrical sophistication, but the actual writing is not up to the concept. But it changed the musical theater, because what happened was that the next show Rodgers and Hammerstein did used a similar technique. Oscar had used a cinematic technique to wipe scenes; instead of the curtain coming down, he wanted to tell the story of a man's life in a complete flow—and that's exactly what he did. When it came time to do the next show, which was *South Pacific,* it was nowhere near as experimental as *Allegro* in terms of the way the chorus was used, but the theatrical technique was the same. Although curtains did come down, there was a sense of cinematic fluidity throughout, which the director of *South Pacific,* Josh Logan, took from Oscar and *Allegro*. *South Pacific* is also the show that changed Hal Prince's perception of theater. He'll be happy to tell you that his approach to directing stems from *South Pacific*. That experience of seeing *South Pacific* and the sophistication he has derived from seeing theater all over the world have blended to form his own techniques—but what started it all for him was *South Pacific*.

Interviewer: *South Pacific* was Hal Prince's *Allegro*, then, wasn't it?

Sondheim: *Allegro* started the musical theater on its way toward cinematic fluidity.

Interviewer: What was it like working with Jule Styne on *Gypsy*?

Sondheim: That was different. It was all done in four months. We started in September, and we had to have it in rehearsal by February because of various schedules. It was different also because while Lenny would argue over every lyric, Jule referred to himself as a tunesmith rather than as a composer. What he meant was that he wanted to write tunes and he recognized that they were going to be tunes in the service of telling a story. Essentially what I did was I wrote lyrics with certain rhythms in them so that he had something to set, as opposed to working together with him the way I did with Lenny, which meant discussing everything. On *Gypsy*, Arthur Laurents, who wrote the libretto, and I would concoct things, and I would write sketch-out lyrics, and then Jule would set them. Not all the time. There were some things that would start from the music, but most of the time they were dictated by the evolution of the story.

Interviewer: In 1965, you collaborated with Arthur Laurents and Richard Rodgers on *Do I Hear a Waltz?* Laurents has said that Rodgers treated you terribly during the preparation of that show. Is that true?

Sondheim: Yes, he did.

Interviewer: Do you think that was partly because he saw you as Hammerstein's protégé?

Sondheim: I think there may have been some of that in it. The reason I did *Do I Hear a Waltz?* was not so much for Arthur, who had begged me to do it; it was for Oscar. Before Oscar died, he said to me, "Look, Dick is going to be feeling bereft, and I know you want to do your own music, but if he ever comes to you with a project, I'd love it if you would write with him." I said okay. Dick kept sending me ideas I didn't particularly like, and then this one came up, and because Arthur was involved I decided to do it. It was a terrible, terrible experience.

Interviewer: Many people feel that the first show in which you really found your musical voice is *Company*. Do you agree?

Sondheim: Oh, sure. My voice is present in *Anyone Can Whistle,* but the show is not a coherent success. *Company* is the first time my voice and a coherent show came together.

Interviewer: Why do you think that is?

Sondheim: Because of George Furth and Hal Prince.

Interviewer: What role did Prince play in your being able to bring out your voice in *Company*?

Sondheim: First of all, it was his idea. These were individual one-act plays by George Furth that George didn't know what to do with. He had a reading of them in New York, and Kim Stanley and John McMartin and Ron Liebman were going to star, I believe. He'd written, I think, seven of them, and that fell through. George wrote me; we had a slight acquaintance. He didn't know what to do with them. I said, "Send them to Hal Prince. He'll tell you what to do with them." Hal called me and said, "I think they could be a musical." So he sent for George and we sat around together; it was Hal's idea to make the plays into a musical.

Interviewer: When you say that the first show in which your musical voice was present was *Anyone Can Whistle,* what do you mean by that?

Sondheim: Well, you have to listen to the music. If you listen to the music of *Anyone Can Whistle,* it doesn't really sound like anybody else who was writing at that time.

Interviewer: Whereas *A Funny Thing Happened on the Way to the Forum* does?

Sondheim: No. There's a good deal in *Forum* of what Lenny called my wrong-note music, the dissonances. I suppose you could say it started with *Forum*.

Interviewer: Would you say that the material of *Forum* was at odds with the music in some ways?

Sondheim: Yes. I've said often that the songs and the book don't quite go together. The book has this elegant low-comedy style, and the songs are sort of salon songs. That's an exaggeration, but there's a disparity between the score and the book. *Whistle,* for all its messiness, is of a piece; there are a lot of extended numbers and extended song forms in that show. *Forum* is a lot of thirty-two-bar stuff, but *Whistle* is experimental in terms of the songs and even in terms of the book, which is surreal.

Interviewer: Putting aside *Anyone Can Whistle,* which wasn't a success, would you say that *Company,* then, is the first so-called Sondheim musical, because it's the first one in which your sensibility really dominates that show?

Sondheim: Maybe so. I think Hal and I were a team. Rodgers and Hammerstein were a team, and you could say that Hal and I were a team in *Company* that way.

Interviewer: How did Prince function in that team?

Sondheim: With *Company,* he had a visual notion of what it should be.

Interviewer: Did he suggest things to be done to the score?

Sondheim: No, not much. He does what all directors have done since it became a director's theater. He does editing. He'll say, "I think that scene is too long" or "I wish that song had a finish" or something like that.

Interviewer: What is it about a project that attracts you to it? I assume you've turned down many more than you've accepted.

Sondheim: No, not at all. There's no answer to that. It's whatever gets to me.

Interviewer: Are you attracted more by the people involved than by the story?

Sondheim: No, but that's part of it. Certainly if they're people I've worked with before or people whose work excites me, I'm more likely to want to collaborate with them. It's like falling in love; it either gets you or it doesn't.

Interviewer: Have you turned down many shows that you've been offered?

Sondheim: Not really. I've turned down things with a "No, that doesn't interest me." But I don't think I've toyed with anything. I certainly have never worked on anything and then decided against it. I'm a slow writer. I don't want to take the time unless I really feel it's worth it.

Interviewer: How would you say your work has evolved over the years? Are you a better composer now than you were thirty-five years ago?

Sondheim: I'm unable to take any kind of bird's-eye view of what I do. I don't even like the word *career.* When your whole body of work is done and you're dead, then someone can look back. People say all kinds of things about me, about what is similar and what is different.

Interviewer: Do you think that you are taking more chances musically than you did earlier in your career?

Sondheim: No, I don't think I am. In fact, *Bounce* is a reversion to a show like *Merrily We Roll Along.* It's traditional musical comedy used in an untraditional way. I'm a firm believer in content dictating form. If the content calls for a kind of musical approach that was *au courant* fifty years ago, then that's what it should be.

Interviewer: Is that one of the things that interests you when a project comes to you, the opportunity to experiment with a new kind of content?

Sondheim: Yes. I think you should frighten yourself. You should try to wade into territory you haven't waded into before. That doesn't necessarily have to be new musical territory; it can be a new approach to the show or to the way of telling a story.

Interviewer: Some people have said that the difference between what you do and what other composer/lyricists before you have done is that you get inside a character musically while they give you only the surface of a character. You've said you almost become those people when you compose, haven't you?

Sondheim: Yes. My approach is closest to that of an actor. I inhabit the character the way I think an actor does. Often by the time we're through, I know the script better than the author does because, like an actor, I examine every line and every word. I query my collaborator on exactly what he means and we discuss it thoroughly. I think musical characterization is something that *is* rare in the theater. One of the reasons is that characters worth musicalizing are rare in the theater. Now we're getting back to book-writing; rich characters in books for musicals are few and far between. The people I've written with can create those kinds of characters.

Interviewer: Doesn't it work the other way, too? Haven't you enriched and enhanced the book-writer's work through your score?

Sondheim: Sure. I'm not being hypermodest about it, but it must start with somebody who can invent characters that are worth exploring. It's the same as the difference for an actor between playing Hamlet and playing Sheridan Whiteside.

Interviewer: You've worked with a lot of different book-writers. You started with Arthur Laurents and Larry Gelbart and Burt Shevelove, then you worked with George Furth and Hugh Wheeler, and most recently it's been James Lapine and John Weidman. Why have you moved around so much?

Sondheim: First of all, it's what they bring me. These things often start when the librettist comes to me. I rarely start projects. In fact, the only ones I've started by myself are *Sweeney Todd, Assassins,* and *Bounce.* Most of the time, people bring me stuff—either Hal or one of the librettists.

Interviewer: Has it been a different experience writing with each of these writers?

Sondheim: No, it's not completely different, because the methodology is generally the same; the personalities are different. Lapine is different from the others because he doesn't write from beginning to end. He starts someplace in the core of the piece and builds outward from it. Everybody else that I've written with starts at the beginning, goes to the middle, and ends up at the end.

Interviewer: What sort of adjustment is that for you as a composer, when Lapine starts in the middle?

Sondheim: None. He starts in the middle, but by the time I start to write, we know what the total outcome will be. It's just that when he plunges in, he doesn't plunge in at the beginning; and I like to plunge in at the beginning, because the opening number has to establish so much in terms of not only exposition but also musical and lyrical style.

Interviewer: You once said that when you listen to the lyrics of *West Side Story,* you hear a writer at work rather than a character. Did you mean that you weren't getting inside those characters, because you hadn't created them musically but were only providing lyrics for someone else's music?

Sondheim: No, it's not that. Those characters, as melodramatic characters, are at most two-dimensional. So much happens in that plot that Arthur didn't have the chance to draw any kind of complex characters.

Interviewer: Would you say that your more recent shows have more complex characters?

Sondheim: Some of them do, absolutely, but not all of them.

Interviewer: *Passion* and *Sweeney Todd?*

Sondheim: Oh, sure. Those are much more complex.

Interviewer: Do you think that the audience today is more willing to deal with more complex characters?

Sondheim: Gosh, I don't know. When you talk about audiences, that type of generalization is hard. Obviously, audiences are more open to experiments and approaches than they used to be, but not all that much. They still would rather have *Mamma Mia!* than *Allegro.*

Interviewer: Doesn't it sometimes seem that there are two audiences out there? There's an audience for your shows and other more serious and experimental musicals, but those are not the same people who are going to see *Mamma Mia!,* are they?

Sondheim: That's right. There *are* two audiences. One audience goes to a musical and expects to have some nourishment, and the other goes anticipating something mindless and easy and expected.

Interviewer: How do you feel about the way your work is received? Some people obviously have difficulty with it. Do you care?

Sondheim: Sure. I'd like everybody to like it, so it disappoints me when they don't; but there's nothing I can do about it.

Interviewer: And, of course, you're not going to write down, are you?

Sondheim: It's not about writing down. I don't think anybody can write down to an audience; because if you're not writing what you believe, the audience is not going to accept that either. Without mentioning any names, the sort of bland, mindless shows that are popular hits are written by people who think they're really good. They're not thinking, "How do we make money?" They're writing from exactly the same impulse that the most esoteric writer writes from. Everybody who writes a musical thinks they're doing their best.

Interviewer: You spend a lot of time, when you talk about your music, stressing that harmony is the essence. Is there any way you can explain that to someone who isn't a musicologist?

Sondheim: No. Harmony for me is the fingerprint of music. It's what gives it character and makes it individual. It's how you distinguish Kern from Gershwin or Beethoven from Brahms. Whether you're trained or not, if you listen to a lot of Beethoven and you listen to a lot of Brahms, and you put on a piece you've never heard, if it's by Brahms you'll say, "That's Brahms," and if it's by Beethoven you'll say, "That's Beethoven."

Interviewer: But if a layperson listens to scores of your various shows, he doesn't necessarily hear that fingerprint in all of them, does he?

Sondheim: That's probably because I do so many different styles, but any musician could find the fingerprint in the harmony.

Interviewer: Isn't the music in *Pacific Overtures* very different from the Oriental music of *The King and I*?

Sondheim: There isn't much Oriental music in *The King and I*. It's actually mostly Broadway music with Oriental orchestrations.

Interviewer: What were you trying to do musically in *Pacific Overtures*?

Sondheim: I was trying to start with kind of faux Japanese-scale music and, as the country gets Westernized, to gradually make the music more Western. The last number is really a Westernization of the opening number.

Interviewer: The opening numbers, then, are much more inflected by Japanese music?

Sondheim: Yes. They're sparse and based very much on open fourths and fifths and certain Japanese styles.

Interviewer: You've said that one of the things you like about theater is that it's a collaborative art and that you in a sense have a family. Again, to the layperson, it's amazing, with all those people involved, that a musical ever gets on. In your experience as a collaborator in the process, when it works, what makes it successful?

Sondheim: The answer is so obvious that it will not seem like an answer. You have to be sure that you're writing the same show. That's something that I didn't discover about *Forum* until too late. We weren't writing the same show, even after we'd spent the better part of four years on it. They were writing a certain kind of show, and I was writing a certain kind of score, and none of us recognized that they were slightly different. I learned from that, and so the preliminary discussions for any show I do with my collaborators are to be sure that we're writing the same show. That's what makes it work.

Interviewer: If, as you say, you take on new projects in order to enter new territory, what was the impetus behind *Bounce*?

Sondheim: *Bounce* was an attempt originally to tell an epic story, to tell the history of a period of fifty years of an aspect of the United States and these two lives. That's something I hadn't tried before, with the exception of *Gypsy,* which covered a twenty-year period. I really would have liked *Bounce* to have been *Citizen Kane*—not in its weight, because John and I wanted to do a comic piece. We wanted to do a comic piece that had an epic sense and sweep to it. That's not the way it turned out, but that was what the attempt was.

Interviewer: What do you think happened?

Sondheim: A lot of things happened. We wrote a very comic, quite wild, farcical piece that was a sort of a Hope and Crosby *Road to. . . .* Then we got a director, Sam Mendes, who said, "You're not taking it seriously." Under his guidance and prodding we wrote what amounted to a very lugubrious piece, not without its comic aspects but Serious with a capital S. When we changed directors and got to Hal, Hal tried to blend the two, although he didn't like Sam's production very much. He encouraged us to keep some of the weight that Sam had brought in and at the same time restore some of the comic bounce of the original—so in the process it lost some of its epic quality. Hal also liked the whole idea of the epic quality, but it got lost in the shuffle.

Interviewer: Did it become a hybrid of the two kinds of shows and never really got an identity of its own? Is that the result of the process of working on it?

Sondheim: I think we just worked on it too long. What it all comes down to is that we shouldn't have spent so much time on it.

Interviewer: Do you mean that you should have stopped at a certain point?

Sondheim: No. I don't know how we could have compressed the time, but we didn't. I have no idea, if I had to do it over again, how to make that happen. The irony is that we like it. It's just that other people don't agree with us as enthusiastically as we would like.

Interviewer: What about *The Frogs*? What was the challenge there?

Sondheim: The challenge there was to write a show for the Yale swimming pool in one month.

Interviewer: Now what happens when it goes to Lincoln Center?

Sondheim: Now it's an expansion of that, but that's what interested me to begin with. Nathan Lane's and Susan Stroman's sensibilities certainly encouraged me to go ahead and write more songs.

Interviewer: Is it a different show?

Sondheim: It's different in the sense that the other one was fifty minutes long and this one is two and a half hours. Nathan Lane has emphasized certain colors in it that give it a balance, but its spirit is the same.

Interviewer: Do you think it's better?

Sondheim: Yes, much better.

Interviewer: Was it difficult to get back to that sensibility?

Sondheim: Yes, it was very hard to get back. I had the same trouble with *Merrily,* trying to get back to the spirit of being a twenty-five-year-old in the 1950s.

Interviewer: I meant going back to that style of music when you've gone on to other styles.

Sondheim: Oh, sure. I had the same problem when Cameron Mackintosh wanted some new songs for the revival of *Follies* that he did in London. I wrote four songs, and that was very, very difficult.

Interviewer: Can you tell the difference between the new and the old songs?

Sondheim: In *The Frogs*, yes. In *Follies*, out of the four, certainly one of them stands out like a sore thumb and the other three are okay.

Interviewer: Where does your dislike of opera come from?

Sondheim: From being brought up on movies and wanting action and story. I grew up on movies that tell their stories in ninety minutes, and opera lingers on every moment. That's the whole idea. That's what it's about; opera is for people who love the human voice above anything else.

Interviewer: What happens when your shows are done in opera houses as operas?

Sondheim: Sometimes they work and sometimes they don't. I've said before that an opera is defined as what is done in an opera house. Therefore, when *The Medium* and *The Telephone* are done on Broadway, they're Broadway shows. The expectation of the audience affects the reception.

Interviewer: When *Sweeney Todd* is done at the New York City Opera, is it seen as a Sondheim musical or an opera?

Sondheim: No, actually, when it's done at an opera house, it's an operetta, a black operetta. Opera is designed to show off the human voice, but *Sweeney* is about telling a story and telling it as swiftly as possible.

Interviewer: Do you have an appreciation of the genius of an opera composer?

Sondheim: In the case of Puccini, who had a real sense of the stage, and Britten, yes, the genius is in the music itself.

Interviewer: That's what I mean. As a musician, you can hear Puccini's music and say, "That's brilliant music"—but, at the same time, you can find a Puccini opera deficient as a theater piece. Is that the distinction you're making?

Sondheim: Even at his operas, I get restless.

Interviewer: If you were so great a fan of movies as a young man, why have you done so little work in films?

Sondheim: Because movies are not a writer's medium. They're a director's medium.

Interviewer: Surely you could arrange to have artistic control on a movie, couldn't you?

Sondheim: No, absolutely not. In fact, any studio would be foolish to give control of a movie to a writer. Think about it. You're a hired gun.

Interviewer: Who is the Stephen Sondheim to your Oscar Hammerstein? Where are the new composers?

Sondheim: They're all over the place. The trouble is they're not getting enough chance to be heard, so they're not learning. You've got to write a lot to learn, and by "write a lot" I mean write and get the work on in front of an audience.

Interviewer: Musicals are much more expensive to get on than straight plays.

Sondheim: Of course, they're much more of a gamble, and therefore producers are much less willing to take a chance. And if you limit yourself to Off-Broadway and regional productions, then you have to confine yourself to limitations on members of the orchestra, number of actors, and so forth.

Interviewer: Regional theaters don't often take the risk of doing new musicals, do they?

Sondheim: No, it's even more than that. You also don't get the professional personnel, so it's a dead end. Young composers and young writers for the musical theater can only learn by doing. By the time Rodgers and Hammerstein had gotten together, they had each done a lot of shows.

Interviewer: You've done a lot of shows.

Sondheim: I never think of it that way. People have pointed it out and I suppose it's so, certainly compared to the generation we're talking about. But Rodgers and Hammerstein did a show every two years.

Interviewer: During the 1970s, you did five or six shows, which is incredible. You probably couldn't have that many productions of your work in a decade now, could you?

Sondheim: No. That *is* every two years.

Interviewer: Can you give us an example of something you learned through doing? In other words, an example of the sort of experience that young composers and lyricists don't have the opportunity to have now.

Sondheim: It's amorphous, but one example is that in *West Side Story* Jerry Robbins kept insisting that the so-called quintet, which is actually a quartet, should be after the bridal shop scene. "No, it's about recruiting," we said, "so it's got to be done before the bridal shop scene." Jerry said no. Every logical argument we made fell on deaf ears. We had a run-through in which he did it before the bridal shop scene and one in which he did it after it—and he was absolutely right. In other words, there's a certain theatrical truth that sometimes overrides logical truths.

Interviewer: Somebody could tell you that at a musical theater workshop and you could say, "It sounds good, but how do I know it's going to work?"

Sondheim: Like so much in the performing arts, certain things can be taught and certain things can't. Certain things in the performing arts have to be done in the theater simply because the performing arts involve the final collaborator, the audience. Nothing exists without the audience, and you can't learn it until the audience is there. And it has to be put on well; if it's put on poorly, you don't learn anything. But it doesn't matter how talented the performers are, working in the theater requires that eventual collaboration with the audience.

Interviewer: A few years ago, you compiled a list of the songs you wished you'd written and Barbara Cook has been singing some of them in her concerts. I thought I detected a pattern in them that I don't see very much in show music anymore, and that is really good and often very clever lyrics. I feel today when I go to a musical that lyrics have disappeared almost entirely. Of course, that doesn't apply to your shows.

Sondheim: It's partly because pop music has deafened the ear to lyrics, but in the last hundred years there really haven't been that many great lyricists. Also, the leading lyricists in the first half of the century—Ira Gershwin, Yip Harburg, Lorenz Hart, and the others—didn't have to write to tell a story. They were never tested in that way; and my guess is that if they had been, they wouldn't have been very good at it. Hammerstein was the sole exception—and Dubose Heyward, who only wrote one show. Nowadays, to be a good lyricist you not only have to be good technically but you also have to have a sense of drama—and you have to apply that. All Harburg and Cole Porter and Berlin had to do was write good songs, touching songs, sentimental songs, or whatever they wanted to write. They didn't have to do anything but entertain. Now storytelling is what it's about. On the other hand, guess what, the more successful shows are the ones that don't bother to tell a story. The songs are just songs. If any song from a musical becomes popular, it's the one that's just a song.

Interviewer: How have you managed to do both? If you can do it, why can't other people do it?

Sondheim: Again, apart from proficiency, that goes back to experience—and the fact that I was trained by Hammerstein. And you have to have characters worth writing about.

Interviewer: You don't really make much of a distinction between a drama and a musical play, do you?

Sondheim: Music, because it's so rich, can enhance and amplify what is in a play, but a play can be much subtler. Musicals can't be as subtle as plays because there's not that much time to develop complexities. Musicals have to be in broader strokes.

Interviewer: Can a performer sometimes take something you wrote and make it better than you thought it was?

Sondheim: I can't give you specifics, but if you get really good performers they can make you shine.

Interviewer: What about critics? Do you find them helpful?

Sondheim: No. I only read the *New York Times* because it's the one that affects the box office. I learned long ago not to read the critics. When I first started reading them, I wanted to read nice things about myself. But for years they either sneered at or ignored me; so I learned not to care, and I stopped. How can it make any difference if you've already opened anyway? The piece is done. If criticism has any function at all, it should be the notion of looking back at a body of work. But judging a piece on one hearing is absurd.

Interviewer: Do you have any interest in a musicologist looking at your work?

Sondheim: They already do. Generally they see things that aren't there. But I don't want to make fun of them. It's nice to be taken seriously.

Susan Stroman

Susan Stroman was born on October 17, 1954, in Wilmington, Delaware. She was educated at the University of Delaware (B.A., 1976). She has worked as a choreographer, director, writer, and performer. The New York musicals she choreographed include Flora, the Red Menace (1987), A Little Night Music (1991), And the World Goes 'Round (1991), 110 in the Shade (1992), Crazy for You (1992), Show Boat (1994), A Christmas Carol (1994), Big (1996), Steel Pier (1997), Contact (2000), The Music Man (2000), The Producers (2001), Thou Shalt Not (2001), Oklahoma! (2002), and The Frogs (2004).

She directed the New York musicals Contact, The Music Man, The Producers, Thou Shalt Not, and The Frogs. She performed in the New York musicals Whoopee! (1979) and Musical Chairs (1980). She received Tony Awards for Crazy for You (Best Choreography), Show Boat (Best Choreography), Contact (Best Musical and Best Choreography), and The Producers

(*Best Director and Best Choreography*). *In 2001, she received the George Abbott Award for Outstanding Achievement in the Theatre.*
This interview took place on July 18, 2002.

• ───────────────────────────────────── •

Interviewer: I heard that you started taking dance lessons at five.

Stroman: That's true. I grew up in a house filled with music. My father was and still is a wonderful piano player. Although he was a salesman by trade, he played the piano every day, and he still does. My brother also played the piano, so the house was always filled with music. I believe it was really a passion for music that drove me to dancing school. I started out as a child of five taking ballet and tap. Then as I grew older, I reached out for every dance form I could—ballet and classical and jazz and ballroom and even baton lessons. I took lessons in anything I could that had to do with dance and music. I also took piano and guitar lessons. It really had to do with the music in the household. My father was the real music man of my life.

Interviewer: Was there show music played in your house?

Stroman: Oh, sure, a lot of show tunes. He introduced me not only to classical music but to the old standards and the classic theater composers like Rodgers and Hammerstein, Rodgers and Hart, and Gershwin.

Interviewer: If somebody had asked you at the age of ten, "What are you going to be?" would you have said a dancer? Would you have said a performer in musical theater?

Stroman: I think at ten I probably would have said a dancer, but I have to say choreography has always been part of my whole being. Even though I went to dancing school and learned different routines from teachers, I would then go home and create my own work. Whenever my father was playing piano in the house, I would dance. I think part of why I have become a choreographer is because I visualize music whenever I hear music. Whether it be a classical piece, rock and roll, or an old standard, I imagine hordes of people dancing. Whenever I hear music, I can visualize the entire piece. Because of that, it was either become a choreographer or go crazy, I suppose. But it all started with a passion for music, all different forms of music.

Interviewer: Would you say, then, that even now, when you do a show, it doesn't start necessarily with the movement but with the music that the movement then interprets?

Stroman: Yes. Part of what I do, too, as a choreographer is I develop the music for the dance. For example, Mel Brooks will write the song "That

Face," but what I have to do then is open it up with my dance arranger and pianist to make it into a Fred and Ginger number. Or he will write the melody for a song called "Along Came Bialy," but then I have to open it into a big dance number. What I do is make sure the music is developed with my choreography. The Rodgers and Hammerstein Estate allowed me to do new arrangements for *Oklahoma!*

Interviewer: When you say new arrangements, do you mean dance arrangements?

Stroman: Yes, dance arrangements.

Interviewer: Could you take any liberties with the music?

Stroman: Within the dance arrangements, yes. For example, the dream ballet never had "People Will Say We're in Love" in it, but I took that and turned it into a country waltz for Laurey and Curly, and then I opened it up into a grand waltz so they could sweep across the stage.

Interviewer: So you could do things with the music in order to bring out what you were trying to do with the dance. I was going to ask you if it's different working on a new show as opposed to a revival. With *The Music Man*, what did you do?

Stroman: The same thing. "Seventy-six Trombones" was a whole new arrangement. I took the melody and opened it up to match the choreography. At one point the dancers pretended they were piccolo players, and at another time they pretended they were trombone players. It is doing that and making sure the orchestration matches that. Part of my choreography is also developing the music.

Interviewer: When you did *Contact*, obviously you had complete freedom, didn't you, because the whole show was your conception from the start?

Stroman: That was the first time I was trapped! *Contact* was a contemporary piece with contemporary music, and it took place in a bar with a sound of CDs playing. I was trapped into what "Simply Irresistible" is or what "Sing, Sing, Sing" is. I couldn't open the arrangement.

Interviewer: But obviously, when you chose those songs, you had something in mind, didn't you? After all, you could have picked any song to be playing in that bar.

Stroman: Yes, sure; but with *Contact*, I wanted it to pull on the heartstrings of a contemporary audience, so those are contemporary classics that are used. Not only do they affect the particular character because they're songs in his life, they also affect the audience because those are songs of a sophisticated audience's generation. All those songs were from my personal stash in my living room! But I had to develop the dance to make sure it matched that music, because I couldn't open it up. I was after a different effect in that particular show than I was in, say, *Crazy for You*, where I took the melody of "I've Got Rhythm" and opened it up for a twelve-minute dance number.

Interviewer: Let's go back to your early career. All of a sudden, in the fall of 1976, you're choreographing *Candide* at the University of Delaware. How did that come about? Had you done choreography before that?

Stroman: Sure. I had done a lot of choreography for community theaters—*Cabaret, The Music Man, Applause*.

Interviewer: How old were you at that point?

Stroman: I guess seventeen, eighteen, or nineteen.

Interviewer: That was pretty unusual for someone that young to be given that responsibility, wasn't it?

Stroman: I think they just believed in me. I did a little performing there and I would jump in with ideas—so they gave me an opportunity to try it for real.

Interviewer: You were both performing and choreographing in community theater. Did you ever direct?

Stroman: No.

Interviewer: So when you got to the University of Delaware, you already had done a lot of professional work.

Stroman: Community theater work, yes. But even in high school, I'd done the half-time shows, rallying people together.

Interviewer: When you got to college, did you do a lot of theater?

Stroman: No, I was an English major in college. I took theater classes, but there were no musical classes. It was all straight theater, Shakespeare and the classics, that we studied. The scene work was all from the classics. My musical experiences came from outside, from community theater in the summers.

Interviewer: Did you think at that time that the theater would be your career?

Stroman: Sure. I knew I would have something to do with the theater, absolutely. I just loved it so. I also loved the theater people. Someone who is attracted to being a director or a choreographer is a natural storyteller. I love being able to tell stories, and I ultimately came to telling the stories through dance. I think that was part of the English background.

Interviewer: After you graduated from Delaware, where did you go from there?

Stroman: I came to New York City. Actually, I didn't really come to New York City. I came on a day trip to New York City because there was an open audition for the Goodspeed Opera House. There seemed to be over four hundred girls auditioning for this particular show called *Hit the Deck*. They were only going to choose two non-Equity girls, and I got chosen. I got a call and they said, "You now have an Equity card and you're going up to the Goodspeed Opera House." I wasn't even prepared for that information. I had come to New York mainly for experience and to take some classes and hopefully see a show. I went back to Delaware, packed my bags, sold my car, and went up to Goodspeed.

Interviewer: As a performer?

Stroman: Yes, as a performer. In New York City, you really can't have a split focus. You have to be one thing or the other. It's not like in London, where you can write a book, do a movie, and be an actor. In New York— really, in America—you have to succeed at that one big thing. I couldn't really come to New York and say, "I want to be a choreographer," and just take over. I had to assess the situation first. I came as a performer because I could sing and dance, but I did not want to be known as a performer. It was more coming to New York to find out what it was all about. I knew that at one point I would have to stop performing if I decided to go for it as a choreographer.

Interviewer: Did you know when you came to New York that ultimately you wanted to be a choreographer, and you saw being a performer as the first step in that process?

Stroman: Sure, I think so. It was the first step in understanding show business. I would have been too young to be in charge of seasoned professionals. Eventually I did a short-lived musical on Broadway that lasted two weeks. It was called *Musical Chairs*. I met a young guy named Scott Ellis, who also did not want to be a performer. He wanted to be a director, and we sort of bonded in that musical. We got to talking, and we approached Kander and Ebb to ask if we could do a revival of *Flora, the Red Menace* down at the Vineyard Theatre. Scott knew them because he had done *The Rink*, and I knew them because I had done the national tour of *Chicago*. They said yes. We went down to the Vineyard Theatre and mounted this production and got paid about two hundred dollars. It had a cult following for that summer. In fact, everybody saw it. Hal Prince came to see it, Liza Minnelli came to see it, and we became very good friends with Kander and Ebb. From there, Scott and I asked Kander and Ebb if we could do a retrospective of their work. That became *And the*

World Goes 'Round, which was very successful Off-Broadway. Then I ended up doing *Don Giovanni* and *Show Boat* with Hal Prince and *Liza: Stepping Out* with Liza Minnelli at Radio City Music Hall. So *Flora* kind of exposed me to the masses. It's one of those things that, if you believe, you just take a chance, even if it means you're going to make two hundred dollars for four months. It's that old rule about taking a chance.

Interviewer: How much time was there between Goodspeed and *Flora?*

Stroman: Maybe five to seven years.

Interviewer: During that time you did a number of touring shows like *Chicago?*

Stroman: And a Broadway show called *Whoopee!*

Interviewer: All as a performer?

Stroman: Yes. But I started to choreograph and direct smaller events like industrial shows, people's cabaret acts, and commercials. At that point I realized, "I can do this. I have to stop being known as a performer. I want to be known as a creator." Even if it meant starving, I was going to go for it.

Interviewer: Where did the transition come, to directing as well as choreographing?

Stroman: *The Music Man* was the first show that I directed and choreographed on Broadway. After that, it was *Contact,* then *The Producers,* and then *Thou Shalt Not.*

Interviewer: Was that a natural transition? Obviously there is a tradition in musical theater of choreographers also being directors.

Stroman: It was a natural stepping-stone for me, because when I choreograph I treat each dance as a scene. Every dance has a beginning and a middle and an end. I treat the dancers as actors. That's why I feel my collaborations with directors like Hal Prince or Trevor Nunn or Nick Hytner have been very harmonious—because the dance is considered more of the scene work.

Interviewer: Was it also a matter of establishing your credentials as a choreographer in order to become a director? Wouldn't it have been hard to have presented yourself immediately as a director of musicals?

Stroman: I think so. I had won the Tony Award for choreography for *Crazy for You* and for *Show Boat,* so at least in the business I had believability. I knew how to get a show up. Yes, because I established myself as a credible choreographer, people then believed that I could direct.

Interviewer: Do you like the idea of having control of both sides—and the responsibility?

Stroman: I do think some pieces need two people. *A Christmas Carol* at Madison Square Garden is in its tenth year, and that is a huge extravaganza that took two people. Something like *Contact* that was created out of my mind has one vision to it, so it was only natural that it was directed and choreographed by a single person. Even with something like *The Producers,* the comedy is nonstop, so the seam work of the choreography is completely comic-oriented. It's the same humor all the way through, so that was quite natural, too.

Interviewer: What do you look for in a musical in deciding to do it? People must bring projects to you all the time.

Stroman: I have to be attracted to the music, really; that's the first thing. I've been offered quite a few things where the music didn't speak to me. Not only that, but I think I need to be able to find a way to make it believable that people sing and dance. There are a lot of musicals out there that really shouldn't be musicals; but if there is a way to make it believable that these people launch into song and dance, then I am attracted to it.

Interviewer: And that can be either an old show somebody wants to revive or a new show?

Stroman: Absolutely. *The Music Man* is a wonderful musical. It's only natural that this man comes to town, to a very stiff town. When it opens, nobody moves at all, and then I get to do a journey of choreography and of movement all the way through as the Music Man revitalizes the town and brings song and dance to it. There's a wonderful line where the little boy says, "Is there a band?" and Harold Hill, the Music Man, says, "There's always a band." That's in all of our minds, all of us in musical theater; so in that way that speaks to me as a very believable musical. When I do a musical, I do research on it, on the decade, on the geographical area, and on the society at that time. *Oklahoma!* is based on the research I've done on the Old West. "The Farmer and the Cowman" is based on square dancing and folk dancing in America at the turn of the century. Even in "Kansas City," the ragtime stuff that he brings back from Kansas City is based on real immigrant clogging steps. I do a lot of research and then make it into my own style.

Interviewer: Even if nobody in the audience knows those steps are authentic Kansas City clog steps, you know!

Stroman: Yes, and then it motivates me to create. So I immerse myself in the history of the piece, of the decade, and of the geographical area. In *Show Boat,* people danced very differently in the North than they did in the South, so I applied that to the choreography.

Interviewer: One of the things that fascinates outsiders about a musical is the mystery of the collaborative process, in which you often have, if it is a new musical, a librettist, a lyricist, a composer, a choreographer, a director, and sometimes a star performer all trying to get their views heard. How has that worked for you? Is it difficult—or is it exciting? Or is it all things rolled into one?

Stroman: The collaboration is the most important process in a musical. It takes a village to put up a musical. It's very important that everyone is on the same page and that everybody is seeing what the director is seeing; so the collaboration with the set designer and the costume designer is very important. It's wonderful actually to feed off one another when you go to these meetings when you are creating a show. With *The Producers*, William Ivey Long, the costume designer, drew me a costume sketch for the girls in the "Prisoner of Love" number. He just happened to draw in a ball and chain on their feet. That inspired me to ask for real balls and chains and to have bouncing balls. I might not have ever thought of that had William not drawn it.

Interviewer: Would you say that in any musical theater collaboration there has to be a dominant figure? In *The Producers*, wasn't Mel Brooks's vision the predominant factor? In *Contact*, your vision was probably predominant. Do you in each case have to have a predominant vision that takes the lead?

Stroman: Sure, but that's always the director's—how you see the set, the costumes, the lights. You could do the most wonderful dance step, but if it is not lit correctly by the lighting designer, it doesn't mean anything. The director should always be the lead person.

Interviewer: Always? Even in a situation like *The Producers*, where Mel Brooks might come to you and say, "That's not what I meant"?

Stroman: Mel wrote a wonderful script. He wrote wonderful jokes. But he was also coming into a different world. What was wonderful was that Mel collaborates.

Interviewer: What you're saying is that he let you show him that world rather than trying to impose his world on a world that he didn't know very well.

Stroman: He's different from a lot of writers because he comes from a world of collaboration. He wrote *Your Show of Shows* with other writers and famous comedians like Sid Caesar and Carl Reiner. He knows how to collaborate. A lot of writers don't. Mel thrives on collaboration. He came to me with these incredible eccentric characters and this wonderful script and then was able to hear how to make that into a musical. He's just a genius.

Interviewer: What about the star in that situation? Can the star either be part of the collaboration or a disruptive force?

Stroman: Yes, absolutely. They're stars for a reason. A lot of them know why they are there and how they got there, because they do a particular thing correctly. It's a matter of using what they have, what has made them stars, and trying to apply that to the piece.

Interviewer: Did Nathan Lane and Matthew Broderick contribute to the design of *The Producers* through their own personalities and ideas as the process went along?

Stroman: Sure. Matthew and Nathan are inspiring to be around. They learn quickly, and they are spontaneous. They'll do something, and it just inspires me to take them somewhere else.

Interviewer: With *The Music Man,* you decided not to go with an established star. Did that make a difference?

Stroman: I needed someone who had real command of the language, and Craig Bierko indeed does. A salesman who has great diction and knowledge of words will always be successful; Craig has both.

Interviewer: How much did the ghost of the original production and movie, both with Robert Preston, haunt you?

Stroman: I didn't watch the movies. I didn't watch *The Producers* or *Oklahoma!* or *Show Boat.* I'm actually inspired by the music, so I don't have those ghosts. I think audience members have these ghosts, but I've never had them.

Interviewer: In a sense, then, you reconceive any show you do, because you start with the premise that you're going to make it into a realistic story. If you do that, then you forget everything that has been done before, because you're thinking of it in terms of it being your show.

Stroman: Yes. Even with a revival. I treat it like a new piece, like it's never been done before. I ask the actors to do the same. All the actors are creating the back story and relationships onstage. Whether it be in a club in New York City or an Italian restaurant in New York City or on the wide open spaces of Oklahoma or in the town of River City, it's about developing relationships within that particular world.

Interviewer: What do you think has happened to the musical historically? It's harder and harder to get a new musical on. There are a tremendous number of revivals, as we all know. Do you think that the future for new musicals is grim?

Stroman: No, but I think financially it's quite tough. You have to be pretty close to being right to ask someone to put twelve million dollars into a musical now; the expense is daunting. It's difficult to have people put money into it and back it. I think that's why a lot of revivals have reared up, because they're tried-and-true pieces; a lot of investors don't want to take a chance. But I do believe musicals change; they take on different forms. When Cameron Mackintosh was at his height in New York with *Phantom* and *Les Miz* and *Miss Saigon, Crazy for You* came in. I think *Crazy for You* caused a resurgence in dance musicals again. For ten years there had been no dance on Broadway; because of that show, musicals started to change. They're never going to go away, but they are going to morph into different variations.

Interviewer: What kinds of morphing do you see going on?

Stroman: I think it changes with the times. Since September 11, people do want happier musicals. *The Producers* has brought great laughter to a lot of people since September 11. I happened to have been in the middle of doing a musical, *Thou Shalt Not,* that wasn't a comedy that opened two weeks after September 11, and that timing was off.

Interviewer: Do you think that the timing had a lot to do with that show not being successful?

Stroman: Yes. People did not want anybody to do anything wrong, and the idea of watching a musical based on Zola's novel *Thérèse Raquin,* where someone commits adultery and murder, the timing was not right for that. Right now people are leaning more toward happier musicals; that might change next year. People might want to go back again to *Rent* and *Noise/Funk.* It changes as society changes, or as current events affect people. Another example of bad timing was *Steel Pier,* the last Kander and Ebb show I did. It opened right after the revival of *Chicago,* and audiences didn't want Kander and Ebb to do anything romantic. They were writing a romantic score, but the audiences wanted an ornery, sparky, and jazzy score like *Chicago;* so they compared us to *Chicago*—and who could have known that the revival of *Chicago* would be playing a block away from us? It was just bad timing, and that does happen with musicals.

Interviewer: You haven't had many failures, but have you learned from them?

Stroman: Even if I've had a financial failure, it's never been an artistic failure. I've always learned and been able to apply what I've learned to the next piece. My whole career has been like a stepping-stone, of balancing onto the next stone and taking that on to the next show and to the next collaboration. The more I learn about other people's departments, the stronger my own department becomes. The more I learn about lighting, the more I learn about costumes, about tech, about sets, it just makes my own talents stronger.

Interviewer: Could you give an example, using a specific instance from a recent experience, where you did something or responded to something in a way that ten or fifteen years ago you might not have?

Stroman: I think I know more about lighting now than I would have known ten years ago. I know how lighting is going to heighten a number, how lighting can help me focus a number, and how lighting can help me set a mood. How lighting adds to my choreography is probably one of the biggest growth points.

Interviewer: What have you learned as a director?

Stroman: As a director, you have to respect the process of every actor. Each actor's process is different. Some are slower, some are faster. Some are unpleasant. Some are completely frivolous. You have to click into that actor's process; you have to respect it, deal with it, and help guide them along so that you are all working the same way. It's a different kind of energy you need to apply to help those actors through.

Interviewer: Is that different from working with dancers?

Stroman: Yes. Dancers are very smart and very fast. Dancers speak the same language. Actors speak very different languages. With actors, you need to find out what piece of terminology is going to make them understand: Do they need to hear a motivation or is it better to do it in imagery or is it better to do it musically? It's finding out how they are going to understand it. For example, in *Contact,* in the second short story, about the abused housewife, when she is lifted into the air for the first time by the headwaiter, she needs to imagine being swept off her feet or she needs to imagine flying through the air or she needs to imagine being touched by a man or she needs to imagine flying herself. I need to use different images or motivated sentences that are going to all of a sudden make that actress hit the right facial expression and find the essence of that particular acting piece and the joy in it.

Interviewer: Have you had an experience where the collaborative process has broken down in some way?

Stroman: September 11 and its effect on *Thou Shalt Not* was quite difficult. Trying to rally the company together to go on to do a dark piece was quite difficult—just because we didn't know what was going to happen to New York at that time. We didn't know whether we were going to continue to be strong. I think people were quite scared all over New York City. Even getting people into the theater was difficult. That was the most difficult time for me, to have to muster up strength to keep actors going, keep the crew going, keep the musicians going. It took a toll on that musical.

Interviewer: Do you think that piece would have a chance five years from now?

Stroman: Absolutely. It's a wonderful story. It gave me the opportunity to act and dance guilt, which one is never really allowed to do in a musical. What would that be if one was to dance guilt? What would that be if one were to really act guilt? As an artist, that musical stretched my mind.

Interviewer: Can you choose one of your shows and take us through the full history of your involvement with it—conception, casting, rehearsal?

Stroman: Okay—*The Producers.* The start of *The Producers* was Mel Brooks bringing the script, which was mainly the screenplay, and it became the question of how to make this into a musical. Mel worked with Tom Meehan, the writer, and we met for a solid year every week on how to make this into a musical. What was great about Mel was that he was the man who invented or conjured up these very eccentric characters and he was also now the man who was going to make them sing. So it was quite natural that he knew them so well, because he actually became them when he wrote them.

Interviewer: So when they were turning a screenplay into a musical, you had a great deal of influence?

Stroman: Yes, but that would be true for any show. With *Contact,* I worked closely with John Weidman; and with *Crazy for You,* I was working with Mike Ockrent, the director, and Ken Ludwig, because that was a whole new book that Ken wrote. The only similarity to the original show is that an easterner goes west; other than that it's all new.

Interviewer: So you as the choreographer and Mike Ockrent as the director were involved with the show from very early on?

Stroman: Yes. From day one, it was how to make this into a musical and how to develop it. The Gershwin Estate allowed me to arrange all the music. I opened up that music with a dance arrangement by Peter Howard. I took "Slap That Bass" and made that number conceptual plotwise. It's how the character Bobby Child gave that town rhythm. So when he goes to leave at the end of act one, they say, "Oh, no, you can't leave, because this is what you gave us." And we saw him give it to them in "Slap That Bass." It was how to make that all believable.

Interviewer: To get back to *The Producers,* you started working with the writers very early on?

Stroman: Yes, and then Mel wrote all those wonderful songs and those wonderful lyrics, but then it became how to write a score, how to open it up. So I brought in a dance arranger named Glen Kelly, who is a wonderful pianist, and we went into a studio. What I did was I took a melody and said to him, "Let me hear what that melody sounds like played in a fast tune." Or "Play it in three-quarter time." Or "Play it like a Mexican hat dance." We did all the different ways you could invoke emotion, build a number, and keep the story in the number. An audience today has a very cinematic eye, and the story has to always be told and the plot has to always be pushed forward. That is true even in transitions. There are no more blackouts in a musical; the story keeps being told as the set changes. It was all about how to build those numbers. For example, Mel wrote the song "King of Broadway." We had to decide who should be with Max, who he should be singing this to. We decided that it would be best if he would sing it to the denizens of Broadway—the street people, the people who are out at night after the shows have ended.

Interviewer: Whose decisions are those? Did you all decide those things together?

Stroman: It's a collaborative process. It was ultimately my saying to Mel, "I'll have a wardrobe mistress on the street and a garbage man." And he said, "You've got to have two nuns; two nuns are funny." So we have two nuns in there. Then it was taking the song and supporting Max's ethnic background, making these denizens of Broadway do a hora and have a big celebratory Jewish wedding in the middle of the street. We do steps that one might find in a Jewish wedding, but they are all celebrating Max's rise again. It's about analyzing the number, analyzing how one would support the lyric. I worked that out in the studio with a pianist and two assistants, and pretty much when I went into rehearsal I had the whole show thought through, choreographed, and blocked. But I also feed off the actors. I find I get the richest result if I do a lot of homework but also act like I have nothing.

Interviewer: After you blocked the whole show in the studio with the pianist, did you then go back to Mel Brooks and Tom Meehan and say, "Here's what I'm doing"? Or did they leave you alone at that point?

Stroman: No. A lot of times I needed something from them. I'd say, "I need an exit line to get out of this scene," and they'd write something for it. It was truly a strong collaboration.

Interviewer: Was there never a point when Mel Brooks said, "That's not what I meant this scene to be"?

Stroman: He might have, but in this case he didn't.

Interviewer: But, generically, that could happen?

Stroman: It could happen; but that's why I have to immerse myself in whatever that world is, whether it's the world of the wide open spaces of Oklahoma or the world of the contemporary club in New York. With *The Producers*, I had to immerse myself in the world of Mel Brooks. That had to be my research. I took no missteps because I immersed myself in that world.

Interviewer: So you had to be creative Susan Stroman doing your thing, but you also had to subordinate yourself to some extent to the vision of the writer.

Stroman: That's why it's important to do that research. You have to become those people. I have to become those characters. Whether I become Curly or Laurey or Max, I have to know how they are going to move and how they are going to exit.

Interviewer: What role did you take in the casting of the show?

Stroman: I think that's probably the hardest, because a lot of departments have to agree on casting: the musical director, the choreographer, the director, often the producer, and of course the writers. It's a lot of departments coming together to finalize on one person.

Interviewer: Does that sometimes cause disagreement?

Stroman: Yes, probably more so than anything else. Everything else, I think, you can kind of understand people's different passions for the collaboration. Casting is the most difficult, because you have to be a real quadruple threat now to be in the theater. You have to sing, you have to dance, you have to act, and you have to be funny. You're asked to do a lot of things and you are asked to please a lot of different departments. And, sad to say, if the producer, who is putting millions of dollars into this show, wants somebody who is not quite as talented, I might have to make compromises. It's quite a big discussion.

Interviewer: But it *is* a discussion, isn't it? It's not the producer who always gets his or her way, is it?

Stroman: The director has to have the last word. If the director doesn't have the last word, the show will go down.

Interviewer: Is that pretty much universally accepted?

Stroman: I think so. When it isn't, there's always a problem.

Interviewer: Speaking of producers, the heyday of David Merrick and Robert Whitehead and the great producers that we all know about is gone. Now musicals are produced by conglomerates. The one dominant producer type is not really around anymore. Does that make it easier or harder?

Stroman: It makes it more difficult, because you have to make sure you have an answer for more people than just one person. *Oklahoma!* was different because it was Cameron Mackintosh and Cameron is a wonderful producer. But yes, it's true; musicals today have up to fifteen or twenty producers, and it's quite difficult.

Interviewer: Now you've cast and you're in rehearsals. What happened then?

Stroman: In rehearsal, even though I've done my homework and have the show plotted out in my head, I don't necessarily share that with the actor. I would rather the actor feel that he has created this whole thing. I would rather an actor feel as if he's choreographed the whole show himself. It's better to look like it has come from a natural place. It is now my role to sort of guide the actor and be there for him.

Interviewer: How do you do that?

Stroman: It's talking through the character and saying things like "What if we tried something like this and see if that feels natural?"

Interviewer: What about with the ensemble? Is it different with the dancers? The dance numbers are pretty set, aren't they?

Stroman: With my choreography, I always have something in unison, which is done and taught to them. But I always allow the ensemble to have their moment in the sun. All the numbers have featured moments so the characters can shine through. In *Oklahoma!* there were the two little girls who chased the little boy, which was a story I wove through the show.

Interviewer: Would there be some freedom allowed to those dancers as you rehearse the show?

Stroman: Absolutely. For example, in *Contact* in that third short story, with all those dancers, one couple's from Westchester, one couple's from Brooklyn, one couple's from Connecticut. That makes you do the same choreography but dance it a different way. It's giving them those characters. One guy's a lonely guy; he doesn't get to dance with anybody—so he dances in a different way. It gives them a chance to create and to make it their own. Then all the choreography and blocking will come from a very natural place.

Interviewer: How often would you say your conception of a moment or a series of moments might change based on how a performer did something?

Stroman: It does change, again because I'm inspired by them. Not only do I do the homework but I do react spontaneously. I am prepared to let that actor take me someplace else.

Interviewer: And that happens?

Stroman: Sure, that happens—especially with someone like Nathan Lane. Some actors come in and give you 60 percent until they've dipped their toes in the water. Nathan Lane immediately jumps completely in the water. It's a different process, but that is exciting for me because then the electricity flies.

Interviewer: He comes to the first rehearsal ready to do the part full out?

Stroman: Full out. He has jumped into the pool. Other actors come with their toes sticking in the pool.

Interviewer: That must have been challenging for you at those first rehearsals when he was in the pool totally and others were not. As the director, you had to keep both going at once and not say to those other actors, "Keep up with Nathan Lane"—because they're doing it a different way.

Stroman: It's interesting. Some people were so excited they jumped right into that pool too! Ultimately you want everybody to jump in the pool, but you don't want them to drown either. You don't want them to be afraid. It takes a lot of your energy—again, it's about respecting the process and trying ultimately to get everyone into the pool. It's just finding what you can say to that actor that's going to help him and make him feel the most comfortable. I'd love to stand in the middle of a room and have an actor feel that he could run at me and jump on me and that I would catch him. That's what you have to make an actor feel.

Interviewer: As the show began to develop, did you have less and less to do?

Stroman: No. It was constant, because then I started to add other elements. I got them on the sets and other ideas happened. I got them in their costumes and other ideas happened. Lights, props, and everything developed in stages. Then, of course, the final thing that you add to this is the audience. Something you might have thought was really, really funny elicits silence from the audience. Then you have to analyze why that's not funny. Or some other moment, which you thought would really be heartbreaking, you feel no emotion. I sit in the house with the audience for the first couple of nights trying to feel what they are feeling. If it isn't working, it's not right. In *Crazy for You,* there's a number called "What Causes That?" The two Zanglers are together, mirroring each other, and they're both drunk. They both put chairs on top of their heads and then walk like Follies girls in headdresses. I thought that would be very funny. I got it out there and there was silence in the audience. I thought, "Why isn't this working? I can't believe this isn't working." Mike Ockrent, the director, said to me, "Why don't you change the spotlight to pink right at that moment?" The minute they put the chairs on top of their heads I changed the spotlight to pink, and I got a big laugh. It was the same move, but I just changed the color of the spot and the audience knew that something was funny. That was reaching into another department to help your own work. But that also coincides with doing research. The more you know about the world that you are supposed to be in, the more you'll know how to apply those other elements.

Interviewer: Do you involve the other craftspeople on the show in your research? Does the costume designer have to know as much about Oklahoma as you do?

Stroman: Absolutely. It's a big part of it—those meetings with those people and making sure we're all researching the same decade, the same time, the same slice of society.

Interviewer: I would think that for a choreographer the costumes can make a tremendous difference.

Stroman: Sure. Who would have thought a yellow dress would have so much power? In *Contact*, William Ivey Long designed a dress that has become theater history. He's very good at making magic clothes. He makes a dress look like it couldn't move at all, and all of a sudden a woman dances and becomes magical.

Interviewer: Did you say to him that you had to have a yellow dress?

Stroman: I said, "I need a yellow dress. I need a girl in a yellow dress." But William came up with the design. We went through about fifteen yellow dresses, because I was asking it to do so much. The dress had to have a little sparkle to it, but it couldn't scratch the men when they picked her up. The dress had to have movement to it, but it couldn't be too long or it would have caught her heel. The dress had to be sexy, but it also had to hold her in so she didn't fall out of it. The dress had to be the right color—yellow meaning "proceed with caution," as opposed to sunshine yellow. I talked to William about what the dress needed to do, what that color yellow needed to say—and then William designed the dress.

Interviewer: After the show has opened and is a success, then what happens?

Stroman: I still go back and see all the shows periodically.

Interviewer: How often do you go back?

Stroman: It depends on the show, on which shows need me more. With *Contact*, they're like lions. They're very strong, very disciplined. It's a mature, more sensual group. The actors at *The Producers* are comedians, so they're very needy. "Can I try this?" "Can I do this?" "Can I have this?" So they need me more than the *Contact* group.

Interviewer: What about *Oklahoma!* and *The Music Man*?

Stroman: They're almost dependent on each other. They're big families out there. *The Music Man* was a family because it was about a community, River City. *Oklahoma!* is about a community. Because you have directed the show as a community, they depend on each other.

Interviewer: What happens when the community changes, when the cast changes?

Stroman: I have to go check on that.

Interviewer: Do you rehearse the new cast very carefully?

Stroman: Yes. But I think if at the beginning you give a company as much information as possible about how to create the community, then they will embrace new actors as they come into it.

Interviewer: Do you do brush-up rehearsals of individual scenes?

Stroman: Yes, even if it's just a particular thirty-second piece of a scene. I think actors really like having notes; they like to know someone is watching them. In every show I do, I also have someone maintain the show.

Interviewer: Those people have been with the show since the beginning, so they know the design and the process?

Stroman: Yes, they know all the motivated moments. They are hired to maintain the show.

Interviewer: And when a show goes on the road, what happens then?

Stroman: I open it in the first city for them, but then they are on their own. They have a main person there who is in touch with me all the time, and occasionally I'll drop in on a touring show.

Interviewer: What do you think of critics? Have you ever learned anything from a critic?

Stroman: One critic will say I'm the greatest thing since Balanchine, and another critic will say too bad Fosse is dead and she's alive; so I can't listen to them. If I listened to the one, I'd have to listen to the other. I listen to the audience.

Charles Strouse

Photo by Chuck Pulin

Charles Strouse was born in New York City on June 7, 1928. He studied at the Eastman School of Music and later took private lessons in composition with Aaron Copland and Nadia Boulanger. His scores for New York musicals include Shoestring Revue (1955), Bye Bye Birdie (1960), All American (1962), Golden Boy (1964), It's a Bird . . . It's a Plane . . . It's Superman (1966), Applause (1970), Six (1971), The Member of the Wedding (1975), By Strouse (1977), Annie (1977), A Broadway Musical (1978), Charlie and Algernon (1980), Bring Back Birdie (1981), Dance a Little Closer (1983), Mayor (1985), Rags (1986), Nick and Nora (1991), and Annie Warbucks (1993).

His film score credits include Bonnie and Clyde (1967), The Night They Raided Minsky's (1968), There Was a Crooked Man (1970), and Just Tell Me What You Want (1980).

He received Tony Awards for Bye Bye Birdie (Best Musical), Applause (Best Musical), and Annie (Best Score). In 1999, he received the Richard

Rodgers Award for Lifetime Achievement, and he was inducted into the Theatre Hall of Fame in 2002.
This interview took place on October 19, 1992.

• ———————————————————————————————— •

Interviewer: Can you begin by talking about how you got started writing for the musical theater?

Strouse: I'm a bit of an anomaly. I studied music academically with some very fine teachers and I did not go into the musical theater early in my career. Instead I wrote what is called serious or abstract music. When I graduated from college, I supported myself by playing in bands and for dance classes; I played in burlesque houses when they used to have those. It was in playing for dance classes that I met a choreographer who invited me to go to a summer stock theater to play what they laughingly called in those days choreographic piano. It was a form of slavery but I did it, and it was something of a turning point in my career because at the time I was very involved in writing a particular serious piece. I had just received a fellowship at the MacDowell Colony and was going to do it, but I gave it up to do this other thing, which I thought would be more fun. Subsequently I grew to love the applause of audiences; and my wishes about musical theater, which I really hadn't admitted to, started to come true when my first Broadway show, *Bye Bye Birdie,* became a success. Obviously, I was hooked after that. I think of myself as a working composer. Interestingly, I have a reputation for being prolific, and yet I know that I am one of the slowest composers imaginable because I do a great deal of sketching but I'm kind of disciplined. I got that from a lot of my teachers. I love doing what I'm doing.

Interviewer: You say you do a lot of sketching. What does that mean?

Strouse: All students of music along the way study other composers. One of the most notable users of sketch material was Beethoven, who had notebooks filled with ideas that were later whittled down to his great compositions but started out very differently. I've always been a sketcher. I'll sit and write an awful lot of crap, frankly, but there'll be some little note in there—or a combination of notes—that I'll later play around with and use. That's my method. Though I'm inspired sometimes, I do more sketching than anything else.

Interviewer: Well, let's start with *Bye Bye Birdie,* which was your first Broadway show and a major success. Can you discuss how that came about?

Strouse: I had been up at summer stock with Lee Adams and Michael Stewart. We had written a revue called *Shoestring Revue,* which emanated from that experience and had a kind of modest success in New York. A producer came to us because he liked our work in this revue and asked us to do what for me was the most unlikely kind of assignment, a show about teenagers. Although I was not that far removed—I was twenty-seven or twenty-eight at the time when he came to me—it was not my background, and it seemed unusual that he liked my work and Lee's enough to ask us. But I researched it as I would a serious project. I listened very closely to the music of Presley, Fats Domino, Annette Funicello, and people like that, and we wrote it. There were five different book-writers involved in the history of *Bye Bye Birdie*. Among them, oddly enough, were Mike Nichols and Elaine May, who I think were number three and number four in the grouping that ultimately was turned down by investors. Finally, Lee Adams and I insisted on bringing in Mike Stewart, with whom we had worked in summer stock. He became the book-writer of record, and it was a wonderful story. It was everybody's first Broadway show, which made it hard to believe and fantastic in a way I couldn't connect to.

I was studying at the time with Aaron Copland. I had studied with him for three years as a composition student after I came back from Europe, where I had worked with Nadia Boulanger. I am one of what I sometimes think of as an army of composers who worked with that woman. I remember that when Aaron came back from London, he called me and said there was a show on Broadway with a composer who spelled his name like I did. He said, "Is that any relation to you?" At the time, everyone called me "Buddy," and he knew me as "Buddy" rather than as Charles. I said no, it was me. He was astounded because he had never heard anything I'd written that had a jazz vocabulary at all. It was a secret part of my life. Maybe I was embarrassed by it; I don't remember, but I kept it a secret in any case. He was delighted for me and encouraged me. I do remember that I was somewhat embarrassed by the show. My credentials were all academic ones, and I thought that it was a kind of rock-and-roll show with a title all of us hated at the time. We really hated it, but we couldn't think of anything else. We did have a lot of other titles, but nobody liked any of them, and the poster had to get printed. To this day, I don't know how we landed on it, but we did. I also remember that we won the Antoinette Perry Award, which meant nothing to me at the time. Now I'm desperate to win it again, but at the time it meant nothing. I was going out with this girl who later became my wife. What I remember about it is that we got this invitation that said I had been nominated for something called the Antoinette Perry Award and that they served dinner, which struck me as very important. I haven't changed that much, actually! I said, "Gee, they're going to give us this meal at the Waldorf!" They didn't hold it in a theater at that time. It was a big thing, so we went; and then we won, which was a dizzying kind of memory. My partner, Lee Adams, and I argued all the time, and when they said, "The winner for the best score, Charles Strouse and Lee Adams," we got up and I said to Lee, "We go that way up to the stage." He said, "No, that's blocked off. We go that way." I said, "We can't go through that way." We argued about even that, and somebody else picked up the award! Typical collaborators!

Interviewer: That's one of the best explanations of collaboration I've ever heard! What was your reaction to the Tommy Tune revival of *Bye Bye Birdie*? How was it different from the original?

Strouse: The Tommy Tune revival did not differ really at all. We did add two songs. It's very easy to explain why we added those songs. The show was really exactly Mike Stewart's book, which is hilariously funny, and all of our songs—but, as I say, we added two songs and took out one. Tommy Tune was wonderful in it, but I didn't feel it should have been brought to New York. What a lot of people didn't realize is something that has always pleased Lee and me very much. *Bye Bye Birdie* has been the most performed musical in America. Part of the reason is that it involves teenagers as well as adults. The same school will do it two, three, four, five times over the years, and it keeps increasing. It was interesting because here it was a first-class tour, and a lot of critics said, "Where has this show been? They pulled it out of mothballs." Actually, it's been around, is performed all the time, and was totally unchanged.

As I said, we wrote two new songs. One was because Tommy Tune loves performing; he's just the opposite of Dick Van Dyke, who hated performing. If we took a song away from Dick Van Dyke, he was the happiest man in the world. There was a moment in the show originally where Albert, the "hero," so to speak, tells his mother off, and he feels like he's a man for the first time in his life. Gower Champion, who directed the original production, had the orchestra play "The Battle Hymn of the Republic" as he stuck out his chest and strutted off. I always hated that cue because it seemed like what we call a television cue. It wasn't my music, but it just seemed a little bit cheap to me. It always got a terrific hand from the audience when he did it. Tommy right away said, "It's obvious that's his song." I had always thought so, too, so Lee and I wrote a song for him. We wrote another song for the mother, who was originally played by Kay Medford, who didn't sing. We took out one song. It was a song called "Spanish Rose." In these times there are very subtle dangers in certain political statements. *Bye Bye Birdie* has a great deal to do with this mother making fun of somebody being Hispanic who is going to marry her son. One of the critics in Los Angeles, where there's a large Hispanic population, actually called Lee and me and Mike (who is now deceased) to task and said that the show was "anti-Hispanic," which was ludicrous to us. We wrote the show for Chita Rivera, and the fact that this woman, who was comic and villainous in a comic way, made fun of Hispanics was all that was on our minds. So we took that out. Since the actress who played the mother in the revival, Marilyn Cooper, sang, we wrote a song for her. Otherwise the show was exactly the same and very good.

Interviewer: You mentioned *Shoestring Revue* earlier. Wasn't Bea Arthur in that?

Strouse: Yes, Bea Arthur was in *Shoestring Revue*. I was the musical director of *Shoestring Revue*, and Chita Rivera and Dody Goodman were also in it. I always feel immodestly that I discovered Chita, in a way, because she was there as an ensemble person. She was going to sing and dance only in the background. As soon as we heard her, I and a lot of the other authors threw every song we could her way. That was her first professional show as far as I know. The show was called *Shoestring Revue* because the producer, Ben Bagley, had no money. I don't know how he was able to get the thing on. For the overture in a mad moment I played "Oklahoma!" The critics liked that. We never asked Rodgers and Hammerstein's permission! It was a show that on opening night, I remember, nobody laughed at. Walter Kerr sat right in front of me, and he was in a terrible mood because it was pouring rain and he was drenched. We got all raves; so much for the vicissitudes of the theater.

Interviewer: Not long after *Bye Bye Birdie,* you did *Golden Boy.* Can you talk a little bit about that?

Strouse: *Golden Boy* was a show I wrote with Lee Adams and Clifford Odets just before he died. He died the first week of rehearsal and William Gibson took over. It was in its way a kind of groundbreaker, I think. In it there was a love story between different races. It was a score I was particularly proud of—not because of its inherent quality, although I did like it, but because for me as a composer it was the first time I had tried to use any depth of technique and also use jazz and pop rhythms. On a certain level, it was a show that dealt with passion and social problems. I felt pleased with myself that I had been able to lend a certain complexity to a score. Oddly enough, it's performed a great deal more in Japan than it is here. I think it's in its fifth year in Japan. Every year it seems another rock star does it there. They do it in blackface, which is really weird to me. A playwright friend of mine, Leslie Lee, who is African American, has loved the score for a long time, and he decided to do a version of it that he called "a street piece." It's a very accurate version of it, but he changed the book totally; it is the classic story of a black kid who comes out of the ghetto and becomes a sort of Sugar Ray Leonard. We did it in a workshop, and I thought it was really, really exciting. It has all new orchestrations.

Interviewer: Workshops are a fairly new phenomenon, aren't they? In the past, plays and musicals had out-of-town runs and then went to Broadway. Now, many of the very biggest and best composers and lyricists workshop their productions. Could you explain what a workshop production is?

Strouse: It's very complicated. If I wanted to waste a whole hour talking about it, I swear you could almost get a course in entertainment law. It started with *A Chorus Line,* when the choreographer/director of that show, Michael Bennett, did a workshop of what became the text of *A Chorus Line.* In this workshop, he used material that the dancers talked about and made that into the book itself; their very words and experiences became that show. At the same time, during a six- or eight-week period, he started putting the dances together, and for that Actors' Equity asked a certain percentage. I think it was 1 percent, to be given to the actors, which was very fair. After the actors' union decided that they would permit this in the case of that show, producers jumped on the bandwagon and decided to "workshop" a lot of things. It's not always the same because most workshops now deal with things that are written by writers. Nevertheless, the break that they give to the producers of paying the actor maybe $350 a week to do this workshop is balanced by the fact that they feel they're going to get a percentage of the piece for the actors. Writers have a certain resistance to this, so another kind of workshop is offered where they pay $450 a week but it can't be done in a theater and there are certain other restrictions. The workshop bandwagon is something that a lot of producers have climbed aboard. I myself think it's a very foolish way to go in many respects. You can see a great deal about the structure of a play in a workshop production, but so much of a musical is production—orchestrations, lighting, makeup, costumes, the very glamour of the musical, which is the thing that I'm very affected by—and you don't get that when you play to an audience of interested people who have not paid any money. They go there with their critical faculties exposed; their antennae are out. In New York, everybody is terribly smart about what you did wrong. As a matter of fact, I said this once to a reporter and I saw it quoted—so I think maybe it was clever. I said, "There are three major drives of man and woman. One is food, another is sex, and the third is rewriting somebody else's musical." I deeply believe that is so. Lee Adams once said to me, "If you listen to everybody at the beginning of the show, you would end up throwing every song out." There are reasons for not doing workshops, but the economics of the musical theater are such that any way one can put a show on and look at it is seized upon by producers.

Interviewer: In addition to writing musicals, you've also continued your interest in classical music by writing an opera, haven't you?

Strouse: I've actually written a number of operas. One was called *Nightingale;* it has been done at Wolf Trap outside Washington, D.C., and in London, and there's a London cast album of it. It's a full-length opera.

When I say full-length, I don't mean it's a grand opera. Grand opera is a difficult exercise for most composers to undergo because there are not that many opera houses that will do them. Most people have rarely heard about any of the grand operas that have been written by composers like Samuel Barber, Howard Hanson, and Bernard Rogers. There are very few opera houses in America, or Europe for that matter, which do American work. *Nightingale* can be done with a large cast, but it can also be done with ten or twelve people; I've seen it done both ways. The London recording is on the bigger scale; there's about forty people in it. As I said before, I'm a bit of an anomaly because my background is a serious musical background and yet my feelings about the musical are very much that it is an American art, which is basically jazzy, fun, parodistic, satirical, and pop. I have strong feelings, though they're not strong feelings pro or anti any other way of doing it, about composing. Basically, I love musicals that are fun and happy. I'm a bit of an oddball that way because my credentials are just the opposite, so I do write opera also.

Interviewer: Is there a difference in how you start or how you work if it's an opera, rather than a musical?

Strouse: In my mind, there's a difference. Aside from the fact that one thinks of opera as being a little bit more complex musically and psychologically, I think of myself very much as a songwriter when I'm writing a musical. I would like to have a hit song in it. I think every composer would like to hear his music played in any kind of arrangement. I've been told Verdi was very flattered to hear his tunes played by an organ grinder—and I would be, too. I'm sure Stravinsky felt that way about some of the tunes he used. I love writing for the human voice, so to have something that could be sung by many human voices is similar to writing for a musical. But the chronology is different. In an opera, time moves much more slowly because people stop and sing about broad subjects—philosophical, introspective, noble, or military. In a musical, time tends to go faster and in real time. I don't know whether that's a rule. I would say that opera has to do with one wanting to do a broader and more complicated psychological and technical kind of exercise in music.

Interviewer: After the great success of *Annie*, why did you do a sequel?

Strouse: A number of reporters in Los Angeles asked me the same question: "Why are you so dumb? Why are you doing this?" One of my answers was "I really think in looking back on it, it probably was a dumb thing to do." But after it bombed in Washington as *Annie 2*, it became a success on the road. The title was changed to *Annie Warbucks*; we had very good reviews, and it's really a good show. One of the things that encouraged me to do it was that, unbeknownst to the critics and certainly unbeknownst to most of the pros in New York, the people in Washington during the show's last week there told us to go on. We worked on the show; we were in Washington for five weeks. With terrific hindsight I can tell you what we did wrong. When we started to straighten it out in Washington, the people who probably very disappointedly held on to these tickets came and started to tell us, "Wait a second. There's a lot that's good about this." By the last week, we even had, dare I say, ovations, and we began to say, "The people are saying something to us." So we continued with it. It became *Annie Warbucks*. We went back to the Goodspeed Opera House in Connecticut, where it and *Annie* had both started, and worked on it for nine weeks, and then we went to Chicago. The reviews in Chicago were unanimous in either their praise or encouragement, and the audiences were lovely to us. We kept going, and now we're doing the California circuit; then we're coming to New York.

Interviewer: Another of your recent shows, *Nick and Nora*, had considerable difficulties. There were all sorts of stories about conflicts between the collaborators. Do you mind talking about that?

Strouse: Actually, it's very easy for me to talk about it because there was such a dichotomy of thought in the end. *Nick and Nora* was taken from a classic American detective story by Dashiell Hammett made into a move called *The Thin Man*, with Myrna Loy and William Powell. It became imbedded in American consciousness. When Arthur Laurents did the script for the musical, he wrote what I called a murderously witty script dealing with a real murder but with people who are outrageous. To my mind as the composer, the only way that this mystery could be told and truly appreciated by an audience was to level it with a great measure of style. I came up with an idea that at one point certainly for me seemed to be a solution to it—and it was for Arthur, too, at one point. But Arthur was the director as well as the author, which is a problem in the power plays that go with such a giant undertaking. In my mind, the only way this mystery could be told was for me to pull a kind of trick of style. I wanted to do the movies of the 1940s, when I grew up. I was particularly attracted to the music of Erich Korngold, Max Steiner, Victor Young, Miklos Rozsa, and people like that. In those days, producers, unlike today, really wanted their money's worth. They had a seventy-piece orchestra, and they wanted the screen always filled with music; it was a very rich tapestry. If there was a scene in which Bette Davis entered a room and she was angry, the music not only described her anger but it described her puzzlement, her doubt, her cowardice, and it described whether she had eaten a meal a moment before. A composer like Steiner went crazy on dancing woodwinds—and all she had done was say hello or something!

It seemed to me that this technique was the only way I could deal with both a real murder and the real dark passions that Arthur had drawn and still capture the humor of these outrageous characters in California whom he knew so well and drew so very well. Musically I could be funny when they were being serious; I could be serious and even murderous to mislead the audience as to who they were. I could dance when they were standing still, and I could stand still when they were dancing. It seemed to me that by exercising this power as a composer I could come up with a stylistic fabric that would not only make the play interesting but express the tensions of this real murder—and at the same time we'd have a unique piece. Imbedded in this would be all these songs. Richard Maltby, the lyricist, and I did something that, as songwriters, I think was very unselfish. Arthur might dispute this. We almost never ended songs. We interrupted songs. I don't think any song was ever played once in its entirety; the lyrics were changed to accommodate certain things happening. As a result—and we knew this would happen—people didn't recognize that there was a score there. It's one of the reasons I particularly like the recording. When we got into rehearsal, Arthur as the director—and I cannot tell you how much I admire him and think he's a great man of the theater—for some reason, whether it was technical, whether it was his own self-interest in terms of the words he had written, found this technique undoable. We had a difference that was so profound that the whole show was done differently and not to my liking; the rehearsal period became quite uncomfortable for me. It turned into about the only fight I've had that I didn't understand. I've dealt with pride and ego, but I wasn't able to deal with him. It's interesting, because I could not admire his gifts more; he's a brilliant, charming, and funny man. This is a work that should have found a level, but I can see now in hindsight that we never could agree on the level.

Interviewer: You mentioned the recording. Is it available? And how did you record it if it had such a brief lifespan? I've heard that some of it was recorded abroad.

Strouse: Jonathan Tunick's orchestrations were recorded in London. Since the show was a failure, there wasn't the kind of backing for a recording that usually exists. It was decided to take the orchestrations to London and record them with a British orchestra, and then the original cast did the voices and lyrics in New York. It's not such an unusual thing technologically; it's done all the time in rock and pop records. There were a lot of union problems, but they were finally solved. It's a recording I'm quite proud of. When we made the recording, we removed the play. As I said, Richard and I with real artistic conviction decided we were going to fragment every song. And we did so with no exceptions, except for one song called "Class," which was written whole and performed whole. There is not one other song in the original script which is done whole. The cast album has for me what was the original impulse of some of the music, what I thought would be the style of the show, which hopefully would capture the tension, the murder, and the glamour of an intensely glamorous piece.

Interviewer: Obviously the collaborative process did not work very well with *Nick and Nora;* but in other instances you've worked very successfully with others. Could you discuss some of your other collaborations and how they differed from one another? I'm thinking specifically of your collaborations with lyricists.

Strouse: With *Bye Bye Birdie,* as I mentioned earlier, we went through five different sets of writers, and we ended up with only four of the songs we had originally written; I can't even remember which ones they were. Mike Stewart wrote a whole story around those four songs, and then we added all kinds of elements. In the writing of the songs themselves for that show, Lee Adams and I worked very closely together. He would actually write some lyrics as I was writing the tune; he would encourage me and I would encourage him. We fed upon one another's ideas. In some ways, that's the way I prefer to work. Martin Charnin, with whom I wrote *Annie,* likes to have a song totally finished before he writes any lyrics. I wrote a show about six years ago with Sammy Cahn, who was the most facile of all lyricists. He was so facile that when we would write together—and this is a bit of an exaggeration but not totally—we would meet at eleven in the morning, and because my hands were stiff I would start by doodling on the piano. He'd say, "What was that?" I'd say, "What was what?" He'd say, "What you just played." I'd say, "I was just trying to stretch my hands." He'd say, "Play it again." I would, and he'd start singing, "I don't know why I love you." I'd say, "What are you doing?" He'd say, "Do it again," and he'd sit at the typewriter, encourage me, and I'd hear him typing. Then he'd pull the lyric out of the typewriter and hand it to me; it was as if a genie had said, "You have now written a song." I hadn't remembered writing it!

I worked with Alan Jay Lerner on a show. Alan would sit with me while I composed the music, which was a very unusual thing. I was very modest about it at the beginning because I'm not used to working in front of anybody. But he insisted on sitting there; one day he sat with me for ten hours. He told me that the reason he did that came from when he worked with Fritz Loewe. Loewe had been a child prodigy whose mother used to chain him to the piano, and he hated it; so Alan would sit there to make him do it. I'm the opposite; I love doing it, so it was a little bit of a strange relationship—but Alan was used to it. It was actually wonderful; I would get an idea and Alan would help me compose. He was a very passionate man and he would push me, which I liked a lot. Richard Maltby is the most unfocused, disorganized person I've met in my life. He'd forget what day of the week it was, but on the other hand he was a puzzle player and the cleverness of rhymes was terribly important to him. So it varies.

Interviewer: One of your least well known shows is one called *A Broadway Musical*, which had a very short run in, I think, 1978. Can you talk a little about that one?

Strouse: That was one of the last shows Lee Adams and I worked on together. It was a very difficult thing for us to face. We loved the show and we loved writing it. What *A Broadway Musical* was about was Lee's and my experience with Sammy Davis on *Golden Boy*. We wrote a musical about writing a musical with a big black musical star. I thought there was a lot that was terrific. It was directed originally by George Faison. He was let go, which was unfortunate because he did some terrific work, and Gower Champion came in, redid it, and did it wrong. George did it perhaps a little clumsily, but there was something to it. Gower changed a great deal of it around. I have found out in a life in the theater that there are certain subjects it is best not to bring up because almost anything one says about them can be interpreted in a way that is going to hurt somebody's feelings. Feminism is probably one, perhaps homosexuality, and race relations. I'm a New Yorker. I went to public schools, where my friends were Asian, black, and largely white. When I got out of school, I had to support myself, and I played for a lot of black acts. I was one of the few guys around that read music and played jazz, so I ended up playing for a lot of black performers. Believe it or not, I toured the South with Butterfly McQueen. We played in high schools for what anybody could afford to pay; people used to give a dollar and we played these poor black high schools. I'm not trying to give you any of my civil rights credentials because they're nothing exceptional, but I was spat upon for eating with a black woman in the South. I worked with another black performer at a very expensive hotel, and she wasn't allowed to use the pool. I've been there; my feelings about race relations are that anybody who's a friend is a friend. In *A Broadway Musical*, we did what was apparently unthinkable to a couple of critics: we treated African Americans as though they were at times dumb, silly, and crazy like all of us. It never occurred to me that anybody would take that and say that that's a statement against black people, but a couple of them did, and it hurt my feelings so very much that I never could in any way revive a feeling about that show. I just kind of slunk away from it.

Interviewer: A show of yours we haven't spoken of is *Applause*. There, as in *Nick and Nora*, you were dealing with another very popular film, *All about Eve*. But, with *Applause*, you had the added factor of it being a star vehicle for Lauren Bacall, who had never done a musical previously. Were there pressures involved in doing that show?

Strouse: Yes, there were pressures. We had written most of the score before Bacall was part of it but then added a great deal. A song like "Welcome to the Theater" was written after she was cast, and I was very conscious that a lot of that could be spoken. A great deal of the show was not written for her, but she absorbed it. The funny thing about Bacall is that she, like Rex Harrison, is a wonderful musician. It's not a great voice, but she has wonderful rhythm and is a terrifically hard worker; so she would absorb the material. When she didn't sing it, she spoke it so crisply that I think the audience was satisfied. As far as the weight of having to write to a masterpiece like *All about Eve,* I felt it very keenly, and so did Betty Comden and Adolph Green, who wrote the book for the show. I consider the Mankiewicz screenplay a playwriting masterpiece, and it was hard to live up to that. I was under tremendous pressure. I had written the music for a film Mr. Mankiewicz directed, *There Was a Crooked Man.* I met him and he was very kind to me, so I felt even more under the gun that I had to please this man.

Interviewer: Didn't *Applause* undergo some changes along the way, before it got to Broadway?

Strouse: Yes. We wrote the ending two ways. The original ending to *Applause* was that the great star says to her fiancé, "Sorry. The theater is what I love," and dumps him. That was very true to life and very true to Bacall herself and that kind of person who is so committed. When the show started to work, the audience liked it but didn't love it. We said, "Let's try the sentimental ending." So we tried the sentimental ending, which is she gets back with her fiancé and gives up the theater and gives her part to Eve. The audience leaped to its feet. It says a lot about America in the 1970s. With the revival we're planning, we're going to go back to the original ending. Everybody now feels very strongly that giving up the theater for love is not what a woman who is impelled to be a great star necessarily would do.

Interviewer: Speaking of endings and going back to *Bye Bye Birdie,* I've always wondered why you decided to end that show with what one might describe as a "quiet ending," rather than with a more traditional ensemble number.

Strouse: It was such a raucous show that we thought it would be a tasty thing to do to settle on what was the center of the piece, the love story. It was a love story that was always hard to get an audience to believe in totally because it was about a man who was almost a cartoon. He was under the domination of his mother and he wanted to make a great rock star; his life was dedicated to making Conrad Birdie. We felt it would lend a measure of humanity; that's all I can say. We could have ended it without that. Indeed, until the show became a hit, it was a very difficult moment for the audience. They were ready to go five minutes before. When the show became a success, it simply then stayed as what we intended it to be, which was a grace note. It was a show that had a lot of bombast in it, and the ending was an echo of another feeling that we wanted to leave with the audience.

Interviewer: What did you think of the movie version of *Bye Bye Birdie?* How much did you have to do with it?

Strouse: The way Hollywood purchases are made traditionally is they pay a great deal of money for the rights with the right to make any changes they want. A lot of authors object to it or insist that they write the screenplay. Because of the amount of money they paid us and the producers, we were encouraged to do it their way—and of course we were disappointed. I feel so hypocritical saying, "They paid me all that money and they didn't do it my way." I did take the money. I feel it was a mistake. But we had worked for six or seven years on *Bye Bye Birdie,* so we weren't about to say, "Do it our way." We were glad that somebody was interested. On *Annie,* however, where they paid us a great deal of money, I really feel it was a mistake to have accepted that money. There was a great deal of argument among the authors and the producers, but there was so much money involved that we felt we would do it. There I felt they screwed it up even more so, but what can I say? I'm not going to sit here and say it was *Hamlet,* but it was a piece we worked very hard on. In *Birdie,* we satirized the American scene very strongly and they turned it into "Teenage Beach Blanket" or something. Of course, because of Ann-Margret more than anything else, it became a great success.

Interviewer: What advice would you give to young people who want to write or compose for the musical theater?

Strouse: Survive—and hang out. I run a free musical theater workshop in New York for ASCAP. Every week we have at least four professionals from the theater who sit and act as a panel. It's the only way new writers can get their works heard, because the economy of the theater is such that there's no more summer stock. There's regional theater, but there's no theater to get new works heard. This is the closest to it or to an audition of this work. We have everybody from Clive Barnes to Hal Prince to Pat Birch to Tommy Tune; anybody who's in the theater and is around comes, and they've been very gracious. They sit and hear these new works. Some of them are half-baked, some of them are very gifted, and some of them are dreadful. What I try to do is encourage everyone to speak frankly. If Hal Prince wants to produce a work that he hears, we're all very proud— and, indeed, a couple of pieces from the workshop have been produced. If he doesn't want to, I encourage him to say what he doesn't like about it, be it the title, the idea, or any number of things. I feel that if the people can survive this—and a great many do and keep going and still have that hunger—some producer may find them. They may fail, but if they can get up off the ground and keep going, that's what's important. BMI has a musical theater workshop, too, but they run it differently. BMI has mentors. They actually take a piece and work along with the composer. Although I'm sure that's very credible, I don't believe in it; I believe ultimately you're going to write what those people want you to write. This other way it's being performed by a group of people for a large audience who come to audit; they simply hear the work, and professionals comment on it.

Interviewer: Finally, a question you may not want to answer. What are your favorite musical theater songs—your own or by others?

Strouse: There's a song in *Golden Boy* called "I Want to Be with You," which is a favorite of mine because—aside from its quality or lack thereof—it was the first time I tried to apply a certain musical technique to what was essentially a pop score. I felt that I solved it and hit certain notes on certain emotional meanings that were important to me. It was a very passionate song, and it took place when people who crossed lines about color and sexuality did so and resolved conflict. To me it was a felicitous solution of a problem. I really do like "Bess, You Is My Woman Now" from *Porgy and Bess*. And there is a song that I always feel is just miraculous that Betty Comden and Adolph Green and Leonard Bernstein wrote for *Wonderful Town* about boredom and Melville and a giant whale. I always thought it was the most terrific musical song because it's about boredom and it's so unboring and really funny. It's called "Conversation Piece," and it's a real favorite of mine.

Tommy Tune

Tommy Tune was born on February 28, 1939, in Wichita Falls, Texas. He was educated at Lon Morris Junior College, the University of Texas (B.F.A., 1962), and the University of Houston. He has worked as a choreographer, director, and performer. The New York musicals he has choreographed in-clude Seesaw *(1973),* The Best Little Whorehouse in Texas *(1978),* A Day in Hollywood/A Night in the Ukraine *(1980),* Nine *(1982),* My One and Only *(1983),* Grand Hotel *(1989),* The Will Rogers Follies *(1991), and* The Best Little Whorehouse Goes Public *(1994).*

He directed the New York musicals The Club *(1976),* The Best Little Whorehouse in Texas, A Day in Hollywood/A Night in the Ukraine, Nine, Grand Hotel, The Will Rogers Follies, *and* The Best Little Whorehouse Goes Public. *He performed in the New York musicals* Baker Street *(1965),* A Joyful News *(1966),* How Now, Dow Jones *(1967),* Seesaw, My One and Only, *and* Tommy Tune Tonite! *(1992). He also appeared in the national tour of* Bye Bye Birdie *(1991), directed the plays* Cloud 9 *(1981) and* Stepping Out *(1987), and appeared in the films* Hello, Dolly! *(1969) and* The Boyfriend *(1971). His memoir,* Footnotes, *was published in 1997.*

He received Tony Awards for Seesaw *(Best Featured Actor),* A Day in Hollywood/A Night in the Ukraine *(Best Choreography),* Nine *(Best Director),* My One and Only *(Best Choreography and Best Actor),* Grand Hotel *(Best Choreography and Best Director), and* The Will Rogers Follies *(Best Choreography and Best Director). He received the George Abbott Award for Lifetime Achievement in the Theatre in 1991 and was elected to the Theatre Hall of Fame in 1991. In 2003, he received the National Medal of Arts.*

This interview took place on June 30, 2003.

•———————————————————————————————•

Interviewer: What were your growing-up years in Texas like? How did they lead to an interest in theater? Were you taken to the theater a lot as a kid?

Tune: No, we didn't have theaters down there. I danced. My parents said that I danced before I walked; I'd be crawling through the living room, the music would come on the radio, I would get up on my hind legs, and I would dance. The music would go off, I would get down, and I would crawl into the den. I hadn't figured out how to walk, but when the music happened I had to dance. My whole entrée into the theater was dancing. I had my first proper class at five, and I studied right through. The first performance that I remember seeing was not theater. The Ballet Russe de Monte Carlo came through Houston. I had an eccentric aunt—she really wasn't my aunt, but we called everybody "aunt" in Texas—Aunt Eunice, who took me to see it, and I was transformed. I went back to dancing class, and that's what I wanted to do; I wanted to be a ballet dancer. But I just grew and grew, and I got so tall that I didn't have the physique for a ballet dancer. Then my mother took me to see *Easter Parade,* and Fred Astaire looked really tall on the screen; so I said, "Okay, I'll do that."

When I went to high school, they said, "What do you want to major in?" I said, "I want to major in dancing," and they said, "We don't offer that"— this is Texas in the 1950s—"but maybe you should go talk to the drama teacher." She realized that I'd never seen a play, so she said, "I have a ticket, and you could go to the Alley Theatre." It was a little tiny theater in a fan factory at the back of an alley in downtown Houston (we lived outside of the city) and my mother dropped me off. It was in the round and the show was *The Glass Menagerie,* starring Faye Bainter. When I went in, I thought, "This is so weird because I'm sitting across looking at people, but the furniture's there, so I guess this is the place the show's going to be." The lights went out, and it was the most perfect blackout I've ever experienced. It was absolutely black, and I was disoriented because it was so black. Then the stage lights came up, and there was Amanda Wingfield speaking on the telephone—and I was transformed. From then on, that was it. I was supposed to call my mother, but I didn't want to call. I didn't want to say anything; I just wanted to stay with that play—with Amanda and Tom and Laura and the Gentleman Caller—so I walked home. It was a long way; I got home after dark, and they were worried about me. I remember being very dramatic; I said, "I can't speak. I have to go to my room and ponder this thing called theater." I was gone on it. The next day I went to the drama teacher and said, "Sign me up!" Then somehow the dancing part and the theater part got joined in high school.

Interviewer: What was the first musical you ever saw? Was it a high school or a professional production?

Tune: We had a community theater there, and there was this girl that I liked in high school. She said, "Do you want to go see a dress rehearsal of *The King and I* at Theater, Inc.?" I didn't know what any of that was—I only knew the Alley—but she was real cute, I liked her a lot, and she had a car. She came by and picked me up and we went. We sneaked into the back row of this little proscenium theater, and suddenly it was very different from *The Glass Menagerie* because they were talking like they did in *The Glass Menagerie* and you got involved in the story—but then they would sing. It made it even better—and then they would dance! I kept saying, "What is this?" She said, "It's a musical. It's the kind of show that they do on Broadway."

Interviewer: The magic word!

Tune: There was that word, Broadway! She was from a wealthy family, and she'd seen musicals in New York. I went back to my drama teacher the next day and I said, "We've got to do a musical!" I had seen that there was a place for me to put the dancing in, because it was not just talking and singing but also dancing. I did it; I didn't even know it was called choreography or choreographing. I didn't know what it was; I just did it.

Interviewer: Was it an original?

Tune: No, it was *The Pajama Game*, and it was totally illegal because *The Pajama Game* was playing on Broadway. I'd gotten the record from the lady next door, who had gone to New York and came home with the albums of *Bells Are Ringing, The Pajama Game,* and one other. I played it over and over and over, and I just saw it all—and we did it.

Interviewer: Did you do the choreography?

Tune: I did it all. I didn't know what I was; I just did it. I choreographed it, but we didn't call it that because we didn't know. I just made up the dances, and I played Hines, the time-study man. Because the girl that played Gladys wasn't much of a dancer, I did the "Steam Heat" number with two girls instead of with two boys and a girl. It was a huge success. It was a very social and high class high school in the best part of town; so the society columnist came and reviewed it: "Roses to the Cast of *The Pajama Game* at Lamar High School." They mentioned my name; it was my first big review as a performer and a choreographer.

Interviewer: After Lamar High School, you went to college?

Tune: I went to Lon Morris Junior College in east Texas, where they were famous for their drama department. It was one woman; her name was Zula Pearson. I went there for two years, and then because of her I got a scholarship to the University of Texas.

Interviewer: Did you continue to do musicals all the way through junior college and college?

Tune: Yes, and plays, too. I did a lot of plays, even after the University of Texas. I graduated and came back to the University of Houston to start work on my master's, and I did plays there—Mr. Antrobus in *The Skin of Our Teeth,* Oberon in *A Midsummer Night's Dream.* I also directed and choreographed a musical that had been done Off-Broadway but hadn't been a success. My master's thesis was to take a show that had not been a success, to study it, to work on it, and to see if I could make it an acceptable thing.

Interviewer: Which one was it?

Tune: It was called *Smiling, the Boy Fell Dead.* Ira Wallach wrote the book, David Baker wrote the music, and Sheldon Harnick wrote the lyrics. I got it through Sheldon's brother Jay Harnick, because Jay had come to Theater, Inc., to direct a show and we made a connection there. He phoned me about this show, and then he helped me get it, because it was in different little pieces around New York. I wrote David Baker and all these different people; I got different versions and I put it all together.

Interviewer: Did you ever look at photographs of the original production?

Tune: No, never. I didn't want to know anything about it. I wanted to see if I could do it with just the written material.

Interviewer: Did it work?

Tune: I think so. It was a delightful score, and it was sort of a Horatio Alger tale. It was sweet and innocent—and I understood it.

Interviewer: After the University of Houston, did you come to New York right away?

Tune: Yes. I didn't even complete my thesis. I had a faculty advisor, and it was difficult for him. He was not from the drama department but from the English department; so he was taking it all from that point of view. I got all bogged down in syntax, and a friend of mine said, "I think it's time for you to go to New York." He threw me in the back of his car and he drove me to New York.

Interviewer: This was on St. Patrick's Day of 1963 that you first came to New York, wasn't it?

Tune: It was either 1962 or 1963.

Interviewer: And you went to an audition for *Irma La Douce?*

Tune: We were driving in, and that's when they used to paint the green stripe down Fifth Avenue for the parade. We crossed Fifth Avenue and we looked at that stripe and he said, "That's the parade route." He said, "You see that newsstand there, Tune? You go and buy copies of *Backstage, Variety,* and *Show Business* and see what's auditioning today." So I did. There was an audition at two o'clock at Variety Arts. I went and I took my tap shoes. Nobody was tapping then, but I had my jazz shoes, too. I auditioned and I got the part.

Interviewer: So you've never been a struggling New York actor?

Tune: Just for one week. That audition was for *Irma La Douce,* and we toured all over. It was supposed to go on for twelve weeks, and it went on for twenty-two weeks because it was a big success. When I got back, I didn't have a job, and I went to work for one week at Young and Rubicam, the advertising agency. I worked in the concept-coding department, and it was Christmastime. Even though I only worked there for a week, they passed out Christmas bonuses and I got one. It's the only Christmas bonus I've ever received in my life! You don't get Christmas bonuses in show business. The job is the gift!

Interviewer: Then you auditioned for *Baker Street* on Broadway and went right into that?

Tune: Yes. I'm trying to think of other things I did. I did a minstrel show at the Shoreham Hotel in Washington around that time. Jay Harnick, again, hired me to be in it— to play one of the end men and to choreograph it.

Interviewer: You were both choreographing and performing at this time?

Tune: Always together. I always did both. I would look in all the theater annuals and find names like Peter Gennaro or Carol Haney and would see that they were in the chorus and then they became choreographers. So I thought, "Okay, that's the way to do it. You start at the bottom rung as a chorus dancer." I did not have aspirations to direct and choreograph; that's just what I did, because nobody else did it.

Interviewer: But you didn't become a chorus dancer because you saw that as a way to being a choreographer?

Tune: No, not at the time; but in retrospect, my subconscious must have been figuring it out. My dream had been to dance in the chorus of a Broadway show, and it happened so fast. The day that I arrived, it came true. I've said this before and it doesn't sound true, but it's so true: Everything that has happened to me—and I've been so blessed and so lucky, and I've worked so hard—has come out of that initial dream, to dance in the chorus of a Broadway show. Everything else is just after. That all just happened because of what I knew how to do, my ability or something; but it wasn't my plan to direct and choreograph Broadway musicals, not at all.

Interviewer: Do you think, in retrospect, that that is the best kind of training to choreograph and direct a Broadway show, to be a performer first?

Tune: Michael Bennett and I used to talk about it a lot, and he said, "The guys that don't come up from the bottom and work their way up the ladder don't know the ins and outs of putting it together." They can be highly skilled people, wonderful directors, but if they don't know how it all goes together (I'm talking about a musical), they don't know. You see it happen a lot. Very high-toned exquisite directors bomb out making a musical.

Interviewer: Why is it so different from directing a play—and so difficult?

Tune: First of all, a lot of directors who aren't choreographers are quite frightened of choreographers. A choreographer can come in and just do things to a show by showing off that can absolutely ruin it. A lot of choreographers show off, and that doesn't help the show. It might be a wonderful flash of a dance for the audience, but it doesn't support the show if you're showing off. You've always got to be serving the core of the show; actually, you should be serving the book. There are great, great musicals that don't really have great scores but because the book's so strong and the music comes in at the right places, they work. It's where a song comes and where a dance comes that's incredibly important to the rhythm of the piece and the telling of the whole tale.

Interviewer: Are you saying that a stage director who tries to do a musical can end up in trouble because the choreographer will take over the show?

Tune: Either that or if he sees that happening, he'll just cut all of the dances out so the choreographer won't take over. Or if he doesn't know, he'll say, "There should be a dance here." Just because it says that there should be a dance doesn't mean that there should be a dance. Dancing is a very abstract thing to insert into lyric theater. If a choreographer gets too abstract with it and they're not people dancing anymore but they're expressing something impressionistically—which on a ballet stage would thrill us to no end—it puzzles us within the frame of a lyric theater piece.

Interviewer: Do you think that's why the director/choreographer combination has worked so well?

Tune: Yes, because we're not afraid of ourselves!

Interviewer: And also you're serving the piece, because you're not just the choreographer, you're also the director.

Tune: Yes, you balance it. What happens, inevitably, when you put on both hats is that the choreography gets slighted, because you have to have the director's hat on all of the time and then make little switches where you take that hat off and put the choreographer's hat on. You try to do that quickly so you can get back to being the director so you don't mess up anything. It's a bit schizophrenic. But it does put the director in the position of knowing where the dance goes. If he's the choreographer, he knows innately, in his soul. The soul of a dancer is so different from the soul of anybody else because we feel it in our musculature. Dancing affects one on a cellular level. It's little dots, and all together it's a dance.

Interviewer: What you're saying is that as a choreographer/director, you're in a much better position to know where dance should be in a musical?

Tune: I think so; Michael and I talked about that, too. He said, "See these guys. They don't know, because they don't feel it." I'd say, "No, that's just because you did it that way." Then we would have arguments about it. But if you look at *My Fair Lady,* Moss Hart directed it, and the dances by Hanya Holm are just so polite and so plopped in. Yes, there's the Embassy Waltz, but anybody who knows how to do waltzing could have done that number because it's a real dance. The interesting part of the dance in a musical is that they dance and they're not dancing, they're just promoting the story. It's not "and then they went to a ball and they danced." But if, while they're dancing, she faints and he tries to revive her and the dance goes on around them, then there's a story of sorts to it.

Interviewer: Isn't that true also of the music and lyrics in a musical? If the show stops for the songs, it's the same problem, isn't it?

Tune: No, because words are being spoken and then words are being sung, so they are intrinsically connected..

Interviewer: You've mentioned Michael Bennett a couple of times. In your book, you say that *A Chorus Line* is one of the three musicals, along with *Oklahoma!* and *West Side Story*, that changed the form forever. What did Bennett do in *A Chorus Line* that was so revolutionary?

Tune: He did something that can't be done again, unless it's in the same form. He made a documentary musical, because it was at an audition; it was taking place on the stage, because that's where auditions used to take place. When I came to New York, you didn't necessarily go to a rehearsal hall. For Broadway shows, the auditions and the rehearsals would be in the theater where that musical was going to eventually play. I don't know why; I think it was a deal with the theater owner. That was a very big help, creating a show in the theater that you were going to perform it in. So there was *A Chorus Line,* taking place exactly where an audition took place, right there with the kids that were vying for the jobs. It was documentary, and we'd never seen that. We'd always watched *42nd Street,* from another time and another sensibility, but this was of its time. They spoke like we spoke, they dressed like we dressed, and they were doing what I'd spent my life doing—going and auditioning for Broadway shows. It was incredibly truthful; they talked about things that we didn't talk about in musicals, sexual things that never came up in musical comedies before—openly frank and honest modern vernacular.

Interviewer: What you're implying is that the whole notion of what we now call the integrated musical, where everything works together, to some extent is a result of having choreographers be directors. In a Rodgers and Hammerstein musical, the show stopped and there was a ballet. Now it's much more seamless.

Tune: I don't know how much the director/choreographer can be held responsible for getting rid of two choruses. When I started in musicals on Broadway, there was a full chorus of singers and a full chorus of dancers. Then they started letting dancers sing. In the beginning, they didn't want us to sing, because our voices were not of that operetta type. Then the songs got rougher, more lusty and with more character, and they started letting us sing.

Interviewer: How and when did that happen?

Tune: It was really before I got here. The show that I saw when I was seventeen years old had the dancers singing and dancing at the same time. Prior to that, the singers would sing and then the dancers would weave through and dance. Then the singers would add on at the end, not being out of wind, from all around the stage, and the dancers would take it through to a finish. That was the shape of a musical number. But in *New Girl in Town*, directed by George Abbott but choreographed by Bob Fosse, I noticed that switch. They were all singing and dancing; it wasn't separated.

Interviewer: Of course, Gwen Verdon, a dancer/singer and Fosse's wife at the time, was the lead in the show.

Tune: Yes, but there was a big tussle on that show because Fosse didn't cast her. George Abbott cast her, and she got Fosse the job as choreographer. Then Fosse was seeing the show in a new way, but Mr. Abbott was doing it the Abbott way, which was great. Mr. Abbott had a real sense of dance, though, because he loved to ballroom dance. But there was this big friction on that show because Fosse wanted it to dance more. We saw the beginnings of the Fosse type of musical in *New Girl in Town*, and it was astounding and original.

Interviewer: Was Fosse the first person to combine the singers and dancers?

Tune: I guess Jerome Robbins was.

Interviewer: Did the dancers in *West Side Story* sing?

Tune: Yes. It was all dancers who sang, and that was a very big deal.

Interviewer: How did you transition from being a performer to becoming a choreographer and a director?

Tune: Let's go back a little bit, because there's a whole area that doesn't exist anymore that was my training ground as a choreographer, summer stock. I've been around long enough now to see summer stock end up on Broadway. The mainstay of Broadway now is that you revive some old show, often with a star, just as we did in stock. I choreographed a lot of stock while I was still performing in Broadway musicals. There were never revivals on Broadway. Michael Bennett kept saying, "You've got to stop going to stock. How am I going to make you into the only male dancing star? How can I do that if you're always out choreographing in stock?" But I had to do both. I was totally intrigued by all the different styles of dance, and I was facile enough at the time to choreograph *Oklahoma!, Carousel, Sweet Charity, High Button Shoes*, and *Gentlemen Prefer Blondes*. I could work in any style. I worked for the Chicago-Milwaukee Melody Tops for about three seasons, and we would do twenty shows a season. We had two companies, and we would get one show ready in Milwaukee, and while we were playing another show with that company, we would get another show ready by day and send it off to Chicago to open. The Chicago company would come and play their show a week, and I would make up a new show for them. I don't know how I did it! I just had to do what I loved to do, and

I had to do it the way I had to do it. Not that I had a plan, but I knew that I was learning so much by watching really good performers. I was learning from them and also playing some parts along the way.

Interviewer: How did you learn to choreograph?

Tune: I had a knack for it. I don't know how I did it. I really don't. I was very well trained as a dancer. I wasn't just a tap dancer. That just happened because of my height; but before I grew to this height, I was a very good ballet dancer. I had all of that stuff, and I think that's really the root of it.

Interviewer: How did you come to do *Seesaw* and then direct *The Club* in New York?

Tune: I had just finished doing the movie of *The Boyfriend* in London. I didn't have a place to stay, so I called Michael Bennett and I said, "Can I stay at your house until I find a place to stay?" He said, "Absolutely." I got there and there was a note saying, "I had to go to Detroit. I'm taking over on a show called *Seesaw*. Don't unpack. Just come to Detroit. I need you." I put a few things in a bag and hopped a plane to Detroit. I choreographed two numbers for *Seesaw*, and then Michael said, "I love these numbers, but I like the way you do them better than the guy that's playing the part; so I'm firing him and I'm putting you in." Then, of course, it clicked, because that's when I won my first Tony, not as a choreographer but as a featured performer.

Interviewer: Were you credited in that show with the choreography that you did?

Tune: I did two numbers, and Bob Avian and I did another number. Then there were a couple of numbers by Grover Dale, who was the original choreographer, that Michael left in the show because Grover said, "Please let me keep this credit because my career is going to be finished if you just wipe it away." So Michael said, "Okay, you'll stay as the choreographer and I'll say, 'Additional choreography by Bob Avian and Tommy Tune.'" I believe that was the billing.

Interviewer: Didn't that also, in a way, launch your career as a Broadway choreographer? When you won the Tony, it was known that you had choreographed those numbers, wasn't it?

Tune: People knew. And that led to *The Club*. The scene designer for *Seesaw* was Robin Wagner, and he had watched me rehearse the company. Michael would send the company off with me while he was working on the story between the two principal characters, and I think Robin saw that. Robin lived in the same apartment building as Eve Merriam, who wrote *The Club*, and she said to him, "This is my idea for a show. Who could I get to direct it?" And Robin said, "Call this guy." She called me and told me the story of the show and I said, "That's very interesting, but there's not a part for me to play in it." And she said, "I don't want you to play a part in it. I want you to direct it." I said, "What gave you the idea that I knew how to do that?" And she said, "Robin Wagner." So I really and truly owe my directing career to Robin Wagner.

Interviewer: After you did *The Club,* did you then begin to get gigs as a director?

Tune: Oh, God, I was the new hot director in town. It was an amazing thing that happened because that show was a scandal. We opened and the carriage trade started coming; there were limousines outside the theater every night. Everybody had to see it.

Interviewer: When suddenly you had this great success as a director, did that frustrate you as a performer, or did you just sort of go along with it?

Tune: I'm very fickle. I just thought, "Well, this is what I'm supposed to be doing. This is great." I never questioned it; that was just it.

Interviewer: As a Texas boy, you must have thought you'd died and gone to heaven when they asked you to do *The Best Little Whorehouse in Texas.*

Tune: It's odd how that came about. In my high school class was this girl named Carlin Glynn, and we became very close friends. Now, years later, they had done *Best Little Whorehouse* at the Actors Studio, and they had somebody choreographing it who had done that abstract thing we talked about earlier. They knew that that wasn't right, and Carlin called me and said, "My husband, Pete Masterson, is directing a show at the Actors Studio, and I think you're the only person to choreograph it, because it's not right and we know it's not right, but Pete doesn't know anything about dancing. Would you come see it?" I went to see it, and the play of it just made me cry. But the musical numbers that were in it seemed to be from another show. They said, "Would you choreograph it?" And at that time, I had just changed agents. My new agent was the late Eric Schepard, who created the whole arc of my career, starting with *Seesaw.* He was the most famous agent in New York. Everybody talked about him, because he was one of the old school agents that didn't just make the deal. If somebody wanted you, he'd make the deal, but he would also figure out what you should be doing so your career grew in an arc. There's nobody that does that now, but Eric did. He had been a chorus dancer before he became an agent. I said to him, "They want me to choreograph a Broadway show called *The Best Little Whorehouse in Texas.*" He said, "You don't choreograph Broadway shows." I said, "What are you talking about? I do that." "No," Eric said, "you're a director now. You've done *The Club.* You do not choreograph Broadway shows. You direct and choreograph Broadway shows." I said, "They have a director and he's fabulous." He said, "Then you'll share the directing credit with him. You'll both direct. Otherwise," he said, "you'll never be able to fix that show. If the director knew about dancing, it would be good now. The problem is not the choreography." It was everything we were talking about earlier in this conversation. That's how it happened, and thank God Pete was generous enough to share the credit. It was because of Carlin that he said, "Okay, I'll take him on." It was very brave of him. But I had always done both, even when I was just choreographing. Even way back with *The Pajama Game,* the drama teacher didn't know too much about directing musicals, and I had a feel for it. I'd say, "Oh, no, they're talking too long here. While they're talking, I'll start bringing the dancers in behind, and they won't disturb it, so by the time they're finished talking we'll be ready for the musical number." I just had a sense of how to keep it moving, because a musical has to move. Otherwise the music becomes an intrusion.

Interviewer: What attracts you to a project? I assume you've been offered lots of shows.

Tune: I always try not to listen to the music, because I'm very easily seduced by music. Really good music just sends me, so I try to always read a new project before I hear it. They always say, "We're going to play a few songs for you to begin with, and then we'll give you the book. The songs are all finished, but we're having a little trouble with the book." And I say, "No, I can't listen to the music first. I have to read the book first, because if there's no book, there's no show." So I guess it's the story.

Interviewer: What's an example of a show that attracted you primarily because of its story?

Tune: There aren't many good stories. I don't think I've had many good stories in my shows; I've had to apply them. The idea for *The Club* was that a group of men come into their club for the evening; they tell hoary old jokes and sing songs about women, degrading comedy songs, actually. What kind of a show is that? I had to go back and listen to all of those songs and all of those jokes and I thought, "What if they all come in at the beginning of the evening and they're all fresh and perfectly dressed and then they drink and get looser and then what happens?" So I had to fashion a whole story that I applied on top of it because it was not spoken; it was implied.

Interviewer: What about some of the shows you turned down?

Tune: I turned down *Annie* because I just couldn't see how Annie could be done. Do you know how the cartoon of Annie looked? I'm not a literal person, but she had great white circles for eyes. How are you going to do that onstage? That's how literal I was, because I had grown up with Little Orphan Annie from when I was a child. The attraction to her was that she didn't have eyes, and neither did her dog. I thought, "Well, you could put Ping-Pong balls, but that would never work." I didn't know how to do it. I didn't know how to humanize it. Boy, did I miss *that* boat!

Interviewer: How did you come to do *Nine*?

Tune: I listened to the music in *Nine* first. I remember it was slipped through the little mail slot in the door. Michael Bennett had moved. I was living in his old apartment, and the guy upstairs, Mario Fratti, slid the tape through the slot with a little note saying, "Mr. Tune, I have a musical based on Fellini's 8½; I call it *Nine*." I laughed out loud. I thought it was hilarious that it was based on 8½ and he called it *Nine*. I took the music and I went out to Fire Island. I had a little tape recorder and I put it on — and I was gone. Maury Yeston's music was magic. Then I went about trying to figure out how to do it, because nothing happened; Mario's book was opera buffa and from another time. I thought, "Oh, God, what are we going to do here?"

Interviewer: What about *Grand Hotel*? What got you into *Grand Hotel*?

Tune: I'm an insomniac, so I watch television to help me go to sleep. I'd never seen the movie of *Grand Hotel,* and it came on one night and I thought, "Wow, this moves like a musical. This is like a musical." There was even a line in the film, "The music never stops in the Grand Hotel." So I called up Maury Yeston, my composer friend, because he's an insomniac, too, and I said, "I want to do *Grand Hotel* as a musical. I'll order the tape and I'll send it to you." He saw it, sort of shrugged, and was not interested. Then I saw *A Night to Remember,* the first *Titanic* movie, with Clifton Webb, and I said, "I see this as a musical." And again Maury wasn't interested. Both of those were my ideas, and he didn't want to do either of them; but eventually he did come in and help me with *Grand Hotel,* and years later he composed *Titanic* for Broadway. With *Grand Hotel,* I was very interested in how all those people weave together, all under the roof of the same hotel, and how all of their stories interlaced like a tapestry. And because of its period, it moved. There was so much movement in it because there is so much movement in a hotel, from the uppers and the lowers. It appealed to me, also, that it danced throughout and the music played throughout. I liked the stories. There were so many; they were a clothesline of episodes.

Interviewer: To get back to *Nine* for a minute, what did you think of David Leveaux's recent revival? That's really the first major Broadway revival of one of your shows, and your shows, in their original productions, all had your personal imprint on them so strongly. How did you feel watching this new *Nine*?

Tune: I didn't want to go see it because I had such treasured memories of the original production. My partner had produced *Nine* and had died. The late Raul Julia had been my muse on it; I would make him sit with me in the audience so he would know about directing, because he needed to be able to direct those women. I had had twenty years of love for that production and I never wanted to touch it again; it was done. I didn't want to go, and then Maury Yeston called me and said, "I want you to come, and David Leveaux wants you to come as his guest to the opening." So I couldn't say no. I was just a mess getting ready: "I don't want to see this. I don't want to go there again. It's going to be so painful." Sometimes I run from high emotion in my life; I would just rather skip it. I've had so much loss in my life—people older than me, a lot of people younger than me; when the first wave of AIDS came, it was devastating to me. Michael Bennett was younger than me and he's gone—and so many people that I danced with in the chorus. But I went, and the moment that that little boy climbed up onto that table, and his shadow was on that screen, I was a goner. I loved it, and I can't believe the originality of David Leveaux. He didn't do one thing that I did. I don't know how he avoided it unless he studied what I did at the film archive at Lincoln Center, because surely sometime he was going to do the same thing just logically. But everything was totally, totally his own and original, and I was so impressed and very moved to visit it all again. I am a huge fan of it. I don't like shows that look like other shows or borrow from other shows. I like originality. That's why I don't do revivals on Broadway. I think it's finding something original that drives me. I don't want to see something I've seen before. This recent production of *Gypsy* is perfectly good, and Bernadette Peters is profound in the lead, but I really don't need to see that show again. I want to see something new, something artful, and something that stretches my imagination, something that's original, that I've never seen before, that doesn't remind me of anything else I've ever seen.

Interviewer: Do you think that as a choreographer you choreograph for yourself as a dancer?

Tune: No, never.

Interviewer: Your dancers don't all have to be six foot six?

Tune: I can't go looking for me because there aren't any out there. But it depends on the show. For *Best Little Whorehouse,* I wanted big boys because they were supposed to be football players; so I got the biggest guys I could get, and I taught them how to dance. The audition was to see if they could learn steps, because I didn't want Broadway dancers; I wanted big guys that could learn steps. For most of them in the original company, that was the only dance they ever knew. They never danced in any other shows. You never saw those guys showing up in somebody else's shows. They only did that dance because they learned it just for *The Best Little Whorehouse in Texas.*

Interviewer: What's happened to the American musical?

Tune: I have no idea. There's nobody writing. It's got to be reinvented in some other way, because it just can't be like it is. The only musical that I'm really in love with right now is *Movin' Out,* and that's not your typical musical. People say it's not a musical, that it's a dance concert. It's not. It's sung through. Yes, they don't speak, but there's a story. I'm terribly moved by it, I'm thrilled by it, and it's epic. It's an amazing, original piece. I've never seen anything like it; it's a masterpiece.

Interviewer: So what's the other side, *Hairspray?*

Tune: When it won everything, I said, "We're doomed."

Interviewer: What's wrong with it?

Tune: What's wrong with it? Nothing's wrong with it, because it makes people happy. It's just not my cup of tea. The shows are lacking in nuance, and what used to make the theater live for me was nuance, be it a play or a musical.

Interviewer: What exactly do you mean by nuance?

Tune: It's a lot of different things. Everybody's wired now. You have the body pack; they can crank you up and it gets louder, and they can make the orchestra louder and then crank you up even louder. That's contributed to the loss of nuance. You can have incredible nuance with sound; it just doesn't all have to be loud. It can be haunting and evocative. I guess artfulness is part of nuance. Heart, soul, feeling, and humanity are all part of nuance. It's that thing that you hear that the Lunts had for sure. There's the story about the last performance of *The Great Sebastians.* This young usher got to the theater early on the closing night. There were Alfred and Lynn onstage; she couldn't see them at first because she'd come in from the bright sunlight, but she could hear Lynn saying, "No, no, Alfred, do it again." Finally her eyes adjusted and she could see that he was lifting a cup; they were still working on that scene. "It's our last chance to get it right," Lynn said. It's funny that when you asked me about nuance, I went to sound, because everybody sings like Ethel Merman now. But Ethel Merman was her own thing, and she in her own way had nuance. It was one strong, fabulous note, but it was nuance because she was the only one doing it. Now everybody has that voice; they all sing like that. It's all big singing now. It's all a blast!

Interviewer: You said in your book that you liked *Floyd Collins* and *Ragtime*. What made you pick out those two?

Tune: They were striving for something. According to some people they reached it, and according to other people they didn't. I was invited up to see the very first performance of *Ragtime* in Toronto, and I was so devastated at the end of the first act that I truly couldn't get out of my seat. I don't know where I was; I was gone. But between the opening in Toronto and the opening in New York, major things happened to that show. It got so cleaned up and perfected that it had lost its impact. In Toronto, it was raw and it was a much better show. For Broadway, it had gotten cleaned up and made better. That's something we never did do with *Best Little Whorehouse*; it was never made better. We kept it raw because it was the right tone. Every show has its own tone, and it gets set in the first five minutes. Then you keep matching that tone, not the dynamics of it. Of course, you have to go fast and slow and quiet and loud and all that, but the evening has a tone. You never change the tone, and then it becomes the thing that you remember. Usually it starts with the opening. It's real hard to launch a musical, because you have to set up all your rules within that opening so that the audience knows what strange world they're being plummeted into that they're going to inhabit for the night. They want to go with you, as long as you don't jerk them around or make them do something that makes them not believe in the world that you want them to believe in. Everybody who goes to the theater wants to believe. Yes, they're sitting there with people next to them, there's a band in the pit, the walls fly in and out, and it's all totally ridiculous. Yet we all love that world that's getting ready to come at us, the latest bit of make-believe. If you establish it and keep it and don't break their hearts or their minds, then you've got something—but it's a real hard thing to find.

Interviewer: You've been called "Doctor Tune" because of the shows you've been called in to save. What are some of the musicals that you've worked on in that way?

Tune: I went in on *Seesaw*, I went in on *Woman of the Year*, I went in on *The Grand Tour*, and I went in on *Hellzapoppin*—I couldn't save that one. But Michael Bennett and I had a saying: "Thou shalt not doctor," because it's a no-win situation. They say they want you; they say they want you to save the show, then when you start, they say, "Oh, no, we already did it that way and it didn't work." You remind them that a lot of times it's "first thought, best thought." And the cast's loyalties are confused because they had one parent and it's like getting a stepfather. They have to be loyal to their original father or what kind of person are they? But they're also afraid that you're going to fire them if they don't do what *you* want.

Interviewer: How did you get around those problems when you did actually manage to do some good?

Tune: The best doctoring that I ever did was on *Hellzapoppin*. I did a brand-new opening number; I did it in three days. It was huge—it was a big cast—and I got it into the show and it was fabulous; but then Alex Cohen, the producer, and Jerry Lewis, the star, knocked heads and the project sank. Doctoring a show is like making a laundry list; you write down all the things that are wrong and just start fixing them one by one.

Interviewer: Can you pick one of your shows and just kind of take us through it from the beginning to the opening?

Tune: I'm going to choose *Nine*, because that's the clearest one to me right now. As I said earlier, the tape came and I listened to the music. I started having visions, and it was wonderful. But the book wasn't any good; so I got Arthur Kopit to redo it. *Nine* all takes place in Guido's head. I knew the point of view; it had to be that this highly creative guy—and I could relate to him—when things weren't right he would fix them. He could change what you were wearing into something else; he could just fix anything. Guido wanted it all to be beautiful; he wanted it all perfect. I knew the way into *Nine* was through him; and Arthur Kopit had written a play that took place in a woman's mind called *Wings,* so I felt he could get into Guido's mind. Then he faltered and I wasn't able to communicate everything that I needed to him to write; so I said, "Let's workshop it. What I don't know how to ask for, I'm going to stage; and instead of speaking, the actors are going to count. I'm going to put them in the body positions and I'm going to move them around so you can tell what's happening. It will be like watching a foreign film and not knowing the language, but you will know what's happening. Then you go back and dub them." So we did that, and he would write scenes. I would stage scenes without dialogue, and he would go away at night and come back and he had written the dialogue. It worked.

Interviewer: Had you ever done that before?

Tune: No, but I had a really important role in a movie in Italy. Except for Shelley Winters, who was there for two weeks, I was the only English-speaking person on the film. They basically make silent movies in Italy and then put in the dialogue—so I did a transference from that and it worked very, very well. Then we started casting. We needed an Otto Preminger type, a German producer, but all the good character men in New York at that time had gone to California to make a living for their families in television. Character men have wives and children. We only saw some bad stock actors. Then Liliane Montevecchi came in. She was French and she was fascinating and I said, "Why couldn't a woman be the producer of the film? Why couldn't she be French instead of German? She's just as threatening. Sometimes women are more threatening than men. Certainly she could be more threatening than any man that we've seen." I thought, "Why not? It's Guido's world. He's not into men. He's into women, all women; he loves them. Why not just make them all women?" But Arthur Kopit and Maury Yeston linked together and said, "Not at all. You just want to re-create *The Club.*" I said, "No, I don't want women dressed up as men playing the part. No, no, no. Women, women, women, only women." And they said no. I said, "I'm not being stubborn, you guys, but I know this is the way to do it. This is the only way that *I* know how to do it. I'm sure somebody else would do it in another way, and you must go and find them. I found a unique way to tell this show and I know it's right and it's the only way I know how to do it." For about two weeks, I was off the project. Then they talked about it and Maury said, "But women's voices all night long will get so boring." And I said, "But you have the lead guy in the middle of it all, and it's going to make him more powerful." So they came back and they said, "Okay. We'll do the workshop and we'll see how it goes."

After that, it was pretty good sailing. Years later, Maury and Arthur, because I was not the writer, did a version with men so they could send it out through Samuel French. They didn't consult me on it, they just did it. That's okay. It was done that way at the Paper Mill Playhouse, with men—gondoliers and other men. But David Leveaux knew a good thing; he did it with the original take. The workshop was really, really good. We rehearsed in a fabulous space, the New Amsterdam Roof. It was a broken-down, decayed theater where Ziegfeld used to do the Midnight Frolics, and there was a ghost in the place. It was mystical—paint peeling, broken proscenium; it was like rehearsing in a Roman ruin. I'm surprised that Equity allowed us to be there but everybody loved it. Barry Diller, who was the head of Paramount, came to see it; he had given us the money to do the workshop, with a promise to come in with a wedge of the pie for the production. He brought Warren Beatty, and Warren Beatty said it wasn't any good, so Barry withdrew his money and we didn't have enough money to open. We scrambled and finally got the money, but we couldn't go out of town. We had to just open. We opened cold in New York. I had done it without an intermission—because it's better without an intermission—but the theater owners said, "We have to break for the concessions." That's why it was performed in two acts.

Interviewer: The only thing you didn't mention was how you got Raul Julia. Did he audition?

Tune: He was the best one. Other people came, but they were all Americans putting on accents, and Raul had an authentic accent. It's interesting that it was the same accent as Antonio Banderas has in the revival, a Latin accent, not an Italian accent. Raul had something more. He had major secrets. He was fascinating.

John Weidman

John Weidman was born on September 25, 1946, in New York City. He was educated at Harvard College (B.A., 1968) and Yale Law School (J.D., 1974). He has worked as a librettist. The musicals for which he wrote or co-wrote the books include Pacific Overtures (1976), America's Sweetheart (1983), Anything Goes (1987), Assassins (1991), Big (1996), Contact (2000), and Bounce (2003). He currently serves as president of the Dramatists Guild of America.

This interview took place on February 9, 2004.

Interviewer: Your father, Jerome Weidman, was a very successful and famous writer, primarily of fiction but also for the theater. Looking at your background, it seems as if you did everything to avoid going into his profession. Is that true?

Weidman: It is true. My dad, who made a very nice life for himself as a writer, felt that it was a poor choice for any other member of his family. He was very eager to have both me and my brother avoid anything that smacked of either being a novelist or being involved with theater. My interests early on took me in other directions. I went to law school after I graduated from college in part because in the late 1960s it was thought of as a way of extending your liberal arts education, which I discovered as soon as I arrived in New Haven was nonsense. I thought I was probably headed for a career in politics. In college, I had taken the foreign service exam and I'd interned at the State Department. It was only after I got to law school that I decided that, although I liked law school, I really didn't want to be an attorney. I found myself back in law school for the second year wondering what else I could do with my life. The two things that I loved were the theater and baseball, and so I wrote two letters. One was to Bowie Kuhn, who was the commissioner of baseball, asking him if he ever hired law students in the summer, and I got a form letter back saying no. I also wrote a letter to Hal Prince saying, "Maybe you don't remember me, but you met me when I was a kid," asking essentially the same question: Do you ever hire interns in your office? As a P.S. I said, "By the way, I have an idea for a play I thought I might write, and I'd love to talk to you about it." The answer to the first part of the letter was "No, we don't hire interns." But I had described the play as being about America's experience in opening up Japan, and that intrigued him. He said, "The next time you're in New York, come up to the office and we'll talk about it." I was at Yale Law School, so I came into town and discussed it with Hal, and there was clearly something even then about the material that intrigued him. He sent me away with a one-page option agreement and five hundred dollars, which was a fortune in those days. To have that kind of professional support for a project I had not yet embarked on and for which I had absolutely no experience at all was heady stuff.

Interviewer: What year was that?

Weidman: It was 1971 or 1972.

Interviewer: Had you written anything at all as a dramatist?

Weidman: At Harvard, my roommate was Russel Crouse's son, Tim Crouse, and we wrote a Hasty Pudding show. That was the sum total of my experience writing for the theater. But there's an innocence that you have early on when you do anything for the first time, when you don't know what you don't know. I'd been going to the theater my whole life, and I knew what a play looked like. I had a typewriter; I could type in capital letters the name of the character and then put down dialogue, so I thought, "Why not?" I sat in the Yale Law School library and wrote a straight-play version of what eventually became *Pacific Overtures.*

Interviewer: Do you think that the example of your father made writing seem easy or difficult or romantic, or did it simply demystify it?

Weidman: I think it demystified it. The example of how my father produced his work was always in front of me, and there was nothing romantic about the way he wrote. He got up in the morning and he went into his study and he wrote until he was finished. He did it in a very workmanlike way, which is to say that he did it all day every day. The doors to his study were always open; you could wander in and talk to him. There was never anything like "Don't interrupt your father. He's working." He was pleased to have somebody come in and talk to him. The idea that you could put words down on paper and that eventually those words would either wind up in print or onstage seemed, without my thinking about it, to be one of the ways the world worked.

Interviewer: Your father was a very productive writer, and I would imagine that virtually everything he wrote got published or produced; so there must have been a sense, not that it was easy, but that it led to something.

Weidman: He was tremendously prolific, but I did live through periods of his career when he was absolutely thriving and periods when things weren't going so good. His career in the theater, which was very compressed, had both; the bad news followed the good news rapidly. *Fiorello!* was produced in 1959, so I was thirteen when it opened. *Tenderloin* was the next season and *I Can Get It for You Wholesale* was a couple of years later, but by the time I was in college in the mid-1960s he was writing a musical and a play that were real failures. The musical was *Pousse-Café,* and it closed rapidly, and the play was *The Mother Lover,* which also failed. After that, he put the theater aside and went back and focused on novels again. By the time I sat down to write something, I had had the emotional experience of how things could work out—great or not so great.

Interviewer: When you wrote those letters, why didn't you write to a literary agent or a publisher and say, "I have an idea for a novel about the opening of Japan"? Why did you think of it as a play? You had both fiction and theater as models from your father.

Weidman: I did; but even as a kid, I was thrilled when I was taken to the theater. It sounds corny, but I can remember the moment when the lights went down, particularly the first musical I was taken to, but the same is true of straight plays.

Interviewer: What was it?

Weidman: The first musical? The first one that I have a vivid memory of is *Li'l Abner*. I'm aware of having been taken to see *South Pacific* when I was very small, and I saw *Peter Pan* like every other kid. But the first one I had a kind of adult self-conscious experience of was *Li'l Abner,* which is actually quite a good show. The overture started, the lights went down, and I thought, "This is wonderful!"—so I think without thinking about it I was pulled in that direction.

Interviewer: As an undergraduate at Harvard, you wrote for the *Harvard Lampoon,* and then later you joined the staff of the *National Lampoon.* What kind of writing did you do for them?

Weidman: When I was a junior at Harvard, I joined the *Harvard Lampoon,* which is as much of a club as it is a magazine. A couple of friends of mine, when they graduated, came to New York to start a national version of the magazine. It was the late 1960s, and it was a very heady and seductive place to work. You could write what at the time was edgy, sort of cutting-edge comedy, most of it about politics; the stuff that wasn't about politics was about social mores. When I graduated from college, I spent several years teaching elementary school in New York as an alternative to military service. The *Lampoon* was a place where I could write at the same time; eventually I became an editor there, and it was a lot of fun. Even when *Pacific Overtures* was produced in 1976, there were two paths to my literary life, and I wasn't sure which one was going to predominate. Believe me, they had nothing to do with each other.

Interviewer: Let's go back to the *Pacific Overtures* story. Did you produce a script for Hal Prince?

Weidman: I wrote a play, I sent it to Hal, and Hal said, "Come into town and we'll do a reading."

Interviewer: At this point, you conceived of it as a play? Did you ever think of it as a musical?

Weidman: I think the answer is no, but the real reason I thought of it as a play is because a play was something I could control completely from my room in New Haven. I could go to the Yale Law School library and sit down and do it—and either it would work or it wouldn't. I didn't have to worry about finding collaborators or having discussions about what should be a song. I finished a straight play, and I sent it to Hal and he decided he would produce it on Broadway, and I was coming into town every couple of weeks for auditions. Talk about heady stuff; it was wild.

Interviewer: And Hal Prince was thinking of it strictly as a play, too?

Weidman: Yes, absolutely. We were casting it, and Boris Aronson was going to design it. Hal called me one day and said, "Boris can't . . . he's not sure . . . it doesn't feel . . ." and then he called me later and said "You know what? I think it needs to be a musical. It needs to have the size it would have if it were a musical." What I heard was Hal Prince saying, "I'm not going to do your play. Thanks, but I've changed my mind." But he was very committed to the material; he twisted Steve Sondheim's arm a bit, and he twisted it some more, and pretty soon we were all sitting in a room together and talking about how to make it into a musical. The content of the play is quite different from the content of the musical, so we really went back and started over.

Interviewer: How did that strike you? Obviously, when you were surrounded by those theater legends, you couldn't very well say, "No, I want to take my play and go to Milwaukee and see if someone there will produce it." But was that a difficult shift for you, or was it easy?

Weidman: It was both. It was easy because of the stature of the people involved. I had been an enormous fan of Hal and Steve's shows up to that point, and here I was all of a sudden writing the next one.

Interviewer: Did you know them at all?

Weidman: I had met Steve, but I didn't know him. I had not met Hal since I was a little kid and he was around the house a couple of times. The other thing that made it easy was that Hal was enormously skillful and generous in managing the process of taking this first-time book-writer and connecting him to this accomplished composer/lyricist and trying to make the whole thing work. If there was a hard part, that was the hard part, too. Suddenly I was dealing with the issues of collaboration and learning on the job how a musical had to get crafted. Hal was always right in the middle of the writing process; that's very different from other shows I've worked on since.

Interviewer: Why do you think that is?

Weidman: In that case, a lot of it had to do with my inexperience; but I think he was right in the middle of a lot of those musicals that were created. They were called Prince/Sondheim musicals, and that's an accurate way of describing them. The moving force behind *Company* and *Follies* really was what happened when those two sensibilities combined—and I got added to that sensibility for *Pacific Overtures*. I did bring with me something that was only mine, a real background in the material the show dealt with. I had majored in modern Japanese history at Harvard. In my sophomore year, I was required to take a course outside my area of concentration, and I took a survey course in East Asian history. This was in the 1960s, and China and Japan had never been mentioned to me in high school. I knew they were over there someplace, but they were not part of anybody's curriculum. The first-year course at Harvard was taught by John

Fairbank and Edwin Reischauer, and it was wonderful. It was like being exposed to a whole other side of the world that nobody had ever told me about. So I brought all that with me into the collaboration. You couldn't get sushi in New York in those days; Japan was a very exotic place that people didn't know about, but I knew a lot more than most.

Interviewer: After that show, did you then see yourself as having a career in the theater?

Weidman: I was an editor at the *Lampoon* at the time, or maybe I was offered a job there immediately after the show opened, and I really wasn't sure what I was going to do. Culturally we were still in the late 1970s, and I had grown up in the 1960s. It seemed to me as if maybe I'd never decide what I was going to do and maybe you weren't supposed to; you were supposed to do whatever came next. It had been serendipitous that I had wound up writing this Broadway show to begin with, so I played around with a variety of different things. Later, when I came back to musical theater in a really committed way, it's where I stayed.

Interviewer: After *Pacific Overtures,* did you have a lot of projects in theater offered to you?

Weidman: I got some phone calls, but not from the most important people in the field. It really wasn't until ten years later, after saying no three times—I didn't have enough therapy to say no a fourth time—that I agreed to write a new book with Tim Crouse for the Lincoln Center production of *Anything Goes.*

Interviewer: Is that what got you back into theater?

Weidman: Yes. I had worked on other things in the meantime. Bob Waldman and Alfred Uhry and I had written a musical together; it was the last thing Alfred did before he gave up being a lyricist. I always had my hand in something, but I would not have described it as the focus of what I was doing.

Interviewer: The focus then was the *Lampoon* writing?

Weidman: Things always seemed to be happening to me. When *Animal House* opened, those of us who were the editors at the *Lampoon* immediately became sought-after screenwriters. I didn't know any more about writing a screenplay than I did about writing musicals in 1976, but I spent several years working on youth comedies of one kind or another. Some of them were pretty good, but they'd go through four drafts at different studios and then they'd stall. It was at the end of that process that I thought, "I hate this. Ultimately this is frustrating, and I don't want to continue with it. What am I going to do instead?" That was when I turned back to the musical theater in a committed way.

Interviewer: How did the assignment to do *Anything Goes* come about?

Weidman: Again, it was one of those happy accidents. Russel Crouse and Howard Lindsay had written the book for the original *Anything Goes* in 1934. Crouse's son, Tim, had been my roommate at Harvard, and Tim's mom, Anna, was convinced that the reason that there had not been a first-class production of the show in decades was the book. She felt that the book just didn't work, that what Lindsay and Crouse had done to try to save what P. G. Wodehouse and Guy Bolton had written originally still didn't work—and she was right. Bolton himself had redone the book for an Off-Broadway production in the 1960s sometime, but he brought in a whole bunch of songs from other Cole Porter shows, and that book wasn't any better. I said to Tim, "Why do this? If it works, people are going to talk about Cole Porter. If it doesn't work, they're going to blame us." He said, "Just shut up and do it!" I agreed, and Gregory Mosher at Lincoln Center was determined to produce it. Greg had a great deal to do with the fact that it wound up in that space; he felt that Cole Porter should be back onstage.

Interviewer: Did you begin working on redoing the book without a firm commitment from Lincoln Center—or anybody else?

Weidman: That's correct. We started on it, we got enough done, and I guess we showed it to Greg. He said Lincoln Center was interested, so we just carried on with it. That was one of those productions where everything just seemed to come together. Jerry Zaks was the perfect director and Tim and I did a lot of reworking with Jerry of what we'd already reworked. The cast was great, and it felt good. It was a hit; everybody liked it. Betty Comden said to me in the lobby one day, "It's very soothing to have a hit, isn't it?" I said "It's a good word, Betty. I never thought of it before. It *is* soothing." It also helped me remember how much I liked the process of making a musical happen, how much I enjoyed the rehearsals and the rewriting and the suffering and the collaborative process of it.

Interviewer: What were the major changes you made in the 1934 book of *Anything Goes* for that 1987 production?

Weidman: We wanted to pretend that we'd been called in to rewrite the show in 1934 but that we needed to do it so that it would work for an audience in 1987. More than anything else, that had to do with pace and length. The 1934 version of the show was long, pages and pages with no music, and I think by 1987 an audience came into the theater, certainly for that kind of show, with an expectation of what the rhythms would be—in talking and singing and talking and singing —and we tried to deliver that. One of the things we did, mechanically, was to restore as much of the original score as we could. There were songs that had been jettisoned over the years for a variety of reasons, and we put them back. We threw out most of the ones that had been interpolated; we kept a couple. That's mostly what we tried to do. We also tried to tell the story so that it would be taken seriously, not that it would be any less silly, because I think that's what drives it in many ways. But we wanted people to be rooting for Billy Crocker to get the girl. We felt that by adjusting the story we could emphasize that aspect of the show, and I think we were successful. Trevor Nunn's production, which is playing in London's West End now and which is wonderful, I think confirms that.

Interviewer: Were there any changes from the Lincoln Center production for the British audience?

Weidman: Not for the British audience. There were a couple of small adjustments that you might not even notice that Trevor wanted, which turned out to be excellent fixes. But we did have one disagreement. Trevor wanted to change the opening of the show so that it started the morning of the sailing. One of the things that we had done was go back to the 1934 structure, in which the show started the night before in a nightclub. We felt it was important to establish the fact that Reno Sweeney was interested in Billy but Billy was interested in the other girl. Everyone was very polite, but we said, "We won't do it." Trevor came up with a compromise, which was to set that first scene on the ship the night before the sailing— so we had to rewrite it for that. We'll rewrite it again because it's not quite right yet.

Interviewer: Was it the experience with *Anything Goes* in 1987 that made you decide which direction to go with your career?

Weidman: Yes. I wasn't a kid at that point, but I thought, "The main thing I want to do between now and however long I get to do whatever I'm going to do is more of this." *Into the Woods* opened that same year, and I called Steve and told him I had an idea for a show. Steve and I had remained friends after *Pacific Overtures*, but I hadn't approached him with a new project. I said, "I've got an idea for something I want to talk to you about." We met, and it was another historical show I had in mind, but he wasn't really interested; he said it felt more like a movie. He said, "What do you think of this, assassins?"

Interviewer: What was the idea you went to him with?

Weidman: I was very interested in Woodrow Wilson and the Paris peace talks and what the tensions are between a certain kind of American idealism and a certain kind of American self-interest and cynicism. Steve had read a musical about a shadowy Vietnam veteran who becomes involved in a conspiracy to kill the president. He had read it when he was one of the judges of Stuart Ostrow's musical theater workshop competition. The play had been decorated with all these historical figures, and Steve had been taken with the idea of this group, so he and I started talking, and that was the next project.

Interviewer: The idea for *Assassins* came from him, then, didn't it?

Weidman: What came from Steve really was the arena and the title. What we eventually brought the show down to being about was something that came out of our conversations.

Interviewer: How did that process work? The first project with Sondheim was different, wasn't it? The first project was your play that you had to fit into how Hal Prince and Sondheim wanted to make a musical. This one was much more of a collaboration, wasn't it?

Weidman: *Assassins* was a very satisfying writers' project. Steve and I finished the show before we ever showed it to a director and before we showed it to André Bishop at Playwrights Horizons. We spent a number of months meeting once a week and talking. I was seventeen when Kennedy was killed, and it was the first real experience of loss that I had had in my life. It was devastating. I went to Washington; I stood there and watched the funeral procession go by. As we worked on the show, I realized that the emotions that were left over from that experience were what was driving my interest in this material. Ultimately, the unresolved questions in my head about where these awful things come from was what the show was about. Steve and I got to that idea. The way we worked, practically, is that I went away and wrote a first draft. We'd already decided that the form of the show probably wanted to feel slightly revue-like. The conventional wisdom about these people at the time was that they had nothing in common with the rest of us and nothing in common with each other; they were isolated nuts. The idea of isolating them in a revue form until finally they all came together and turned the style of the show into something else, which was what happened in the last scene, seemed like the right way to go. I went away and wrote everything that's in the show now up to the last scene in the Texas Schoolbook Depository, while Steve went to work on the opening number. We then did a reading of that material.

Interviewer: Was there any other music at that point?

Weidman: No. There was music just for the opening. I then finished the book and Steve carried on with the score. That was a collaboration in which I don't think I ever wrote a scene that then became absorbed into a song. We had already identified the pieces of the show that would be musical and the ones that wouldn't be; so in most cases Steve would work from elaborate notes that I gave him or snatches of scenes.

Interviewer: In other words, the two of you would decide where the song would go, and Sondheim would take notes on what that song should cover?

Weidman: Yes, or I would give him a couple of pages of dialogue scraps. Just to pick one example, there's a song that's called "The Gun Song," and I said to Steve one day, "I want to write a monologue for Leon Czolgosz in which he talks about his gun as if it were a product, like a shoe or a piece of furniture, a product of the capitalist process by which he feels so brutally oppressed and by which other people similarly situated were so brutally oppressed." That became the verse of the song.

Interviewer: When you said, "I want to write a scene like that," what happened then?

Weidman: I never actually sat down and wrote a finished monologue, just notes.

Interviewer: Did Sondheim say at that point, "I'd like to write a song on that subject"? In other words, did he appropriate your idea?

Weidman: That's correct, although *appropriate* is a loaded verb. There are shows where book-writers have felt as if their best work has been stolen by their collaborator, who was then going to get all the credit. I've never felt that way or had that experience. If you don't want your best ideas and your best work to wind up in the score, then you shouldn't write musicals. That's where they belong.

Interviewer: If there is a choice in a musical of dramatizing a particular moment or musicalizing it, does musicalization usually win out?

Weidman: Yes, it does. But *Assassins* is odd, because the last eighteen minutes of the show is a book scene that resolves into music but has no song in it at all. The Sam Byck character, the guy in the Santa Claus suit, has two long monologues, and Steve and I talked about whether or not one of them would become a song. Other writers approaching that material would have, I think, felt almost obligated to take one of those monologues and musicalize it. Not in *Assassins*.

Interviewer: In other scenes when he opted to musicalize, would you agree to that, even in cases where you had conceptualized a dialogue scene at that point? Would you say that is a common procedure in a musical in your experience?

Weidman: Yes. I don't know what other people's working relationships are like, but, as I said, I think that in most cases the reason to write something as a musical instead of a play is that you have this additional tool that is able to deliver these colors and these emotions that are not available if that tool isn't available—and you want to use it.

Interviewer: To go back to *Pacific Overtures,* there you started with a full script. Were there moments in that process when Sondheim said, "Let's do a song here instead of this dialogue"?

Weidman: Different things worked in different ways with that show. For example, we had a meeting to talk about the scene in the Treaty House when the Americans have finally come ashore to deliver their letter. Nothing happened; they brought the letter, they dropped it off, and they left. Hal was interested in the idea of different perspectives on the event, so the idea for what became "Someone in a Tree" was something that got talked about. I went away and wrote bits and pieces, snatches, and maybe even a clean version of a scene with the Samurai under the floorboards and the kid in a tree. I don't remember. That was a number that evolved from a discussion and a decision.

Interviewer: Was it conceived of as a musical number at that point?

Weidman: Yes. The conversation was about "This will be a song."

Interviewer: If that was the case, why did you have a role in that song? You were the book-writer.

Weidman: Steve relies very, very heavily on his book-writers for tone and for language. In my experience with him, almost invariably the way he works best is that he requires raw material from his collaborator before he can sit down and go to work. He never writes a song without something the librettist has provided. It could be a polished scene or it could be pages of notes, which include snatches of dialogue, which get him going.

Interviewer: Do you sometimes find in a song of his pieces of lyrics that you might well have written originally?

Weidman: Yes. With *Assassins,* for example, at the end of all the scenes that precede the Texas Schoolbook Depository scene, I had written a sequence of declarations for the assassins. I did it because it would bring them back out and fill the stage; we knew that was going to turn into a song. We knew what the dramatic structure of the song was, but I had not written that scene. I was perfectly happy to leave it to Steve and he called me and said, "I can't find the hook for this. Is there anything that you cut from the scene in the Texas Schoolbook Depository that might be helpful?" I said, "I don't think so, but I'll look," and I went back into my computer. I'd cut a page of dialogue that I had written in which one of the assassins referred to the group of assassins as the other national anthem, the one you don't hear at the ballpark, so the idea that drives that song came out of this leftover dialogue that got cut.

Interviewer: Would you say, and this may be reaching, that one of the reasons that Sondheim's shows are so well integrated is just because of the process you're describing? You can't detach his songs as easily from his shows as you can from the musicals of the 1950's, because Sondheim's songs grow so integrally out of the book.

Weidman: Yes, the shows are absolutely organic, and there's no question those were his impulses as a dramatist; that's why he wanted to write for the theater. But on a personal level, his respect for and his eagerness to collaborate with his librettists also contributed to the same thing. I can imagine someone with a different temperament having the same artistic impulse but not being able to work as effectively with a collaborator as Steve can.

Interviewer: You worked with Richard Maltby and David Shire on *Big*. Was that collaboration very different from the ones with Sondheim?

Weidman: Not terribly. Dave and Richard are really accomplished and really smart and collaborating with them was similar to collaborating with Steve. There were two of them instead of one, and Richard tended to be the guy who did the dramaturgical work about what this needed to be, what it wasn't, what needs to happen in the story here, and how this could be a song. More of that came from Richard than from David, but we spent an enormous amount of time sitting around talking about what we would do.

Interviewer: That show was based on the movie, obviously, so it was an adaptation in a sense, wasn't it?

Weidman: Yes. The impulse to do that musical came from David and Richard. I initially didn't think it was a good idea. Not only is it a famous movie with a star performance in it, but it was done beautifully. The film was a completely finished piece of work as far as I was concerned, and I didn't see a reason to do it over. But I really wanted to work with them, and they went away and wrote a really good song that made me think, "There's an emotional approach to this that music will provide that will make telling the story again worth doing and make it effective." So we went ahead and tried.

Interviewer: What was your role in *Contact*? It's hard to imagine where a book-writer entered into that process.

Weidman: It's interesting. The process for me as a book-writer was not terribly different from the standard book-writer's role on other shows. The difference was that the collaborator's spot—the writer's role—that is traditionally occupied by a composer/lyricist in this case was occupied by a choreographer. It's a story-driven show, even though it's divided into three parts; and if the dancing had been language, I don't think my piece of it would have seemed so unusual. There are sung-through musicals, and nobody questions the fact that they have books; *Sweeney Todd* is the best of them, I suppose. In shows like *Phantom of the Opera* or *Les Misérables,* there's precious little talking, but when it stops language continues—so I think it feels as though it's a familiar thing. *Contact* felt unfamiliar because when the dialogue stopped, so did the language.

Interviewer: The music wasn't original either.

Weidman: That's correct. *Contact* was a wonderful experience. Susan Stroman and I had gotten to know each other on *Big*; she was the choreographer. She called me one day and said that André Bishop had called her and invited her to develop something at Lincoln Center. She said, "Why don't you come over and we'll talk."

Interviewer: What did she need you for? If she started with her story about the Girl in the Yellow Dress, which she says she saw in a restaurant, she could have easily done a ballet on that subject as a choreographer who wants to do a ballet about a Girl in a Yellow Dress.

Weidman: If she had been approached by Peter Martins of the New York City Ballet rather than by André Bishop, I think you're exactly right; she probably would never have called me. But Lincoln Center was interested in some kind of theater piece. When she and I first sat down and started to talk about the story—and we were only talking about what would eventually be the third part—we thought that maybe we would approach Lynn Ahrens and Steve Flaherty for an original score. The fact that the fundamental language of the piece became dance rather than music, lyrics, dialogue, and dance was something that grew out of the conversations we had about what the most effective way would be to tell the story. We didn't start out with the idea that this was going to be a dance piece with recorded music. That's where it got to from talking about this guy and this girl and what the story was going to be. Because the people in the room were me and her, we were both predisposed to push it in the direction of dance, but that was not where we started. It was really another situation of where form really does sometimes follow content; it felt like the way to tell that story was to turn Susan Stroman loose.

Interviewer: So Susan Stroman originally was the choreographer/director of a potential musical for which you would write a conventional book?

Weidman: André Bishop said to Stro, "You come here and do something in my theater." It could have ended up as a book musical. The result of that phone call could have been *Thou Shalt Not,* the next new musical that Stro did at Lincoln Center. Because she had the idea of the Girl in the Yellow Dress in her head and because it was a dance idea, that's where we were heading. I don't want to suggest we were two-thirds down the road to writing *Oklahoma!* and suddenly she said, "Let's throw the language out." That's where we started, and frankly, that's what was most exciting. The idea of collaborating with a choreographer in the place that's usually occupied by the composer and lyricist made me think, "I wonder what will happen? I wonder where this will take us?" We did the third part first and said, "Would this story be more effective if it were preceded by something else?" It built incrementally that way, and it was a tremendously satisfying experience.

Interviewer: Can you talk about the kind of conversation you would have with her, past the Yellow Dress scene? Did you become a kind of scenarist for the show?

Weidman: Yes, but always in collaboration with Stro. The two of us would get together and talk in the same way that Steve and I would sit around and talk about what *Assassins* was going to be, and then he would go away and do his part and I would go away and do my part. We workshopped the third part of *Contact* first. It was about an hour and five minutes long, and Lincoln Center Theater was prepared to produce that on its own, but we had already begun to think, as I've said, of ways of ramping the evening up—so that when you started where the third piece started you'd be ahead of the game and you'd have more impact at the end of the evening. We would sit around and talk about how the third piece was going to be constructed, about the scene beats within the story, and about what songs she wanted to bring in for the music. It evolved the way other shows have evolved, through discussion about what the most effective structure was to tell the story, and then the way the structure got expressed was primarily through dance. As I said, from the book-writer's point of view, it wasn't that different.

Interviewer: The only difference is that the audience coming to that show would have a harder time telling what your contribution was.

Weidman: Absolutely.

Interviewer: In *Assassins,* in *Pacific Overtures,* and in *Big,* the audience might think they could tell what your contribution was, but you're saying that what they might think your contribution to one of those other shows was is just as likely to have been Sondheim or Hal Prince or Maltby and Shire. The roles in creating a musical are not as clearly defined as the audience imagines, are they?

Weidman: I feel that I collaborated with Susan Stroman on *Contact* the way I collaborated with Stephen Sondheim on *Assassins,* although, as I say—and this has been true of some collaborations and not true of others—she and I were talking story and structure together from the very beginning. It's not as if I went away and came back to her and said, "This is what the story and structure is," and then she, instead of writing songs, went away and designed dances. It started with her and I got added. And working with her was a collaboration like the collaborations I've had with Steve in the sense that I always felt like there was nobody better than the person I was working with.

Interviewer: This might be an unfair way of putting it, but it sounds like the role of a book-writer, as you've described it, has to be a very "humble" one in a musical theater collaboration. I don't mean this in the way that it's going to sound, but you seem always to be in the service of somebody else.

Weidman: I think that's correct. I think it *is* in the service of somebody else. The cliché is "They don't call them booksicals; they call them musicals"—and it's true. The most powerful parts of a story in a musical should wind up in the score. If they're not in the score, then something's wrong, except in a sui generis piece like *Assassins,* which I think made up its own rules and obeyed them. You are there not to serve the composer/lyricist but to provide the platform on which the composer/lyricist will ultimately stand. If the librettist's work is not done well, it's almost impossible for a musical to succeed; whereas if the librettist's work is done well, a musical can succeed even if the score is a B or B+.

Interviewer: Peter Stone's book for *1776* is often considered an example of just how literate and important a book can be in a musical, isn't it?

Weidman: *1776* was another musical that made its own rules. The work that Peter did was brilliant and the nature of the material itself meant that his were the most riveting parts of the show. There are weaknesses in that score where characters behave in a way that I find vaguely embarrassing given the quality of the way they're drawn outside the songs.

Interviewer: Would you say that the nature of that book was demanded by the material? Wasn't Stone very fortunate that he found a composer who would give him that prominent a role?

Weidman: My understanding of where that show came from is that the composer/lyricist of the show, Sherman Edwards, had done the whole thing and it didn't work, so Peter was brought in to make it work. In that sense, it's ass-backwards—but Peter came in and made it work.

Interviewer: Is it just a coincidence that Peter Stone was for a number of years president of the Dramatists Guild and that you are now the president? Is it perhaps because librettists work well with others?

Weidman: In my case, it probably has more to do with the fact that I went to law school.

Interviewer: Seriously, though, isn't working well with others a major requirement for a librettist, especially because, as you've said, you are there to provide a platform for the composer and lyricist?

Weidman: Peter is an interesting case study; he worked fast and he worked well. He was a consummate professional who wrote screenplays and books for musicals. I don't think he ever wrote a play. There clearly was something about the collaborative process that I'm sure he enjoyed, but there must have been something else about it that was important to him and that he needed. Peter had the facility and ability to write anything, but I'm not aware of his ever having written something in which the only voice you heard was entirely his.

Interviewer: What about you? Are you comfortable with this role?

Weidman: Yes, absolutely. In part, it's because I have been lucky in my collaborators. I started out collaborating with Steve Sondheim; I didn't work my way up to Steve Sondheim. I've worked with Lynn Ahrens and Steve Flaherty, I've worked with Maltby and Shire, and I've worked with Susan Stroman (as I said, in that show she occupied the place of the other writer). When you're working with people of that caliber, it's exciting and stimulating.

Interviewer: Okay, but the bottom line is everybody says that it's a Sondheim musical; they don't say it's a John Weidman musical. Don't you have to be comfortable with that or else you couldn't do it?

Weidman: Yes, I think you have to be comfortable with that.

Interviewer: Along those lines, you said somewhere that musical book-writers are like barrel-makers. What did you mean?

Weidman: Writing the book for a musical is an odd profession. In the days when musicals had a fixed form—say, in the 1950s; it's hard to figure out what the fixed form would be today—there were people who did this work and nothing else. Peter was a kind of survivor from another era. It's an odd little profession—like making barrels.

Interviewer: One of the great mysteries about the musical theater for those of us who see a lot of musicals is how they ever happen, much less succeed, when there are so many people involved in their creation. We imagine a room in which everyone tries to be heard. What role does the librettist play in that room? Especially when you're trying to fix a musical, what role does the librettist have?

Weidman: I think shows reach a certain point where almost all decisions become the result of a collaborative process in which the book-writer and the composer and the lyricist and the director and maybe the choreographer are in a room together figuring out why this doesn't work and what we can do to fix it. At that point, everybody is pitching in. Eventually, the meeting is over and everybody has to go do their individual thing, but at that point it's not as if, when there's a story point, everybody shuts up and turns and looks at the book-writer; or if there is a staging issue, everybody shuts up and turns and waits for the director. It becomes "What do we do?" and everybody has something to say about it. For different shows that I've worked on I've contributed in a variety of different ways.

Interviewer: Could you elaborate on that? You've described some of the processes, but what are a few of the characteristic differences?

Weidman: As I said, *Assassins* was a show in which, although Steve and I went away and each of us wrote our own part of it, we operated as co-authors before anybody else got involved. *Big* already existed as a finished piece of work, so Maltby, Shire, and I talked about "How do we take this thing and turn it into something that will work onstage?" In essence, David and Richard, particularly Richard, were making book-writer's contributions from the very beginning: Does it go this way? Does it go that way? Does it want to be taller, shorter, more red? Is this part of the story important? Is this part of the story not important? When you're dealing with somebody of Richard's experience, that's going to happen. There have been some book-writers—it's never been me—who want to go away and write the book almost as if it were a play and bring it back and let the composer and the lyricist put in their material. I don't think anybody does that anymore.

Interviewer: Is it your impression that that used to be more often the way it was done?

Weidman: I think so, in part because shows used to get written so much more quickly.

Interviewer: "Let's plug a song in here" was the idea.

Weidman: Yes. It was "You go write the book and then we'll talk about it and we'll write some songs." People used to get one up every couple of years. Now it takes so long to do it that there's plenty of time for everybody to get in a room together and talk about what to do.

Interviewer: The stakes are so much higher now, too, aren't they?

Weidman: With Broadway musicals, that's especially true. There's so much more money involved—that's a relatively recent development—and because the stakes are so much higher, producers are more inclined to look for something that an audience is already familiar with, so there are many more adaptations now than there used to be. Musicals have always been adaptive works for the most part, but they tended to be adapted from plays or maybe a novel or a short story. I was astonished; there was some movie that was a huge hit three years ago, and they couldn't wait to try to turn it into a musical. That's new, but it does mean that if that's what you're starting from you do tend to start from a place where everybody gets in a room and tries to figure out how we're going to do this.

Interviewer: What I meant when I said the stakes are much higher is that you can't really afford not to get everybody's input. Forty years ago, when a musical didn't succeed, you wrote another one the next year. Now you can't afford not to have everybody's input be part of the process, because the stakes are so high and the risks are so great.

Weidman: The danger is that what you wind up with is a slightly homogenized safe product rather than something that is the product of the idiosyncratic point of view of one or two writers. The route that *Urinetown* followed to get to Broadway is probably what more and more interesting musicals are going to follow, because there were no expectations from those guys. They wrote what they wanted, and then it got moved along.

Interviewer: It created an audience gradually, and then by the time it got to Broadway audiences were waiting for it.

Weidman: With *Contact*, which is a sort of an odd example because it was an odd musical, if Stroman had gotten a call not from Lincoln Center but from commercial producers, and they had said, "We want you to create a new musical," we never would have come up with what we came up with. It would have been something else, and it might have been good, but it would not have been this thing that grew incrementally, spinning out of her head and out of my head. There would have been meetings about who the audience was and how much it was going to cost and what star we were going to get.

Interviewer: Let's talk about *Bounce*. How do you feel about it? What do you think went wrong?

Weidman: It got better and better, and by the time that we opened it in Washington I was pleased with the quality of work we had done on it. Arthur Laurents has said that things can get better without ever finally getting good. I still feel like I'm too close to it to give you a smart answer to the question of what does or doesn't work about it. The ultimate impact of the experience of being in the theater and seeing the show was never quite what we wanted it to be and it's difficult to figure out why that was.

Interviewer: What prompted the several changes of the title?

Weidman: *Wise Guys* was an original title that was hung on it when it was more about Wilson Mizner and his sensibility than it was about the relations between the two brothers. In the end, I would say that the show was really more about Addison Mizner than it was about Wilson. Addison was the character who had a clear drive and ambition to do something wonderful and the show was about how it got subverted. *Gold* was always an interim title, although it was useful because it described what these two guys were after their whole lives. *Bounce* finally seemed like it was correct, plus Steve was writing a new opening number called "Bounce," which felt like a title song.

Interviewer: When I saw it, I didn't feel that I had enough of an investment in the characters. I didn't care about Addison and Wilson very much, and I think for a musical to succeed, you have to care about the characters, even if they are the most unreal people in the world.

Weidman: I think that's fair. *Candide* is an example of a picaresque musical that's completely unreal but in which that investment exists. We were dealing with picaresque material in the sense that we were going to follow these guys over a sweeping period of time through a variety of different adventures, but the reaching out and really grabbing and gripping the audience clearly did not happen to the extent that it needed to to really make it work.

Interviewer: In some ways, it's a total mystery as to why some musicals work and some musicals don't, isn't it?

Weidman: There *is* something mysterious about it. Steve and I would talk about *Bounce* and say, "All right, let's take it piece by piece." We'd be satisfied with each piece as we went through but we'd get to the end of the conversation and say, "Wait a minute. Why did we have this conversation if we're completely satisfied?" It's frustrating.

Interviewer: When you saw it in Washington, did you say to yourself, "There's something missing here," or did you say, "I don't understand why they don't think it's better than they think it is"?

Weidman: No, I feel that the show doesn't have the impact that it ought to have, and when other people say that to me, I nod. I do not feel that the show was underappreciated, although I do think that if it had not had the history that it had, it might have been received better.

Interviewer: And there were the names attached to it. If it had been three promising newcomers creating a musical, rather than Sondheim, Weidman, and Prince?

Weidman: Yes, and if they'd only started on it, say, three years before it opened and if this time around was the first time that it was being seen: I think it's hard to know what the response would have been under those circumstances. But I'm being completely honest with you. The experience that the audience is supposed to have falls short of what it ought to be.

Interviewer: As a creator of the show, that must be very frustrating.

Weidman: It *is* frustrating, because I feel like we fixed what we tried to fix one thing at a time. That's always the rule when you're out of town. I think we did that, but you get so wrapped up in it that it's difficult to have a clear sense of what needs to be done and what doesn't need to be done. If there had been a third city after Washington, I don't know what else we would have changed. That doesn't mean that six months from now I won't be able to say, "We need to throw this out and do this."

Interviewer: Where do you see the American musical going in the future—and where is it now?

Weidman: I think that what's happened on Broadway these last few years is irreversible. The Broadway musical has become a very different animal from what it was ten or fifteen years ago. The audience has changed and the real estate has changed. When I saw *Thoroughly Modern Millie* a week or two after it opened, I looked around and the audience in the theater was the audience you once would not have seen at a new Broadway musical for a year or a year and a half.

Interviewer: Can you elaborate on that?

Weidman: It was a tourist audience that would ultimately have worked its way into the theater to see a new hit musical. But ten or fifteen years ago, what you saw at the Shubert Theatre for the first six or seven months of a new musical was a sophisticated New York audience seeing the next new show. I think a certain kind of tourist musical that can be replicated and run around the country is going to take over Broadway. But at the same time, a couple of years ago Ben Brantley wrote a piece in the *Times* about the changing landscape of new musicals and he talked about *The Dead, Hedwig, Contact,* and one other musical that season. There were four musicals that did not obey any of the rules that had applied to musicals in the past, and it seemed as if there was going to be a push into new territory. Then, of course, you went into the next season when there was nothing new—so there is no real trend. I would like to think that the success of current shows like *Avenue Q* means that there is a developing audience even in Times Square for more peculiar, adventurous, and unexpected kinds of musical theater experiences. If that's not the case, then musicals based on movies, which are what commercial producers are almost exclusively interested in, will occupy the field and the alternatives will be pushed further to the fringe, which is also not such a terrible thing. People who want to write these more experimental musicals will starve and be miserable and have to find another job but they'll find a place to do their shows. A big established theater like Lincoln Center did

Contact, and *Caroline, or Change* came out of the Public Theater. I don't know how to answer your question in a definitive way.

Interviewer: Can you talk about the history of one of your shows and your involvement in it, from beginning to end?

Weidman: I'll do *Assassins,* because the revival is about to go into re-hearsals—and it's part of the story. That was a show, as I said, that started with me approaching Steve Sondheim with another idea. He bounced one back at me and it struck a chord. I would not even have been able to tell you at the time it struck the chord why it did. With respect to process, as I also said, it was a real authors' work and started with no preconceptions about what we wanted to write or really what we were going to write about except in the most general sense. We decided we would meet every week and talk. There was a certain amount of underlying material that we re-searched, but not much. You can read forever about Lee Harvey Oswald and about John Wilkes Booth, but as far as the rest of them are con-cerned, there were only a couple of books that were useful.

Interviewer: Did you both do research?

Weidman: I did. Steve will admit that one of the things that he likes to rely on his collaborators for is research. I love to do research; it's work, but it's painless. You sit around, you read; it's not like trying to write. We spent a couple of months talking, and as we talked, as I said, the shape and the form and the content of what we wanted to write about emerged. It was enormously satisfying because we didn't design a topic sentence first and then try to fit the material in underneath; we just let it go. I felt very free to write whatever I wanted, and I was drawing on a lot of different styles in which I had written in the past because that seemed to be what the material required. The scene in which Sara Jane Moore and Squeaky Fromme try to assassinate Gerald Ford is the kind of thing I might have written for the *National Lampoon,* but here I was writing it for a musical that I was writing in collaboration with Steve.

Interviewer: How would you say the tone of *Assassins* evolved? There's a definite tone to the show that I think is one of its great virtues.

Weidman: Again, it was not a result of a deliberate decision to apply a certain tone to the material. Once we decided we were going to take these characters and have them encounter each other across the ages, that sug-gested comedy in many cases—not in all cases, but in many cases. That's simply where it took us. Steve had recently done *Sunday in the Park with George* at Playwrights Horizons and liked working there. When I had finished a first draft of everything other than the final scene, we took it to

Playwrights. André Bishop said we could do a reading there; we did, and that confirmed to us that we were on the right track.

Interviewer: Was this the reading that only had the introductory song and most of your book?

Weidman: Yes. That was a midpoint in the writing process, so we went back to work with the expectation that we would ultimately do the show at Playwrights, although I don't think we had a commitment from them, nor had we made a commitment to them. They simply were making the space available to us when we needed it. When I finished the book, I don't recall how much of the score was done. Let's say it was a third or maybe a half. At that point, Steve and I started to talk about finding the right director. I had just worked with Jerry Zaks. Jerry has a tremendous ability to entertain, and he had done wonderful work at Lincoln Center, where he had just done *Six Degrees of Separation* and *The Front Page*. We thought he would be right for us, so we approached him; Jerry suffered for a long time over whether or not it was right for him before he said yes. Then we did a workshop at Playwrights; at this point, the book was done and I would say maybe two-thirds of the score, not the whole thing. Jerry rehearsed the actors for about a week, and then we did three or four presentations for invited audiences.

Interviewer: What happened as a result of that? Was there feedback that you then interpreted?

Weidman: It was tricky. Because they were all our friends, we got individual personalized feedback. But we also got the more valuable feedback, which was to have an audience for the first time and to see how they reacted, as a group, to the material in front of them. The reaction we got pleased us and confirmed us in the idea that we were heading for what we had originally set out to accomplish, so we persevered. Jerry Zaks had to move *Six Degrees of Separation* from the Newhouse downstairs at Lincoln Center to the Beaumont upstairs, and that delayed us for a while. We recast and went into rehearsal, and the expectation was that we would run the show at Playwrights and then move to a larger theater. The show opened and the critics were angry. We got a set of reviews that we've never gotten anyplace else for the show. Neither of us was naïve; we knew we were dealing with incendiary material and that by applying this variety of different tones to it, including a comic tone, we were taking a risk. But I don't think we were prepared for this more or less across-the-board rejection. David Richards in the Sunday *Times* loved it, and that made us feel better. The issue then became "Can it move? Should it move?" Ultimately, the money that was required to move it did not come together in time to get the show out of Playwrights, which I feel in the end was fortunate. That was a great cast and a good production. Some people got to see it, but a lot of people didn't—so it remained a kind of unknown quantity. The next place it turned up was in London. Very quickly, Sam Mendes decided to do it as his first production at the Donmar Warehouse, and he did a terrific job. The reviews there were the exact opposite of the reviews in New York; they were all good.

Interviewer: Did you do anything to the show between New York and London?

Weidman: Steve wrote one new song, which has been part of the show ever since. It's a song that matters, but the difference between the response here and the response there was not because of the new song. Since then, the show has been performed continuously, mostly on college campuses and in smaller theaters. We've been approached a couple of times over the years by different directors who wanted to do it in New York, and neither Steve nor I ever felt like we wanted to fix it. We felt that we had written the show that we wanted to write. Its failure in New York would ordinarily feel like an invitation to the authors to do something so it wouldn't be a failure in New York again. We really felt, particularly with the new song added, as if our work was done. We had one relatively well known director approach us who wanted to pull it apart and put it back together.

Interviewer: Didn't anybody want to do a New York production without making any changes?

Weidman: A couple of people did, but they didn't feel like a good fit with the sensibility of the show. Joe Mantello seemed perfect. I'm a big admirer of his work; he called and said he wanted to do it—so here we go again. As we were heading for what was going to be the production in 2001 (it was ultimately called off after 9/11), Joe wanted to have a couple of readings so he could see whether there was anything we had to work on, and there really wasn't. He had a smart idea for one very small adjustment in one of the scenes early on, and that was it. That represents fixing *Assassins,* so now we'll see what people make of it.

Interviewer: What was the adjustment?

Weidman: I don't know how well you know the show, but it starts in the shooting gallery and then there's the scene in which Lincoln is assassinated and Booth is dealt with in the burning barn. Then there's what in some ways would conventionally be the first book scene, with all the guys sitting around in a saloon. Joe asked, "Once you come back to these people, why aren't the women in the scene?" I said, "The first impulse was that this was the guys' scene and we'll get to the women later." He said, "I think it would help the audience if they had the sense that they'd all been gathered together and were staying together." I said, "All right, let me see," and I wrote a half-page piece for Sara Jane and Squeaky; we did it at the reading, and he was absolutely right.

Interviewer: That's a good example of how a fresh eye on something can often see something that you would not have thought of, isn't it? You don't always know everything there is to know about your own show, do you?

Weidman: No, and until the material is in front of an audience, you really don't know what you've got. It's not a book; it's not a painting. Until you see how a lot of people respond to it, you don't know what you may want to rewrite and what you think you will never want to rewrite.

Interviewer: On what basis do you decide which suggestions and responses to reject and which to consider?

Weidman: It has to do with what resonates. Someone will say something and you'll go, "Yes, that will help me express more effectively what I was trying to express in the first place." If you're in previews and listening to people who are simply saying, "This is wrong," that's another issue; then you have a real problem.

Interviewer: Is the audience always right? If you write something that you think is an absolute scream and nobody laughs, is it then not funny?

Weidman: It could be that you need a different audience, but it's treacherous to tell yourself that the audience is wrong. Plays and musicals are collaborations between the audience and what's going on onstage. Everyone has been in a meeting where someone says, "I can't wait to get this show to New York, where there's a hip, smart audience." I don't think so. That's why shows have previews. You don't really know what you've gotten right and what you haven't gotten right until an audience tells you.

Interviewer: Do you ever learn anything from a professional critic?

Weidman: Yes, but usually too late. There are critics whose opinions seem more interesting over time than others; but it's such a highly charged arena, the relationship between criticism and this work that we do, that I tend to read reviews simply to see if they're good or bad and that's it. I feel there is something fundamentally antithetical between what the critic does and what the rest of us are trying to do.

Interviewer: There are stories of old-time critics like Elliot Norton in Boston and Richard Coe in Washington actually having had an effect on shows, perhaps because they wrote a different kind of theater criticism. They weren't the stars. They wrote as theater lovers who were honestly trying to be constructive rather than clever. Do we have that kind of critic writing today?

Weidman: Not in the same way, no. Those guys you're talking about were still around when *Pacific Overtures* was done. Because of the way shows worked, because of what New York meant and how shows made their way to New York, they had a certain role to play, which they were really good at. It wasn't thumbs up or thumbs down; it was "I'm taking a look at this on its way to someplace else. I'm going to see if I can say something useful about it." Those guys were generous men. The relation between the critic and the creative community has gotten worse. The idea of a theatrical community is a very healthy thing, and the arms of the community should be large enough to embrace many different kinds of family members. There is no real reason why critics shouldn't be part of that, rather than adversaries, as I think for the most part they are perceived to be today.

George C. Wolfe

Photo by Julia Maloof

George C. Wolfe was born on September 23, 1954, in Frankfort, Kentucky. He was educated at Pomona College (B.A., 1976) and New York University (M.F.A., 1983). He has worked as a director, librettist, and playwright. He has written, co-written, or conceived the musicals Paradise! *(1985),* Queenie Pie *(1986),* Jelly's Last Jam *(1991),* Bring in 'da Noise, Bring in 'da Funk [Noise/Funk] *(1996),* The Wild Party *(2000), and* Harlem Song *(2002). He was the lyricist for* Paradise!, Noise/Funk, *and* Harlem Song. *He has directed the musicals* Jelly's Last Jam, Noise/Funk, On the Town *(1998),* The Wild Party, Harlem Song, Radiant Baby *(2003), and* Caroline, or Change *(2004).*

He has written the plays The Colored Museum *(1986) and* Spunk *(1989), and he has directed the plays* Spunk, Angels in America: Millennium Approaches *(1993),* Angels in America: Perestroika *(1993),* Twilight: Los Angeles *(1994),* The Tempest *(1995),* Elaine Stritch at Liberty

(2002), and Topdog/Underdog *(2002). From 1993 to 2004, he served as producer of the Public Theater in New York City. He has won Tony Awards for* Angels in America: Millennium Approaches *(Best Director) and* Noise/ Funk *(Best Director).*
This interview took place on December 11, 2002.

•────────────────────────────────•

Interviewer: How did you, as a boy growing up in Frankfort, Kentucky, get interested in the theater?

Wolfe: That is an impossible question to answer because I don't know what it was, past life or what, but from as early as I can remember I've always been obsessed with theater. I went to a private black grade school. My town was segregated back then, and each year we would put on plays at the end of the year in which the entire school would be involved, and I remember being very obsessed and focused during that time, thrilled by the whole process. My cousins told me a few years ago that when people would play house, instead of just playing I would give people lines to say. So I was functioning as a director when I was four or five years old! Frankfort, Kentucky, is not the cultural center of the world; but from the very beginning for me, the dynamics of theater were already a part of me— crafting space, trying to create a world. In retrospect, I remember watching television or talent shows and not watching as an audience member, but as a director.

Interviewer: Even then, do you think you were looking at things more as a director than as a performer? You were primarily a performer then, weren't you?

Wolfe: When I went to college, my focus was going to be acting and design. Then it became acting and directing. And in my last year at college I wrote a play, so that by the time I finished college, I had functioned as an actor, a director, a designer, and a writer. Oftentimes, things seem so random, but if you look back on them within the context of your life, you realize how organized and in some respects how efficient certain experiences and choices were.

Interviewer: Was there a certain production that you went to when you were young that made a particularly strong impression on you?

Wolfe: I cannot point to a magic moment when I saw a Judy Garland movie, or some such revelatory moment; the desire to create theater has always been a driving energy inside of me. My mother was a teacher, and she would get all these copies of teaching magazines, and in the back there'd be plays, which I'd read. When I was eleven, I forced myself to sit down and read *A Midsummer Night's Dream,* because we had all of Shakespeare's plays at home. I also read encyclopedias, poring over any entries that had to do with theater.

Interviewer: Did you have much experience of professional theater when you were a child? Did you see many shows?

Wolfe: The first "professional" theater that I saw was when I came to New York at age thirteen with my mother. She was doing some advanced degree study at NYU, and we went to see a production of *Hello, Dolly!* with Pearl Bailey and a revival of *West Side Story* at Lincoln Center. Also at that time I saw a production of *Hamlet* by the Mobile Unit of the New York Shakespeare Festival in Washington Square Park, directed by Joe Papp. It was sort of a mock *Hamlet,* with Cleavon Little. I realize now that there was something so incredibly efficient about my seeing each of those three productions at such a formative time. With *Hello, Dolly!* it was seeing people of color on Broadway; with *West Side Story* it was the spartan brilliant staging and social relevance; and in seeing a show from the Public directed by Joe Papp, it was meeting an institution that some nineteen years later would become my artistic home. So, as I said, there's been this bizarre kind of economy in my experience that led me to my journey to create theater in New York City.

Interviewer: Speaking of studying, what made you go to college at Pomona?

Wolfe: Because it was in California and I was tired of cold weather! My mother was at Miami University in Oxford, Ohio, getting her doctorate. I was in high school at the time, and my younger brother was in a production of *Oliver!* at Miami University. They also had a summer theater workshop there that I had been in for two summers during high school, working as an actor. It was a crucial point, because I was starting to think about theater in a more serious way, performing in one-acts by DeGhelderode and Pinter. Anyway, my brother was in *Oliver!,* and I took him to a cast party, and there was this girl there who was going to Pomona, and she told me that they had a great theater school. I said, "Send me the information." Then her mother tracked down my mother on campus and gave her this little piece of cardboard with the admissions office address written on it. My mother brought it to me; I said, "California, warm weather! Done." I went out there and it turned out to be the perfect place for me, because at Pomona it wasn't so much about teaching you how to do theater as much as engaging you in a conversation about what theater is and about altering the form to fit the content of what you are creating. I was a very aggressive student; so by the time I graduated, I had acted in a number of plays, directed five shows, and written two plays. Productions were staged in rock quarries with giant puppets. I studied Kabuki; I took classes in religious theater. I wasn't interested in nor was I allowed to live in just one place in terms of my comprehension and understanding of what theater was. It was an incredibly idealistic and expansive time.

Interviewer: When you finished at Pomona, were you tempted to stay on the West Coast?

Wolfe: My first year out of college, I was hired to come back to Pomona to be an artist-in-residence and direct a new play that I had written there my senior year. So I moved to Los Angeles and started working at a theater called the Inner City Cultural Center, which was a very nurturing environment. I was teaching acting and creating plays. I did about four shows in L.A. that got very good reviews in the *L.A. Times,* but I didn't figure out how to traverse the landscape, because there was no Off-Broadway to speak of. Then at one point I went for an interview to write on some sitcom. In the meeting, I said something clever, and the head writer said, "Oh, he's quick. We're going to have to tie one hand behind his back." I literally saw myself showing up for work and them literally tying my hand behind my back. That's when I decided to move to New York.

Interviewer: Did you see yourself then as a writer or as a director?

Wolfe: I saw myself as a writer/director.

Interviewer: Of plays?

Wolfe: All the plays I had done were plays with music. I had done a play that was adapted from folk tales and set to music. I had worked on a musical called *Back Alley Tales,* which was set in New Orleans and was probably a precursor to *Jelly's Last Jam.* They all had music, they all tried to bend and twist the form, and none of them was stylistically realistic.

Interviewer: Would you say that you've always been attracted to combinations like that?

Wolfe: Absolutely! I'm sure it probably had something to do with having seen *West Side Story* at such a young age, the fact that it was material that had weight and joy and substance all built into it. I think that as an artist you have your understanding of the world and then you see plays or meet people who affirm it. Joseph Papp was like that. He had this ability to affirm your vision of yourself as a serious or important artist. Him affirming a quality that you felt inside yourself gave you permission to resolve all your inhibitions, thereby allowing those qualities to come shining through.

Interviewer: Are you a fan of the old-style musicals that one can't produce now because, although they often have great scores, the books are so weak?

Wolfe: As an audience member, I can celebrate their good craftsmanship. But given who I am and when and where I was born—black and southern at a time of segregation and the fact that I'm gay—has dictated the kind of theater I want to craft. It's a theater that's full of delight but also has edge and a sense of responsibility to the world.

Interviewer: Did you ever have any sense, as a black man in the majority white culture, that you were at any disadvantage in terms of the possibilities within the world of theater? As you say, you did grow up in a segregated city.

Wolfe: Yes, but everyone in the black community that was a part of segregated Frankfort, Kentucky, told me I was amazing and marvelous. The town became integrated by the time I was eight or nine, and my high school was predominantly white. So moving from a very sheltered environment to a not as sheltered environment was very traumatic for me. Theater was the ultimate way I gained—for a lack of better words— power and recognition inside of that school, so by the time I left that school I was viewed as being talented and amazing. My sophomore year in college I spent a summer at the Williamstown Theatre Festival. There was a production of the musical version of *Juno and the Paycock*; I came in to audition and later found out they didn't cast me because I was black. Up to that point, clearly I had encountered racism, but my intelligence and my talent had always cut through. The mantra that was given to me early on was "They think you're less than, which means you've got to be better than." What fueled me then and has fueled me since—and I have encountered racism throughout my career in New York City—is: Do I believe in my vision? Yes. Do I believe in the power of theater to heal and transform and empower people? Yes. Do I work hard? Yes. Am I skilled? Yes. Do I think that I have something to say? Yes. That's the fuel that has driven me past whatever obstacles I have encountered.

Interviewer: Did the situation at Williamstown discourage you?

Wolfe: No. At the time it had a significant emotional impact on me, but I think it was supposed to. While I didn't get into those shows, I did get into John Guare's play *Rich and Famous,* which is how I met John. And so many other people that I met during that summer were these amazing artists who I've since worked with here at the Public or on Broadway. Being an apprentice there, in retrospect, I realize was not about my being an actor. I watched those huge productions being done to varying levels of success, and I realize now that I was there studying as a director.

Interviewer: Would you say—and this is a deliberately provocative question which you can dismiss if you want—that because as your career has developed you've become a creator rather than being subject to someone else's decision, that has in some ways gotten you past the problems of not being cast because you're a person of color?

Wolfe: I got out of college in 1976, and in 1986 *The Colored Museum* happened, so I struggled economically, really struggled, for ten years. In L.A., I evolved my vision. In New York for the six years that I was first here, it was about learning the rules of the landscape so that I could incorporate those rules into my vision so that my vision would have that level of muscularity to it. Through the NYU musical theater program, I took a book class with Peter Stone, who became an early supporter of mine. Arthur Laurents was also very supportive of my writing, and Richard Maltby let me observe the creation of *Baby*. It was a time in which I absorbed a tremendous amount of information. Also, when I was at the NYU musical theater program, very unsubtle, or not so subtle, racist things would be said, by one administrator in particular, and I chose not to deal with them, because I was there to get information. I was there to empower myself so that I could be in charge. I felt that if I spent my time being angry, I was not spending my time being productive; if I expended my time trying to attack somebody or trying to make them a better person or, even more to the point, defending something, I was not spending my time acquiring essential information. By putting the work out there, that was going to be the staunchest weapon that I could use, because it would reach so many people.

Interviewer: Can you talk a little bit about the evolution of *The Colored Museum*, which was the first big splash you made?

Wolfe: When I first came to New York as a writer/director, people would say to me, "You can't do both." So I said, "Okay, let me focus on the writing." I tried to get into NYU's directing program, but I got put on the wait list. I did get into the dramatic writing program, and later the musical theater program. The woman who was running the musical theater program kept me out for a whole year. It's only because of Peter Stone insisting that I be in his class that I got into that program. While I was at NYU, three writers were writing plays about old black tap dancers—and they were neither old nor black nor dancers. It got me to thinking, "Somewhere along the way, somebody has defined what 'black' is. Hell, I don't know what 'black' is, because to me it's an ever-changing identity." In so many respects, on a purely didactic racial level, I wanted to explode, literally put dynamite underneath, any predetermined definition of "black." That was the impetus for *The Colored Museum*. In essence, I wrote *The Colored Museum* in order to give myself permission to write any play, because, with rare exceptions, most of the plays that were being done in New York at the time about black people were social realism, and that never appealed to me. When I would show people early versions of my writing, I had all sorts of theatrical influences in my work, everything from Kabuki to commedia, and people would say that it wasn't a black play. But I was not interested in three walls, a chair, a table, and suffering. I was interested in theatrical influences that had absolutely nothing to do with the definition of what somebody else, black or white, perceived my world to be. I had a much more expansive and freer and messier definition of my world. My imagination was not defined nor limited to somebody else's definition of who I was. My imagination was beyond those boundaries, and so writing *The Colored Museum* was an act of freeing myself.

Interviewer: As I look over your work, it occurs to me that everything you've written and many of the things you've directed have in a sense been political with a small *p*. Would you say that is one of the motivations that attracts you to projects, that they say something?

Wolfe: I think every single piece of theater is political, because every single piece of theater either affirms the status quo or challenges the status quo. If it's affirming the status quo, that's political; if it's challenging the status quo, that's political. If you have two people onstage engaging in just about any kind of conversation—I'm sure there are rare exceptions—you're either affirming what the status quo thinks or you're not. I think there is a fundamental component in my personality that is subversive, wickedly subversive. I remember when I was writing *The Colored Museum,* I felt like sometimes I'd be writing it very innocently and there was a little demon on my shoulder saying, "I can't believe you're going to do that." I'm not doing it to be provocative, but it's accessing a component that is an integral part of my personality.

Interviewer: I was going to say that at almost every show of yours I've seen I can hear myself say, "He can't do that"—and that's probably exactly the reason you do it!

Wolfe: My very first memory, literally—and I think it's defined and very possibly damaged me for the rest of my life—is I was sitting on a yellow rug, and when my grandfather would pile up these blocks, I'd knock them down, and he would applaud. Thus began my relationship with the world!

Interviewer: What particularly attracts you to the musical theater form?

Wolfe: Its rhythms. I'm fundamentally a writer of rhythms. From the time the audience takes its seat, the whole evening is nothing but a series of rhythms. If the lights go down and you're in the dark too long before the lights come up, it screws up the rhythm of the event. The way the scenery moves, the way an actor walks onstage, every single thing that happens in the theatrical event is defined by rhythm. I remember seeing a terrible production of *Othello* in college, but it was deeply moving because with Shakespeare the power of the rhythms of storytelling and the language are so brilliant. I also think that when you do a play, it can take you anywhere from three minutes to an hour before an audience will surrender to it. In a musical, the first three notes of an overture can hit, and the audience is yours.

Interviewer: What about the collaborative aspects of a musical? When you write a play, even though you have a director, stars, and all the tech people, it's still your script. In a musical, you have to work with many people in a very different orientation from a play. Is that an attraction for you or is it difficult?

Wolfe: I think I'm a really great collaborator. I can be very opinionated and at times dictatorial, but I'm very collaborative because I love the aspect of theater that's about community. One of the things that makes me a good collaborator is I'm not driven by *my* sense of right and wrong, but I can locate the *material's* right and wrong. I believe that if you write one perfect scene or if you can find one perfect moment in a play, that it's almost like DNA, like finding the hair of some animal. You can then reconstruct what the whole animal looks like. If you can locate a perfect moment or the moment that is close to perfect in a play, that gives you the rules for every single thing that comes before and follows after. I have very specific kinds of analytical skills—only because I've had so many wonderful experiences in working with so many smart people—that enable me to go to that moment and say, "Does this scene over there have the same integrity, truth, buoyancy, depth, and outrageousness as this perfect scene?" It's important to have not just an intuitive sense, but also a craft-like understanding of how it's all connected.

Interviewer: How has the collaborative process worked with the musicals you've done? When you wrote the book, did you work very closely with the composer and the other creators of the piece?

Wolfe: Yes. On *Jelly's Last Jam,* we worked very closely—composer/arranger Luther Henderson, lyricist Susan Birkenhead, and I. In preparation, I listened to Jelly's entire musical canon, and I did tons and tons of research on New Orleans, Creoles, the geographical journey of jazz, etc. When I'm working as a writer, I'm also functioning inside my head as a director and as a designer. I'm trying to bring all the various crafts that I've worked inside of into play when crafting a moment. Susan and I would be on the phone and she'd read a lyric and I'd read the scene. We'd go back and forth that way for hours on end, with the goal being to make everything as seamless as possible. In *Noise/Funk,* I'd come up with rough scenarios and then come in and give assignments to various people—the composers, the choreographer, the researchers—and they'd go off to work. On that show, I dreamed about three or four of the numbers, and the next day I would come in and give theatrical language to that image. One night I dreamed the guys who played the buckets in the show were beating on the bottom of Savion Glover's feet. I asked the production department at the Public to rig up a bar structure so that Savion could hold on to it, lifting himself up so the guys could hit the taps on his shoes with their drumsticks. Seeing the bar, hearing the rhythms, I realized it was a chance to explore urban industrialization, how rural rhythms got turned into industrial urban rhythms. When I was an actor, when I would read a play for the first time, I believed that something inside of me knew exactly how every single line should be done and that the rehearsal process was about me getting out of the way so that that understanding could come through. In many respects, I think that's how a lot of artists work. It's instinct or talent or gut or whatever that knows. The writing or the rehearsal process is working so that the smallest part of you gets out of the way so the larger part of you, the intuitive, the inspired, can be fully present.

Interviewer: Can you give us an example of trying for the perfect moment in *Jelly's Last Jam*?

Wolfe: There was this song called "Lovin' Is the Lowdown Blues," and I had this image in my head, in which three Storyville whores were going to be pushing a large brass bed around while Jelly and Anita were lying in bed, and through a series of scenes we were going to see the course of their relationship. As the piece evolved, the three whores turned into the Hunnies, a sort of Greek chorus who stalked the scene, commenting on the relationship and waiting to see it turn from something euphoric to something deadly. It was funny and smart and dark, and sexy and dangerous, all at the exact same time.

Interviewer: How about *Harlem Song*? Is there a key moment in that piece?

Wolfe: There was a riot in Harlem in 1943, which I wanted to deal with—and I also wanted to deal with the Lindy, because as a dance it's astonishing, not just in terms of its energy, but in its seductive physical aggression. Then, as I got further into the research about the '43 riot, I found out that the week of the riot, the police shut down the Savoy Ballroom because black and white couples had started dancing together. And then I read this social theorist who believed that if the Savoy had been open, the riot wouldn't have happened—because every night three thousand people would have been able to release their energy. So then I decided to put the Lindy and the riot together and used hipster, zoot-suit language from the period to tell the story. The language is sexy, and the dance is energetic, theatrical, and aggressive. Instead of the riot as blood, blood, scream, it was what I love—history meeting theatrical dazzle.

Interviewer: What attracts you as a director to a musical that you haven't written? Most of the musicals you've directed have been your material, but what about a project like the revival of *On the Town?* How did that come about?

Wolfe: With *On the Town,* at the Public we'd finished a marathon of all of Shakespeare's plays, and we had to come up with a second production in the park. I said, "No more Shakespeare. Let's try to find something celebratory, something that celebrates the city. What about a musical?" And so we set out to do *On the Town* as a little love valentine for New York City.

Interviewer: What about *The Wild Party?*

Wolfe: We had commissioned Michael John LaChiusa to create a piece, and he brought in this wonderful poem, *The Wild Party.* I heard a couple of songs and they were incredible. Then we had a reading—this is sort of a terrible story—to which we'd invited a very famous director to consider directing the piece. He was sitting there in the room listening to the material, and I was there, and halfway through listening to the material, I was saying to myself, "Oh, God, *I'm* supposed to do this show." It wasn't even "I *want* to do this show"; it was "I'm *supposed* to do it." It pulled me in that way.

Interviewer: Can you define in a more generic way what quality in a musical pulls you in, whether it's an already written one or one that you're just seeing for the first time?

Wolfe: I think it's very different reasons. Sometimes you don't even know why. I was working on *Jelly's Last Jam* for about three years before I really knew why I was doing it. After *The Colored Museum,* all these people wanted to hire me to do everything, and I said yes to a whole bunch of projects because I was so used to people saying no to me. After about six months a lot of that stuff just died because I wasn't supposed to do it, but *Jelly* hung around. The reason I wanted to do *Angels in America* was that I couldn't figure out how to do it. How the hell do you do a seven-hour play? Generally, I'm drawn to things that scare me, because I know that at the end of the day I'm going to end up with muscles that I didn't have prior to that experience. I think that in a musical the score is the soul, and if the score doesn't have a soul you can't live there. I directed a piece that I did for very nice, noble reasons, but ultimately I couldn't find freedom inside the soul of the piece—so it was just a craft experience. It wasn't an "I'm inspired! I'm enthusiastic! I'm amazed!" experience. It was an experience where I did only craft because the soul of the piece, the music, didn't speak to me, didn't excite me. A lot of musicals tend to have fake feelings, so I can't live inside of them.

Interviewer: I'm not sure that forty years ago directors of musicals thought in terms of making them have a soul. What you're talking about is, in many ways, the aim to make a musical real, to make it believable and serious even though performers are singing and dancing.

Wolfe: Musicals have really great qualities, and straight plays have really great qualities. A straight play has the audacity to take an audience on a journey, and if it goes down a dark alley, it goes down a dark alley—which is great because when you come out of that dark alley into the light, the light is so astonishing. That's what I love to try to bring to my musicals. My theory about musicals is that there is a dark world just waiting offstage and the people are singing and dancing to keep that dark world from coming onstage. When you turn into the 1960s and 1970s, you've got Fosse in terms of the dark sexual energy; you've got Michael Bennett's work; and you've got the Prince/Sondheim musicals. They started to let that dark world move onstage more and more. But it's still basically on the periphery waiting to come in and take these characters. What I'm really intrigued by is what happens if you put the dark world completely onstage. That's what *Jelly* was. If you put the dark world onstage, the audience is engaged in this perpetual struggle: Is the light going to soar up or is the darkness going to devour? At the end when the light soars up, you feel as though you've gone through this cathartic experience with the characters, because in life that's what we all do; we negotiate a relationship with our fears. They're driving us to do the good deeds that we do, and they're driving us to do the bad things that we do. To me that dichotomy is a primal and exciting source of music. The main thing you have to do as a writer or director with this kind of material is to keep things buoyant.

Interviewer: But aren't many of today's writers and directors more interested in style than in truth, perhaps because of the predominance of film in our culture?

Wolfe: But style needn't be at the expense of truth onstage. I'm intrigued by the rhythms of film. In *Noise/Funk,* the opening number has the rhythms of an MTV video—with lights and staging married to create quick edits. And then when we go back in time to the slave-ships sequence, the rhythms are slower and it's almost done as if in one take. Then as the piece starts to move forward in time, the visual rhythms change and there are the equivalents of jump cuts and fast editing because as our society was evolving, so was our ability to edit, to edit out truths. When I did *The Wild Party,* I watched tons and tons of silent movies, because I was intrigued by how people could pose and why people pose—by how people want to live inside of a pose and then what happens when moments don't allow you to pose, when you can't do these long gestures; you can't smoke those cigarettes and you can't put them out slowly, because you're starting to fall apart. Silent films were the popular culture when that play was set; so I always think about what the technology was that existed when this scene or this play is set and then I try to incorporate that into the rhythms of storytelling.

Interviewer: What is the experience like directing your own material, as opposed to someone else's material? Is there any difference, and do you have a preference?

Wolfe: I always try to surround myself with as many smart people as I possibly can, so that I get smart questions about my material. Collaboration is two very strong forces coming together to try to come up with the smartest possible vision. I don't think collaboration is synonymous with compromise at all; that's a huge mistake that people make. I made that on my first show; I compromised my integrity because I wanted to be a nice guy in the rehearsal room and the show was ultimately damaged as a result. It's difficult but essential in collaboration to believe passionately what you believe while being completely open to others. Elaine Stritch told me she told a director one time, "It's not that I won't do what you're saying, it's that I can't." That was an incredibly brilliant statement to make. In many respects, I think there's a part of me that, in my work as a writer and as a director, approaches material emotionally, like an actor. That's why I always take actors very seriously, because they have these barometers inside of themselves that are based on their truth, on having lived on the planet as long as they've lived on the planet, and on craft. If somebody's talking bullshit, you can tell right away; but if they're really trying to understand something, even if they don't have the language for it, you've got to help them find it because it's connected to something that's valuable to the play.

Interviewer: If they say to you, "I can't do that," do you accept that?

Wolfe: I have a saying: "If the elephant doesn't want to tap dance, you don't make it." If after about three days of teaching the step, the elephant's not doing it, you need to come up with something else. Either you explain it so the person can feel free to do it, or you've got to be flexible. I remember when I was in tech with *Noise/Funk* on Broadway. We were zooming along and then we came to one sequence and I spent literally half a day trying to do a very short sequence the way it had been done downtown. I kept on saying, "What's wrong? What's wrong?" and then I finally realized, "I need to change it"—and what had been taking half a day we finished in forty-five minutes. I remember when I was in college I was directing a play that I had written and the opening number in it wasn't right. I was with the composer, trying to find a solution, and the actors were over on the side making noise around the piano. I kept saying, "Quiet, please. We're trying to work," but the actors just kept on making noise. I turned around, was about ready to yell, when I realized they had solved the problem. It was one of the most brilliant lessons I had ever learned, because as a director you have a responsibility to hear and see and be open to the entire room; you have no idea where the solutions are going to come from. That to me is collaboration. It's somebody saying, "Well, what about this"—and it transforms a whole moment. That's what's wonderful about theater and about the community of theater. It could be a chorus person, it could be the star; anybody can contribute an idea that will be the missing ingredient, the pinch of salt that transforms the seasoning for what you're trying to create. And it's thrilling when it happens, because that means everybody's in the play together.

Interviewer: What about critics? Do they serve any function for you as a creator?

Wolfe: No, they're a marketing tool. It's really wonderful when they say nice things, and it's really painful when they say bad things. Over time you realize that there are smart ones who can say incredibly smart things, there are dumb ones who can say incredibly smart things, and there are smart ones who can say incredibly dumb things. So I can't engage in a conversation with what they say and what they do. I can only create the work. What I listen to more than anything else is audiences, not individuals but the collective audience. They're the smartest group you can listen to—and your collaborators. Because of the death of newspaper culture in New York City, we don't have five papers. We have one, and as a result the power has shifted to a realm that is completely ridiculous and not healthy. I feel as though my healthiest response is to not engage in an intimate relationship with something whose fundamental structure is unhealthy.

Interviewer: What do you think the current state of the American musical is?

Wolfe: I think there are some wonderful composers working now—and that's exciting. I think there are very few people who know how to write books; that might be due to the rise of the director/choreographer. I feel very fortunate that I got to talk early in my career with and learn from Arthur Laurents, Peter Stone, and Richard Maltby, people who've spent a lifetime crafting musicals. And then there are the economics of the day, which are just hateful, and the critical climate is, more often than not, very severe.

Interviewer: Do you think that there are two kinds of musicals today, the kind that you would be attracted to do at the Public Theater or some other regional or nonprofit theater and the Broadway musical?

Wolfe: I don't think there is such a thing as a Broadway musical anymore. I mean, Broadway still exists, but there's no guiding aesthetic, i.e., a Prince show, a Fosse show. What is guiding Broadway is the economic realities. The challenge is to figure out how to duck beneath the economic barbed wire and deliver a daring, innovative musical. It's all about ducking under the barbed wire and either surviving the critical reaction or having enough marketing money, which is what the corporations have, to survive.

Interviewer: Can you choose one of the shows you've done, preferably one where you were writer and director, take us through it from the beginning to the end, and tell us how the process went?

Wolfe: I don't know which one to choose. *Noise/Funk* was the most intense and most compacted; *Jelly* was spread out over such a period of time; and *The Wild Party* was the most violent—so let me talk about that. Michael John LaChiusa had found this sexy, dangerous epic poem about Jazz Age Manhattan. He did a presentation of about four songs based on the material for Wiley Hausam, associate producer at the Public in charge of musicals, and myself. We were very excited by them, gave him the commission, and he went off to work. Months later, there was a presentation with a bunch of actors and probably about eight songs. We had invited the director I mentioned earlier to come watch, and afterwards everybody kept coming up to me, and saying, "*You're* supposed to direct this"—and I was thinking the exact same thing, so I signed on to direct it, and Michael John went off and did more writing. During the summer we did a five-week workshop with me directing. At the end of that workshop, I had figured out how to stage it; I knew it was going be on a revolving stage. Maybe two or three actors from that workshop, if that many, ended up being in the actual piece. During that five-week workshop, I had also gotten inside the piece emotionally, and I felt I knew the characters very well.

At the end of that process, Michael John and I talked, and I became the co-book-writer. There's a book called *Terrible Honesty,* which is this brilliant study of the New York City cultural landscape in the 1920s, and it became an invaluable source for us. I've done lots of research about the 1920s. All over the world—Berlin, Paris, New York—it was just an extraordinary period, this dance between the wars. The worst war had just happened and all of a sudden humanity was celebrating—and then came the Depression and fascism. It's an incredibly exciting period for me, and Michael John's music and lyrics were so dangerous and had such electricity to them that I wanted to try to match that energy and bring in as much wit as I possibly could with the book. Then we did another workshop, and something like eight or nine months after that we did a staged reading in which Vanessa Williams joined the show, along with Mandy Patinkin, Eartha Kitt, and a number of other people who ended up in the production. The staged reading was thrilling, exciting, and amazing; and Scott Rudin, a producer I had gotten to know through *On the Town,* saw the workshop and expressed interest in joining the project.

Michael John and I proceeded to move forward, doing rewrites and planning the full production. At one point in the design of the show, working with the designers—Robin Wagner, Peggy Eisenhauer, and Jules Fisher, whom I'd worked with on *Angels* and on *Jelly*—we came up with a design for a space that was larger than the Public Theater (we have a very small pit here). It became apparent that, for this show that had been nurtured by the Public, its physical demands were bigger than any of our theaters. So we contacted Rocco Landesman at Jujamcyn, and he agreed to give us the Virginia Theatre. The Public Theater then formed a relationship with commercial producers Anita Waxman, Elizabeth Williams, Roger Berlind, and Scott Rudin, something that the theater had never done before. It was set. We were going to go into rehearsal in the fall, and so I went away to Spain on vacation. The day I got back, Vanessa's manager called to tell me that she was pregnant and asked if we could rush and go into rehearsal right away. We couldn't do that because Mandy had a series of concerts and was not free until January. I went to see Rocco Landesman and he said, "I made a commitment to you, not just to a star, so you still have the theater if you want it." Then, through Scott Rudin, I met Toni Collette, who was in New York doing promotion for *The Sixth Sense*. We instantly got along; she went into a room with Michael John and the music director, learned an entire song in one minute (mind you, she had never taken singing lessons in her life), and we were all thrilled because we had our Queenie again.

We went into rehearsal sometime around January. The designs were exciting; the cast was amazing. We had huge trouble casting one role, Black, the guy who becomes Queenie's lover. I had a very specific look that I wanted, and Michael John had a very specific sound. The person that we ultimately settled on, a very talented guy, ultimately couldn't fill all the demands of the role; but everything else seemed to be going quite well. At a certain point, Scott Rudin and I started butting heads; and then about two or three weeks into rehearsals, I realized that Mandy and Toni were not getting along well. In fact, a lot of people in the company were having trouble with Mandy, feeling that he was not acknowledging anybody's boundaries other than his own—and that started to create a certain dynamic. The energy between Scott Rudin and me just kept on intensifying. Toni and Mandy and all the actors were doing brilliant work; what was happening onstage was very exciting. Michael John was continuing to work, we were making changes throughout, and the ensemble was building in a really extraordinary way. But a number of people in the cast were also having issues with the choreographer.

Then we moved into the theater and began the teching process, which is always very tedious, and the Scott Rudin tension kept on building, and the tension between Mandy and the company intensified. By the time we had our first preview, I knew it was going to be rough. I always use previews, because then the other collaborator, the audience, is there, so I can gauge what's working and what isn't. When I did *Jelly*, I was oblivious to the gossip machinery of Broadway. All of a sudden, I was made aware that there were gossip columns and chat rooms, and that the word-of-mouth on the street was this or that. For *Jelly*, I redid seven numbers in a four-week preview period, oblivious to the chatter. With *The Wild Party*, I was acutely aware of all the rumors that were swirling around. The situation with Scott Rudin continued to be something that was very troublesome, and Mandy's behavior became more and more intense. I think he had trouble playing such a dark character. In the readings it was fine, but when he was living inside of it, I think, it just became very difficult for him. His behavior started to become very complicated onstage for a number of the actors. Then in the papers every day there were articles about people walking out of *The Wild Party* or about what Mandy was doing. There were also rumors within the company that people who were connected to the show were feeding information to the gossip columns because if they couldn't have things their way they wanted to see the show closed. So in addition to working on the new show, I was dealing with the major issue of company morale. The work was progressing and changing, and we all remained very excited by the ambitions of the piece.

In most musicals, characters announce what they've been doing. But with this show, with its incredibly brilliant score—I think it's one of the best scores that's come along in the past twenty years—we were trying to do a behavioral musical. The storytelling existed in the behavior. It was similar to the dynamic in *Follies*, where the character is singing "In Buddy's Eyes." She's singing one thing, but through behavior and emotion, you realize she really means the exact opposite. A lot of *The Wild Party* was like that. The one thing I feel as though, creatively, I was not able to do with the show was develop enough spectacle. Spectacle is that one pure element that allows an audience to experience a show without thinking, and the spectacle in this production should have been present in dance. If I get to do the show again, I will increase the dance factor. At one point, one of the general managers remarked that she felt that ultimately the most damaging dynamic about *The Wild Party* was that because of a certain adversarial relationship that evolved as the show did, I was forced into a relationship where I felt I had to defend the show—and I was not allowed to devote my pure analytical energy to working on the piece.

Interviewer: That's a great example of how the realities of producing a musical today can interfere with its artistic aims.

Wolfe: It was the violation of a collaboration. I'd done *Jelly* on Broadway, I'd done *The Tempest* on Broadway, I'd done *Noise/Funk* on Broadway, I'd done *Twilight: Los Angeles* on Broadway; but all of a sudden, it was a new and a very different Broadway. It all felt very mean-spirited, and I had never experienced it that way. In the beginning, we'd gotten a certain resistance to *Noise/Funk* from people saying it was an entertainment, not a musical (I still don't know what that meant). But with *The Wild Party*, we were in a situation that felt like perpetual assault.

Interviewer: So you slunk back to Lafayette Street, where you could be comfortable again.

Wolfe: I don't slink! But I did go back downtown to the protective environment of the Public.

Interviewer: After you've done it there, if somebody wants to take it to Broadway, you've already worked on it and gotten it to the artistic point you wanted to reach.

Wolfe: Exactly. A year or so after *The Wild Party*, that's what happened with *Topdog/Underdog* and *Elaine Stritch at Liberty*. Those shows were nurtured in the same environment that nurtured *The Tempest, Twilight: Los Angeles, Noise/Funk*, and *Take Me Out*. It was also the same environment that nurtured *The Wild Party*. The difference with *The Wild Party* is that we took the baby out of the incubator way too soon.

Index

About the Editors

Jackson R. Bryer is a professor of English at the University of Maryland. He is the editor of *The Playwright's Art* and co-editor of *The Actor's Art*.

Richard A. Davison is a professor of English at the University of Delaware. He is the co-editor of *The Actor's Art* and has published books on Frank, Charles, and Kathleen Norris and numerous articles in major literary journals.